CHRISTOPHER THACKER

The Wildness Pleases

*THE ORIGINS OF
ROMANTICISM*

CROOM HELM
London & Canberra
ST. MARTIN'S PRESS
New York

© 1983 Christopher Thacker
Croom Helm Ltd, Provident House, Burrell Row,
Beckenham, Kent BR3 1AT

British Library Cataloguing in Publication Data

Thacker, Christopher
The wildness pleases: the origins of romanticism.
1. Romanticism
I. Title
809'.914   PN751
ISBN 0-7099-2409-7

© Christopher Thacker 1983

First published in the United States of America in 1983

Library of Congress Cataloging in Publication Data

Thacker, Christopher.
The wildness pleases.

1. Nature (Aesthetics) I. Title.
BH301.N3T47 1982   111'.85   82-10769
ISBN 0-312-87960-1

Printed and bound in Great Britain by
Biddles Ltd, Guildford and King's Lynn

Contents

List of Plates

Foreword

I wanted to write this book over twenty years ago, but those older and wiser said 'You haven't read enough. Wait until you're as old and wise as us'. Well. I've waited, and read, and been and seen. In the meanwhile the subject has grown, and 'eighteenth-century studies' have become an industry, with workers, foremen, directors and even *chevaliers*. 'What cheek', they might say, 'to write so broadly. It's *superficial*.'

But a book is its own length. It dictates what you use, and what you leave out – and, dear *chevaliers*, to change the proportions of what I have put in and what I have left out would not alter my theme, direction or conclusion at all. That at least – after twenty years – is sure. You could have chapters more on Hutcheson, Helvétius, Kant and Schiller, on Richardson and Mackenzie, on Marivaux, Lenz and Klinger, on Gessner and Caspar Wolff and Goya. The book would be longer – but what it says would be the same.

I wish to thank the British Academy, who helped to finance the search for stony hermits and garden volcanoes in Czechoslovakia and East Germany; and my splendid teachers at Indiana University, Horst Frenz, Wadie Jwaideh, Henry Remak, Newton Stallknecht and Ulrich Weisstein, who said 'read a bit more', and Rainer Gruenter and the members of the eighteenth-century centre in Wuppertal, whose enthusiasm urged me, at last, to write the book.

ACKNOWLEDGEMENTS

My deep thanks are due to the following individuals and institutions, for kindly permitting the reproduction of many of the illustrations: Mr Maldwin Drummond, for the illustration of a proposed hermitage (plate 20), and for the accompanying text; Mr C.W. Thacker, for the illustration of *The Falls of Tivoli* by Gaspard Poussin (plate 5); the British Library, London, for plates 1-4, 12, 14, 21, 26, 28-9, 31, 41; the Tate Gallery, London, for plates 6, 16, 25, 36; the National Museum of Wales, Cardiff, for plate 17; the Derby Museum and Art Gallery for plates 22, 23, 30, 37; the National Maritime Museum, Greenwich, for plate 34; the Institute of Arts, Detroit, for plate 47; the Kunsthaus, Zürich, for plates 45-6. Photographs for plates 5, 13, 15, 20, 24, 38-9, 43, 49-50 are by the author.

1

The Status Quo

Aristotle claimed that all poetry was 'the imitation of men in action' (*Poetics*, 1448a). By poetry, he implied all forms of art, from sculpture to drama, from epic poetry to history, to painting and even to music. Aristotle resolutely associates poetry, or art, with human beings and their dealings with one another. He sees man as an ethical and social animal, and art as the presentation of man's dealings with other men – whether it be the tension between two people, the story of a family, or the concerns of a town or state, and whether these matters are comic, passionate, domestic, political, military or philosophical. It is the essence of the classical attitude. On a large scale, David's painting of the *Oath in the Tennis Court* (1791) is an admirable example of the 'imitation of men in action', showing a throng of people united in a moment of political determination. On a smaller scale, almost any comedy by Molière – for example, *Le Tartuffe* (1667) or *L'Avare* (1668) – shows a similar concern in representing the activities of a single family.

Aristotle's definition of the scope of poetry cuts out many matters which we might consider wholly proper, indeed desirable, as the subject of a work of art. Above all, the depiction of 'nature' is a subject which we, living two centuries after the romantic explosion at the end of the eighteenth century, have come to accept almost without thinking. To us, Samuel Palmer's *In a Shoreham Garden* (*c.* 1829), or *Landscape of the Vernal Equinox* by Paul Nash (1943), Claude Monet's paintings of water-lilies, *Les Nymphéas*, in the Orangerie (1914-25), or James Ward's *Gordale Scar* (1810), are all acceptable as parts of the depiction of 'nature', large or small, wild or gentle; yet to Aristotle, I believe they would have seemed, if not incomprehensible, at least not worthy of serious attention, and outside any consideration as 'works of art'. This change of attitude towards 'nature' is immense, and its implications, its effects, its ramifications, extend far beyond a simple question of whether 'birds and bees' may be accepted as the subject-matter of

1

poetry or painting; it is as vast a change as any in the whole history of human attitudes, influencing not only all forms of art, but also our attitudes in sexual, social and political affairs. This change of attitude took place in western Europe in the eighteenth century. It is the subject of this book.

In the seventeenth century, Aristotle's view of the proper subject-matter of poetry as 'the imitation of men in action' was accepted widely in western Europe. It is the centre of the classical attitude, an implicit or explicit part of the general view of man — a creature distinguished by his ability to think reasonably, and to exist in the context of society — in contact with other people, in the family, the city, the state, and a morally conscious entity in God's creation. The attitude coincides with both Christian and non-Christian views. 'Man in action' is, for the Christian, acting under the aegis of his Creator, and indeed can be seen — as by a Pascal — in terms of his success or general failure to act fitly towards God. In a fallen world, the re-ordering and improving of a man's acts — to love his neighbour as himself — comes high in the list of the Commandments. To a pessimist such as Hobbes, man may have been abandoned by his Creator, and be living in unhappy spiritual isolation, fearing and feared by his fellow men. Yet the gloomy Hobbesian phrase, *homo homini lupus*, while it says that man is a wolf, implies also that he exists through his actions towards other men-wolves. He is a social wolf, not one living singly in a forest.

The classical view is of man among men, not in isolation. In 1637, it is implicit in Descartes' 'Je pense, donc je suis,' 'I think, therefore I am,' seeing man as a creature who is able to *reason*, and it is abundantly evident in La Fontaine's *Fables* (1668-93), with the anthropomorphic presentation of the animals and the direction of each fable towards some human, and usually social, failing. Contemporary with La Fontaine is Molière's insistent depiction of middle-class family situations, and the perils which arise when someone — a member of the family, or an outsider — behaves in a self-centred and therefore anti-social way. For Molière, the healthy middle- or upper-middle-class Parisian family is the centre, the focus of 'men in action'; whoever threatens this centre is dangerous — the greedy, lecherous, hypocritical or eccentric person — and even such a man as Alceste, in *Le Misanthrope* (1666), though his intentions may be noble, must be expelled or corrected, since his views, if tolerated, could only disrupt the established ways of society. In England, much of Ben Jonson carries a similar, if less optimistic, view — we may think of *Volpone* (1606), or *The Alchemist* (1610), where the villains are at least punished or expelled, though their victims in society are so stupid, wishy-washy or mean-spirited that we cannot give them our whole approval. Yet, willingly or with misgiving, Molière and Ben Jonson both see society — the family, the town — as the only centre, and this holds true as a general attitude throughout the century, especially in France. In La Bruyère's *Caractères* (1688-94), for example, the analysis of different kinds of men — the courtier, the nobleman, the judge, the financier — sees each and every one as a member of society. The overall improvement of society is the goal. Again, Boileau's *Satires* (1666-1711), like those of his model Juvenal, run through the many weak, foolish or vicious types who flourish in the capital of his day, to show how they mar the proper union of 'men in action'. When writing of the duties of a poet, in his *Art poétique* (1674), Boileau sees him specifically as a wise and sociable member of society and not — as we post-romantics might do — as a solitary and unsocial person. Do not sit alone, says Boileau to the poet. Instead,

'Cultivez vos amis, soyez homme de foi. . . Il faut savoir encore et converser et vivre.'

['Cultivate your friends, be a man to rely on. . . And you must know the art of conversation, and the social life.']

(*Art poétique*, iv)

And again, after recommending to the budding poet 'let nature be your sole study', he links this to the advice 'Study the court and know the town' (iii) — the court and the town being the most likely places where nature — in Boileau's sense *here*, 'human nature' — may be studied. When men lived in their primitive state, it was poetry which first brought order, harmony and reason into their lives, and enabled them to leave the forests, and come together in a civil state.

Looking back again from two centuries of nature-worship, and from a similar period of increasingly assured control over the dangers of the natural world — safer, faster travel by whatever means, fewer wolves, bandits and cannibals — it is easy for us to underestimate both the indifference and the hostility of earlier centuries towards nature. A great many activities which some of us now undertake for pleasure — for example mountaineering, skiing, potholing, camping generally, or even 'going to the seaside' — were then both practically unknown and unthinkable. Until late in the seventeenth century, the only acceptable part of the natural world was that which was cultivated. Further afield, it was seen with indifference, suspicion or fear. This attitude was even

3

given theological backing in the 1680s in the *Telluris theoria sacra*, the *Theory of the Earth*, of Thomas Burnet (Latin, 1681-9, English 1684-90). Considering the jagged, precipitous shapes of mountains, and the irregular and unsymmetrical coastlines of the continents, Burnet concludes that such roughness, such ugliness, could not have been the work of God in the creation of the world. Rather are these the signs of God's displeasure — visible proof of the chaos which occurred at the time of the Flood. Truly, we live in a fallen world, from which much of God's original perfection, the smoothness and symmetry, has been lost.

Thomas Burnet's theory is neatly echoed by his namesake Gilbert Burnet in 1686, in his *Letters . . . in the years 1685 and 1686*, when he passes from the rural lakeside near Lausanne to the Alps. The first scene shows nature tamed, and brought within the control of society:

> The Banks of the *Lake* are the beautifullest spots of ground that can be imagined; for they look as if they had been laid by art, the sloping is so easie and so equal, and the grounds are so well cultivated and peopled, that a more delighting prospect cannot be seen anywhere (*Letters*, p. 11).

A while later he views the Alps, and these are so high, so irregular, that the traveller is

> apt to imagine . . . that these cannot be the primary productions of the *Author* of Nature; but are the vast ruins of the first *World*, which at the *Deluge* broke into so many inequalities (ibid., p. 12).

Nature in the raw: the evidence of an angry God, irregular, broken, unlovely — and therefore to be tamed, and made part of an ordered, social scheme.

Above all in France the ponderous edifice of Versailles, elaborated by Louis XIV from the early 1660s until the end of the century, is a symbol of attitudes — political, religious, aesthetic — designed to celebrate 'men in action', or, more precisely, Louis XIV controlling all other Frenchmen, and dominating the rest of Europe. The château and its gardens are a symbol of his authority, of the completeness of his rule, of the single religion within whose doctrine he is God's most powerful temporal ruler, and of the unified aesthetic outlook which brings royal order to the rest of Creation. Sanctioned by God, Louis XIV's system was absolute and intolerant of deviation. The king's subjects and admirers might emulate, but they should not differ from his views. It is entirely consistent that the revocation of the Edict of Nantes in 1685, which ended the toleration of Protestants in France for a century, should occur in the years of the greatest glory of Versailles, when the completed château and gardens were proclaiming the absolute authority of the king over society, the arts and the natural world.

Though other countries might not accept Louis' political domination, there was general agreement that in worldly matters the centre of interest could only be man, and that other aspects of the material universe were only important in so far as they were useful to man. In his *Essay Concerning Human Understanding* (1690) Locke remarks 'our business here is not to know all things, but those which concern our conduct' — i.e. our actions in relation to one another — and again he speaks of the need to distinguish 'what may be of use to us', i.e. things which are important in influencing our conduct. This necessarily excludes many other matters, in particular all those areas of the natural world which have no connection with man's social and ethical conduct. It is a view which has a long ancestry — we may see it in the ethical attitudes of Greek and Roman writers, from Sophocles to Marcus Aurelius, and again in Dante, and numberless others in between; while at the end of the sixteenth century, it is nobly uttered by Montaigne, when he says characteristically that a good teacher should possess, and should impart 'good conduct and right understanding' rather than a collection of unrelated and meaningless facts. I dare to say that such an ethical, classical and Aristotelian concern with 'men in action' is at the very centre of Shakespeare's plays, though his reference and his sympathies extend so wide that we may be tempted to read, and mis-read, an uncritical and wild enthusiasm for the whole of nature into his work.

In the last decades of the seventeenth century the 'aesthetic of Versailles', if not the political domination, was widely accepted and imitated. All over Europe palaces and gardens were adapted, or built from scratch to ape, to out-do what Louis XIV had created at Versailles. Within France, his own courtiers did so, and abroad even his rivals and enemies did so. No sooner had William of Orange settled in England (and his predecessor on the English throne, James II, escaped to France) than he set to work at Hampton Court to have the gardens made more imposing — the diarist John Evelyn wrote on 16 July 1689, 'I went to Hampton Court about business... A great apartment and spacious garden with fountains was beginning in the park at the head of the canal.' In the same period King Billy had employed an *émigré* Frenchman, the Huguenot Daniel Marot, to design a formal garden for him as the fitting horticultural extension of his new palace of Het Loo

in Holland; and meanwhile, great and less great noblemen followed suit
— in England, Le Nôtre may, or may not, have come over to consider
re-shaping St James's Park, but in 1694-5 the Frenchman Grillet certainly designed the great cascade at Chatsworth *à la St Cloud, à la
Marly*; and at the far less grandiose estate of Melbourne, in Derbyshire,
in 1696, the owner Thomas Coke was offered designs for his garden 'to
suit with Versailles'. All over Europe, from the 1680s, and in many
ways, right through the eighteenth century, the aesthetic of Versailles
was imitated; balance, symmetry, control over nature — right up to the
French Revolution such formal gardens were made and maintained.

Enough of formal gardens. The more general, and far more important
classical ideal of Molière, La Fontaine and Boileau, was a mighty force,
existing beside the newly born and struggling impulses of romanticism,
and often enough mixed, jumbled together without apparent strain in
the work of a single artist, and even in a single work of art — so that we
may see, for example, in the Abbé Prévost's *Manon Lescaut* (1731) an
acceptance of society-as-it-is (corrupt, possibly to be reformed, but
without any conceivable alternative) as the background for the
passionate, impulsive (and 'unclassical') adventures of the hero, Des
Grieux. Seventy years later, Benjamin Constant's *Adolphe* (written in
1807, published 1816) describes the adventures of another young man,
who has endeavoured to play just such an impulsive and passionate role,
but without real conviction; the narrator looks back at a passion which
was false — a betrayal of an ill-conceived romantic ideal — and at a
society which, though patently mediocre, was none the less *real*, and
the only possible milieu for persons of birth and education.

Most often, the classical ideal continued in a fairly 'pure' form, and
we may see it as the 'alternative' or even the 'opponent' of the new
romantic ideal of the eighteenth century. Above all, it is established in
the eighteenth-century view of the *citizen*, derived from Molière and
Locke. Usually, he is a married, balanced, considerate, productive and
middle-class man — that is, someone who lives in and for his society.
Though the exact components of the recipe vary, we may see this type
of man in many eighteenth-century plays and novels — the comedies of
Holberg, or Sheridan; or Lessing's *Minna von Barnhelm*. or the novels of
Fielding or Smollett — and the citizen is incontestably the 'centre' of
the immense *Encyclopédie* directed and edited by Denis Diderot, and
published between 1751 and 1772. When, in the article 'Encyclopédie',
Diderot asks what the *centre* of the assembled mass of universal knowledge should be, he replied to himself, 'Man is the sole point from
which we must begin, and to which everything must return.' When we

examine the *Encyclopédie*, we discover that this 'man' is not any abstract, naked, ideal creature — nor Adam, nor a Christian man, nor indeed the ideally proportioned Vitruvian man of the Renaissance, with a matching completeness of interests and activities such as were displayed by Alberti, or Leonardo — but a bourgeois man, hard-working and responsible: a citizen. We may still admire this kind of man today.

To illustrate this classical attitude in the eighteenth century both quickly and fairly, we may see its reflection in many writings which deal with travel and with 'foreign parts'. Today, the idea of 'abroad' appeals to many of us since it is different from our own surroundings. This appeal is a romantic one, and we shall witness its birth and amazing growth in the eighteenth century. But while the classical attitude was still vigorous, 'abroad' was not of interest first and foremost for its palm trees and exotic fragrance. Not at all. In 1719 Daniel Defoe published *Robinson Crusoe*, expanding in fictional form the experiences of Alexander Selkirk, marooned on the Pacific island of Juan Fernandez. Though Defoe fascinates us with Crusoe's adventures, he does not show his hero revelling in the 'delights' of a desert island. That is reserved for his imitators. When Crusoe finds himself shipwrecked on a lonely shore, his first action after a prayer of thanksgiving to be still alive is 'to get up into a thick bushy tree like a fir, but thorny . . . and where I resolved to sit all night' — he is terrified. And almost all the rest of his stay on the island is concerned with his attempts to build round himself a one-man, later two-man, form of the working household in which he had lived in England. His recurrent fears on the island are all to do with things — wild animals, cannibals — which are unfamiliar and hostile in the affairs of 'men in action', and his moments of satisfaction come when he has successfully reproduced some part of his earlier middle-class surroundings.

The classical view of travel is not disapproving, but governed by a man-centred interest which is often overlooked today. When Dr Johnson — the greatest English representative of the classical outlook — was in France in the company of the Thrales in 1775, Mr Thrale remarked one day on the quality of the landscape, and Johnson replied. This exchange was recorded by Mrs Thrale, who wrote:

Mr Thrale loved prospects, and was mortified that his friend [Dr Johnson] could not enjoy the sight of those different dispositions of wood and water, hill and valley, that travelling through England and France affords a man. But when he wished to point them out to his companion: 'Never heard such nonsense', would be the reply: 'a blade of grass is always a blade of grass, whether in one country or another: let us if we *do* talk, talk about something; men and women are my subjects of enquiry; let us see how these differ from those we have left behind' (Hester Piozzi, *Anecdotes of the late Samuel Johnson*, ed. S.C. Roberts, 1925, p. 66).

Johnson is here almost paraphrasing the words of Socrates, talking to his friend Phaedrus during a similar 'excursion' to the country outside Athens: 'I am a lover of knowledge, and the men who dwell in the city are my teachers, and not the trees or the country' (*Phaedrus*, 230, d). Johnson was not averse to travel, and undertook several arduous journeys in the British Isles. His principle is clear in his remark made in 1776, that 'the grand object of travelling is to see the shores of the Mediterranean'. This 'object' is not to be able to lounge in warmer sunshine than that available in the British Isles, but to inspect the region which gave birth to the religion and culture of western Europe — since 'almost all that sets us above savages, has come to us from the shores of the Mediterranean'. One travels 'in search of men' — as in Johnson's novel *Rasselas* (1759), where the young prince leaves his Happy Valley in Abyssinia to travel into Egypt, in order to make the 'choice of life', i.e. to decide what kind of life to lead. Once in Cairo, Rasselas does not often go out and about as we might do, seeing the sights of the greatest city in Africa. Instead, having reached the metropolis, he is content to stay most of the time where he is, conversing with the many different people who come to visit him. In this way the purpose of his travelling is fulfilled. The main characters in Voltaire's *Candide*, published in the same year as *Rasselas*, also travel, far more widely than Johnson's hero. Between them they visit a bewildering variety of places covering most countries in the world. Yet Voltaire tells us little of the flora and fauna, the *exotisme* of these foreign places, for he is in this respect firmly with Johnson in the classical tradition. The hapless Candide is not willingly in 'search of men' (except when he tries to find 'la perle des filles', Cunégonde); but Voltaire makes it his business to bring Candide into violent contact with unnumbered representatives of the human race, so that the book is a profoundly Aristotelian study of 'men in action'.

Such attitudes necessarily continue — essential parts of human culture. Though by 1800 the forces of romanticism had pushed much that was 'classical' to one side, classical attitudes could not possibly disappear, and they re-emerge in the nineteenth century, side by side with the — by now equally respectable — attitudes of romanticism. In 1836 Nicolai Gogol wrote *The Government Inspector*, in which the foibles of 'men in action' are the very centre of the play. In the 1890s, we see a man who is, as-near-as-dammit, the epitome of all Descartes, Johnson, Aristotle or Voltaire could have wished: Sherlock Holmes — the man of reason. Characteristically he remarks in *The Sign of Four* (1890), 'But love is an emotional thing, and whatever is emotional is opposed to that true cold reason that I place above all things.'

Then we find Bernard Shaw, and Galsworthy, and later the dreary Sartre. And in 1949, an incomparable play, Arthur Miller's *Death of a Salesman*, tells of 'men in action' as truly as did Sophocles (while, five years later, Dylan Thomas' *Under Milk Wood* is as pure a romantic vision as any in the century). Since then, we have had the Red Guards. What would Molière have made of Mao Tse-tung? Today, romantic and classic run neck-and-neck. If we are honest, we know that they are restless bedfellows, verging on oil and vinegar. But they are both with us, in the blood and in the brain; they'll live as long as we do.

2

Reaction

Agreeing with Saint-Simon, we may see a general weariness with the regime of Louis XIV, a tiredness with formality, with what Montaigne called the 'vertu lâche et catarreuse' of an old man. It shows, for example, in the little-known *bosquet* of 'Les Sources' at Trianon, where in the 1680s the greatest of all formal garden-designers, Jean Le Nôtre, made a small and irregular garden, shaded by trees, to the side of the palace of the Trianon, in which streams flowed gently through the *bosquet*, their course interrupted by the big trees. In 1694 Le Nôtre siad of it that, with the Tuileries, it was his favourite garden, and in it the ladies could sew at their ease, while 'the streams meander without order, and turn in the open spaces around the trees, with fountains irregularly spaced'. Again, in the paintings of Antoine Watteau (1684-1721), the ladies, lovers and musicians are portrayed in garden settings which reveal the beginnings of ruin — trees no longer clipped, but over-grown; statues shadowed with ivy, like the pillars and walls which would, once, have stood free and clear to mark boundaries, the proper extent of order. Yet greater uncertainty is felt in the tragedies of Racine. Set in royal palaces, strongholds of order and discipline, the characters find themselves ill at ease, prisoners, despairing. The confidence felt among Molière's characters, or Corneille's a generation before, in the strength and rightness of society has vanished, and so, for a Racinian hero, vital Cornelian words like 'gloire' and 'honneur' and the 'honnête' of Molière have no more power than last year's journalistic jargon.

At a philosophic and political level, the waning of French absolutism is apparent in the spirit of questioning which pervades the *Dictionnaire historique et critique* (1697) of Pierre Bayle. In this massive dictionary, the ponderous mass of information available concerning past persons, places and events is examined, piece by piece, to assess where — if anywhere — truth is to be seen. Though exercised mainly in the scrutiny, and rejection, of fabulous accounts of mythological happenings, Bayle's scepticism is fundamental, and rejects the unquestioning acceptance of both political absolutism and religious dogma. Bayle *questions*, expecting claims to be justified; if no logical justification can be found, then we should suspend our judgement; or reject any claim which cannot be adequately supported. Such 'rational enquiry' is obviously at the centre of the eighteenth-century enlightenment, and not part of the beginnings of romanticism; it is the attitude of the true *philosophe*, and will lead to the questioning of French absolutism which underlies Montesquieu's *Lettres persanes* (1721), the *Lettres philosophiques* (1733/4) of Voltaire, and the host of lesser writings which contain comparisons between French society and other real or imaginary 'utopian' societies. Paradoxically, some of these alternative societies will be presented with an uncritical enthusiasm which Bayle himself would have eschewed, based on an *a priori* assumption, that of the innate goodness of the 'noble savage', every bit as unprovable as the fabulous or superstitious beliefs which are exposed by Bayle.

In the British Isles opposition to French absolutism came in other ways. Long warfare between the French and the English led, especially after 1688, to the development, fostered for political reasons, of the view that France was a tyranny, while England was the home of liberty. It was not the first, nor the last, occasion for this propaganda, but its importance encouraged the rejection of more than just the political pretensions of the French. The genuine and permanent difference between the two monarchies after 1688 was in part behind the halting attempts to find native 'English' or 'British' characteristics which could be opposed to French ones, whether political, literary, architectural or horticultural. If the parliamentary system went back to the time of the Anglo-Saxons, and they were the fathers of freedom, then their form of architecture might also be remembered with respect, as being equally different from the architecture of the modern French (the early eighteenth century was not versed in the assessment of pre-Renaissance architecture. Approximately, 'battlements', 'pointed arches', 'fan vaulting' implied old, medieval, gothic — and so, by an easy extension, 'Saxon'). In the theatre, Shakespeare would not lie down. Awareness of his greatness was a continuing obstacle to the acceptance of the French classical drama. Indeed, his independence from the 'classical unities' made these rules seem less than dogma, and more a form of aesthetic tyranny.

Already, while the 'aesthetic of Versailles' was exerting its most dazzling appeal, and 'order', 'symmetry', 'control' over what was untidy and irregular in existence was being urged, an English thinker — scientist and philosopher — was establishing a system which was to challenge whole areas of the French attitude, and lead to its rejection for most of the eighteenth century. In proving that the universe was perfectly constructed on logical, mathematical principles, Isaac Newton (1642-1727) convinced most western European thinkers that each and every part of the Creation must embody an equal and comparable perfection. This view led to far-reaching conclusions, one of which, transferring the 'perfection' of abstract principles of mathematics and physics to the human part of the Creation, maintained that an all-wise, all-powerful and consistent Deity would surely create a 'perfect' world at the human level as well; and that our world must be 'the best of all possible worlds', in which all that happens must be 'for the best'. This philosophy of Optimism, some decades and several thinkers removed from Newton, is only slightly and briefly connected with the development of romanticism; but a related view, also descended from Newton's demonstration of the perfect construction of the universe, was central in the defeat of the 'aesthetic of Versailles'. This view saw God's perfection not only in the laws of mathematics and physics, but in the rest of God's physical creation — in the natural world. Echoing Newton, the philosopher John Locke claimed, 'The works of Nature everywhere sufficiently evidence a Deity.' Man may be a fallen creature, and — *pace* Thomas Burnet — some parts of nature may have been affected by his fall. But — in opposition to Burnet's general view — the works of nature are as much the handiwork of the Creator as the structure of the universe, and equally evidence of His perfection. From this, it is the tiniest step to saying that, if God is perfect, and God is good, then nature, likewise perfect, must also be good. We have reached one aspect of Shaftesbury's thought. And Shaftesbury is the father of romanticism.

*   *   *

We must accept as a general rule that Art embellishes Nature; that palaces are more beautiful than caves, that well cultivated gardens are more pleasing than a barren waste (Madelène de Scudéri, *La Promenade de Versailles*, 1669).

The wildness pleases. We seem to live alone with Nature. We view her in her inmost recesses, and contemplate her with more delight in these original wilds than in the artificial labyrinths and feigned wildernesses of the palace (Anthony Ashley Cooper, Third Earl of Shaftesbury, *The Moralists*, 1709).

Madame de Scudéri's remark occurs near the beginning of a panegyric upon the gardens of Versailles, which, in 1669, were well advanced in their magnificence, though they were not to be completed – and then only approximately – until the late 1680s. In England, the full impact of the French formal garden was not felt until the dynastic change in 1688, when the still vigorous forms of the Italian Renaissance garden were for a while arrested. (The last Renaissance garden in Italy itself, Isola Bella, was completed in 1671.) John Evelyn noted the new garden works at Hampton Court in 1689 – these were in particular the execution of the great *parterres de broderie* on the park side of the palace. Among lesser gardens of a formal kind laid out in England, it is proper to mention the small but totally French creation of Maréchal Tallard. He was taken prisoner at the battle of Blenheim in 1704, allowed to live in some style in Nottingham, and laid out two symmetrical parterres in his garden. This he must have done in 1705 or the year following, as a detailed description, with a plan, is given of 'M. Tallard's garden' in the 1706 edition of *The Retir'd Gard'ner* by George London and Henry Wise. In 1709, the nature of the formal French garden was fully codified in A. J. Dézallier d'Argenville's *La théorie et la pratique du jardinage*. It was translated into English in 1712.

I catalogue these dates since they indicate the years in which the formal French garden was without serious challenge or competitor in the whole of Europe. It is only a short time, some forty years; and it corresponds, somewhat ironically, with the life-span of the man whose ideas were to bring about the death of this kind of garden, and of the entire 'aesthetic of Versailles'. Anthony Ashley Cooper, Third Earl of Shaftesbury, was born in 1671. Serious, learned and highly intelligent, he was held back from public and political life by his poor health, and from the turn of the century he lived a life of relative retirement, his main interest being the broad study of philosophy. Those of his works which concern us are the *Letter concerning Enthusiasm*, written in 1707, published in 1708; *The Moralists* (1709); *The Characteristics* (1711), which include the earlier texts together with his *Advice to an Author* (1710) (quotations are from Shaftesbury, *Characteristics,* ed. J.M. Robertson, 1964); and his notes on philosophical matters which date from 1698 until 1712, but which remained unpublished until this century (*The Life, Unpublished Letters, and Philosophical Regimen of Anthony, Earl of Shaftesbury*, ed. Benjamin Rand, 1900: a fascinating book, but edited in an unsatisfactory and eccentric way). He travelled to Naples in search of a more congenial climate in 1711, but his health still declined, and he died there in 1713.

Following the thought of Newton (Shaftesbury's tutor was the philosopher Locke), and most deeply influenced by Greek and Roman Stoicism – Zeno, Epictetus, Marcus Aurelius – his philosophy includes an enthusiastic admiration for the physical universe, through which we may glimpse the perfection of God. The natural world – Nature – is God's creation, and therefore shares in God's perfection. God may be glimpsed in every part, however 'rough' or 'wild' it seems to us city-dwellers.

Shaftesbury is in this one of the founders of eighteenth-century Optimism, and Leibniz acclaimed the thought of the *Characteristics* when this work was published, saying that Shaftesbury had anticipated much that he himself had written in the *Essai de Théodicée* (1710). Yet his optimism is far away from the greasy *laissez-faire* which more complacent thinkers were soon to propose, culminating in the world-wide 'tout est bien' which Voltaire was to annihilate in *Candide* in 1759. For Shaftesbury, the qualities of the Divine were to be perceived rather *through* than *in* the natural world. He is a deist, rather than a pantheist, though his admiration for nature is so profound that it is at times tempting to think his attitude is pantheistic. In *The Moralists*, he argues through a dialogue between Philocles and Theocles, who walk together in the country in order to pursue their discussion in congenial surroundings. 'We fell naturally into the praises of a country life,' says Theocles, and remarks on the unity – and fitness – of nature. 'All things in this world are united,' he says, and exclaims, 'See there the mutual dependency of things!' (*Moralists*, II, iv, 61, 64, 65). But his aim is not mere praise of the natural world. To walk in the country is good, a necessary preliminary to deeper thought – 'invoking first the genius of the place, we will try to obtain at least some faint and distant view of the sovereign genius and first beauty' (II, i, 40). The 'genius of the place' may be paraphrased as 'the ideal spirit of the natural world around us', ideal yet subordinate to the 'first beauty' of the Creator. Again Theocles exclaims, as they walk into the country,

> Here ... we shall find our sovereign genius, if we can charm the genius of the place ... to inspire us with a truer song of Nature, teach us some celestial hymn, and make us find some divinity present in these solemn places of retreat (III, i, 97).

A few moments later, reaching 'the most beautiful part of the hill', he is inspired by 'the open scene of Nature in the plains below', and is launched by his poetic feeling into rapturous praise of nature, and nature's divine Creator:

O glorious nature! supremely fair and sovereignly good! all-loving and all-lovely, all-divine! ... O mighty Nature! wise substitute of Providence! impowered creatress! O thou impowering Deity, supreme creator! Thee I invoke and thee alone above ... be thou my assistant and guide me ... whilst I venture thus to tread the labyrinth of wide Nature and endeavour to trace thee in thy works (III, i, 98-9).

With such a view of nature, 'supremely fair and sovereignly good', Shaftesbury here turns his back on the suggestion that nature might be 'fallen', a physical reminder of God's anger with the world. Instead, nature is a vision 'whose looks are so becoming and of such infinite grace; whose study brings such wisdom, and whose contemplation such delight; whose every single work affords an ampler scene, and is a nobler spectacle than all which ever art presented!' (III, i, 98).

Shaftesbury never approaches the universal optimism of Leibniz' followers (such as Christian Wolff, or the poet Brockes of whom more must be said later), since he is most deeply convinced of the inadequacy of human beings. He sees human tampering with nature as the great flaw; and human attempts to 'improve' the existing beauties of nature as puny and misguided. So, when Philocles is at last fully convinced of the divine presence in the works of nature, his praise of Nature is made more forceful by a condemnation of human attempts to improve nature in artificial ways. His outburst is famous. Speaking to Theocles, he says:

Your genius, the genius of the place, and the Great Genius have at last prevailed. I shall no longer resist the passion in me for things of a natural kind, where neither art nor the conceit or caprice of man has spoiled their genuine order by breaking in upon that primitive state. Even the rude rocks, the mossy caverns, the irregular unwrought grottos and broken falls of waters, with all the horrid graces of the wilderness itself, as representing Nature more, will be the more engaging, and appear with a magnificence beyond the formal mockery of princely gardens (III, ii, 125).

'Things of a natural kind' have beauty and virtue for Shaftesbury even if they are wild. The quotation from *The Moralists* at the head of this chapter, beginning 'The wildness pleases', comes from Theocles' description of the deserts of Egypt, after a passage on the terror of the crocodile. Escaping these monsters, he says, let us 'fly to the vast deserts of these parts', and he proceeds to *admire* them. 'All ghastly and

hideous as they appear, they want not their peculiar beauties. The wildness pleases' . . . The contrast between the scenes of nature and 'the
artificial labyrinths and feigned wildernesses of the palace' is now far
greater. Here nature appears in the form of deserts which are 'all
ghastly and hideous', with 'scaly serpents . . . savage beasts, and
poisonous insects', which may be 'terrible' and 'contrary to human
nature'. Now these 'are beauteous in themselves, and fit to raise our
thoughts in admiration of that divine wisdom, so far superior to our
short views'. Nature contains what is *terrible*, and yet this leads to the
divine wisdom — 'we are yet assured of the perfection of all' (III, i,
122).

How different from Mme de Scudéri's 'palaces are more beautiful
than caves'! In his time Shaftesbury must have seen much of the
'formal mockery of princely gardens', and he may even have read, and
rejected in his mind, the lines by Mme de Scudéri. In his notes he
attacks the elaborate structure of court life and its extension by means
of theatrical, musical, architectural and horticultural artifice. These he
calls 'rattles', much the same as Pascalian *divertissements*, keeping men
'busy', to save them from seeking the real and the divine, *'tranquillity,
serenity, retreat, peacefulness, silence, order, beauty, majesty*, and the
rest that is found in nature at those times when the temper leads that
way, and seeks the romantic places, the rocks and seashores, wood,
caves, etc.' (Rand, *Life of Shaftesbury*, p. 218).

Shaftesbury is not only the originator of reaction to the formal
French garden. He is also, more than any other person, the originator of
the eighteenth-century cult of the sublime, the belief in the beauty of
terror; of the belief that the poet derives his inspiration from what is
sublime, rather than any other source; and of the belief that through
such inspiration, the poet is — if only temporarily — different from
other people, and superior to them.

Shaftesbury's view of the poet — his nature, and his relationship to
God — develops from book to book. In the *Letter concerning Enthusiasm*
he tries to disentangle the conduct and attitude of a true *poet*, who is
'inspired', from that of a fanatical, falsely 'enthusiastic' or 'superstitious' person. Yet they work in similar ways. 'Poets are fanatics too,'
he writes, since, for their *poetry* to be inspired, *they* must first be
seized with inspiration from above. The poet is possessed by 'a noble
enthusiasm', and his inspiration, coming from the 'divine presence', 'may
be justly called divine enthusiasm' (*Enthusiasm*, vi, 36, vii, 37, 38).

In *The Moralists*, Shaftesbury considers the true enthusiast, the poet.
Theocles is shown as one granted poetic inspiration, and this comes to

him when contemplating the unspoiled works of nature. These may often be wild — the wondering Philocles exclaims to him 'the very storms and tempests had their beauty in your account' (*Moralists*, I, ii, 15) — and they must be set apart from the bustle of the town. Evening or night are favourable — Philocles remarks that 'the approaching objects of the night were the more agreeable to you for the solitude they introduced' (I, ii, 12). Even the reader, the listener must bring himself to a mood of the sort such surroundings would induce in order to 'relish these diviner poets'; we must be 'contemplative', with a disposition 'as that in which they writ themselves' (I, iii, 27).

When Theocles bursts into his rhapsodic praise of nature, he is *inspired*. Philocles, watching him, sees that he is ready, and says

'Begin: for now I know you are full of those divine thoughts which meet you ever in this solitude . . .'
Just as I had said this, he turned his eyes away from me, musing awhile by himself; and soon afterwards, stretching out his hand, as pointing to the objects round him, he began:
'Ye fields and woods . . .' (III, i, 97)

His ecstatic outburst is uttered 'sous le charme', as Diderot will put it when paraphrasing this passage in his *Entretiens sur le Fils Naturel* in 1757. This Shaftesbury confirms when Theocles awakes: 'Here he stopped short, and starting as out of a dream: "now Philocles", said he, "how have I appeared to you in my fit?" ' (III, i, 99). In Theocles' second, and much longer, outburst (III, i, 110-24), the poetic inspiration is even more clearly separated from everyday behaviour in the manner of his awakening. His speech tails off, and he is silent. Shaftesbury explains, 'Here he paused a while and began to cast about his eyes, which before [i.e. during his period of inspiration] seemed fixed. He looked more calmly,' so that his friend Philocles could deduce that 'whether I would or no, Theocles was now resolved to take his leave of the sublime'. When Theocles speaks again, in a more normal mood, he changes 'to a familiar voice'.

For Shaftesbury then the poet is an exceptional person, who is inspired rather than calculating; he is inspired by 'things of a natural kind, where neither art nor the conceit or caprice of man has spoiled their genuine order by breaking in upon that primitive state'; these 'things of a natural kind' can inspire him both with delight, and horror, and apprehension, as in vast woods where 'the faint and gloomy light looks horrid as the shade itself'; and his inspiration may indeed verge on melancholy, enthusiasm and madness, 'while an unknown force works on the mind, and dubious objects move the wakeful sense' (III, i, 123).

Shaftesbury's final position, in the *Advice to an Author* (1710), is firmer still. Here the true poet is seen as the great creator, the true Prometheus who creates for the benefit of mankind, and whose creation is inspired by that of God himself. 'Such a poet is indeed a second *Maker*; a just Prometheus under Jove.' The poet is the only one who has this gift of fully harmonious creation – and it is modelled on, and inspired by, the creative nature of God. 'Like that sovereign artist or universal plastic nature, he forms a whole, coherent and proportioned in itself with due subjection and subordinacy of constituent parts' (*Advice*, I, iii, 135-6). How different from Boileau's poet, whose task is to 'study the court, and know the town'.

The Moralists appeared in 1709, the same year in which Dézallier d'Argenville's *La théorie et la pratique du jardinage* was published. Dézallier d'Argenville's work was popular, and was re-issued as late as 1760. But, even before it appeared in English in 1712, Shaftesbury's 'passion . . . for things of a natural kind' had taken root, and was becoming more popular than 'the formal mockery of princely gardens'. In 1726, in his *Tour through . . . Great Britain*, Defoe described that parterre which Maréchal Tallard had made in Nottingham soon after the battle of Blenheim. Twenty years had passed and Defoe commented, 'it does not gain by English keeping'. He might have added, 'for in these days, only the wildness pleases'.

While Shaftesbury was elaborating his thought, other writers were discussing the quality of the created world in roughly parallel terms. Though Shaftesbury's thought is only Christian by courtesy, there was in his time a current of Christian opinion which adopted the Newtonian view of the mathematical perfection of the universe to use it as a double proof of the existence of God, and of God's excellence in making so perfect a world. An 'accurate' God must be a benevolent God – and since God is 'accurate' in all his works, all his works must therefore be 'good'. Two English theologians with such views were John Ray (1627-1705), whose *Wisdom of God in the Creation* appeared in 1691, and William Derham (1657-1735), who published *Physico-Theology, or a Demonstration of the Being and Attributes of God from his Works of Creation* in 1713. The former might have been read by Shaftesbury, the latter might have read what Shaftesbury wrote, and all three could have been known to slightly later writers, such as Addison or Thomson.

In Switzerland in the same period another scientific theologian combined a passionate interest in the natural world with equal interest in justifying the truth of the Bible. Johann Jakob Scheuchzer (1672-1733) was a deeply learned natural historian, whose scholarship was backed by considerable curiosity of an experimental kind. His early *Beschreibung der Natur-Geschichten des Schweizerlands* (3 parts, 1706, 1707, 1708) is a truly remarkable work in which he discusses — rather in the manner of a *Spectator* essay — a host of different topics to do with the natural history of his country, which he has patently studied *on the spot*, and by means of investigations which leave the generalities of Ray, Shaftesbury and Derham far behind. Mining, mineralogy, fossils, forestry, cheese and wine, rainbows by moonlight — topic after topic is examined with detailed comment on what he himself has observed. For our purpose it is especially important to notice his interest in *mountains*, which appears with an essay on mountain travel in paper 17 of part I, and continues with a score of studies of Alpine topics. The third part (1708) has as the general heading of each paper 'Schweizerische Berg-Reisen', mountain journeys which were in the early eighteenth century both rare and dreaded by educated people. In I, 17, he shows that these were neither so difficult, nor so dangerous, as town-dwellers think — indeed, the peasants who live in the mountains may be both fitter and more contented than ourselves. Then, in part III, he describes 'a journey over the highest Alps made in 1705'. He is proud of this — one paper is called *Summae Alpes* — and two papers, numbers 7 and 11, describe mountain scenery with a detail and an excitement which is absolutely new, and unmatched in Europe for many years. Number 7 describes the 'Panten- oder Banten-Bruck', and it is illustrated by an engraving of the bridge by Melchior Füssli. Scheuchzer's admiration is mainly for the visual spectacle — which he sees in terms of a painting:

A landscape painter will not regret the time it takes him to get here, since the prospect is so exceptional. . . Below the bridge is a drop of a hundred feet, while to the south and north there is a long *perspectiv'd* steepening of the cliffs, which gets darker and darker as the light fails to penetrate, while the *Sandbach* rushes and foams below the cliffs at a fearful depth. . . Even the boldest people can be overcome with giddiness at such a view, extending from such a height to such a depth (III, 43).

And then Scheuchzer adds, 'I found it so *curious* that I had several sketches made of this bridge.' In paper 11, he discusses the valley of the river Reuss, near the Teufelsbrück or *Pons Diaboli*, again illustrated by one of Melchior Füssli's engravings (see Plate 1). His description here is longer and more complex. He notes the contrast and variety —

> the road is at times joyous and pleasing, at times wild and fearsome; you reach the lower parts of the mountain through an attractive forest; now you glimpse through a dark and natural *perspective* many trees, some upright, and others tumbled one over another into the depths of the roaring, foaming Reuss; now you see streams dashing down the mountains, pouring down towards the river; now you hear the sound, sometimes delicious, sometimes terrifying, of the forest cataracts which, from the height of the fall or from the rocks in the way are dissolved into spray — in which the glancing sunbeams are transformed, as in a work of art, to become many-coloured rainbows (III, 43).

This cheers the damp and weary traveller, who is then filled with fear and horror at the sight of 'pendant, often wholly overhanging and shattered sections of cliff, which may break loose at any moment and carry the traveller from this world into the next'. And then, Scheuchzer ends his mountain-picture by saying that their slopes,

> rarely covered with all sorts of uncommon mountain plants, provide manifold delight for a curious mountaineer, which sweetens the arduous difficulties for him, and gives him frequent cause to admire the great works of almighty God, best creator of the natural world (III, 43).

Elsewhere in the mountains Scheuchzer had found marine fossils (III, 5), which, he said, were left over from the Flood. They were a sign, like the 'rare mountain plants', of God's guiding hand, and in his next work, *Herbarium diluvianum* (1709), he concentrates on the evidence of fossils, found in the Alps and other rocky parts of the world, to re-establish the truth of the biblical Flood; and through this, to confirm the authority of the Bible and the wisdom of God the creator. The fossils are relics of this biblical event, and in concentrating on this aspect of the anger of God with sinful man, Scheuchzer is able to side-step discussion of the moral Fall, and the depressing inadequacy of humankind, while admiring the 'relics of the most wise and eternal geometer'. Scheuchzer was not the first to see fossils deposited on mountain tops as 'proof' of the Flood — he had translated John Woodward's *Specimen geographiae physicae* in 1704 — and the arguments for and against were to be heard in England, France and Germany for most of the century; but he *is* important in going on from this to discuss the whole of Creation as evidence of the truth of the Bible. In 1721 he published *Jobi Physica Sacra, oder Hiobs Natur-Wissenschaft verglichen mit der Heutigen*, a heavy volume which goes verse by verse through the book of Job to show how accurate the biblical picture of the physical world had been. Numerous references to other books of the Bible confirm their accuracy as well. And then, from 1731 to 1735 he produced the four volumes of his huge and sumptuous *Physica sacra*, which was published simultaneously in Latin, German and French. This work combines his years of study of the natural world with a parallel consideration of the Bible, to produce the fullest and most learned proof that our entire natural surroundings, from the remotest stars to tiny spiders, are God's handiwork, and that the evolution of human activities from earliest times is truly and accurately portrayed in the Bible. Scheuchzer's text goes side by side with detailed engravings, all showing, as St Bernard had said long before, that *natura codex est Dei*. The plates and text concerned with the Creation show this to perfection — for example, for the Third Day, the plates include one (VI) of mountains and the sea, and another (VIII) showing these bare and rugged shapes clothed with trees and plants; then Plate XII shows the landscape of hills and valleys, adorned with vegetation, overlaid with insects of many kinds, bees and butterflies, and with a magnificent spider's web stretching over one corner of the frame (see Plate 3). Later in the Fifth Day, Plate XIX shows a coastal scene with a rocky archway in which shells are embedded, and this (related to Scheuchzer's earlier *Herbarium diluvianum*) is backed up by Plate XLVI, entitled *Cataclysmi reliquiae*, the 'relics of the Flood', with a view of stratified rocks in the mountainside. Plate LXXV, *Stellae innumerabiles*, 'countless stars', could be an illustration, not merely to Scheuchzer's biblical exegesis, linked to Newtonian astronomy, but to Addison's lines (*Spectator*, no. 465, 23 August 1711):

The Spacious Firmament on high,
With all the blue Etherial sky,
And spangled Heav'ns, a Shining Frame,
Their great Original proclaim.

God is apparent in every part of the Creation — however 'misshapen' or violent. Plate CLXVII illustrates Exodus, xix, 16-18, showing 'thunders and lightnings' on Mount Sinai when 'the Lord descended upon it in fire . . . and the whole mount quaked greatly'. Here the wildness of the scene reflects the terrible presence of the Almighty. Scheuchzer's text (I, p. 188) points out the link between what happened on Mount Sinai, and what *we* might witness were we present at a volcanic eruption. Volcanoes may thus be understood as God's handiwork, and therefore admired. This point is most clearly put in his text to Plates VI and VII (I, p. 12), showing the creation of land and sea:

> Stand here, o friend of the divine, and adore the signs of GOD the eternal geometer, in exquisite proportion from the height to the depth, from the summits to the caves, from the deserts to the oceans: admire the supreme symmetry in this confusion, the order in the ruins of the Divine Architecture.

Like Thomas and Gilbert Burnet, Scheuchzer agrees that the world was shattered at the time of the Flood. But he maintains that what remains is not just 'a World lying in its rubbish', but still a creation of infinite order and beauty. He is affected both by Newton and by Leibniz — God's creation is 'accurate', and it is good. When he discusses the rainbow (*Iridis demonstratio*, vol. I, Plate LXVI, text p. 81), the illustration shows a *modern* spectator looking at a rainbow, overprinted with a network of lines demonstrating the optical process. His text indicates the scientific side, then adds:

> I cannot refrain from warning, or at least requesting any preacher who might wish to use the objects of nature as edifying topics, and who would explain them in an allegorical or mystical way, to base his explanations not on false and invented principles, but on true principles founded in nature itself.

The rainbow therefore is not 'miraculous', but part of a logical and comprehensible creation — and therein lies its 'wonder'. The rainbow is a neat and telling paradigm to isolate when discussing the early romantic interest in nature, since it is both firmly tied to biblical thought concerning the Flood and the Fall of Man, and to Newtonian optics and subsequent theories to do with the mathematical perfection of the universe. (Newton had consolidated earlier discoveries by establishing that the chromatic order of the colours was necessarily fixed and demonstrable; which served for later speculators as a symbol of *all* that Newton had discovered. Looking back, we may note that as late as *c.* 1636, Rubens' *Rainbow Landscape* (in the Wallace Collection, London) presents the rainbow in an improbable position *vis-à-vis* the sunlight, an error which would have been unlikely a decade or so later.) Scheuchzer's lengthy discussion of nocturnal rainbows derived from moonlight, in his *Beschreibung der Natur-Geschichten des Schweizerlands* (part II, 1707, paper 11, pp. 41-4), says nothing to encourage a mystical attitude, and everything to explain how they are scientifically possible, even the 'Exempel ohne Exempel' of a double moon-rainbow which independent witnesses had recently seen, and to establish the precise and extremely rare conjunction of circumstances which would allow such rainbows to appear.

Following soon after Scheuchzer's first books come the poems of two other writers, who share similar, if not identical, attitudes to God and to nature. They are the German Barthold Hinrich Brockes (1680-1747) and the Swiss Albrecht von Haller (1708-77), and between them they take the appreciation of nature a long way beyond the generally abstract theory of Shaftesbury and Scheuchzer's scientific curiosity.

Brockes is the first 'nature poet' to write in German in the eighteenth century. From his first volume of poems, published in 1721, to the ninth, published in 1748, a year after his death, his writing is distinguished by a vision of particular details of the natural world — remarkable at any time, and outstandingly so in the early eighteenth century. His descriptions have the perception of minute detail which we expect from Dutch still life paintings of the period, and Brockes was in fact a close friend and admirer of the painter Willem van Mieris. His descriptions are of natural objects and scenes, mostly small ones, studied in his garden or in gentle rural surroundings. His vision lingers most willingly on details seen close to — the blossom on a single tree, a bunch of flowers, the petals of a single flower, or the shimmering, iridescent wings of a beetle. Compared with Scheuchzer and with Scheuchzer's illustrators, his view of nature is minute — no grandiose mountain scenes, no panoramas of the Creation, Flood or crossing of the Red Sea — yet its exactness is convincing.

As well as this, Brockes inevitably conveys a 'message'. He is, following Leibniz and his disciple Christian Wolff, an Optimist, wishing to see all for the best in a world made by God for the benefit of mankind. He is a *teleologist*, seeing all things made for one end or purpose — i.e. for man — and so his entire *œuvre* is a hymn of praise — man's praise for God's goodness. The first volume of his own poems was called *Irdisches*

Vergnügen in Gott — 'Earthly Contentment in God' — and each of the eight following volumes had the same title. Entirely in tune with this attitude is his translation in 1740 of Pope's *Essay on Man*, the most notable statement of the optimistic creed to come from England. Brockes' whole-hearted acceptance of the Wolffian attitude leads to grotesque and unpoetic perspectives in many of his weaker poems, as each poem carries the 'message' of optimism at some point. Considering the summer sunshine, or the flowers of spring, it is not hard to say, 'All things bright and beautiful . . . the good Lord made them all.' But the winter? Snuff? The wolf? The wolf, he concludes, is *useful* after all — its glands are valued as medicaments, its skin is an important trading commodity (*I. Vergnügen*, IX). The cold winter is a blessing, since it makes beggars jump up and down to keep warm (IV). And snuff? Even this contains a 'message' — 'Man, thou are but dust.'

He is the great poet of colour, aware of its subtle nuances; and aware too of its changing and complex quality when affected by passing lights, shadows or reflections, by movement, by the impinging force on one colour of other, adjacent colours. In 'Kirschblüte bei der Nacht' — 'Cherry-blossom in the Night' (II), he talks first of the whiteness of cherry-blossoms in the moonlight,

> Ich glaubt, es könne nichts von grössrer Weisse sein.
> Es schien, ob wär ein Schnee gefallen.
> . . .
> Est ist kein Schwan so weiss, da nämlich jedes Blatt,
> Indem daselbst des Mondes sanftes Licht
> Selbst durch die zarten Blätter bricht,
> Sogar den Schatten weiss und sonder Schwärze hat.

> [I thought that nothing could be more white than this,
> It seemed as though the snow had fallen.
> . . .
> No swan could be as white when every single leaf
> — while the moon's own gentle light
> pours through the tender leaves —
> has white for shadows, such special white for black.]

As white as could be imagined, he thinks, 'Unmöglich . . . kann auf Erden Was Weissers angetroffen werden' — 'nowhere on earth can anything more white be found'. But not so. He looks upward through the branches, loaded 'Von zierlich weissen, runden Ballen' — 'with dainty white round balls' —

Und ward noch einen weissern Schein,
Der tausendmal so weiss, der tausendmal so klar,
Fast halb darob erstaunt, gewahr.
Der Blüte Schnee schien schwarz zu sein
Bei diesem weissen Glanz.

[I sensed a brightness still more white,
a thousand times as white, a thousand times as clear,
and I looked up again amazed.
The blossom's snow appeared now black,
before this white splendour.]

Not moonlight, but light from a star, a light 'which shone straight into my soul'.

He can also describe a broader scene, as in 'Die auf ein starkes Ungewitter erfolgte Stille' — 'After a violent storm: the calm' (I), where he tells of a downpour following a month of burning summer. This poem — to my mind one of his best — is one of the first to depict a storm in detail. Brockes is obviously fascinated by the storm, observes it closely, and is *relieved* when it has gone by. Colours again are prominent — as the sky becomes overcast,

         die Luft ward plötzlich dick
Das Licht ward allgemach von Schatten überwunden;
Es stieg ein grauer Duft und Nebel in die Höh;
Des Tages Gold erbleicht'; es schwand das heitre Blau;
Die dicke, dunkle Luft beschattete die See;
Die Bäche schienen schwarz, die Flüsse braun und falbe;

[suddenly the air grew thick
and all at once the light succumbed to shade;
grey haze and mist rose in the air,
the gold of day grew pale; the cheerful blue had disappeared,
and all the lake was shaded with a thick, dark air,
the streams seemed black, the rivers brown and dun;]

When the storm breaks, the colours change,

Ein fürchterliches Braun färbt die erzürnte Flut,
Die Luft ein grässlich Grau.

[a fearsome brown stains the angry flood,
a hideous grey tints all the air.]

Wind, rain, thunder and lightning wildly alternate, and at long last pass by. And then, after the terror of the storm, people come out from the shelter of their cottages, and find the damage to be less than they had feared — 'Ist alles wohlgemut,' 'it is a cheerful scene,' as the farming activity begins once more:

> Dort wendet mas das Heu; hie mäht, da bindet man,
> Ja das Gefilde lebt, soweit man sehen kann

> [There they turn the hay; here they mow, and there they bind,
> the fields alive once more, as far as eye can see]

— and the land, properly moistened for the first time for a month, surges with fresh life and beauty, crops, cattle, birds and fish, clover, rushes by the stream. We are suddenly in high summer, as the cattle browse in the rich water-meadows:

> indem das glatte Vieh
> Wenn es mit schlankem Hals oft bis an Bauch und Knie
> In Klee und Blumen geht, von den gespaltnen Füssen
> Die dunklen Zeichen lässt.

> [while the smooth-coated cattle
> bend their sleek necks in the knee-high clover and grass;
> dark in the moist soil, the traces of their cloven hooves.]

The storm — God's strength — has done no serious harm, and with the returning sun — God's love — the country is renewed in its first beauty — 'still the old Eden, yet a world renewed'. Though Brockes' verse is sometimes made clumsy by the insistent rhyme, and though it is often spoiled outright by the exigent 'message' at the end, he has the most perceptive eye for the gentle natural scene, for the vivid and tiny detail of garden and farm, until the nineteenth century; and in his feeling for colour — its variety, complexity, delicacy and mutability — he has, I think, a most special place. (I doubt if Turner, or Monet, or Proust had ever heard of Brockes. But on the subject of colour, they would all four have understood each other.)

In 1745, two years before his death, Brockes published 'as an appendix to the *Irdisches Vergnügen in Gott*', a complete translation of Thomson's *Seasons*. Brockes' version comes as a parallel text with the English, and has William Kent's four original engravings. In a few pages, Thomson's *Seasons* are discussed as part of the British response to

Shaftesbury's 'the wildness pleases'. It is enough here to note that Brockes' and Thomson's writing of poetry about the world of nature was both independent and contemporary — Thomson's first version of 'Winter' was published in 1726, Brockes' first volume of the *Irdisches Vergnügen* in 1721 — and that Brockes saw there was sufficient difference between his detailed, and Thomson's broader, approach to nature for him to call the *Seasons* an 'appendix' to his own work.

Albrecht von Haller's poem 'Die Alpen' was written in 1729, after he had made a plant-hunting journey into the Alps, and also after he had come under the influence of English literature, having travelled to England in 1727. 'Die Alpen' was first published in Haller's *Versuch Schweizerischer Gedichten* in 1732.

Haller's Alpine journey seems to have impressed him as deeply as did Scheuchzer's over twenty years before. Indeed Haller visited Scheuchzer towards the end of his journey, and wrote with respect of his encyclopedic production — in 1728, Scheuchzer must have been well advanced with the preparation of his *Physica sacra*. What marks Haller out from Scheuchzer is his vision of particular detail in the natural world, combined with an especial admiration for the rugged, inhospitable and uncultured Alpine regions which goes beyond Scheuchzer's biblically supported scientific explanations of natural wildness, and also goes further into the realm of *untamed* nature than anything in the poetry of Brockes. His travel-journal, written in French in 1728, the *Récit du premier voyage dans les Alpes*, contains two passages which show the way his attention is directed. First, he *admires* the wildness of the mountains — in the vicinity of Lausanne, where he is placed between farmland and mountains, he writes, 'this blend of the fearful and the pleasing, of wild and cultivated land has a charm unknown to those who have no interest in nature'; and, second, he *admires* the peasants, as being happier and better than townsfolk — of one group, who lived in a primitive fashion without even the knowledge or use of forks and spoons, he says, 'Happy race, preserved by ignorance from so many of the evils which come with the refinement of the town.'

In 'Die Alpen' these points provide the focus. The mountains are wild, beautiful and *good*; while their inhabitants are not only healthy — this much Scheuchzer had seen — but possess happiness and virtue which have vanished from the life of city-dwellers. The poem opens with a contrast between the unhappy, ambitious men of the town, and the happy shepherds of the mountains, who, taught by Nature, live still in an age of gold. O happy age, Haller writes, 'Beglückte güldne Zeit, du Erstgeburt der Jahren' — 'blessed golden age, thou first-born of the years' — this first age of mankind lives still in the Alps, though not in the unreal form the poets have described. The 'güldne Zeiten' to be found in the mountains are not 'arcadian' — the Alps are 'hardly the vale of Tempe' — the seasons are harsh with snow and ice, the fields are stony. But here virtue reigns, freedom, equality and simplicity, and having these qualities, the city's vain, extravagant material needs may be ignored. This happiness comes from a life led in the country, in the bosom of nature. Nature is the teacher, and Haller repeats the words 'die Natur' in contexts which add to the idea of 'abstract virtue' or 'ideal conduct' (which the seventeenth century would have approved), an indisputable sense of 'the surroundings of the natural world'. So, when he exclaims, 'Ihr Schüler der Natur, ihr kennt noch güldne Zeiten,' 'You, pupils of nature, still you know an age of gold,' he explains that the natural surroundings in which they live protect them from the uneasy ambitions of the town, and guarantee their simple, happy life. They learn this, not from books, but from their — natural — surroundings. Reason itself is 'led' by nature: 'Hier herrschet die Vernunft, von der Natur geleitet.' Haller's line is extraordinary in the attempt to combine the two ideas, like the later line of Pope 'the feast of reason, and the flow of soul' (*Epistles and Satires*, 'To Mr. Fortescue', 1.127). Yet at the end of the same stanza, he is every bit as 'ahead of his time'; combining Shaftesbury's praise of 'things of a natural kind' with an appreciation of *instinctive* behaviour:

> Was Epiktet getan und Seneca geschrieben,
> Sieht man hie ungelehrt und ungezwungen üben.

> [What Epictetus did, and Seneca wrote,
> This we see here, and done untaught and unconstrained.]

Haller is remarkable in his praise of Alpine simplicity, which is again and again set in contrast with the effete and luxurious life of the town. The happiness of individuals is better assured 'hier, wo die Natur allein Gesetze gibet' — 'here where nature alone gives laws' — since the prejudices of class or possessions do not exist. There is no artificiality in a shepherd's wooing, for his ardour is fed from purer stuff:

> Natur und Liebe giesst in ihn ein heimlich Feuer,
> Das in den Adern glimmt, und nie die Müh erzwingt.

> [Nature and love inspire his secret fire,
> wholly unforced and glowing through his veins.]

This peasant poetry comes from an inspiration which is hard to distinguish from the 'divine enthusiasm' which Shaftesbury saw as the privilege of all true poets. Haller does not go further – he does not, for example, say that *all* poetry, not just the shepherd's songs of love, should be so inspired – but turns to other characters whose worth is superior to that of city-dwellers. There is first the old man, representing the warrior, defender of freedom; then the wise old man, who is 'a living law', the living memorial to law and justice, preserved by such as William Tell, while tyranny rules in foreign lands; and then a third old man is described, a repository of nature-lore. Here Haller launches into the most coherent section of his poem, describing the beauties, glories, value and *goodness* of the mountains. All that 'playful nature' has united here is good – 'Der Bergen ewig Eis, der Felsen steile Wände; Sind selbst zum Nutzen da und trinken das Gelände' – 'the mountains' eternal ice, and the sheer cliff walls; even these are useful, and water all the land'. All therefore is worthy of study and admiration. As a post-Newtonian, he praises the rainbow above a foaming waterfall – as did Scheuchzer – and as a botanist he is thrilled by the Alpine flora, so abundant that

Ein ganz Gebürge scheint gefirnisst von dem Regen,
Ein grünender Tapet, gestickt mit Regenbögen.

[All the mountainside seems embroidered by the rain,
a green and growing carpet, tricked out by rainbows.]

And last the treasures of stone and ice and water are described – minerals, crystals, 'O Reichtum der Natur!' – 'o wealth of nature!' – and the sources of the great rivers of Europe. Europe, down below, exists in slavery, wicked, envious and betrayed, while in the mountains, a simple people still live modestly, virtuously and in happiness, in the world of nature – 'die Natur allein kann glücklich machen' – 'nature alone can bring content'.

Though several of these writers have praised the natural world, none before has ventured to say that those who live by force of circumstances in simple natural surroundings – i.e. country folk, peasants, *as opposed* to townspeople – are living better, more virtuous and happier lives. This is new. It may be implicit in Shaftesbury's writing, but it is not stated. In Ray's *Wisdom of God manifested in the works of the Creation* (1691), the entire universe may have been made by a benevolent Creator – the text at the head of Ray's book is from Psalm 104, v. 24.

'O Lord, how manifold are thy Works! In Wisdom hast thou made them all' – but Man exists to 'plant' and to 'adorn' what the Creator has made for him. The way of savages, in 'a Barbarous and Inhospitable Scythia' or 'a rude and unpolished *America* peopled with slothful and naked *Indians*' is to be scorned, since man has had 'Wit and Reason' bestowed on him.

Again, Haller's admiration for the 'virtue' and 'beauty' inherent in the mountains is expressed far more strongly than in any other earlier author. While Ray in 1691, and more fully in 1701, and Woodward, in 1695, praise mountains, and even volcanoes, for their usefulness, they do not really see their beauty. Ray's 1701 edition of *The Wisdom of God* has seven sections on mountains, rejecting Burnet's view of their ugliness. Of these six praise their usefulness, and only one their beauty. 'They are very Ornamental to the Earth', he writes, 'affording pleasant and delightful Prospects' – i.e. *down* into the plain, and *up* from the plain. Looking closer at Ray's text, we see that he gives as examples the view *down* from 'the Downs of Sussex', and the view *up* of any higher place for those 'who have lived in the Isle of Ely'. However much he praised the 'Counsel, Wisdom, and Design' of the Creator in making mountains, Ray might have found it hard to share Haller's love of the Alps. Though his theory looks forward, his practical view is still that of the previous century, akin to Pepys, crossing Salisbury Plain by night in 1668, and worried by the height of the earthworks of Old Sarum, 'prodigious, so as to frighten me', or to Johannes Praetorius, in his *Blockes-Berges Verrichtung* of 1669, with the long, careful description of the journey up and down the Blocksberg, where the band of 15 people and 12 horses proceed with discomfort and observe 'not without amazement and fear'. Praetorius and his companions are obviously intensely *interested* in what they see, and in what they fear they may experience in exploring the pathless mountain; but they *admire* only at one point, when the clouds part for long enough to reveal 'God's great and marvellous works' down in the plain. Bestehorn's engraving of the Blocksberg, drawn in 1732, shows witches and demons cavorting on the top (see Plate 4). We may reflect, more or less seriously, about *them*, but we cannot be frightened by the mountain itself – it isn't wild or jagged enough. Yet Praetorius was frightened, as was Pepys on Salisbury Plain – while Haller, in the Alps, was not. Here is one of the main changes of the century – and it will not rest with Haller's 'Die Alpen'.

In Britain, following the writings of Shaftesbury and the lesser optimists, there was a swift acceptance of the thesis that formality and artificiality were inferior to a 'freer' approach to the natural world.

This acceptance was — like the acceptance of any important idea — both progressive, spreading and strengthening with the passing of time; and partial, since it did not embrace all aspects of life with equal strength; indeed it was often paradoxical, when the new delight in nature was cherished beside the old approval of formality in some other sphere; it was affected by personal considerations — the age or the innate temperament of X or Y, when these developments occurred (and this is as true of the wildest, frenzied stages of these enthusiasms, at the end of the eighteenth century, as it is of their first twitchings at the beginning); and this acceptance did at first run gently parallel in several channels, only slightly overlapping and running into one another, in gardening, in poetry and painting. Above all, it appears at first as a new way of seeing the countryside, the English countryside of farms and villages, fields and hedges, rivers and woods.

The earliest signs of this 'discovery' after Shaftesbury's theoretical writing are in the widely read papers of Joseph Addison, in the *Tatler* and the *Spectator* in 1710, 1711 and 1712. Much of what Addison says is negative, disapproving the 'unnatural' artificiality of formal gardens seen in *parterres de broderie* (*Tatler*, no. 161, 20 April 1710), and in the clipped bushes and hedges of topiary work, which pervert the 'Luxuriancy and Diffusion of Boughs and Branches' of the naturally growing tree into 'a Mathematical Figure'. Our gardens are filled with 'Cones, Globes and Pyramids', and 'we see the marks of the Scissars upon every Plant and Bush' (*Spectator*, no. 414, 25 June 1712). A year later, this attack is taken up more violently by Alexander Pope in the *Guardian*, no. 173, 29 September 1713, when he lists an imaginary 'Catalogue of Greens' (i.e. items of topiary work) which are offered for sale. The first three items are:

Adam and Eve in Yew; Adam, a little shattered by the fall of the Tree of Knowledge in the great storm; Eve and the Serpent very flourishing.
Noah's ark in Holly, the ribs a little damaged for want of water.
The Tower of Babel, not yet finished.

We should remember that these criticisms are prompted both by Shaftesbury's 'Passion . . . for Things of a *natural* kind', and by disapproval of Dézallier d'Argenville's *La théorie et la pratique du jardinage* and its translation into English in 1712, a work which, as I have said, codified the practice of the French formal garden.

On the positive side, Addison's proposals are gentle and wishful rather than vigorously practical. He describes his own (imaginary) garden in which there is 'a Confusion of Kitchin and Parterre, Orchard and Flower Garden', and which nearly resembles 'a natural Wilderness' (*Spectator*, no. 477, 6 September 1712). But this is more hope than reality – in the *Spectator* essay, no. 414, where he attacks the fashion for topiary, his own proposal is theoretical: with some small 'Additions of Art', one's estate, with its rural and informal characteristics, 'may be thrown into a kind of Garden', and in so doing the whole might come to resemble a painting – 'a Man might make a pretty Land-skip of his own Possessions'. But how d'you do it? Addison is caught in his own belief in order and control – his 'spangled heav'ns' are 'a shining Frame', and he is both the author of these *Spectator* essays, and of the formal verse tragedy *Cato* (1713), in which he consciously set out to write a tragedy in English which would satisfy the most rigorous of French critics, and provide a basis for a genuinely 'classical' theatre in England. Though we do not often see *Cato* performed in the West End these days, it had a notable *succès d'estime* in the early eighteenth century. Voltaire saw it when he was in London, and praised it lavishly in his *Lettres philosophiques*. He called the play 'a Masterpiece', and said that Cato himself was 'the greatest Character that was ever brought upon any stage' (letter xviii, Voltaire's English version of 1733), and a few years later, the German writer Gottsched adapted Addison's text, with the admixture of lines from Deschamps' *Caton d'Utique*, to make his own tragedy, *Der sterbende Cato* (1732), which was intended, in emulation of Addison's play in 1713, to found an indigenous 'classical' theatre in Germany.

Addison then was on both sides at once, hankering after 'a natural Wilderness', and admiring the controlled construction of classical drama. In garden matters, the impasse was surmounted – or breached – with speed and success, though in the theatre it needed another fifty years. Ironically, the solution came from Dézallier d'Argenville's *La théorie et la pratique du jardinage*, where there is a brief reference to 'une claire-voie qu'on appelle autrement un *ah, ah*, avec un fossé sec au pied' – a phrase translated by John James in 1712 as 'an Opening, which the *French* call a *Claire-voië*, or an Ah, Ah, with a dry Ditch at the Foot of it'.

The *ha-ha* was a ditch or dry moat, serving as a substitute for a wall, hedge or fence along those parts of a garden where a view into the countryside was desired. So long as your garden was closed by a visible barrier, such as a wall, it was impossible to make one's 'own Possessions' into 'a pretty Landskip'. By means of the ha-ha, the visual barrier was eliminated. Ha-ha's were so called because of their unexpectedness, their virtual invisibility — as Horace Walpole put it in 1770, their invention was so successful, and 'so astonishing that the common people called them Ha! Ha's! to express their surprise at finding a sudden and unperceived check to their walk'. The earliest record of the ha-ha being used in England is at Blenheim, where in 1712 William Stukeley observed that

> the garden is . . . taken out of the park, and may still be said to be part of it, well contriv'd by sinking the outer-wall into a foss, to give one a view quite round and take off the odious appearance of confinement and limitation to the eye (*Itinerarium curiosum* (1724), p. 44).

With this invention, the way was clear for 'the formal mockery of princely gardens' to be replaced by 'a natural Wilderness'. But it took some while — most of the century — for this to happen, though at every stage there were observers who imagined that this or that garden scene had achieved a perfect representation of untamed nature. And when at last this was — more or less — accomplished, as at William Beckford's Fonthill estate in Wiltshire, there was nothing left for the garden to do except to return to and to experiment with the various forms of formality, which previous ages had produced.

At first, when the ha-ha was new, the attempts to embrace 'Things of a *natural* kind' were guided by the pastoral, arcadian background to the dialogues in Shaftesbury's *Moralists*, and not by the direct imitation and incorporation of the English countryside. The pastoral tradition, with supreme literary backing from Greece and Rome — Theocritus, for example, Bion, Moschus, Virgil, and a stream of Greek and Roman novelists — had barely faltered in western Europe since the early Renaissance, flourishing in poetry, drama, opera, music and painting. Though shepherds and shepherdesses are a genuine part of the country scene, their use in the many forms of pastoral from the *Idylls* of Theocritus to moments in *As You Like It* or the *Midsummer Night's Dream*, from *Daphnis and Chloe* to the paintings of Claude Lorrain is always slightly, or heavily, tinged with artifice. They belong, be it wholly or never so little, to an arcadian fiction, and to the same extent they are separate from the directly observable and real world of nature.

It was principally to the visual forms of this pastoral tradition that the first landscape gardeners turned. Though the term 'landscape gardening' was not coined until the middle of the century, the idea is implicit in Addison's 'a Man might make a pretty Landskip of his own Possessions' — a man might make his property *resemble a landscape painting*. And the landscape paintings which Addison probably, and later gardeners certainly, had in mind were scenes of the Italian countryside, wooded, hilly, adorned with a ruin or two, peopled by men and women wearing the clothing of another age, and taking part in stories from ancient history and older myth (see Plate 5). These pictures — by Claude Lorrain (1600-82) and Gaspard Dughet (or Gaspard Poussin if you prefer, 1615-75), and by contemporaries or followers such as N. P. Berchem ('Orizonte', 1620-83), B. Breenbergh (*c*. 1598-1657), A. M. Crivelli (d. *c*. 1730), J. A. Eismann (1604-98), A. Magnasco (1697-1747), V. V. Reiner (1689-1743), Marco Ricci (1679-1729) and Salvator Rosa (1615-73) — were studied, bought, copied and imitated throughout the eighteenth century; and from Addison's 'pretty Landskip' until the 1750s, most of the 'new' gardening, and much of the new writing and thinking about nature reflected their attitudes and ingredients. Towards the end of his life Shaftesbury was much concerned with these paintings, in particular with the work of Claude Lorrain, at the same time that he was discussing the emblematic vignettes which he wanted for the revised edition of his *Characteristics* (2nd edn, 1713). Shaftesbury's emblems are far removed from Claude's paintings, and yet his concern with both has a common basis, in that each for him portrayed, not the immediate physical reality, but some aspect of the ideal world.

The influence on the English of these paintings, and of the Italian scenes behind them, was immense. The young painter William Kent was sent to Italy from 1712 until 1719 to study painting, and in 1713 one of his patrons, Burrell Massingberd, told him to obtain copies 'after Poussin and Clodio Lorenzo'. When he came back to England, Kent's first published work, in 1720, was a frontispiece to the *Poems* of John Gay, in which he showed a view of the temple of the Sibyl at Tivoli, a building which both Claude and Gaspard had delighted to depict, either in its original hillside situation, or in imaginary settings, combined with other buildings, alone, ruined or complete, in wooded, marine or lake-side scenes. When Kent turned to the designing of gardens, he was the first of many gardeners to have a real version of this temple built — at Stowe, in the 'Elysian Fields', where his temple of Ancient Virtue was built in 1734, modelled on the temple of the Sibyl. Not long after, he sketched a design to replace the formal cascade at Chatsworth, in which Grillet's water-staircase would have been utterly abolished, and a rough, wooded slope substituted, enlivened by irregular falls of water, and with a version of the Sibyl's temple perched high up, like the original temple on the hillside at Tivoli. Certainly Kent was producing scenes of some wildness — no one could call them 'formal' — and their original in Italy was 'natural'. Yet they were not 'English', and their Italian associations kept them from being so. When not precisely pastoral, these scenes alluded also to the villa gardens of the ancient Greeks and Romans. It is no accident that Lord Burlington, who had his house at Chiswick modelled on Palladio's villa Rotonda, who employed Kent as a garden designer, and who adorned the *exedra* in the garden with statues from the ruins of Hadrian's villa at Tivoli, had in the same period encouraged his protégé Robert Castell to publish Pliny's letters describing his villa gardens (*The Villas of the Ancients Illustrated*, 1728). In discussing the 'representation of the countryside', Pliny's *imitatio ruris*, Castell harks back to Addison when he suggests that these parts of Pliny's garden 'were possibly thrown into such an agreeable Disorder, as to have pleased the Eye from several Views, like so many beautiful Landskips'. For us, two and a half centuries later, it is hard to appreciate the grounding which educated eighteenth-century people had in Greek and Roman culture; and it is therefore easy for us, looking at a temple, an urn, a classical statue or inscription in a garden such as Stowe or Chiswick to see these only as *architecture*, ornamenting the composition of grass and water and trees, while we overlook the associations which told the original beholder: 'Reflect. It is as if you had stepped into Arcadia; or into the grounds of Hadrian's, or Pliny's villa. You are in an antique world.' What Kent did, so did scores of others, setting up temples, bridges, monuments of a 'Grecian' or 'Roman' kind in gardens where formality was diminished, but where allusions to paintings and scenery of the Italian landscape remained strong. Kent's finest garden, at Rousham in Oxfordshire, is outstanding for its cleverly created scenes, like 'so many beautiful Landskips', contrived in the garden; and virtually all these scenes, framed in the 'natural' surroundings of the Oxfordshire countryside, with woods and fields and the irregularly meandering river Cherwell, are given a feeling of antiquity — Italian and Claudian — by the tactful incorporation of statues, a Roman arcade, the glimpse of a temple. Horace Walpole felt this atmosphere most strongly. 'The whole', he wrote in 1770, 'is as elegant and antique as if the Emperor Julian had selected the most pleasing solitude about Daphne to enjoy a philosophic retirement.' Rousham is still much as Walpole described it, if we can open our eyes to see as he did — it is 'the most pleasing solitude', of a sort Shaftesbury would have approved, and so apt for 'a philosophic retirement' that I at least could imagine Philocles and Theocles discoursing there. But it is not entirely 'natural'.

Pastoral, antique, a 'Landskip' of an Italian scene. Later in the century, Walpole summed up the way in which 'nature' had been embraced, yet kept at a distance. 'This country exhibits the most beautiful landscapes in the world when they are framed and glazed, that is, when you look at them through the window.'

The pastoral tradition continued throughout the century, and was gradually separated in the minds of painters, poets and gardeners from the increasingly intense approach to nature. When, in the mid-1730s, Philip Southcote adorned his *ferme ornée* at Wooburn in Surrey with representations of antique farming implements, such as Romans would have used, his contemporaries did not cry 'artifice'; but when in the last years before the Revolution the elaborate Hameau — mill, farmhouse, cottages and the rest — was constructed for Marie Antoinette, and when Thévenin's astonishing *laiterie* at Malmaison was built, including as part of its décor a series of Sèvres porcelain milk bowls whose shape — so it was said — was modelled on that of one of Marie Antoinette's breasts, no one was fooled.

The most vivid illustration of this pastoral approach, to show its early association with 'nature' and its gradual drift back to 'artifice', concerns the Æolian Harp. This instrument — essentially a resonant box, over which strings are tightly stretched so that they may vibrate and produce musical notes when the wind blows across them — was invented by the scholar Athanasius Kircher, and first described in his *Musurgia universalis*, vol. II, book ix, pp. 352-5 in 1960. Though the surrounding section of the work is entitled 'Æolias Cameras fabricari', 'On the making of Æolian chambers', the instrument itself is not called an Æolian harp, but merely 'aliam machinam', 'another harmonic and automatic instrument . . . which by means of wind and air alone produces a perpetual harmonious sound'. He explains how to make it, and then describes ways of amazing the ignorant by attaching such harps to figures of dragons, fish and even angels, which are erected outside — like weather-vanes — over summer-houses. Then he discusses the theory. Kircher's attitude is unemotional. He is in search of knowledge, a scientist, and sees the invention as a phenomenon to be investigated rather than wondered at.

In the early eighteenth century, the attitude changed profoundly. The idea that the random, rather eerie, sounds which this instrument produced were 'nature's music' — i.e. a spontaneous music created without human agency — made the Æolian harp popular among the

growing public of nature-lovers, while its Greek name, referring to
Æolus, god of the winds, was easily and erroneously taken to mean
that it had been known to the ancient Greeks, and an original part of
the pastoral tradition. And so the Æolian harp became part of the
apparatus, the *staffage*, of the 'natural' garden. When, in his *Castle of
Indolence* (1748), James Thomson described a rural scene as containing
the essence of the qualities of the three best-known painters of the
Italian landscape − it had 'Whate'er Lorrain light-touched with soften-
ing hue, Or savage Rosa dashed, or learned Poussin drew' − he completed the arcadian character of the scene by adding 'Aerial music in
the warbling wind'.

Although the earliest responses to Shaftesbury's 'passion for things
of a natural kind' were in Addison's remarks to do with gardens, these
run parallel with an increased liking for nature in literature and painting. In some writers this admiration exists happily beside a genuine
acceptance of formality in other spheres. It is fashionable at present to
see Pope as a lover of nature, an enthusiast for the new gardening − yet
he remains the author of the *Rape of the Lock*, of the *Dunciad* and
other large and splendid poems which are as wholly imbued with
classical town-centredness as anything by Molière or Boileau. But the
poetry of James Thomson (1700-48) has an understanding of nature
which is far deeper and less equivocal, and which could plausibly be
presented as 'the truer Song of Nature' which Shaftesbury's
Theocles might have sung in his 'noble enthusiasm' in Shaftesbury's
Moralists. Looking back through the rough-and-tumble directness
of Wordsworthian nature poetry, we may be disappointed by Thomson's
Augustan circumlocutions − 'the plumy race, the tenants of the sky',
for birds-in-flight, or 'the household feath'ry people' for cock-and-hens.
We may also, and with better cause, regret the additions which he made
in the years of his fame to his main work, *The Seasons*, swelling out its
British references with descriptions of all sorts of foreign scenes. That
said, Thomson remains the first great poet of nature in the eighteenth
century, and the first poet in Britain fully to express Shaftesbury's
vision of the beauty of 'wildness'.

This is triumphantly apparent in his first long poem, *Winter* (1726).
From the start he puts forward Shaftesbury's view that the natural
world embodies the wonder, beauty and sublimity of God. Thomson is
the first British poet to take 'nature' as the subject of a long poem. He
says in the preface to his second edition, 'I know no Subject more
elevating . . . than the Works of Nature. Where [else] can we meet with
such Variety, such Beauty, such Magnificence? . . . But there is no

thinking of these things without breaking out into Poetry.'
In *Winter*, he combines rapturous admiration with fear:

> *Vapours*, and *Clouds*, and *Storms*: Be these my Theme
> These, that exalt the Soul to solemn Thought,
> And heavenly musing. Welcome kindred Glooms!
> Wish'd, wint'ry, Horrors, hail!

The storm is welcome, as a sign of the immensity and immanence of
God. This is stated more fully in the 'Hymn on the Seasons' (1730),
where he begins

> These, as they change, Almighty Father! these
> Are but the varied God

— lines which suggest a near-pantheism again resembling Shaftesbury's.
Going through the seasons, and the ways in which they reflect the
Creator, 'the God of Seasons', winter shows a divine and fearful
strength,

> In Winter dreadful thou! with clouds and storms
> Around thee thrown, tempest o'er tempest rolled,
> Horrible blackness! On the whirlwind's wing
> Riding sublime, thou bidst the world be low,
> And humblest nature with thy northern blast.

'Riding sublime' — Thomson here uses the word 'sublime' in a way
which will become special to the eighteenth century, and which will, by
the time of Burke's *Enquiry into . . . the Sublime* (1756), be seen as
exactly that quality in 'the wildness' which 'pleases'. Not only is it
'great', 'majestic' — so much so that it is beyond our feeble comprehension — but it is associated with 'fear', 'dread' and 'horror'.
    Yet Thomson can admire and even enjoy what he sees. In *Winter*, he
writes

> Pleas'd, have I wander'd thro' your rough Domains

and goes on to describe several storms in different situations. Some
have tragic results. In 1730, Thomson adds to *Winter* the episode
(II.276-321 in the final version of 1746) of a shepherd who loses his
way in a blizzard, and dies — 'In his own loose-revolving fields the

swain / Disastered stands'. In *Summer* (1727) — a summer thunder-storm is the cause — he describes the death by lightning of a wholly innocent maiden (see William Williams' painting of this scene, Plate 6). Passages like these separate Thomson's attitude from the kindlier, blinkered theological view of Brockes — in *his* summer storm all danger passes safely by, and the country blooms refreshed, 'still the old Eden, yet a world renewed'.

Thomson's view of nature is enthusiastic, like Shaftesbury's; it is also Newtonian, seeing the universe as a creation of matchless perfection and exactitude. In *Spring* (1728), therefore, a shower of rain is followed by the rainbow:

> Meantime, refracted from yon eastern cloud,
> Bestriding earth, the grand ethereal bow
> Shoots up immense;

and on to the different colours of the rainbow, 'running from the red / To where the violet shades into the sky'. Newton is the unraveller of this phenomenon:

> Here, mighty Newton, the dissolving clouds
> Are, as they scatter round, thy numerous prism,
> Untwisting to the philosophic eye
> The various twine of light, by thee disclosed. . .

As in Scheuchzer's *Physica sacra*, what *was* a mystery is now a beauty scientifically justified. A year earlier, in 1727, when Newton died, Thomson had published 'To the Memory of Sir Isaac Newton', in which he praised Newton for his discovery of 'the SYSTEM', in which 'by the mingling Power / Of *Gravitation* and *Projection*', he saw 'the whole in silent Harmony revolve'. Passing from one to another of Newton's discoveries, Thomson reaches the rainbow. Its beauty seen in the sky over Greenwich is described, as a marvel in the natural world, and yet one which is scientifically understandable:

> Even now the setting sun and shifting clouds,
> Seen, Greenwich, from thy lovely heights, declare
> How just, how beauteous the refractive law.

When, in 1730, the *Seasons* were published with four illustrations by William Kent, it was almost inevitable that the engraving of 'Spring' should contain a rainbow (see Plate 7); and when Brockes' eighth volume of the *Irdisches Vergnügen in Gott* appeared in 1746, a year after Brockes had translated the *Seasons* into German, it is no surprise to find among the poems one called 'Der Regenbogen', 'the Rainbow'.

Thomson added to the *Seasons* to fill out his composite picture of the world. Part of his survey — in *Summer*, from line 100 onwards — resembles the vision of Theocles in the *Moralists*, passing from the heavens to the earth, and visiting 'horrid' climates and regions before alighting in the temperate countryside of England and Scotland. We should note that it was in the deserts of Africa, after fleeing 'the noted tyrant of the flood', that Theocles-Shaftesbury exclaims, 'The wildness pleases,' and Thomson is as convinced of this as Shaftesbury. Like Shaftesbury, however, Thomson is no great admirer of men who remain 'wild', when they need not do so. Nowhere does he approach Haller's view that the simple, honest and healthy way of life of the Alpine peasants is *superior* to life in the city. In Thomson's passage to do with the rainbow, for example, its meaning, discovered by Newton, is *understood* by 'the philosophic eye', while the peasant looks at it with incomprehension:

> Not so the swain;
> He wondering views the bright enchantment bend
> Delightful o'er the radiant fields, and runs
> To catch the falling glory; but amazed
> Beholds the amusive arch before him fly,
> Then vanish quite away.

Similarly, on the appearance of a comet (*Summer*, 1744 version, II.1700ff), 'the enlightened few, / Whose godlike minds philosophy exalts, / The glorious stranger hails'. In contrast, 'fearful murmuring crowds', 'the guilty nations' and 'the fond sequacious herd' can only see this phenomenon as 'portentous', since they are enslaved by 'super-stitious horrors'. In *Winter*, Thomson draws the picture in a slightly different way, which is also one which Shaftesbury would wholly approve. Here (II.253-300 in 1726) he describes how he likes to spend the winter evenings — in a wild countryside, amid wild weather, reading and studying the histories of the great men of the past, such as Socrates, Lycurgus, and Cato:

> A rural, shelter'd solitary Scene
> . . . there let me sit,
> And hold high Converse with the mighty Dead.

This attitude is, clearly, that of 'the enlighten'd few', not that of ordinary countryfolk. The difference is made absolute when, in 1730, he adds a passage telling what peasants do at this time of year, beginning with 'meantime' to distinguish them from himself. They listen credulously to tales of ghosts, 'goes the goblin story round, / Till superstitious horror creeps o'er all'; or they play simple games, tell 'the simple joke', 'arousing rustic mirth' in shepherds who are 'easily pleased', and play at catch-and-kiss. Haller writes of this kind of thing in Alpine villages, praising the villagers for their innocence and wisdom. Thomson did not, though later lovers of nature admired and envied the simple, even primitive, people who inhabit the remote and wilder parts of the world.

3

The Primitive

While the new and exciting world of nature was being explored in the first decades of the eighteenth century, two related interests were also receiving more and more attention. These interests are, first, in things — objects, architecture — of a *primitive* kind; and second, in the role *man* himself might play in natural and sometimes primitive surroundings.

The interest in the *primitive* is unmistakable in the studies of 'pre-classical' architecture published in the seventeenth and eighteenth centuries. Much of the time, this interest was firmly antiquarian and historical, as in Camden's comments on Stonehenge in his *Britannia*, or architectural and antiquarian, as in Inigo Jones' *Stone-Heng* (1655), where aesthetic appreciation is limited to wonder at the builders' skill in transporting or erecting the stones. Inigo Jones' illustration of Stonehenge is almost crude in its simplicity, while his other engravings are all of a speculative kind, considering the geometrical and architectural implications of the remains. Then, in 1721, the German architect J. B. Fischer von Erlach (1656-1723) published his *Entwurf einer historischen Architektur*, a lavish, exuberant and amazing work which surveys the notable architecture created in the world so far, and then illustrates some of the architect's own projected schemes. The latter — late-baroque extravaganzas of a generally impractical kind — are not important in this history (unlike the late-baroque sculpture of his acquaintance and contemporary Matthias Braun — see p. 60), and one might argue that the idea of the main first part was not especially new — other architects with historical leanings had described the buildings of the past before going on to show what they could offer in the present — Sebastiano Serlio, for example, or Andrea Palladio. But Fischer von Erlach not only illustrates the architecture of the ancient Greeks and Romans, but places these beside, and gives them no more prominence than, the architectural marvels of other parts of the world. Some of these, like the hanging gardens of Babylon, the temple at

Jerusalem, or the island-garden of Isola Bella, may be 'justified' by saying that they are precursors or followers in the main Greco-Roman tradition. This would allow Fischer von Erlach to be retained, albeit uncomfortably, within the 'aesthetic of Versailles'. But in presenting even the Greek and Roman monuments, he endows them with such monstrous size and complexity; and in presenting the Ka'aba at Mecca, and a variety of Chinese bridges, monuments, temples and palaces, he gives them qualities of such an intriguing, gorgeous and stupendous kind; and, above all, in presenting three primitive monuments, one in China, one, Stonehenge in England, and one, the rock theatre at Salzburg, in German-speaking Europe, he so extends the range of 'memorable' works of architecture that he steps outside the limits of classical orthodoxy.

Though many of his illustrations are taken from earlier books, and his sources are usually acknowledged, his work is original in the extra dash of extravagance which he adds to these illustrations, and in the bringing together of such widely varied creations as specimens of 'world architecture', to be considered and respected beside the buildings of Greece and Rome. The presence of the three primitive monuments is, I think, amazing. The view of 'Cliffs made by Art' (see Plate 11) comes originally from Jan Nieuhof's *Gezantschap ... aan den grooten Tartarischen Cham* (1665, French 1665, English 1669, Latin 1668), the description of the Dutch embassy to China in 1655-7. This book provided the visual stimulus for many of the chinoiserie objects, large and small, produced in the middle decades of the eighteenth century, including Chambers' pagoda at Kew (1762), and Fischer von Erlach is in part responsible for making this material known. The 'Cliffs made by Art' was the only picture in Nieuhof's book to show an example of the Chinese admiration for irregular stones, which is a central part of their garden tradition. Such stones could be small enough to stand on a table indoors, or so large as to dominate an entire garden. Though the Nieuhof picture may exaggerate the size of the crags, it is not impossibly untrue, and the scene must have seemed rather outlandish to Europeans in 1665. In 1721, in Fischer von Erlach's book, it was still the only picture of such a scene to have been reproduced in Europe, and the erection of irregular rocks with a specifically 'Chinese' character did not occur in Europe until the nineteenth century, in England, at Biddulph in Staffordshire. The 'Chinese' elements in European gardens were in contrast one of the commonest aspects of imported *exotisme* from the middle years of the eighteenth century, but were invariably restricted to architectural ornaments set in gardens or landscapes which were otherwise firmly European. The picture of 'Cliffs made by Art' cannot therefore have encouraged similar 'Chinese' style rocks to be set up (though the other pictures of pagodas and the like certainly encouraged architectural chinoiseries), but must be considered beside the general appeal to interest in the primitive of the two other primitive monuments I have mentioned. The picture of Stonehenge, by David Loggan, was taken from J. Beeverel's *Délices de la Grande Bretagne* (1707), and the picture of the rock theatre at Hellbrunn near Salzburg was published about the same time. Fischer von Erlach brought these two pictures together on the same page (see Plate 8), although the monuments were from different countries and cultures, and the combined effect stresses the air of immense age, of crude, gigantic size, and of remoteness from everyday town life which will come to be admired in 'primitive' objects and scenes from this time onwards.

Contemporary with Fischer von Erlach was the English antiquarian William Stukeley (1687-1765), who made several tours in different parts of the British Isles to investigate the remains of past ages, whether medieval, Saxon, Roman or prehistoric. Though his fascination with the debris of history stemmed from the jackdaw curiosity of the seventeenth century (and is related to the universal studies of men like Athanasius Kircher), Stukeley was also emotionally moved by the consideration of ruins in a way which is true of the eighteenth century – going, when he was in his teens, 'to sigh over' the ruined remains of Barnwell Abbey in Lincolnshire. During his excursions, he was especially interested in ancient British and Roman remains, and made such extensive (and peculiar) studies of the prehistoric circles in Wiltshire that he published two books on the subject, *Stonehenge* (1740) and *Abury* (1743), and the 1748 edition of Daniel Defoe's *Tour* (I, p. 336) reports that Stukeley had been consulted by the Earl of Pembroke about 'a Design ... to erect a *Stone-Henge* in Miniature, as it was supposed to be in its original Glory' in the gardens at Wilton. This project was not executed, but it marks the beginning of a succession of monuments of a *primitive* kind which were planned or executed in British gardens, distinct from the urns, statues, columns and temples within the pastoral landscape tradition.

In a mid-way position between monuments of a Greco-Roman and monuments of a primitive kind, there are 'Gothic' monuments, which were seen – first in England, and not until much later on the Continent – as a form of architecture native to northern Europe, and so, by an unhistorical extension, as the original primitive architecture of Germanic lands, to be contrasted with the 'imported' architecture of Greece and

Rome. As with prehistoric architecture, so antiquarian interest in gothic architecture goes back well before 1700, but a *liking* for it does not begin until the 1700s with people such as Stukeley. In 1709 the architect Vanbrugh suggested that it would be appealing to retain the old fragments of Woodstock Manor in the landscape which he was designing at Blenheim, and the later, more fully romantic landscape parks at Studley Royal (begun *c*. 1720) and at Duncombe (begun in 1713) in Yorkshire were both planned to embrace the medieval remains of Fountains Abbey and of Rievaulx Abbey respectively. The deliberate building of gothic-looking structures also began in the 1720s, with 'King Alfred's Hall' in Cirencester Park, Gloucestershire, in 1721, a curious pavilion at the end of the garden canal at Shotover, in Oxfordshire, and extensive walls and towers, designed by Vanbrugh (1725), round parts of the estate at Castle Howard in Yorkshire. These first gothic buildings in the eighteenth century are nowhere near historical accuracy – they have battlements, pointed arches, and, if there is an interior to the building, there may be a form of ribbed vaulting. At first battlements are the especial sign of the gothic, even if they are attached to a fabric which is otherwise anonymous, or supported with pillars of a classical kind. 'Gothic' architecture was seen as the *ur*-architecture of northern Europe, and so in England it was occasionally called 'Saxon', to contrast it, in a patriotic way, with the architecture of Versailles. In 1742 Batty Langley published his *Gothic Architecture Improved*, in which he writes about 'the ancient Saxon Architecture', and at about the same time James Gibbs designed the Gothic Temple at Stowe, in Buckinghamshire, which was at first called the Temple of Liberty, since it was built in an aggressively irregular, gothic and un-classical style, and contained busts of Saxon kings – the defenders of liberty.

By the late 1740s the gothic is thoroughly restored to favour. In 1747 Sanderson Miller built a section of ruinated castle wall at Hagley, in Worcestershire, taking the desideratum of visible antiquity to its logical conclusion. (Horace Walpole was to say of this 'folly' in 1753 that 'it has the true rust of the Barons' wars', i.e. that its appearance was that of a dilapidated and therefore genuinely antique construction.) In the same year, 1747, Walpole himself took over a small property at Strawberry Hill in Twickenham – a property which he was to 'improve' continuously until his death in 1797. In the grounds, his 'improvements' were in the form of landscape gardening. With the buildings he acquired, the 'improvements' were wholly related to a 'gothic' conversion and elaboration matched only by William Beckford's creation of

Fonthill Abbey at the end of the century. Walpole's building was not *ruined*, save when his earliest, flimsy battlements were destroyed by winter storms and had to be replaced — his enemies said that they had been made of *papier mâché* — but it was more and more thoroughly filled with the elements of the 'gothic', carvings, fan-tracery, stained glass, antique armour and heraldic adornments. Walpole may have begun all this in a somewhat tongue-in-cheek manner, and he always preserved a certain degree of detachment — there is little gothic, and an immense amount of the *philosophe*, in his witty, malicious and copiously *social* correspondence — but by the early 1760s he had so immersed himself in what he believed to be genuinely medieval that it is not in the least surprising that he should have the dreams, or dream-like fantasies, which lead to his writing the first 'gothic novel', the *Castle of Otranto* (see p. 111).

In seeing gothic architecture as the true style of northern Europe, people in the early eighteenth century were tempted to imagine a simple and primitive, indeed a 'natural' origin for this architecture — viz. the intertwined and crossing branches of forest trees, which, they thought, could have suggested the shape and construction of the pointed arch, and the complexity of late medieval fan-vaulting. By the end of the century, this theory is worked up into a sizeable — and rickety — case, with a string of advocates from Goethe to Victor Hugo, who expatiate on the inspiration of the great germanic forests, and cite as examples of gothic 'tree architecture' the late-gothic Royal Oratory by Benedikt Rieth (1493) in the cathedral at Prague, or the carved wooden altar-pieces by Tilman Riemenschneider at, say, Bad Rothenburg, or Creglingen, or Detwang in Bavaria, where the ribs of the tracery are clearly and deliberately carved to resemble the many-branched, budding and leafing stems of trees. But this is at the end, or even after the end, of the eighteenth century. At the beginning, the views are sporadic and tentative — William Stukeley, visiting Gloucester Cathedral in September 1721, writes admiringly in his *Itinerarium curiosum* (1724) of the cloister, saying 'nothing could ever have made me so much in love with *gothic* architecture (as call'd)', and explaining that the design might well be imitated:

> I judge for a gallery, library or the like, 'tis the best manner of building, because the idea of it is taken from a walk of trees, whose branching heads are curiously imitated by the roof.

A few years later Pope spoke of his idea of planting 'an old Gothic cathedral . . . in trees' (Joseph Spence, *Observations*, ed. J. M. Osborn,

1966, no. 619). 'Good large poplars' would serve for the columns.

In 1753 such speculation about the origins of architecture comes up in connection with *classical* buildings, in the *Essai sur l'architecture* of M.-A. Laugier. Laugier is concerned with greater simplicity and purity of style, a concern at the heart of neo-classical architecture, and firmly within the purlieus of the Enlightenment, seeking to eliminate the ornamental trimmings which the baroque and the rococo had added to classical architecture. But Laugier takes as his starting-point not 'men who dwell in the city', but men at a time when there weren't any cities, and when men lived in a state of nature. Laugier explains, in his first chapter, that the principles of architecture are based 'sur la simple nature'. Man in his first state has no guide except his natural instinct. He needs somewhere to rest, and, after trying the bare ground, the damp shelter of the forest and the enclosed but stuffy shelter of a cave, he appreciates that what he needs is 'a dwelling which covers him without burying him', and this leads him to build his 'petite cabane rustique':

A few fallen branches in the forest suffice for his purpose. He chooses four of the strongest, which he puts upright, setting them in a square. He places four others across, at the top; and above these he sets up other sloping branches, which come together to a point from either side. This kind of roof is covered with leaves ... and in this way, your man is housed ... This is the simple way in which nature proceeds: and art is born from the imitation of nature's methods. The small rustic hut which I have described is the model from which all the glories of architecture begin (*Essai*, pp. 12-13).

Laugier repeats that 'our small rustic hut' is the first and purest form of building, and then goes on to discuss the need to restore this original simplicity to the architecture of the day, a call which is central to the idea of 'noble simplicity and quiet greatness' put forward by J. J. Winckelmann a year later, in 1754, in his *Gedanken über die Nachahmung der griechischen Werke in der ... Kunst*. Both Laugier and Winckelmann are on the side of the Greeks in the controversy which began in the 1750s over the relative merits of Greek and Roman styles of building, which was stimulated by the discoveries of Roman architecture, furniture and decorative motifs at Pompeii and Herculaneum; by the re-discovery of the ruins of Palmyra, built in Roman style; by the study of Greek architecture at Athens, and finally by the virtual re-discovery by western artists and architects of the Greek temples at Paestum in southern Italy. As I have said, most of this debate is to do with the growth of the neo-classical movement, and it leads to the almost obsessional interest in 'pure' architecture of late eighteenth-century designers and architects such as Boullée and Ledoux, a concern which has nothing to do with the origins of romanticism, and everything to do with the rational and town-centred preoccupations of the Enlightenment. Once again, we should not forget that this current of thought continues beside the romantic stirrings which are our subject here, and that both currents occasionally and briefly flow together.

They come together, from opposite sides as it were, in their interest in the Greek or 'primitive' Doric column. The Greek form of the Doric order is in essence much simpler than Tuscan or Roman Doric, since the column has no base or plinth at the bottom, and no superfluous lines or decoration round the capital. Greek Doric came to the attention of western architects — was virtually 're-discovered' — with the publication of J. D. Le Roy's *Ruines des plus beaux monuments de la Grèce* in 1758, and James Stuart and Nicholas Revett's *Antiquities of Athens* in 1762, and was imitated in the garden temples, with primitive Doric pillars, at Hagley (1758) — designed by Stuart — and Shugborough (*c.* 1758), and in the painting on the ceiling of the villa Albani in Rome by Mengs in 1760-1, which depicts the subject of 'Parnassus', and has in its centre Apollo, god of the arts, standing beside an altar-column in the primitive Doric style. For the neo-classicists, this interest led on to a purification of over-elaborate architectural design. But for those who were fascinated by the *primitive* origins of man's history, it led to Laugier's 'small rustic hut' and more of the kind. From the 1750s, such buildings were imagined in ever cruder forms, made from rough-hewn tree-trunks, knotted, knobbly and still covered with bark, or made even from the contorted, misshapen roots of trees, where the interstices between the writhen irregular roots were to be filled with moss or clay.

I think that the most fascinating of these meeting-points between neo-classical and primitive comes in an illustration to the *Voyage round the World . . . by George Anson*, compiled by Richard Walter, published in 1748. Anson, circumnavigating the world in 1740-4, came into the Pacific from Cape Horn in a state of exhaustion, and his expedition paused for life-and-death succour at the uninhabited islands of Juan Fernandez, off the coast of Chile, and Tinian or Tenian, near to Guam, east of the Philippines. At each stopping-place Anson and his sailors found water, food, health and tranquillity — the islands were fertile, yet uninhabited — and at the second, Tinian, there were mysterious monuments left by long-departed earlier inhabitants (see Plate 9). These monuments, we know, were not all that different from the monuments found on Easter Island, in the south Pacific, when first Roggeveen's and then Cook's sailors arrived there in 1722 and 1774 (see p. 166). But Anson's artist did not know this, nor the subsequent engraver of the artist's sketch, and the 'View of the Watering Place at Tenian' shows the British sailors, a tent and a few barrels set among 'exotic' trees; and then to the right, two exactly parallel rows of identical standing stones, six on each side. If we were to cut them out of the jungly background, we might in the late twentieth century think that they had a vaguely 'Egyptian' look — something from a version of *Aïda*. But this was not in the mind of Anson's artist. Far more likely was the idea of the Greek or 'primitive' Doric. Artists involved in topographical work have often been tempted to interpret what is there — in this case, stone monuments of profoundly un-European nature — in terms of what their patrons and customers would like to see, or, simply, could understand. In the late 1740s hardly any living Europeans apart from the surviving members of Anson's expedition could have seen the jagged, irregular stones on Tinian, and so no one, not even the engraver, knew what they were. But the form of the Greek Doric was just becoming known, and would be in the minds of interested readers. The change was not a great one — mainly the simulation of a regularity-in-simplicity which was not really there — and it was understandable. The exactness, clarity and balance of these rows of columns has the very spirit of neo-classical simplicity, as if a Laugier or a Winckelmann were inspiring the artist's interpretation of this primitive scene. Commodore George Anson was, I am certain, willing to see, to accept, to interpret the monuments in this way, for when he returned to England in 1744, he soon occupied himself with gardening at his brother Thomas Anson's estate at Shugborough, and had built there, not only one of the first 'genuine' Chinese pavilions (Anson had stopped for several weeks at the port of Canton), but the second, if not the first, garden temple in the 'primitive' Doric style, designed by James Stuart and built *c*. 1758.

Commodore Anson — Lord George Anson, as he became — must retain our attention in one more anecdote to do with the primitive — the interest in *ruins*. Anson had arranged for an artificial ruin to be built at Shugborough, and his workmen had — not understanding the reason for its construction — carried on 'building' the ruin until it had become a complete edifice. 'Then comes Mr Anson with axes and chissels to demolish as much of it as taste and judgement claimed; and this without affectation, for he is very disciplined, grave, and sensible' (Sneyd Davies, letter of 30 July 1750, in John Nichols, *Illustrations of the Literary History of the Eighteenth Century*, I, p. 639).

The interest in ruins is an essential part of early romantic enthusiasm, fed by the theme of ruined classical buildings in landscape paintings of a Claudian kind, and by the sight of real ruins all over the British Isles. I have already mentioned Sanderson Miller's logical step in 1747, when putting up a stretch of 'gothic' castle wall, of making it partly ruinous. I say 'logical', yet it was *emotional*, since such buildings were justified by the increase in *feeling*, of melancholy, mystery and even fear at the crumbling grandeur of another age. No wonder such creations were called 'follies' by the unbelievers. They cost money to put up, and were admired by their emotional owners often in proportion to their degree of 'ruination' — a quality directly opposed to the usefulness which a rational society would expect from financial outlay.

It is probable that classical ruins were built slightly earlier than gothic ones. Batty Langley's *New Principles of Gardening* (1728) suggests that 'artificial ruins in the Roman taste' could be painted on canvas and set up on frames. Langley adds that the ruins need not be painted, but 'actually built in that manner with brick and covered with plastering in imitation of stone', and this followed soon after. In 1735 the cartographer John Rocque produced a plan of the gardens at Wanstead in Essex, adorned with pictures in the margin. These include 'the Mount in the Great Lake', composed of heaped-up earth and rock, backed by pine-trees, and with a crumbling façade of a classical kind — pillars, doorways, urns and statues. Though the interior contained several rooms, intended for entertainment, the outside view is that of a *ruined* building, since a statue is overturned on the ground, columns are broken, and an obelisk is shattered at the point.

This ruin had pine-trees as a background — a proper setting with their sombre colouring. There was ample support for the use of pine-trees, whole or shattered, leaning with roots partly exposed, in the mountainous and storm-wracked paintings of Salvator Rosa, the most 'savage' of the three landscape painters whose Italian scenes were the ideal of so many landscape gardeners in England. Since his paintings were wilder than those of Claude or Gaspard, the idea of translating such scenes into garden landscapes was not attempted until later, just as the building of ruins came after the building of unruined structures.

The more ruined the ruins, the more isolated and primitive they were, the more likely they were to convey the desired emotions. The 1740s are a decade of experiment in these feelings, with Edward Young's *Night Thoughts* (1742-5), the poet's melancholy nocturnal reflections on death, set in a churchyard, Robert Blair's poem 'The

Grave' (1743), which aims 'to paint the gloomy horror of the tomb'; and Thomas Gray's 'Elegy, written in a Country Churchyard', begun in 1742, finished in 1749. In England churchyards are usually 'gothic', and often ruinous; considered at night, they are lonely, melancholy, mysterious:

> from yonder ivy-mantled tower
> The moping owl does to the moon complain
> Of such as, wand'ring near her secret bower,
> Molest her ancient solitary reign.
>
> Beneath those rugged elms, that yew-tree's shade,
> Where heaves the turf in many a mould'ring heap,
> Each in his narrow cell for ever laid,
> The rude forefathers of the hamlet sleep. ('Elegy', II. 9-16).

These graveyard poems may seem tame to our seasoned twentieth-century taste, and the gloom- and ghost-ridden gothic novels which were written from the 1760s onward were to be far more sensational. The ghost — a highly primitive ingredient of these scenes — was hardly to whisper until the Celtic spectres in Macpherson-Ossian's poetry arose in 1760 (see p. 103).

While these graveyard poems were being written in England, Giovanni Battista Piranesi (1720-78) was gathering material for two collections of engravings which are fundamental in the growth of romanticism. Piranesi's *œuvre* consists in engravings, with their preparatory sketches. His subject-matter is architectural, and to do with the architecture of Italy, either Roman (ruined or in reconstructed form) or as elaborated by the architects of the Renaissance, or by Piranesi himself. His representation of gothic architecture is minimal, and incidental in the depiction of Roman or Renaissance monuments (as in his view of the Pyramid of Gaius Cestius in Rome, which has a glimpse of late medieval battlements), while there is no trace of other *exotismes*, such as Chinese or Turkish architecture, with the exception of 'Egyptian' motifs in his late collection of interior designs, the *Diverse maniere d'adornare i cammini* of 1769. His concentration on Roman architecture obviously makes his work of importance in the neo-classical movement, and he is understandably in the forefront of the battle between the pro-Greek and pro-Roman camps. For many years Piranesi had no interest in the 'simpler' or 'purer' Greek forms, and until the publication in 1778 of his *Différentes vues ... de Pesto* his significance in the history of romanticism is to do with the manner of *presenting* the classical buildings which are his subject-matter, the *atmosphere* with which he surrounds them.

In his collection *Alcune vedute di archi trionfali ed altri monumenti* (first published in 1748 as the *Antichita romane de' tempi della Repubblica e de' primi Imperatori*), Piranesi shows Roman ruins in a way which entirely forsakes the arcadian manner of Claude and Gaspard. Piranesi has a new, vibrant and almost violent vision of the greatness of the past. Throughout his career Piranesi was passionately concerned to prove the superiority of Roman architecture, and in *Alcune vedute* this appears in the characteristic exaggeration of the *size* of the monuments — by reducing the size of the human figures who are shown beside them, and, as in the view of the temple of Jupiter tonans in Rome (Plate 10), by showing the huge upper parts of the antique building rising from the debris of subsequent ages. This device leads the viewer to reflect, almost automatically, 'were the debris to be cleared away, how tall, how majestic the temple would be'. In *Alcune vedute* the artist also shows the human figures as inferior to the original creators of the buildings. Usually the inhabitants of Piranesi's scenes are peasants, ignorant shepherds and goatherds unworthy of so great a legacy; or, if they are more prosperous, curious travellers, for example, they are shown gesturing with amazement at what they discover. Last, Piranesi shows the ruins as if they are engaged in mortal struggle with the forces of nature. Grasses, weeds, bushes, trees grow wherever they can find roothold, lifting, cracking and overthrowing the Romans' still massive, and once superbly aligned, blocks of stone. This 'overgrowth' which appears so prominently is itself a part of the antiquities, with a strength and knotted permanence which make the creepers and trees look of equal age with the buildings — and thus, like the buildings, infinitely older and stronger than the puny creatures, peasants and dilettanti, who visit them today. Piranesi drew practically no straightforward landscapes — the view of the *cascatelle* at Tivoli (*c*. 1766) is his only non-architectural engraving — yet 'nature' is a principal actor in nearly all his intensely dramatic views of ruins in their present state. There are only two actors, of course — the ruins, and nature. Man, modern man, is the audience, overawed and even frightened. Piranesi, more than any other, sets off the theme of Shelley's 'Ozymandias', 'look on my works, ye Mighty, and despair'. It is one of the main themes of romanticism, in which man, modern man, is saddened, frightened, or crushed by the strength and relentlessness of forces outside him — time, or nature, or simply 'life'.

Around 1745 Piranesi issued another, small series of fourteen plates, the *Invenzioni capric di carceri*. These engravings, to be altered and re-issued in the early 1760s as the *Carceri d'invenzione* (see p. 119 and Plate 19), are unlike *Alcune vedute* in that their subject-matter is not antique, nor ruinous, nor viewed from the outside. Instead, they are interior views of modern prisons, apparently complete, and in active use. They lack therefore any sense of ruined antiquity, and lack too all reference to 'nature'. No plants grow in Piranesi's prisons. But they share with his views of Roman ruins the sense of immensity, a scale greater than that of the inhabitants. These prisons — 'fantasies', Piranesi calls them — are of nightmare vastness, all the more depressing because there is no 'outside' visible in the engraving, but ever-receding vistas under ponderous sections of archway, along galleries whose end is concealed by another cyclopean arch, up wavering wooden staircases whose top leads only to another gallery returning to the centre of the prison. And the inhabitants, like those of the Roman ruins, are tiny — scurrying along the galleries, or carrying weapons in a purposeful way, or standing, cloaked and with shoulders bowed, silhouetted against the monstrous masonry which rises far above their thoughtful figures. Frightening though these visions are, he will make them still more sombre and compelling in the 1760s. The emotion will become far wilder, just as his interpretation of the monuments of the past is to become even more gigantic — and sublime.

The object with greatest potential for development of a primitive kind was at this time the cave or *grotto*. During the Renaissance grottoes had featured as an element of the pastoral tradition, a representation of the rocky cave originally inhabited by river gods or water spirits. Built in a deliberately rough and 'cave-like' manner, with mossy rocks and incrustations of shells, they served to provide contrast with the regular and symmetrical parts of the house, and were also an appropriate place for fountains and waterworks. These grottoes had in the seventeenth century a fairly general characteristic of being showplaces for mythological sculpture, surrounded by glittering stones and crystals, and enlivened by 'curious' waterworks. The origin of the grotto was both natural and primitive, but by this time it had become highly artificial. The 'grotte de Tethys' at Versailles, built in the 1660s, was indeed connected with the sea-goddess Thetis, and Girardon's statuary was appropriate. But the grotto as a whole was elaborately ornate, symmetrical and artificial.

In the early eighteenth century, grottoes began to be made more 'natural'. In 1724 Aaron Hill has a lengthy description of a grotto which he would like to create in a London garden, where the pomp and extravagance of Versailles have been exchanged for a complicated symbolic scheme representing the different parts of the natural world.

Somewhat similar is the grotto which Pope made at Twickenham between 1719 and 1725. Pope's grotto, which was not large, was lined with shells and flints and lumps of crystal, with coral branches and even with stalactites which friends had shot down for him from the roof of the caverns at Wookey Hole. Pope conveniently discovered a spring there, and to increase the light and to multiply and confuse the glittering and twinkling images there was a lamp hanging from the centre of the ceiling, and 'pieces of looking glass in angular forms' stuck to the roof and walls. Friends sent Pope shells and mineral fragments from distant and exotic places — Mexico, Peru, Germany, Cornwall — and Pope himself clearly thought that the grotto was a miniature repository of the world's marine and mineral rarities. 'Approach! Great Nature studiously behold!' he wrote, in the spirit of Shaftesbury's statement that 'the rude *Rocks*, the mossy *Caverns*, the irregular unwrought *Grotto's*' were 'representing NATURE more' than did 'the formal mockery of Princely Gardens'. It was not long before less sophisticated and wilder grottoes came into favour. The landscape gardener William Kent is noted for a characteristic design of a grotto-cum-cavern-cum-cascade nature. It first appears at Chiswick, where in the 1730s he designed a cascade to go at the end of the Serpentine lake. This relatively formal and firmly architectural design was rejected and replaced by one which was much more primitive, and which was executed. Kent often re-used this design, and at Rousham and at Claremont his crude, rocky cascade arches, apparently made from irregular boulders, still look like ruined or roughly hewn or even natural cavern entrances.

Grotto-builders were often in two minds about this, wanting the outside to look ruinous, and then having the interior set out in a sophisticated and contrasting manner. The tiny shell-temple at Goodwood, in Sussex, begun in 1739, had originally an irregular outside surface, but within it was, and is still, adorned with tens of thousands of shells in a totally formal way. I suspect that the rooms within the 'ruined' classical mount erected at Wanstead may have been lavishly decorated, and such deliberate juxtaposition goes on throughout the century — the simple thatched cottage at Malmaison, built for Marie Antoinette, has its main room wholly covered with a sumptuous decoration of shells. The two most renowned grotto-builders in England were Joseph and Josiah Lane, father and son, and the earliest work by the father was ornate. But the fashion for wildness became stronger, and by the late 1740s his grotto at Painshill in Surrey, built for Charles Hamilton, had a wildness which Pope might have found perplexing. The favourite material for the outside of the Painshill grotto and its nearby 'excrescences' was a limestone tufa perforated with large and irregular holes (something like grey, gigantic Gruyère), and which was called *pierre antidiluvienne*, 'pre-diluvian stone', since it had an aged, water-worn air suggesting thousands of years' submersion in the sea. Primitive indeed.

Most primitive of the cave and grotto works in this period was the strange and beautiful *Felsengarten* or 'cliff garden' of Sanspareil, near Bayreuth in Bavaria. In a hilly and undulating countryside, the wooded area known since the 1740s as 'Sanspareil', almost a mile long, and some two hundred yards wide, is crowded with rocky outcrops. These are the centre of the landscape garden which Wilhelmine, Margravine of Bayreuth, began to shape in early 1744, and finished in late 1749. It is a garden with a mythological theme (like Stourhead in England, made in the same period, where the walk was so arranged that visitors could follow the events and thoughts of book iii of the *Aeneid*), since the region was adapted to create the scenes on Calypso's island, when young Telemachus (the son of Odysseus) and his tutor Mentor were shipwrecked there. The episode is from book vii of the prose epic *Télémaque*, by Fénélon, published in 1699.

The whole of Sanspareil is therefore embraced by this mythological scheme, like a series of three-dimensional scenes from Claude, all related to one story. But such a comparison is not altogether correct, since within the beech groves of Sanspareil there are many Claudian cliff and grotto scenes, but none of his pastoral ones. Sanspareil is both simpler, more arcadian, than the courtly world of Bayreuth, and much, much more primitive – to an extent which might even, on reflection, have surprised its creator, the Margravine Wilhelmine. In September 1749, she wrote that 'its situation is unique . . . the buildings which have been erected are in exceptional taste. Nature herself was the architect' – 'Die Natur selbst war die Baumeisterin.' Her last phrase can be matched with others, especially from England, before and at this time. But in 1793 or 1794, half a century later, views of the scenes at Sanspareil were published by J. G. Köppel, only slightly different from those of his father J. T. Köppel in 1746-8, and still strikingly 'primitive' in comparison with the scores of 'sublime' garden scenes created in the intervening years. For us, looking back with two centuries' experience of wild and wilder gardening, it is still exceptional. These cliffs are real, and the rough hollows scooped out in their sides – the 'grottoes' of Calypso, the Sibyls, of Æolus, of Diana, of Mentor and of the Sirens (and also Vulcan's cave) — are not tricked out like a magpie's nest with a mixed bag of assorted crystals. The appeal of these places is in their wildness, and their association with the story of Telemachus enabled the Margravine to envisage adapting the site in a way which would have been impossible had she wished to make a garden in more ordinary circumstances. This fact appears in the engravings of the 1750s and 1790s of the three buildings erected at one end of the rock area, and therefore just outside the confines of the goddess Calypso's 'magic island'. While the main building, the 'oriental building', has an outside encrustation of sparkling stones, like that used on artificial grottoes in England at the time, its form is symmetrical, and it is flanked by smaller symmetrical pavilions. These three buildings then embrace a rectangular garden area whose centre was filled with a *parterre de broderie*. By the 1790s, the *broderies* have gone, but the symmetry of the grassy space is still maintained, as indeed it is today. To make it 'wild' would have been ridiculous; yet in the engravings, and still today, we may see behind the 'oriental building' the rising mass of rock and trees, dense, irregular, impossible to tame. In this main area, paths and stairways were made to meander between the cliffs, and some parts have an uncanny resemblance to Nieuhof's view of 'Cliffs made by Art' which Fischer von Erlach had re-published in 1721 (see Plates 11 and 12). The resemblance between these Chinese 'garden rocks' and the cliffs of Sanspareil must have been even stronger in the eighteenth century than it is today. As an example, the engraving of the 'grotto of Æolus', with its broad, curving stairways and airy bridges, leading circuitously to the flimsy and pagoda-eaved building perched on the cliff-top, the wild and top-heavy rocks and the glimpses of caves within these rocks, might have been sketched with Fischer von Erlach's view as a principal inspiration. The possibility of this influence is all the more interesting when we consider that next to 'Calypso's grotto' at Sanspareil is the extensive and extraordinarily 'primitive' *theatre*, built in 1746, combining deliberately ruined arches over the stage with an immense natural rock arch over the auditorium. Another such ruined theatre — larger, but less primitive — had been built for the Margravine Wilhelmine at Eremitage, on the outskirts of Bayreuth, in the previous year, and both are undoubtedly inspired by the massive rock theatre at Hellbrunn, near Salzburg, used as early as 1617 for operatic performances, and built in and under the rocky arches of a hollowed-out quarry area. This rock theatre at Hellbrunn also appears in Fischer von Erlach's work, and, it must be stressed, the illustration is on the same page as the picture of Stonehenge (see Plate 8). The theatre at Sanspareil combines the rocky arches of the Hellbrunn theatre with the equally primitive ruins of Stonehenge, the 'Chorea gigantum' or 'dance of the giants'. The theatre at Sanspareil, approached through the low arch of Calypso's grotto, looks as if it could be the home of Calypso's nymphs, who might have performed dances and entertainments in a setting half-cave, half-rough-hewn rocks, so crude as to be coeval with the very invention of architecture. The landscape garden was called Sanspareil — 'incomparable' or 'peerless' — by one of its earliest admirers, in 1746. At that time, there was no other artefact to compare with Sanspareil for originality, and for its representation of the primitive world. 'Nature herself was the architect.'

4

Man-in-nature

The growing passion for 'things of a natural kind' was necessarily connected with views of man's place in a more natural environment. I have discussed the awakening interest in nature first, as historically it seems to come slightly before, and with slightly more strength, than the consideration of where man should see himself *vis-à-vis* nature. With Shaftesbury, the two concerns are simultaneous, but many of Shaftesbury's contemporaries or followers are content to expatiate on nature, without saying so much about man. If we look at, say, the poetry of Thomson or Brockes, we may note the sensitive description of nature and yet be aware that the poets themselves are far from relinquishing their status as educated townsfolk. But this is gradually modified, above all in the growing approval of rural, and even solitary, rural existence.

The idea of 'rural retirement' is of respectable antiquity – by the 1700s it was easily two thousand years old – and has its advocates even in the most town-centred decades of the seventeenth century. In the eighteenth century this idea takes a fresh dimension, since the experience of living alone in the country is now seen not as a denial of refinement and luxury, but as a fuller way of existence; and as the attraction of uncontaminated rural life grows stronger, so approval becomes more absolute, and more at odds with the life of the city.

The *hermit* is a favourite model for this idea of man living in the heart of nature. Already Milton had written in 'Il Penseroso':

> And may at last my weary age
> Find out the peaceful hermitage,
> The hairy gown and mossy cell,

and there are many variants on this theme from the 1700s onwards. Sometimes the hermit serves just as a convenient 'repository of wisdom', as in Thomas Parnell's poem *The Hermit*, published in 1721 (a principal source for Voltaire's *conte philosophique, Zadig*). It is obvious here that neither Parnell nor Voltaire wishes to recommend any life other than that of the town. But elsewhere there is much more enthusiasm. In the 1730s, the Abbé Prévost treats the theme several times, varying the ingredients in ways which suggest that it had considerable appeal for him. In the *Histoire du chevalier Des Grieux et de Manon Lescaut* (1731), the hero considers a celibate rural life, with good books and the company of like-minded friends. This, he imagines, could make him perfectly happy, but he lacks the company of Manon – and so the scheme fails. In Prévost's *Philosophe anglois, ou les aventures de M. Cléveland, fils naturel de Cromwell* (1731-9), the hero has several periods of country life, when he lives more or less happily, or could do so, were it not for his ill-managed and ill-fated passions. Once Cleveland lives rather as Des Grieux planned to do, as a scholar-in-the-country – not all that different from Thomson's way of passing the winter (p. 40 above). For another period Cleveland lives far more roughly, within the gloomy shelter of 'Rumney Hole', a Devonshire cavern like Wookey Hole in Somerset. Pope had stalactites from Wookey Hole in his grotto, but he would not have considered the hermit-like process of living in such discomfort, and so far away from the metropolis.

None the less, the hermitage – and a hermit to go with it – does become a part of the 'natural' garden, as the garden becomes less arcadian, and more wild. In the 1730s the name 'hermitage' begins to be given to garden structures which are, to our eyes, no more than summer-houses (as at Philip Southcote's *ferme ornée* at Wooburn), and which gradually acquire roughness and antiquity as the parallel tastes for the gothic and the grotto increase. It is on the Continent that the two first full-blooded examples of garden hermitages and hermits occur, with a rigour and suddenness which are astonishing.

The first example was in Bohemia, north of Hradec Kralove (some 150 miles north-east of Prague, and only a few miles from the present frontier between Czechoslovakia and Poland). Here, near the village of Kuks or Kukus, Graf Franz Anton von Sporck first endowed four hermitages for real hermits. This was between 1711 and 1720. One was in honour of St Francis, one of St Paul, one of St Anthony and the fourth of St Bruno. Praising the appropriateness of their location, a contemporary wrote that 'all around, the spirit of turbulence itself would find tranquillity' (G. C. von Stillenau, *Leben des . . . Grafen von Sporck*, 1720). This writer described many other religious foundations Sporck had set up in the village of Kuks (see Plate 14). Here Sporck had tried to create an entire religious and cultural community, and his buildings have a certain connection with the hermitages in the nearby woods.

Graf von Sporck (c. 1662-1738) was an extraordinary man. A deeply religious Roman Catholic, he was a man of intense energy, and passionate in prosecuting his charitable but egregious schemes, to the extent that he often clashed with those with whom he had dealings. When he was nineteen, he travelled to Italy and other parts of Europe for nearly two years, and made at least one further journey to Rome later in his life. He was also a fanatical lover of hunting. Stillenau wrote of him that 'he would often choose the wild forests as a pleasant place to dwell, for weeks on end', and that on occasion, he would ride on ahead of the others, lose them, and spend the night in the hut of a charcoal burner. This solitary disposition appears also in a liking he had for exploring the mountains of Bohemia – an enthusiasm which makes him one of the first mountain-climbers of the time.

In 1695, he founded an order of chivalry, the Order of St Hubert, a society both noble and religious, and connected with hunting – St Hubert was converted to a godly life when the stag he was hunting sprouted a cross on its forehead. And in 1704 or 1705 he met the young sculptor, Matthias Braun von Praun (1684-1738), and persuaded him to come to work in Bohemia. Braun had trained in Italy, coming under the influence of the school of Bernini, and his entire work seems to breathe the spirit of the late baroque, tense, agitated, with swirling draperies and muscles contracted in moments of nervous spiritual exaltation. A few of his sculptures are in Prague (a Jupiter, and a St John the Baptist, in the National Gallery) and – a most striking example – his bas-reliefs adorn the façade of the Clam-Gallas palace, which was designed by Fischer von Erlach. On the Charles bridge, there are the groups of St Ludgard and of St Ivo, and there are other statues in the beautiful but neglected remnant of the Schönborn garden. Otherwise most of his work is scattered widely across northern Czechoslovakia, still on the sites which Sporck commissioned Braun to adorn.

Since neither Sporck nor Braun is known in western Europe, these details are necessary to ensure understanding of what the two men achieved.

While Sporck was setting up his hermitages, Braun had already worked for him for some years. He had, in particular, sculpted for Graf von Sporck the prancing, grimacing, menacing and generally wind-blown figures of the vices and the virtues which line the balustrade – 150 yards long – of the hospital and its central church at Kukus, looking across the valley of the Elbe to the spa and other buildings beyond (see Plates 13 and 14). This hospital, its statues and its overall situation are powerfully reminiscent of the Renaissance villas Sporck would have seen on his Italian travels, particularly the villa Aldobrandini at Frascati. At Kukus, the central axis of the hospital is carried down to the river, and up some distance on the other side, where an elaborate staircase flanked by two small step-cascades rises up the opposite slope. Today, this pair of cascades — recalling the cascade at, say, the villa Garzoni at Collodi — is completed at the top by statues of reclining river gods. Originally, yet more sculpture and more buildings formed a striking balance to the mass of the hospital. Braun's share of the sculpture, mainly the statues in front of the hospital, seems to have been completed by 1719. Among the activities which Sporck had fostered was the publication of religious pamphlets, and in the 1720s this led him into conflict with the authorities. In 1729 the community at Kukus, visitors to the spa, residents, hermits and all, was suddenly arrested by the military and interrogated. Suspicion of heresy was a problem which Sporck had to face for a good few years.

The soldiers left, the spa survived. But Sporck's hermits did not. They were sacked. Although Sporck's religious convictions were unchanged, their expression at this point took on a different form. Instead of new hermits, Sporck installed stone ones, sculpted by Matthias Braun. In the years 1731-3, Braun created a host of hermits, saints and penitent sinners, most of them well over life size, to populate the woods beyond Kukus. Like the weird giants and monsters in the sixteenth-century garden-park at Bomarzo, near Viterbo, which Sporck or Braun might have seen in Italy, these sculptures are carved from natural rocky outcrops. Some, single or in small groups, stand, crouch or stretch freely on the ground. Others are carved in deep relief on the face of larger outcrops, so that they appear to be emerging from some primitive rock shelter. Other groups of statues were carved against the tall cliffs which line the upper edge of the woods, but these were destroyed when the sandstone was quarried in the 1780s. The entire area is now known as 'Bethlehem' from the most extensive group of these sculptures, which represents several parts of the story of the Nativity — the three kings, travelling with their camels, the birth of Christ, the adoration of the shepherds and the presentation of gifts, with St Hubert and the stag as additional spectators to one side.

A mile away, in another wood called Grossbock or Bukovina, Sporck had had over a hundred beech trees carved with hermits and saints, and also one tree showing Sporck himself in a magician's cloak, and, among

other details, the inscription FALLITVR ARTE MAGVS STABIT SVB
NVMINE FAGVS ... 1730. 'The magician is deceived by art. The
beech will stand under the protection (of the saints).' 'FAGVS' serves
also as the initials of Franz Anton Graf von Sporck. The wood-carver
Andreas Schübler was the main artist involved, and the area became
known as the 'Hubertiwald', from the importance which St Hubert had
for Sporck. A catalogue of the subjects was made 47 years later, with
the comments that the carvings and the paint which had been added to
them had expanded as the trees had grown, and that a saying had
arisen, 'that here the Saints grow on trees'.

Sporck's living saints at Bukovina have disappeared, and no pictures
survive to show whether the carvings were aesthetically related to their
surroundings. At Bethlehem, however, several groups of sculpture remain,
and these are still amazing, both in themselves, and in their setting.
Were they exhibited in a museum, the best of them would be distinguished for their wildness and agitation — like Braun's St John the
Baptist in Prague. Seen as they are in the wild, their total effect is
superbly savage, and historically unique. If Kent's landscape at
Rousham, say, or the 'Felsengarten' of Sanspareil can be proposed as a
three-dimensional version of scenes from Claude or Gaspard, it is just as
likely that Sporck and Braun had wished to emulate the scenes of
hermits set in primitive, stormy landscapes, painted in Italy in the
1660s by Salvator Rosa. There is a St Onuphrius by Rosa which could
have been the model for Braun's Onuphrius at Bethlehem. The saint
(patron of weavers) grew his hair so long that it served as his clothing,
but Braun's version is far more hirsute than Rosa's (see L. Salerno,
Salvator Rosa, 1963, fig. 92).

The masterpiece at Bethlehem is the massive figure of St Garino (see
Plate 15). He appears on his hands and knees, just outside his cave,
portrayed at the moment when the hounds (which will destroy him)
have discovered where he is. He looks up, tense with fear. Matted hair
falls down on either side of his emaciated face. His clothing is rough,
barely distinguishable from his hair and shaggy beard. At a distance, he
could be a bear, a monster, and it is only at close quarters that you can
make out what he really is: a wild and frightened man. The primitive
quality of the man himself takes Braun's sculpture far beyond Rosa's
hermits. Rosa's interest is usually in the setting, in which their hooded
or shadowy figures and features are *staffage*. For Braun, the natural
wilderness provides the proper setting to enable him to concentrate on
the solitary man.

In 1795 William Blake painted his 'Nebuchadnezzar' (Plate 16).

Blake cannot have been to Kukus, and Braun's sculpture is unknown in western Europe. But Braun and Blake were trying to portray — approximately — the same kind of person, the man who has chosen to live in solitude, away from other men and the comfort, security and elegance of the town. Hermit, madman, saint or savage, the details and the occupation may differ, but the artists' interest is the same. For Blake to paint Nebuchadnezzar with the mossy, green-blue matted hair of a sloth in the jungle is striking enough in 1795; for Braun to sculpt St Garino as he did in the 1730s is amazing.

'Ich bin allein, wenn ich vergnügt sein will' — 'I am alone, when I want to be happy.'

This was the personal motto of the Markgraf Georg Wilhelm, of Bayreuth, who ruled from 1712 to 1726, and had the Schloss or *Eremitage* built near Bayreuth in 1715. (This building is known now as the 'Altes Schloss' to distinguish it from the nearby 'Neues Schloss' built in the 1740s by the Margravine Wilhelmine — the creator of Sanspareil — whose extensive garden-work at Eremitage obliterated or overshadowed a great deal of what Margrave Georg Wilhelm had made.) Bayreuth is not too remote from Prague, or from Kukus and the activities of the Graf von Sporck. While the Margrave Georg Wilhelm was creating his 'hermitage', Sporck was busy endowing his hermitages in Bohemia (between 1711 and 1720). We must assume that the simultaneous activities of the Protestant in Bayreuth and the Roman Catholic in Bohemia were prompted by a general *Zeitgeist*, formed by influences from Italy and England. To add to the similarities is the foundation of a chivalric order — like Sporck's order of St Hubert — the order of the Red Eagle, originally the 'Ordre de la sincérité'. For the Margrave Georg Wilhelm, a Protestant, who was himself the Superior of the order, this can only have been a harking-back to the departed spirit of medieval simplicity, paralleled by the awakening nostalgia in England for the 'gothic'. The members were supposed to wear monk's clothes, and to sleep in small, simple wooden 'hermitages' near the Schloss. There were seven of these little buildings, 'without any symmetry indeed', and each was reached, not by a central avenue, but by its own narrow and meandering path, 'in the middle of a thick wood' (K. L. von Pöllnitz, *Memoirs* [1723], 1737, I, p. 207).

The idea of the simple life, however limited and fragmentary it might have been at Eremitage, clearly implies the desirability of solitude, and the narrow, winding paths which now proliferate are a physical proof of this. Walking along a broad *allée*, you can be one of a group — say half a dozen, or more. Walking down a narrow *allée*, you may be obliged to walk more or less alone, but you are visible the whole way along. Make the *allée* into a path, and let it be a winding, irregular path, and you may walk alone, or *à deux*, and be unperceived by the rest of the world once you have passed the first bend and the first clump of trees. 'I am alone, when I want to be happy.'

The idea of the *hermit* was an excuse for retreat to the country. It was soon seen that certain moods, and indeed certain kinds of men were best satisfied in the country, and in primitive country at that. Enthusiasm, inspiration, the qualities of the poet in short could only flourish *away* from the town, and in the heart of nature. Shaftesbury had shown that the poet was possessed by 'a noble enthusiasm' which emanated from 'the divine presence', and that this could only be felt in solitary communion with God's creation, the natural world. And it was *felt*, not *thought*. Others had developed this idea in slightly different directions — the Abbé J.-B. Du Bos (1670-1742), for example, in his *Réflexions critiques sur la poésie et sur la peinture* (1719) had elaborated the concept of an indefinable 'sixth sense' which enabled the critic to discover the quality of 'je ne sais quoi' which differentiated the good or great work of art from the mediocre. Taste, the 'sixth sense', was a matter for personal decision, and therefore open to subjective variation; and genius, the quality which marked the greatest works of art, was something which was subjectively *felt* and in essence beyond rational definition. While critics had agreed for centuries that taste was a personal matter — *de gustibus non disputandum* — Du Bos was the first to say so with such emphasis.

With such views, it is not surprising that the general conception of the artist, the painter, the poet, should change. For several decades there had been argument about the relative merit of Homer and Virgil — with the claim that Homer might be superior in some ways, but that his verse was imperfect, cruder, less sophisticated than that of Virgil, who lived in, and benefited from, a more cultured society. The dispute was given an entirely new emphasis at the beginning of the eighteenth century, first by Richard Bentley's discovery of the *digamma* — an unwritten but voiced consonant — whose addition to the written text of the Homeric epics destroyed at a single blow the theory that his verse was metrically crude and imperfect; and second, by Du Bos' proposition, in the *Réflexions critiques* of 1719, that criticism was not only influenced by personal and therefore indefinable preferences, but was relative, and not absolute, in yet another way, viz. that all works of art should be considered and assessed in the context of the culture in which they were first created. Therefore – to return to Homer – we should try to understand what sort of society he lived in, and what sort of audience he was writing for.

In the 1720s and 1730s Homer benefits from the combination of these opinions. Quite suddenly, Homer is approved for his virtual illiteracy, his status as a peripatetic singer, his blindness, and for the remote and savage conditions of the world he describes. These views are assembled by Thomas Blackwell. His *Enquiry into the Life and Writings of Homer* was published in 1735, with a second edition in 1736. Blackwell's presentation of Homer himself – his reconstruction of what Homer's life, education and character might have been – is remarkable. His big question is, *'How a blind stroling Bard'* could possibly write great poetry? His answers show a new regard for the quality of primitive existence, and for the supposed nature of a *primitive* poet as opposed to a *modern* one.

He begins by considering the region of the world where Homer lived, and the conditions which prevailed there in his time. These were rough and violent, and in their maritime affairs piracy was the general practice. In his poems to do with the siege of Troy and the wanderings of Odysseus, Homer was therefore describing *'natural* and *simple Manners'* little different from those which prevailed in his own day. Blackwell claims that 'he took his plain natural Images from *Life*; He saw *Warriors*, and *Shepherds*, and *Peasants*, such as he drew' (section I). In his poetry, 'there is not any single Character marked out or distinguished by *acquired* knowledge' – their wisdom has come from 'their converse among Mankind'. In stressing the simplicity of the Homeric heroes, and of Homer's contemporaries, Blackwell draws comparisons with other societies in the Middle East, as shown in Arabic, Turkish or biblical literature, to demonstrate how different all of these are from the urban, literate and artificial ways of modern Europeans (III, IV). Homer's primitive surroundings were matched by his own life. In section VIII of the *Enquiry* Blackwell develops his principal thesis, *'That Homer's being born poor, and living a wandering indigent Bard, was, in relation to his Poetry, the greatest Happiness that cou'd befall him'*. Being poor and blind, he was forced to wander from place to place, as a *'Stroling Bard'*. Blackwell then defines what a 'bard' was, and he makes it clear that such a person was vastly different from the educated 'poet' in modern Europe. The modern poet is 'learned by Books', while Homer, though maybe not illiterate, gained his education from 'Converse among Mankind'. Blackwell's comment here is, for 1735, exceptionally forward. Cautiously, he begins, 'Tho' I do not say that *Homer* . . . had no learning of this sort' — book-learning, that is — and then he continues, 'But perhaps. . .the less of it the better.' In other words, Homer wrote greater poetry since he had little education. Formal education would have been a disadvantage. The bard's compositions were again presented differently from modern poetry, which would either be *read* silently or aloud, from the text. Homer, the bard, did not *read* his poetry, he *recited* it. Probably, he did not *speak* his poetry, but *sang* it to the company round him, and a great deal would be improvised to suit the occasion. He might begin calmly, but inspiration would seize him, and 'like a Torrent, he wou'd fill up the Hollows of the Work' — and in section IX Blackwell briefly compares the ecstatic singing of the bard with the performance of a sibyl, inspired to prophecy, and with forms of madness still respected in eastern countries as containing something divine. And the subject-matter of the bard was both familiar to his audience — about persons not much different from themselves — and exalted. 'Their Subject must be . . . *The Deeds of Gods and Men.*' (It is proper to note that Rembrandt had already appreciated much of this when he painted his 'Homer' in 1663 (in the Uffizi, Florence) although his painting did not have any immediate effect on the general European conception of Homer or of 'the bard'. Rembrandt's poet is blind, impoverished and infirm. A frail old man, his blindness has allowed him a deeper, tragic vision. Blind, he listens or remembers, and his mouth and hands are tense and fearful with what he is compelled to tell. A traditional view, in contrast, is the 'Homer' by P J Mola (1612-66) in the Zwinger, Dresden. Mola's portrait shows a respectable, reasonably affluent man playing on a stringed instrument in excellent condition, and obviously 'dictating' his verse to a young male secretary, who is, like his master, clean, well fed and literate. Mola has tried, as it were, to paint Homer as the seventeenth century wanted to see him — an earlier Virgil, inconvenienced by blindness, but certainly an educated man.)

How accurate Blackwell's speculations were does not matter here — though they compare well with modern theories, such as those in Albert B. Lord's *The Singer of Tales* (1960). What is important is his approval of this kind of poet, and the distinction he draws between the bard and the modern poet, and between the life of Homeric times and our own. Apart from a grudging reference to the *Irish* or *Highland Rüners* (writers of runes, thus *poets*), he maintains that there is 'no modern Character' comparable with the Homeric bard. The entire fabric of modern society is so secure that the surprising adventures which happen, say, with the Trojan horse, or during Odysseus' many years of journeying, just do not come within our experience.

'The *Marvellous and Wonderful* is the Nerve of the Epic Strain' writes Blackwell (section I), 'But what marvellous Things happen in a well-ordered State?' He contrasts the adventure of Homeric times with modern security in terms which Diderot will repeat in 1758 in his *Discours sur la poésie dramatique* (see p. 89 below). In Homer's world, 'the Manners are *simple*, and Accidents will happen every Day: Exposition and Loss of Infants; Encounters; Escapes; Rescues; and every other thing that can influence the human Passions'. But today, 'these are not to be found in a well-governed State' — and therefore, poetry such as Homer wrote is also beyond our power to re-create. 'For Peace, Harmony and good Order, which make the Happiness of a People, are the *Bane* of a Poem that subsists by Wonder and Surprise.'

Blackwell has isolated the problem. The town-centred modern world is inimical to heroic poetry. Blackwell himself does not wish to rejoin Homer. Instead, he turns smugly to his patron, and remarks, 'Yet I am persuaded your Lordship will join in the Wish, *That we may never be a proper Subject of an Heroic Poem*.' Peace is better than poetry. Two decades later, Young and Diderot will look with greater longing at 'The *Marvellous* and *Wonderful*', and with less respect at the well-ordered State, which inhibits the creation of poetry like Homer's.

In 1760, Macpherson will publish the first fragments of 'Ossianic' poetry, supposedly the creations of a Celtic bard — in whom an ecstatic public will see a 'northern Homer' (see p. 104 below); and by the 1790s much of the 'Peace, Harmony, and good Order' which Blackwell saw around him will have gone, exchanged for 'the proper Subject of an heroic Poem' — the French Revolution.

In England, people were quick to remember that there had been native bards among the ancient Britons, the Druids, and to remember as well that such bards had continued to practise their craft in Wales until relatively recent times. The study of Druids was well-established on the 'historical' side with the continuing speculation about the construction and purpose of Stonehenge, culminating in Stukeley's *Stonehenge* in 1740. Wholly in line with this interest is the discovery and encouragement of 'primitive' poets, whose work was thought to have special merit simply because it was written by a ploughboy, a milkmaid or a shoemaker. The most famous was Stephen Duck (1705-56), who was 'discovered' in 1729 working on a farm in Wiltshire, and found to be writing verses in his moments of leisure. He was taken out of his rustic obscurity, and in 1735 installed by Queen Caroline as the 'Cave and

Library Keeper' of a special building named Merlin's Cave and erected for him in Richmond Park. It was designed by William Kent in 1735, and was a strange confection of the elements thought most appropriate for a 'thresher poet' — a thatched roof, a façade with a gothic feel to it, and inside, in gothic niches, the wax figures of Merlin and his secretary, Queen Elizabeth, her nurse, the queen of Henry VII, Minerva, and a witch. Only a short distance away was the 'Hermitage', also by Kent, and put up in 1734. 'Merlin's Cave' looked out, appropriately, over a small lake called 'The Ducks Pond'. Duck's poetry did not benefit from his fame and he suffered from fits of depression. In 1756 he drowned himself in a stream near Reading.

Related to the hermit and the poet is the *passionate* man, who, though he may not wish to live in a root house, or to declaim spontaneous verse, none the less feels rather than thinks, and is moved more by impulse than by reason. Already Shaftesbury had shown Theocles in a trance-like state of inspiration, essential for him to appreciate the truth and beauty of nature. Now such inspiration is received from persons of the other sex, and is seen as good.

The eighteenth century did not discover the strength of sexual passion. This had been known for several thousands of years. But in western Europe there has been at least since Christian times a firm tradition of disapproval of liaisons which exist 'for themselves alone'. Husband and wife, yes — provided that the attachment between them is *part* of a broader responsibility, upholding a marriage and family within society; mistresses, lovers, yes — provided that such attachments do not threaten the structure of family and society. Should these attachments lead to the destruction of a marriage, then, albeit grudgingly, society has tended to allow its wealthier members to re-marry, and so restore a degree of order and social connection to their establishment. What society has not condoned has generally been the liaison which takes no account of society. Since the beginning of the Renaissance and until the early eighteenth century this was true almost without exception.

In writers within the classical tradition, the responses are characteristic. With Corneille, for example, love is properly subordinated to duty and honour in *Le Cid* (1636), and when — in *Horace* (1639) — a person shows that her love for her betrothed is greater than her patriotism, she is killed by her patriot brother Horace, and the audience is told that his action was right. Corneille's response is optimistic. While acknowledging the existence of sexual passion, he enables his nobler figures either to overcome it in favour of more worthy forces, such as honour, duty or

68

religion, or else to bring it into an alliance with these forces so that tragic conflict is avoided. In the comedies of Molière the aspirations of his young lovers are inevitably presented favourably, as if they were so matter-of-course that no reasonable person could possibly disapprove. Should some other and unsuitable person attempt to form a *mésalliance* he or she is made to look ridiculous, frustrated, and either expelled from the family group or rendered harmless. Yet these young lovers are, for the most part, a pallid and unimpressive collection and their 'happily ever after' is usually achieved not through the strength of their own passion, but thanks to the resourcefulness of their servants. In contrast, Racine sees sexual passion dominating his characters' lives to an extent which is unthinkable in Molière, and with a lack of balancing virtues — duty, honour, self-sacrifice — which is unthinkable in Corneille. In Racine's plays sexual passion is easily the most important theme, and characters afflicted with it are doomed — it is a madness, a disease, a curse from which there is no escape. By the end of the tragedies — *Andromaque* (1667), *Britannicus* (1669), *Bajazet* (1672), *Phèdre* (1677) — the main characters are dead or isolated from their companions, driven to death or wretchedness by a passion which cannot be returned or fulfilled. None of them is happy, nor could any of them find lasting 'happiness' with the object of their desire, or a 'place in society' were they to remain together. To imagine Néron living into a tranquil old age in the company of Julie, or Phèdre happily married to Hippolyte, is grotesque, since their passion is both obsessive, solitary and destructive.

With the Abbé Prevost's *Histoire du chevalier des Grieux et de Manon Lescaut* (1731) (first published as vol VII of the *Mémoires et aventures d'un homme de qualité,* 7 vols., 1728-31) we come abruptly to an attitude to passion which is profoundly different. The hero, the young *chevalier* des Grieux, sees the young Manon Lescaut, and falls in love with her 'at first sight' — literally so. Des Grieux, studying philosophy at Amiens, is destined for the church. He is about to leave for Paris, to visit his father, in the company of his friend Tiberge. The day before their departure, he and Tiberge are strolling in the street, when they see a coach arrive from Arras, and idly follow it to the hostelry where it will pull up:

> We had no other reason to go there but curiosity. Several women got out of the coach, who went indoors straight away. But there was one remaining, who was extremely young, who waited on her own in the courtyard, while an elderly man, who seemed to be her

companion, busied himself collecting her baggage from the back of the coach. She seemed so delightful to me that I — a person who had never thought about the difference between the sexes, nor looked at a girl with any attention — that's right, me, praised by everyone for my wisdom and discretion — I suddenly found myself smitten with passion. In those days I used to be excessively shy, and I was easily put off; but far from being held back on this occasion by my timidity, I walked up to the mistress of my heart. (F. Deloffre and R. Acard (eds.), *Histoire de Manon Lescaut*, 1965, p. 19).

So far, this is not so remote from the meeting of Romeo and Juliet. The brisk elopement of Manon and des Grieux is equally understandable — Romeo and Juliet might have done the same. Yet within a few pages, a difference appears which is irresolvable — the love of Romeo and Juliet is frustrated by the feud between the Montagues and Capulets, warring families of equal nobility. Were the parents not so perverse, no obstacle should stand between the union of these admirable young creatures, and the sympathy of the audience lies with the lovers. But the love of des Grieux for Manon is frustrated by the social distance between his known and noble family — he is a *chevalier* — and hers, which is unknown, even base — her brother is a ruffian. Here, the readers understand, as clearly as did Shakespeare's audience with Romeo and Juliet, that there is a barrier between des Grieux and Manon — and in 1731 they understand that the barrier is both real, and indestructible. A marriage between the two would be unthinkable. Yet des Grieux does not care — precisely because he does not *think* about it. While able to 'reason' about virtually anything else, his attitude to Manon is entirely irrational and impulsive.

Des Grieux' father intervenes, separates the two, sends his son back to his studies, while Manon — far less attached to the young des Grieux — soon becomes the paid mistress of another man. Des Grieux is overwhelmed with chagrin. None the less, though persuaded that Manon has betrayed him, he still loves her, fickle though she is:

Doubtless I no longer felt any respect for her. How could I have respected so flighty, so faithless a creature? But I kept her picture, her charming features, deep in my heart, and there they continued to survive (ibid., p. 36).

Reason tells him she is no good. But this doesn't matter a bit. Des Grieux' father has no idea of the depth of his son's feeling, and cheerily offers to provide him with a mistress, as compensation (i.e. a female companion for his amusement, but with whom there would be no question of marriage). The *chevalier* is not cooperative, so he is kept as a virtual prisoner, studying theology and becoming tempted by the idea of a studious, rural, bachelor retreat (see p. 59 above). Time passes, the memory of Manon fades, and, on the brink of an ecclesiastical career, he gives a public lecture in the Theology School. Manon learns that he is to give this address, and comes to see him privately afterwards. He is — at first — speechless, she is enchanting. She asks, begs him to live with her again. He hesitates, filled with apprenhension at the feelings which rise within him:

> What a change, indeed, from the tranquil state I had been in, to the tumult of emotions which stirred again inside me! I was terrified. I shuddered, as you do at night in a lonely countryside, when you imagine that you've been carried off into a different world; and a secret horror seizes you, which doesn't go away until you've looked round about for quite a time (ibid., p. 45).

It is a moment of terror, exactly comparable to the instant when Racine's Phèdre sees her young stepson Hippolyte for the first time:

> Je le vis, je rougis, je pâlis à sa vue.

And yet the responses of Phèdre and of des Grieux are poles apart. Each is instantly and wholly aware of their passion for the person they have just met; each is filled with horror. But while Phèdre then struggles to the point of death, vainly trying to stifle her desire for Hippolyte, des Grieux goes on from this point to live solely for the delicious but fickle Manon. She likes him — 'loves' is too charitable a word — well enough while he has the cash to keep her, but leaves him when it's gone. On one occasion, having left to take up with a man of means, she sends him a pretty young girl to be a consolation, a substitute mistress for herself. Yet des Grieux is unshakable in his devotion, and, from the point when he perceives the 'different world', he remains dedicated to Manon, in spite of her infidelities, and in spite of the terrible obstacles which his father, his friend Tiberge, and society as a whole set in his way. Were he a Phèdre, he would be tormented with guilt, aware constantly that he was damned. But he is not, and after the initial shudder, his reaction is one of rapture, with only intermittent moments of regret. After one such twinge of remorse (when he has sponged on Tiberge), he says, 'But this struggle was slight and of short duration. The sight of Manon would have made me leap down from Heaven itself.' While Phèdre suffers the torments of the damned, des Grieux consciously rejects the promises of heavenly bliss for the brief but real and incomparable delights of his love with Manon. On earth, he says, 'the delights of love. . .are the most perfect bliss we have'. Having come to appreciate this truth, Manon is his life, and he follows her till she dies in America. His passion has carried him into a new dimension of experience, so powerful that it takes the place of glory, happiness and fortune, the conventional rewards offered by society. Not that des Grieux *rejects* society — that will come later, with Rousseau's version of the 'passionate man' — but he considers society, its rewards and its obligations less important than his devotion to Manon. While he and Manon are able to live peacefully within the social scheme — when they are tolerably solvent, for example, and not being pursued by those who wish to separate them — des Grieux is entirely willing to go on in the same way. He, like Manon, enjoys the life and entertainment of the capital. But if society's demands should clash with his life with Manon, he is ruthless — to the point of fraud, violence, even murder. 'There are many things, I am sure, for which I would give my life — either to have them, or avoid them; but to value something more than my life is still not a reason to value it more highly than Manon.'

In all this, reason is totally on the side of society, and of des Grieux' father and Tiberge; des Grieux himself rejects these for a happiness which he does not understand, but merely — and passionately — enjoys. His entire approach to Manon is emotional, as if the indefinable 'je ne sais quoi' which the Abbé Du Bos had postulated as deciding ticklish aesthetic problems — the intuitive verdict of the individual — had become the sole means of judgement, rather than an accessory beside criteria of a rational and objective kind.

5

Primitive Man

In the *Nouvelle Héloïse* Rousseau will return to the theme of the passionate lovers frustrated by their social differences (see p. 94 below), and will associate this with the theme of nature and virtue in conflict with society and corruption. But *Manon Lescaut* has no trace of approval of 'wild nature' — des Grieux and Manon are both thoroughgoing town-dwellers, and when they arrive in Louisiana they are aghast at the rough and primitive country they find there. When they escape into the wilderness outside New Orleans, Manon wilts through exposure and exhaustion and dies. Nowhere does Prévost suggest that the lovers *wish* to live further from Paris than a nearby village — close enough to allow Manon regular visits to the theatre. Although this presentation of the young lovers makes for a far more convincing book, it is slightly puzzling that Prévost should have excluded all traces of his undoubted liking for scenes and themes of a foreign, exotic or primitive kind, which appear in his other novels, as well as in his publication of the immense *Histoire générale des voyages*. But in his novel *Cléveland* (see p. 59 above) he indulges a taste, not merely for life in wilder parts of the world, but for the primitive people who live there, and for the ways in which their life is different from that of European city-dwellers. The interest in the life of 'savages', with a certain hesitant approval, goes back many years — we may think of Montaigne's 'Des cannibales' (*Essais*, I, xxxi). But such an interest could not flourish under Louis XIV — when Dryden first uses the term 'noble savage' in his *Almanzar* (1670) — 'I am as free as Nature first made man, When wild in woods the noble savage ran' — the speaker's 'nobility' comes from his dignified conduct, comparable to that of an antique Roman, and superior to that of modern Europeans, who have declined from the ancient pattern. Dryden's praise is not for his nobility as a savage — and as much can be said of Oroonoko, the 'noble savage' who is the hero of Aphra Behn's novel *The History of the Royal Slave* (1688), and

73

again, in another context, of Shakespeare's Othello at the beginning of the seventeenth century. In this period none the less there begins a series of descriptions of foreign peoples, their culture and customs, which includes not only the Chinese or the Japanese (peoples with a history and culture which Europeans might fail to understand, but must admit to be considerable), but also wilder, lesser and primitive races. Some of these descriptions come in the writings of travellers and explorers, others in missionary reports, especially those of the Jesuits. In the long series of their *Lettres édifiantes* the latter had described their work in many parts of the world, often stressing the amiable and positive qualities of the peoples whom they were trying to convert, and thus suggesting that such conversions were likely to be sincere and worthwhile. Their optimistic reports from Canada in the 1690s led free-thinkers to argue that some native peoples might in fact enjoy a life — culture, customs, government, even religion — which was equal or superior to that of many European Christians. An early example of such anti-clerical travel literature was the *Nouveaux voyages, Mémoires* and *Supplément aux voyages* of the baron L.A. de La Hontan (1703), which was one of the first works after Montaigne's essay 'Des canni-bales' in the 1580s to say outright that a primitive society — in this instance, Red Indians — had much in its way of life which was admir-able, healthy, virtuous, even though these natives had never been influ-enced by Europeans, and even though they were in fact 'savages'. Little by little different aspects of the life of primitive peoples attract Euro-pean attention, as the absolutist attitude of Louis XIV loses its compul-sion. With the publication of Montesquieu's *Lettres persanes* in 1721, the temptation to read about and even write fantasies about the ways of other people in contrast to the ways of Europeans becomes irresist-ible. Interest in the more primitive races, who might be scantily cloth-ed, or cannibals, or vegetarians, or tattoo themselves in unexpected ways is paralleled by the interest in 'wild' children who were occasion-ally discovered in Europe, having lived alone since childhood in some amazing yet intriguing way. With the classical example of Romulus and Remus before them, Europeans were fascinated that such young savages could still be found, and when they were discovered — a selec-tion includes one in Lithuania in 1694, two in the Pyrenees in 1719, 'Peter the Wild Boy' in Hanover in 1725, and, in 1731, a girl in Cham-pagne — this led to further speculation on the primitive state of man, on the earliest forms of language and the discussion of what man's earliest, basic necessities really were. Some of this speculation is so bookish (like the antiquarian Stukeley's about Stonehenge) that it cannot readily pose as a *liking* for savages; and some so fanciful that the rougher aspects of primitive existence which appealed to romantic spirits are totally neglected — as in the play by Marivaux, *La Dispute* (1744), where the audience is to suppose that two children, a boy and a girl, have each been brought up separately, from birth until adolescence, in entire ignorance of society in general, and the other sex in particular. An enlightened prince has done this, to find out in a practical way whether the 'first man' or the 'first woman' was the original backslider at the beginning of the world. Marivaux' two wild children are both beautiful, innocent and articulate, and each falls instantly in love with the other. Had Matthias Braun's wild sculpture of the savage St Garino shambled on to the stage, Marivaux' sweet young wild girl would not have fallen in love with him. Marivaux is using a theme of general interest at the time, but has treated it in a way much closer to the outlook of the Enlightenment than to the outlook of early romantics — just as Voltaire uses a fashionable eastern setting for several of his *contes* in order to express his views about Paris, and just as Voltaire will discuss the simple Quaker society in Pennsylvania in the *Lettres philosophiques* (1733/4) and several simple or wild societies in south America — the Jesuit theocracy, the cannibal Oreillons, and the ideal state of Eldorado — in *Candide* (1759) in order to attack one or another form of European complacency. I labour this point once again, since the city-centred classical attitude continues, via the *philosophes* and the Enlightenment, until the end of the eighteenth century, and my history would be false, were this continuing current to be forgotten.

To return to Prévost's *Cléveland:* in this long, emotional novel, the hero not only spends much time in a cave in Devonshire, but even longer abroad, especially in wild parts of America. As is the way with unhappy heroes, he is often separated from those he loves, and so, when re-united, he and the reader are both treated to the stories of what these loved ones did while they were kept apart. In this way, Prévost is able to describe aspects of at least four different societies which are met with in the course of his story, and which leave an overall impression of fascination, no less, with *other* ways of life than the European, and especially with ways of life which are primitive. The first of these societies is the least wild, though it is 'simple' — an exiled group of Huguenots is discovered living on the island of St Helena. Then Cleveland reaches America, and in the nation of the Abaquis he finds a near-ideal group, worshipping the sun in a manner which he is easily able to direct towards pure deism; elsewhere, there are ferocious cannibals, and then again a society, the Nopandes, which was once Christian, but which has lost contact with European missionaries and lapsed into idolatrous superstition. On most occasions Cleveland and his elderly friend Madame Riding, who tells her part of the story, are content merely to relate what they observe, as curious, approving or frightened spectators. But sometimes they are themselves caught up in the ways of these primitive peoples, so much so that they must willy-nilly follow a part of their customs. And they sometimes suggest that these are as good as, or even better than, what prevails in Europe. So, among the deist Abaquis, Cleveland is happy to go through their form of non-Christian marriage with his beloved Fanny (book iv). Much later, Madame Riding is walking on her own in the American wilderness, carrying the baby girl Cécile who has been born to Fanny. Separated from the others, frightened that she will be captured by hostile savages, yet determined to preserve the life of her young charge, she is forced into a solitary existence which resembles that of the savages. Hiding in the woods, she catches fish from a stream with her bare hands, and eats them − not raw, but slightly cooked. 'A gnawing hunger forced me to eat the fish, without any other preparation than to lie on top of them for one or two hours, to make them less raw by the warmth of my body. This wretched meal did me as much good as the very finest of dishes.' But the tiny Cécile cannot stomach the fish, and so Madame Riding opens a vein in her arm, collects the flowing blood in her cupped hand, dilutes it with water, and feeds the baby girl to their mutual satisfaction. After this crisis has been overcome, Madame Riding carries Cécile with her 'for most of a year', walking steadily towards the eastern coast, and becomes so skilled and contented in supporting herself in the wilderness that had she not hoped constantly to rejoin Cleveland and his wife Fanny, she would have been happy to stay for ever in these savage and natural surroundings (book xiii).

Although these anecdotes from *Cléveland* may seem crude, naïve and improbable to us, they display a fascination with forms of wildness, and with the wild people who live in the wilderness, which has moved on a long way from Robinson Crusoe's first horror at being cast upon a desert island, and his further fears on discovering the single naked footprint. Yet little more than a decade separates the two books (1719, 1731-9). Wild nature, once dreaded, has become attractive − even an inspiration; and man, once anxious to live in the town, is learning to shed his sophisticated ways, and to think of living simply, naturally, and to become a part of the wildness he now admires.

6

The Heyday

In the years following 1709, when Shaftesbury wrote 'The wildness pleases,' his view of the beauty, inspiration and divinity of wild natural phenomena had become generally known and appreciated. By 1759, Oliver Goldsmith could write in *The Bee* that Shaftesbury 'had more imitators in Britain than any other writer', and indeed in the mid-1750s several books appeared which 'codify' the developing approval of wildness. The principal writers are Burke, Young, Diderot and Rousseau. They are all indebted to Shaftesbury. None of them, therefore, is wholly original, but in their different ways, their summaries of what has happened, or their indications of what should now be done, are vital points in the development of romantic thought; and together, they form the central moment of my history.

As a 'codifier' Burke is easily the most important. Edmund Burke (1729-97) published his *Philosophical Enquiry into our Ideas of the Sublime and the Beautiful* in 1756 (revised edition, 1757). It is Burke who sorts out the meaning of 'sublime' for succeeding romantics, and it says much for the firmness of his definition that the meaning has not changed much since. For earlier writers — Longinus, for example, or Boileau, or even for Shaftesbury himself — it had meant principally the quality of wonder in a deed, in a work of art, or most often as an attribute of the Divinity which was so great as to be beyond human expression or comprehension. From this point, once Shaftesbury had shown the way, the wildness of nature could be classed as sublime, since it too was a part of the Divinity, and had qualities of terrible greatness which were beyond description. The wildness of nature being something which had not been admired before, the word 'sublime' served excellently to indicate the indescribable attraction of savage scenes, and came quickly to mind when these and related matters had to be set in contrast with 'beautiful' things of a traditional kind. Burke establishes this contrast, and shows that while what is *beautiful* has always a basis in what *pleases* us, the *sublime*, from its associations with what is great or violent, is necessarily based to some extent on *fear*. What is *beautiful* is still to be admired, but it is absolutely different in its origins. There is, says Burke, 'an eternal distinction between them' (III, xxvii), and for many romantics in the second half of the century, there was little doubt that they not only preferred the sublime to the beautiful, but often thought it was 'better' as well.

Things which are beautiful are *small, smooth* and *delicate*, and are gently varied in their construction or composition. For example, 'in fine women, smooth skins' are beautiful (III, xiv), as is the gentle transition in contour from a woman's neck to shoulders and breasts. Things which are beautiful are clearly visible, and distinct, like the smoothly changing, but unambiguous S-shaped 'line of beauty', the 'serpentine' line which William Hogarth had postulated in the 1750s as the most beautiful abstract shape, neither straight nor irregular, yet combining variety with smoothness and symmetry. Most of Burke's treatise is aridly theoretical, but in summing up the quality of *beauty* he gives a memorable example:

> Most people must have observed the sort of sense they have had, on being swiftly drawn in an easy coach on a smooth turf with gradual ascents and declivities. This will give a better idea of the beautiful. . . than almost any thing else (IV, xxiii).

The example is even more memorable, when we connect it with Dr Johnson, the greatest advocate of the classical attitude in England. Usually unwilling to admire the 'sublime' scenes of wilder nature, he would generally approve what was 'beautiful', including the gentle modulations of the female neck and shoulders, and I fancy that he had both these and Burke's 'easy coach on a smooth turf' in mind when, in 1777, he told Boswell what he would enjoy doing most of all, were it possible:

> In our way, Johnson strongly expressed his love of driving fast in a post-chaise. 'If (said he) I had no duties, and no reference to futurity, I would spend my life in driving briskly in a post-chaise with a pretty woman; but she should be one who could understand me, and would add something to the conversation.'

Enjoyable indeed, and infinitely remote from the sublime. 'For the sublime', said Burke, is 'the strongest emotion which the mind is capable of feeling' (I, vii), so strong that in its purest form it 'effectually robs the mind of all its powers of acting and reasoning' (II, ii). For the sublime is derived from the apprehension of *terror* — 'indeed terror is in all cases whatsoever, either more openly or latently, the ruling principle of the sublime' (II, ii). *Terror* — Burke uses the word several times, alternating it with 'fear', 'horror', 'danger' and 'pain', depending on the circumstances. A violent storm might make us aware of danger, a savage animal about to bite would lead us to expect pain, and so forth. Most of his examples are drawn from the physical world, some concern animals, and a few are to do with situations which might be depicted in a work of art, or in which people might find themselves.

Things which are sublime are, for example, *solitude* — a most romantic quality, since it is the negation of *social* existence:

> Absolute and entire *solitude*, that is, the total and perpetual exclusion from all society, is as great a positive pain as can almost be conceived . . . *pain* is the predominant idea . . . death itself is scarcely an idea of more terror (I, xi).

Solitude, therefore, is a foretaste of death (we may think of the hermits and hermitages which flourish at this time), and so is darkness and obscurity. If we wish to produce a feeling of the sublime in a poem or a painting, then it may be given a nocturnal setting — 'how greatly night adds to our dread' — to give full play to the terrors aroused by 'ghosts and goblins', or 'druids. . .in the bosom of the darkest woods' (II, iii). The opposite qualities, naturally, are allied to beauty — light and clarity — since they *dispel* the feelings of uncertainty which darkness and obscurity encourage. 'The obscure idea' is 'more affecting' than a 'clear' one, and 'a clear idea is therefore another name for a little idea'. How scornful of the 'Enlightenment', the 'Siècle des lumières', this phrase appears! And what a change from the admiration of light, of clarity, of rational *understanding* in Pope's

God said, 'Let Newton be!' and all was light.

If, in Burke's phrase, a clear idea is a little idea, then size — vastness, immensity, infinity — and *power* are necessarily sublime. 'I know of nothing sublime, which is not some modification of power' (II, v). The words 'some modification' should be noted, for an object can display degrees of the sublime. The useful domestic horse, for example, 'has nothing of the sublime', but when, in biblical language, it *'swallow-*

eth the ground with fierceness and rage' (II, v), then it is sublime indeed — as in George Stubbs' paintings of a horse attacked by a lion, discussed below (p. 133). In these scenes, as Burke says, the sublime 'comes upon us in the gloomy forest, and in the howling wilderness, in the form of the lion, the tiger, the panther, or rhinoceros' (II, v).

The last qualities of the sublime which should be quoted from Burke's analysis are *deformity, irregularity* and *ugliness* (III, v). He takes some pains to justify these, explaining that they are not necessarily sublime, unless 'united with such qualities as excite a strong terror' (III, xxi). Burke is trying to get away from the Renaissance idea that all satisfactory works of art and architecture are based on mathematically verifiable proportions, related in turn to the proportions of the 'perfect' human body. No, says Burke, for the men and women whose features and form we most admire are never exactly 'regular', but are instead distinguished by individual characteristics. Deformity or ugliness in an object — what is considerably different from the regular and 'beautiful' — is therefore not simply a kind of minus quantity, leaving the object less good, less 'beautiful' than it might be, but is merely a difference from what he calls the 'complete, common form'. And *that* could be an advantage, since the 'complete, common form' could well be so common that it was lacking in interest. 'Ugliness', on the other hand, when 'united with such qualities as excite a strong terror', may well be sublime. Burke does not give examples, but I imagine that he was thinking of characters such as Shakespeare's Richard III, deformed, malign and powerful, or natural objects such as the shattered trunks and stumps of trees so common in the paintings of Salvator Rosa. Certainly later practitioners of the sublime were to think along these lines, finding the thrill of horror, danger or possible pain to be increased if a soupçon of ugliness was added to the brew.

So much for Burke and the sublime. I have used the word sparingly until now, preferring to avoid it until Burke's own phrases could be brought to bear. From this point until the end of the century 'Burke on the Sublime' is known directly, or indirectly, to almost everyone who has a smattering of education; his concept of the sublime is *felt*, in such terrible, alarming and amazing forms that western Europe takes fright at what it has come to create; and the effects are still with us today.

Edward Young's *Night Thoughts* have already been mentioned in connection with graveyard poetry (see p. 50 above). In his old age Young produced an essay which had even greater influence, since it summed up and directed the thought of the period on an important topic — the *genius*. Young's *Conjectures on Original Composition*, begun in 1756, were published in 1759. The essay is deeply indebted to Blackwell's *Enquiry into the Life and Writings of Homer*, and is related — the influences were possibly mutual — to Thomas Gray's poem 'The Bard', begun in 1755, published in 1757. Young brings the discussion of the 'bard' into the present age. With little reference to Homer, Young argues from modern examples, Milton and Shakespeare. These are 'originals', writers of genius, who may be contrasted with 'imitators', writers who may be worthy enough, but who lack the blaze of genius. The villain in Young's essay is Pope, in his translation of Homer. Pope's fault is twofold — his efforts in translating the *Iliad* leave us with 'a *Translation* still', a work which Young feels to be unworthy of Homer's poetry, since Pope's version is in rhyming couplets, which jingle ('Had *Milton* never wrote, *Pope* had been less to blame'), and at the same time it was a labour which kept Pope from writing an original work. Young says little about the artificiality of rhyme — with Milton and Shakespeare as the great originals, he need not develop an argument. He puts a question in the mouth of the reader. 'Must rhyme then, say you, be banished?', and answers crushingly, 'I wish the nature of our language could bear its entire expulsion.'

Shakespeare, in contrast, is 'the divinely-inspired enthusiast' (a phrase straight from Shaftesbury!), with little formal learning, yet 'master of two books, unknown to many of the profoundly read... the book of nature, and that of man'. Young echoes Blackwell's doubts about Homer's education, but transfers them to Shakespeare: 'Who knows whether *Shakespeare* might not have thought less, if he had read more?'

Not only does Young bring the question of the bard up to date, but he makes the question a general one, looking into the future, by drawing an eternal distinction between the genius and 'the well-accomplished scholar'. Young separates impulse and enthusiasm and inspiration (all good) from the humdrum (and tedious) virtue of study and hard work. 'A genuis differs from a *good understanding* as a magician from a good architect; *that* raises his structure by means invisible; *this* by the skilful use of common tools.' Already in the *Night Thoughts* Young had separated the admired, instant and near-magical quality of 'instinct' from the step-by-step and somewhat despised processes of reason:

> *Reason* progressive, *Instinct* is complete;
> Swift *Instinct* leaps; slow *Reason* feebly climbs (VII, 142-3).

In the *Conjectures* he repeats the comparison, and then warns 'but by that leap, if genius is wanting we break our necks'. Diderot's article 'Génie' in volume VII of the *Encyclopédie* (1757; see p. 86 below) might seem to be Young's source for this image, had not Young already written the lines in the *Night Thoughts* long before.

Genius also has spontaneity. Speaking of the *original* work of art, Young sees in it an organic quality, which needs no premeditated labour: 'An *Original* may be said to be of a *vegetable* nature; it rises spontaneously from the vital root of genius; it *grows*, it is not *made*.' We have already seen Shaftesbury's Theocles speaking with the rapt enthusiasm of inspiration, in a markedly different way from his normal speech. Young now separates the laboured work of the imitator from the creation of the genius. With Diderot's help, most of the justification for the impulsive, wilfully erratic drama of the *Sturm und Drang* is now provided: nature, Shakespeare, genius. Aristotle's *Poetics* are likely to be neglected, when we accept that a great work of art is 'of a vegetable nature'.

'The Bard' by Gray was published in 1757. Gray's bard is Welsh, and he sings defiantly as the country is invaded by the English king Edward I. Most of the ode is the song of the ancient bard, half singer, half magician, who curses the invader, and prophesies the doom of Edward's successors. He stands on a cliff overlooking the river Conway, and invokes the forces of nature and the attendant spirits of past heroes to witness his spell:

> Robed in the sable garb of woe,
> With haggard eyes the poet stood;
> (Loose his beard and hoary hair
> Streamed, like a meteor, to the troubled air).
> And with a master's hand, and prophet's fire,
> Struck the deep sorrows of his lyre.
>
> . . . 'They do not sleep.
> On yonder cliffs, a grisly band,
> I see them sit, — they linger yet,
> Avengers of their native land.'

When his wild survey of Edward's forthcoming cares is complete, he stops:

> He spoke, and headlong from the mountain's height
> Deep in the roaring tide he plunged to endless night.

The scene of Gray's bard standing by the precipice, his hair streaming in the storm, as he plucked prophetic notes from his lyre, was to be painted again and again (by Thomas Jones, for example, in 1774 (see Plate 17), by P. J. de Loutherbourg, Fuseli, Blake, Richard Westall, and last of all by John Martin in 1817). This poet is far removed from Boileau's pupil, who is told, 'study the court and know the town'. Gray's bard, like Blackwell's Homer, or Young's Shakespeare, knows little of these. He is the 'master' of 'the book of nature, and that of man'; and with his power of incantation, the 'grisly band' of ghosts and his own perpendicular exit he is a model for all sorts of poet-bards to come — we may see him, shadowy, behind Macpherson's Ossian and Beattie's 'Minstrel' (1771), and even the 'Last Minstrel' of Sir Walter Scott in 1805.

In 1757 and 1758 Denis Diderot (1713-84) makes his main contributions to the discussion of the sublime and the genius. (Quotations are from Diderot, Œuvres esthétiques, ed. P. Vernière, 1965). The years from 1755 until 1760 are the *anni mirabiles* of this subject, with a flood of writings coming so close together that it is often impossible to say which author influenced which at what point. What is certain is that Burke, Young and Gray in England, and Diderot and Rousseau in France, were all considering the sublime; that they all had knowledge of Shaftesbury's writings; and that their interest was often communicated to friends before the actual publication of their writings. In 1757, the position is at its most complicated — the second edition of Burke's treatise on the *Sublime and the Beautiful* appears, Young is maturing his thoughts on Shakespeare, Gray's 'Bard' is completed, Diderot's *Entretiens sur le Fils naturel* appear, followed by the article 'Génic', and in the background Rousseau is deep in the composition of the *Nouvelle Héloïse* (see p. 94 below).

Diderot was profoundly indebted to Shaftesbury. Already in 1745 he had translated Shaftesbury's *Inquiry concerning Virtue*, and his writings in 1757 and 1758 are especially marked by the influence of the *Moralists*, coupled with the influence of Rousseau whom he had met in the 1740s, and with whom until mid-1757 he had been closely associated. In February 1757 he published his play, *Le Fils naturel*, the text of which was followed by a series of three *Entretiens avec Dorval*,

generally known now as the *Entretiens sur le Fils naturel*. These 'entretiens' or 'discussions' are dialogues between Diderot himself and Dorval,
the hero of the play, who is an emotional, sensitive and talented man
modelled partly on Rousseau and partly on Shaftesbury's Theocles.

The *Entretiens* take their form from the *Moralists*, being discussions
on nature, life and the theatre, held in a framework of country walks.
In this setting, Diderot ('moi') has the role of Shaftesbury's Philocles,
questioning, and at last convinced by the passionate Dorval. The tone
is soon set when 'moi' observes the reunion, after the play, of the
characters who have just 'acted out' their story — all, that is, save one,
who had died and had been represented in the play by another old man.
The sight of this second, tottering old man reminds the company of
their departed friend, and they all burst into tears, including the servants, and including 'moi'. As 'moi' walks away afterwards, wiping his
eyes, he says to himself, 'I must be a simple fellow to get so upset. It's
only a play after all.' Dorval then convinces him that his tearful reaction was right. Tears, sentiment, 'feeling' come from our instinctive
reaction, and, in so far as this reaction is instinctive and emotional
rather than rational, it is good. Dorval, himself a 'genius', experiences
such expansive and emotional reactions with facility, and in the *Entretiens* 'moi' not only talks with Dorval, but has the opportunity to
watch him in moments of emotional inspiration.

As in the *Moralists*, where Theocles descants rapturously on the
beauties of unspoiled nature, Dorval is inspired by the countryside.
'Moi' and Dorval have agreed to meet again, at the foot of a wooded
hill — a lonely spot, overlooking the fertile plain, with jagged mountains
on the horizon. Dorval is there first, and 'moi' arrives without Dorval
noticing, for Dorval is caught up in admiration of the scene:

> He had given himself up to the contemplation of nature. His bosom
> heaved, his breath came in gasps. . . I began to share his enthusi-
> asm, as I cried out, almost involuntarily 'He's under a spell' ('Entre-
> tiens' in *Œuvres esthétiques*, p. 97).

Dorval hears this, turns to 'moi', and replies in terms which paraphrase one of Theocles' outbursts to Philocles,

> It is true. Here is where nature is to be seen. This is the sacred abode
> of enthusiasm. What does the man do, who is gifted with genius?
> He will leave the town and its inhabitants. . . Who is it, who joins
> his voice to the torrent, as it falls from the mountain-side? Who

84

feels the sublimity of the wilderness? Who listens to his inner prompt-
ings in the silence of solitude? It is he. O Nature! All that is good is
held within thy breast! Thou art the fertile source of every truth . . .
Only virtue and truth in this world are worthy, that I should occupy
myself with them. . . Enthusiasm is born from the objects of nature
(ibid, pp. 97-8).

Dorval goes on to describe how inspiration, 'enthusiasm', seizes the
poet, and forces him to pour out the torrent of his ideas. Dorval speaks
ecstatically, and then falls silent. 'A while later he asked me, like a man
waking from deep slumber, "What did I say? What was I saying to you?
I can't remember what it was."' Not only are Dorval's trance-like state
and awakening copied from Theocles ('Here he stopped short, and
starting as out of a dream: "now Philocles", said he "how have I
appeared to you in my fit?"'), but Diderot will repeat them in the
Neveu de Rameau, written some years later (c. 1761-c. 1775), when he
has to some extent turned against the cult of genius and the sublime
(see p. 261 below). Here, though, Dorval speaks with the approval of
'moi', and we may see his praise of nature as the 'fertile source of every
myth' coinciding with Diderot's opinion at this moment. I have tried to
phrase this as accurately as possible, since Diderot is, however great his
praise of nature and genius in the writings of 1757-8, still the same man
who has been working at the *Encyclopédie* since 1745, who has always
shown deep interest in the improvement of the affairs of 'men in
action', and who will from the mid-1760s be one of the first to turn
away from the sublime to concentrate wholly on 'the men who live in
the city'.

In the *Entretiens*, however, this division in Diderot's allegiance is
only slightly apparent. It shows in a fascinating way at the start of the
third discussion. 'Moi' and Dorval had agreed to meet again at the same
place, but there was a thunder-storm, and 'moi' imagines Dorval exult-
ing in the experience:

In my imagination, I saw Dorval in the centre of this sombre scene,
as I had seen him the day before in the rapture of his enthusiasm;
and I thought I could hear his melodious voice, rising above the wind
and the thunder (ibid., p. 135).

But 'moi' himself stays at home until the storm is over, and then,
when the worst has gone by, he says, 'I would have gone to look for
Dorval among the oak trees, but I reckoned that the ground and the

grass would be too damp and soggy.' Dorval for his part has anticipated 'moi''s dislike of wet grass, and waits for him in his house; and there, in Dorval's garden, 'along the sanded borders of a broad canal' they finish their discussion. For 'moi''s sake, uncomfortable nature has been exchanged for a formal garden.

Out of Dorval's enthusiasm for nature and genius comes a dramatic theory of an only moderately adventurous kind. The *Fils naturel* itself preserves the 'three unities' with a correctness which later German critics will find positively pusillanimous, and the play has little that is unconventional or experimental apart from being in prose, with occasional soliloquies of a 'natural' and disjointed nature, and a setting which is clearly contemporary and middle-class: not revolutionary. In the *Entretiens* Diderot proposes a 'tragédie domestique et bourgeoise', a 'genre sérieux' — 'a domestic, middle-class tragedy', a 'serious genre'. This will bridge the gap between tragedy and comedy, exclude violent or farcical extremes, have a contemporary middle-class setting, and obviously be written in prose; and it will have a moral and improving effect. When, in 1758, Diderot published his *Discours sur la poésie dramatique*, which was prompted by his play *Le Pére de famille* (1758), there is an even greater division between his visions of genius and sublime nature, and his timid play with its domestic setting. In Germany, where Diderot's influence was far stronger than in France, the effect is noticeable in two distinct areas corresponding to the two sides of Diderot's approach. The 'tragédie domestique et bourgeoise' is rapidly identified with the 'bürgerliches Trauerspiel', best represented in the plays and criticism of Lessing (who translated Diderot's dramatic writings into German in 1760, as *Das Theater des Herrn Diderot*), while praise of the genius is taken up by the younger writers of the Sturm und Drang (see p. 212 below).

In November 1757, nine months after the *Entretiens sur le Fils naturel*, volume VII of the *Encyclopédie* was published, in which the article 'Génie' appears, which is principally the work of Diderot. This article extends Dorval's excited speeches, while continuing Shaftesbury's view that the genius acts upon inspiration coming from nature. His imagination is so strong that he can 'feel', and be moved by the situations in his mind:

> The *genius*, surrounded by the objects with which he is busied, does not remember, he sees; he does not merely see, he is moved: in the silence and obscurity of his study, he delights in a smiling, fertile countryside; he freezes in the howling wind; the sun burns him,

and in the tempest he is seized with fear ('Génie' in *Œuvres esthétiques,* pp. 9-10).

Diderot then makes a distinction which Young also makes in his *Conjectures* (possibly Young had read Diderot?), between the qualities which a writer may possess, either of *goût* ('taste') or of *génie* ('genius') The one can be acquired by study, while the other is 'a pure gift of nature'; this corresponds to Young's 'imitators' and 'originals'. Again Diderot comes near to Burke and to Young when he claims that 'le goût' will produce works which are beautiful, elegant, polished, while a work revealing 'génie' will sometimes be 'careless, and with an irregular, rugged and wild appearance'. Diderot continues with examples of each: '*Genius* and the sublime shine in Shakespeare like lightning during a long night, while Racine is always beautiful; Homer is full of *genius,* and Virgil of elegance' (ibid., pp. 11-12). Though the details vary, the distinction is exactly that made by Burke between the sublime and the beautiful, and that made by Young between Shakespeare and Pope. A while later, Diderot makes a similar contrast between the careful, correct and balanced writings of Locke, and the sometimes faulty, but sublime, creations of Shaftesbury. To illustrate this comparison, he writes in words which echo Young in the *Night Thoughts* (VII, 142-3),

> *Reason* progressive, *Instinct* is complete;
> Swift *Instinct* leaps; slow *Reason* feebly climbs

but adds — as does Young in the *Conjectures* of 1759 — a warning that the 'leap' of genius can lead both upwards, and into the abyss. The genius 'rises with an eagle's flight towards one shining truth, source of a thousand truths which the mass of wise observers will reach — in the end — by crawling' ('Genie', p. 14). This is splendid; but the leaping genius 'cannot walk along the beaten track', and in government especially Diderot has reservations about the value of so independent and so impetuous a creature: 'There are times when he may save his country; and which he would subsequently bring to ruin, were he to remain in power' (p. 16). In the *Neveu de Rameau* Diderot will expand these doubts, showing the ambiguous situation in society of a man who is far more talented than most, yet who lacks the full fire of genius. But this is still some years away, and in the 1750s Diderot is fairly consistently an admirer of genius. More than any other theoretician, Diderot unites the ideas of the sublime and the genius, and he does this particularly in the *Discours sur la poésie dramatique* of 1758.

The *Discours* is no more successful than the *Entretiens* in bringing Diderot on the theatre and Diderot on nature and the sublime together; indeed by the end of the book he has managed, *sans le vouloir*, to show that the kind of play he wants, the *tragédie bourgeoise*, must of necessity lack the fiery and poetic qualities of genius which he describes with so much enthusiasm.

At an early point (ch. ii) he bursts out with the question 'Then human nature itself is good?' — which he proceeds to answer with the Shaftesburian and Rousseauan reply, that *everything* in the natural world is good, however violent:

> Yes, my friend, very good. Water, air, earth and fire, everything in nature is good. Even the gale, at the end of autumn, which rocks the forests, beats the trees together, and snaps and separates the dead branches; even the tempest, which lashes the waters of the sea and purifies them; even the volcano, casting a flood of blazing lava from its gaping side, and throwing high into the air the cleansing vapour. ('Discours' in *Œuvres esthétiques*, p. 195).

Here we may catch a distant echo of the post-Newtonian teleologists, Derham, or Ray, or Scheuchzer, finding 'usefulness' even in the most violent of nature's manifestations (see p. 30 above); Diderot's contemporaries were not concerned with this, but loved the praise of wild nature. And in Diderot's next sentence, this praise was turned into an attack on society, which cuts men off from these things: 'Man is perverted by the wretched customs of society; we must not lay the blame on human nature.' By 1758, this is an echo, not of near-forgotten writers from England, but of Rousseau, alive and writing in France, and his contribution to romantic thought must soon be discussed.

Violent nature and the genius are akin. If nature, even when wild, is 'good', and the genius has an instinct to leap to the highest truth, then rules, 'les règles', are an encumbrance. A year earlier, Diderot wrote in the *Entretiens* that the 'three unities' might be hard to observe, but that they were 'sensible'. Now, he has changed his ground. The rules, he claims, were made by those who are too small to create the greatest works of art. Men of genius are free to ignore these rules whenever they please (ch. xi).

In ch. xviii, 'Des Mœurs' — 'Concerning Manners' — Diderot sums up his view of the sublime, the true environment for the poetic genius. Like Blackwell, Diderot not only sees a great difference between the conditions favourable for the growth of the genius and the life of his own times, but agrees that his own times are fundamentally opposed to genius; and he takes Burke's analysis of the sublime as the framework on which to hang examples, either of sublime conduct, or of sublime natural phenomena, both of which are the essence of poetry (the creation of genius), and both of which are lacking, indeed harmful, in our own society. Diderot's remarks are amazing. He has, as it were, given flesh to Burke's theory, and provided a catalogue of human or natural wildness, of *extremes* of emotion, action or situation which can serve as an index of what most subsequent romantics will admire, and of what society, by and large, must reject.

The opposition of poetry — including 'genius', 'nature', 'the sublime' — to society begins his argument: 'In general, the more a nation is civilised, the less poetic are its manners' — and he proceeds to list manners which *are* poetic, and which are patently uncommon today:

> when a mother bares her bosom, and implores her son by the breasts which have suckled him; when a young man cuts off his hair, and scatters it over the body of his friend; ... when meals are sacrifices which begin and end with cups filled with wine, and cast on the ground; ... when pythian sybils, their eyes rolling, foaming at the mouth, tortured by some demon, squat over a tripod, and make the gloomy caverns echo with their prophetic utterances; ... when other women strip themselves shamelessly, open their arms to the firstcomer, and prostitute themselves, etc. ... (ibid., pp. 260-1).

Diderot, himself a cheery fornicator, adds carefully, 'I wouldn't say these were *good* customs; but they are poetic.' Remembering Burke, we may add that they are wholly sublime. So too are the examples Diderot gives of *poetic* nature, which he contrasts with nature of an uninspiring kind. He asks, 'What does a poet need? Nature which is wild, or cultivated, peaceful or disturbed?' His examples of what is poetic are all wild, and could, I think, have been appreciated by Shaftesbury; possibly by Thomson, though hardly by Brockes. Diderot sets his examples one by one in opposition to what is 'cultivated' and 'peaceful' — Burke would have used the word 'beautiful', since 'cultivated' and 'peaceful' means small, smooth, regular and gently varied:

> Will a poet prefer the beauty of a pure and cloudless day to the horror of a murky night, where the hoarse roaring of the wind is joined to the rumble of faraway thunder, and where he sees the

sky aflame with lightning over his head? Will he prefer the sight of a calm sea to the sight of lashing waves? The silent, chilling view of a palace to a walk among ruins? A building which is complete, a patch of ground cultivated by human hand, to the dense thickets of an ancient forest, or to an unknown cavern in a lonely mountain? (ibid., p. 261).

At the end of his list, Diderot sums up the requirements of poetry in one sentence, which is a paragraph in itself:

La poésie veut quelque chose d'énorme, de barbare et de sauvage.

[Poetry demands what is enormous, barbaric and wild.]

In its direction, it is barely distinguishable from Burke's claim, that 'terror is. . . the ruling principle of the sublime'.

Diderot had certainly read Blackwell. The paragraphs in the *Discours sur la poésie dramatique* which follow enlarge Blackwell's view that 'Peace, Harmony and good Order, which make the Happiness of a People, are the *Bane* of a Poem that subsists by Wonder and Surprize.' Diderot asks, 'When are poets born?', and replies to the reader 'after a time of disaster and great misfortune'. Blackwell said firmly that he would rather forgo a Homer, and avoid such civil calamities; Diderot, seeing what he believes to be the same alternatives, remains silent. He died in 1784, five years before the beginning of the Revolution. This most turbulent chapter of the *Discours* ends, characteristically, for Diderot, neither with a question for the reader to answer, nor with an exhortation, but with a puzzled statement, a paradox: 'We find these contradictions everywhere' (p. 263).

To sum up Diderot's views: nature is good. Genius is good. Society, in contrast, is bad. True, Diderot has his doubts, and they will grow — and they grow as the gap between himself and his erstwhile friend Rousseau widens. It is the moment to see how Rousseau fits into the wild, natural and passionate scene.

Almost everything written by Jean-Jacques Rousseau (1712-78) has its place in the development of romanticism. For more than twenty-five years, from his *Discours sur les sciences et les arts* of 1750 until the *Rêveries du promeneur solitaire* written in 1777-8, he said that nature was good; that society was corrupt, and was a corrupting influence, and that man's happiness was dependent on his living a life which was 'natural' and which had therefore rejected the ways of society. His writings explore the different aspects of this difficult view of life — some of them concentrating on nature, some considering society, and others discussing man's past, present or possible situation *vis-à-vis* nature and society. Like Burke and Diderot, Rousseau brings together thoughts which had already been expressed by others, though without Rousseau's overall completeness; and in some of his writings the synthesis is so complete and so wholly absorbed into what Rousseau himself wants to say that he creates works which are, as nearly as makes no difference, original. Unlike Burke or Diderot, however, who both have deeply social leanings, Rousseau never goes back on his allegiance to nature and his condemnation of modern society.

Rousseau's taste is for the gentler aspects of nature, such as he would have known round the shores of lac Léman in Switzerland, and as were admired by Gilbert Burnet in the 1680s, while the wilder, barren mountains of the Alps do not attract him. It is a cliché when talking of Rousseau and the discovery of nature to say that he climbs only half-way up the mountains. The gentle, wooded slopes are fine, with their prospects of 'a smiling countryside', but once the trees thin out, and rocks push through the soil; and higher up, when there is no life, but only rocks, and snow and ice, then Rousseau is not interested. Certainly Rousseau's descriptions of the Alpine *countryside* brought countless tourists to the Alps, and no doubt helped them towards the mountain-mania which flourished from the 1780s. But there is nothing in Rousseau's writings to suggest that he himself would have wished to scramble to the top of Mont Blanc with Saussure in 1787; to share the ecstasy of Senancour's hero Oberman, in 1804, as he indulged in solitary *rêverie* on the top of a glacier; or to join with Byron and Childe Harold in 1816 in wishing to be united with God in the annihilating plunge of an avalanche. No. Rousseau is a lover of gentle, pastoral nature, and remains so from his naïve and artificial small opera or 'intermède', *Le Devin du village* of 1752, via the ideal rural community described in book iv, letter 10 of the *Nouvelle Héloïse*, written in 1756-7, published in 1760, until the last of the *Rêveries* and his death in 1778. Though Rousseau probably knew nothing of Brockes, he would, I am sure, have been wholly in sympathy with Brockes' delight in the tiniest details of individual plants and flowers, and with Brockes' view that the beauties of nature were the work of a benevolent Creator. In his last twenty years, Rousseau turned increasingly to the pleasures of 'herborising' — we would say 'nature study' or 'plant collecting' — as a scientific and therapeutic activity. He collected flowers and grasses, and preserved them in several volumes, some of which still survive with his detailed annotations, and his *Lettres sur la botanique* were published in 1772. His herborising was most often a solitary pursuit, which led beyond the study of plants to a personal communion with nature. Nature — *this* kind of nature — is good, the source of virtue, and a living proof of a kindly Creator. Rousseau's most compelling writing on this subject is in the *Rêveries*, but already in the *Nouvelle Héloïse* there is a passage which unites solitary communion with nature with virtue and with supreme happiness. In book iv, letter 11, the hero St Preux describes the garden — the 'Elysée' or 'elysium' — made by Julie, his erstwhile lover. St Preux has been away for several years, sailing round the world with Commodore Anson, while Julie has married, become the mother of three children, created a happy rural community, and, in the old orchard near the mansion, she has fashioned the 'natural' garden of the 'Elysée'. St Preux is shown round the 'Elysée' by Julie and her husband. Delighted, St Preux imagines he is back on an uninhabited island, such as Juan Fernandez or Tinian, both visited by Anson on his voyage through the Pacific, and asks for permission to return to the 'Elysée' on his own, for he is still in love with Julie, and he wants to wander amid the garden-scenes she has made, and to indulge in daydreams about her. Meanwhile, her husband has remarked tartly to St Preux that he should *repsect* the 'Elysée'. He tells him, 'Learn to respect the place where you are now; it has been planted by the hands of virtue.'

Next morning St Preux returns to the 'Elysée', intending to dream about Julie. But he remembers her husband's words, and his entire attitude is changed. From the proposed contemplation of pleasure, he turns to the contemplation of virtue, in Julie herself and in her 'Elysée': 'I said to myself, "Peace reigns in her heart, as it does in this refuge, called by her *Elysium*."' So St Preux, expecting 'a pleasing reverie', experiences in the natural and virtuous groves of the 'Elysée' two hours of incomparable reverie, 'which I value above any other time in my life'.

Though natural, there is nothing wild in the 'Elysée'. Rousseau trails behind the new landscape gardening which was flourishing in England. The 'Elysée', natural and untouched by human hand though it is intended to appear, is patently a garden which has been most carefully contrived, and which not only excludes unwelcome visitors, but also all but the pleasing and gentle aspects of nature itself. The 'Elysée' not only lacks the fuller approach to nature as a whole which English gardeners were attempting; it contains the beginnings of Rousseau's own progression towards a private and solitary relationship with nature which is essentially opposed to the idea of the garden.

To explain further: The description of the 'Elysée' in the *Nouvelle Héloïse* is Rousseau's only extended passage on what a garden should be like. It is a garden which is normally uninhabited, shut away from all but three or four occasional visitors, and which makes its profoundest impression upon St Preux as resembling a 'desert island', the uninhabited paradises of Juan Fernandez or Tinian. The allusions refer back to St Preux' earlier brief account of Anson's visit to these islands (book iv, letter 3), echoing phrases from the original *Voyage autour du monde. . . par George Anson* of 1749, which Rousseau read in 1757 (a French translation of Richard Walter's *Voyage round the World. . . by George Anson* of 1748). For Anson's sailors, the islands were found at moments of vital importance – without these landfalls, they would have died. For Rousseau, for St Preux, the 'Elysée' is essential as a spiritual refuge which enables the hero to sublimate his passion and continue living. The 'Elysée', Juan Fernandez and Tinian are valuable because they are uninhabited. Were people to frequent them, the tame birds or animals would be frightened, their gentle charm would be lost and their virtue would be destroyed.

Within a few years Rousseau had clearly outgrown all interest in gardens. In 1766-7 he spent sixteen months in England, in which time he describes only one garden, Wootton Park, in Staffordshire. Nor does he seem to have discussed gardens with his acquaintances, even though he must have visited several near London or in the neighbourhood of Wootton. Instead, the references in his letters (when *nature* gets a chance – his stay in England was tormented by his growing fears of general conspiracy against him) are to his love of 'herborising', and to his preference for doing this out in the country (usually in Dovedale), not in the artificial confines of a garden. On 12 February 1767, he writes to the Duchess of Portland in terms which mark the end of gardening for himself:

> The plants growing in our woods and on our hills are still as they were when they left the Creator's hands, and it is there that I love to study nature – for I must admit to you that I no longer feel the same delight in botanising in a garden. I find that nature, in a garden, is not the same: she has more brilliance, but she does not move me as much. Men say, they make nature more beautiful – but I believe they disfigure her (letter 3265 in Rousseau, *Correspondence générale*, ed. Th. Dufour, 1924-34).

Rousseau's direction is clear. The garden is artificial, since people have shaped it; and since people *use* it, it is also social. In the last years of his life, his thought moves to countrysides where his contact with nature is even more absolute, and society less able to spoil his delight. This is in his *Rêveries*, written in 1777-8. Discussion of them must therefore take place at the proper moment (see p. 225 below), when the other developments urged on by the thoughts and writings of Burke, Diderot and Rousseau himself are in their most tempestuous and passionate form.

The romantic belief in passion is also boosted by Rousseau, so much so that he seems almost its originator. In the *Nouvelle Héloïse* Rousseau takes from Prévost's *Manon Lescaut* the theme of 'total love at first sight'. St Preux, the tutor, and Julie, the young lady, fall in love with nearly as much promptness as the *chevalier* des Grieux. But − note the difference − *they* fall in love. When des Grieux falls in love with Manon, her response may be prompt, but it is not sincere, and her devotion to des Grieux may be measured again and again by the length of des Grieux' purse. That is, as it were, a one-way affair. But Rousseau presents a love which is not only instant, but mutual, and complete. Both St Preux and Julie love each other wholly, and when separated still love each other, so that, years later, when they meet again (involving the episode of the 'Elysée') St Preux comes to the brink of suicide and Julie at the last is burnt out by her continuing passion within her. This will inspire generations of romantics, and their opponents. In France alone we may think, for example, of Chateaubriand and *Atala*, Senancour and *Oberman*, Hugo and *Hernani*, Fromentin and *Dominique* on the one hand; and of Constant and *Adolphe*, Musset and the *Confession d'un enfant du siècle*, and Flaubert and *Madame Bovary* on the other.

No one could doubt that des Grieux is passionately devoted to Manon. But the language used by Prévost, either in description or in des Grieux' own words, is clear, complete and analytic: 'I shuddered, as you do at night in a lonely countryside, when you imagine that you've been carried off into a different world.' Rousseau sees that such accurate prose is not for passionate lovers. And so, following the example given by the epistolary novels of Richardson, his lovers write, in their more excited moments, in a language which is abrupt, incoherent, and punctuated with expressive silence. A fair example is in book i, letter 14, when St Preux writes to Julie describing the moment of their first kiss:

But I don't know what happened to me next when I felt... my hand shakes... that tender trembling... your rosy lips... Julie, it was *your* mouth... touching mine, pressing my mouth, and you hugging me in your arms! (*Julie, ou la Nouvelle Héloïse*, ed. R. Pomeau, 1960, I, xvi, p. 38).

St Preux may seem excited — but Julie, who does the kissing, goes pale, closes her eyes and falls unconscious. Two centuries later, our jaded taste demands either more, or less, of this. Rousseau continues happily with more of the same, phrases which are short, and rather a set of exclamations than connected and coherent prose:

A favour, you think?... it's torture, dreadful... No, keep your kisses. I can't bear any more... they're too fierce, too penetrating; they go right in, they burn me right to the marrow... I'd go mad with them (ibid.).

Here Rousseau has joined forces with the supporters of the sublime. St Preux' agitation is akin to Burke's *terror*, which 'effectually robs the mind of all its powers of acting and reasoning'. Connected prose, then — the product of a 'reasoning' mind — is impossible, and we are left with gasps, grunts and silence — the vocabulary of passion. Burke had already claimed that, in certain circumstances, deformity, irregularity and ugliness could be sublime, while Diderot had praised the 'naturalness' — or truth — of the inarticulate wailings of Sophocles' Philoctetes, rolling on the ground before his cave, and crying 'Apapapai, papa, papa, papa, papai.'

Bring these three together, Burke, Diderot and Rousseau, and the romantics who follow them have every excuse for incoherence. Once a passion soars, then connected words are a hindrance. Words cannot express our feelings. . . .

In the new picture of passionate love, Rousseau adds one other important element which was absent in *Manon Lescaut*: nature. While des Grieux and Manon loved and half-loved in Paris or out of Paris, and worried only when they were short of cash, St Preux and Julie love each other 'at the foot of the Alps', and these rural surroundings are the proper setting for their deep, innocent and rightful affection. Left to themselves Rousseau's lovers could — the reader feels — only be happy. So what should prevent their marriage? Not nature, says Rousseau, but society. Julie is a lady, St Preux is her tutor — no more than a servant — and their marriage, like that of des Grieux and

Manon is out of the question. Prévost in 1731 did not take umbrage at this. For him it was a fact of existence, and it provided, simply and acceptably, a reason why des Grieux *could not* marry Manon. For Rousseau, however, society is the great villain, the stumbling-block to the happiness of St Preux and Julie, and through them, to the happiness of us all. St Preux' seduction of Julie is not condemned by Rousseau — it is the 'natural' outcome of their natural affection — but when she becomes pregnant, St Preux is expelled and, travelling to Paris, is easily corrupted by the vicious gamblers and actresses whom he meets, while she, after a miscarriage, is forced to marry an older but socially acceptable man. Such pressures, outside the control of innocent lovers, will be used by later story-tellers to the point of tedium and beyond, bringing the threat and excitement of suicide, elopement, midnight marriage or breathless escape into the welcoming arms of nature. Happy the pair who live together as children, and grow up together, in such a natural surrounding, like Bernardin de Saint-Pierre's Paul and Virginie — and woe betide the pair — like Paul and Virginie — when one or other of them has, perforce, to return to society, and is destroyed!

Already in the *Discours sur les sciences et les arts* of 1750 Rousseau had shocked his contemporaries by claiming that man was worse, not better off, for the inventions of the arts and the sciences, and in the *Discours sur l'origine et les fondements de l'inégalité parmi les hommes* of 1755 he blamed man's unhappiness on the general and particular institutions of society, which he sees, *in itself*, as essentially bad. In this Rousseau is contrary to earlier *philosophes,* such as Montesquieu and Voltaire, who, though they might attack the institutions of society with a terrible vigour, wished always to reform society, not to destroy it. They wished to clean up the city, not to abolish it.

In the *Discours sur. . . l'inégalité* Rousseau establishes an immediate and total contrast between man's original state, the 'state of nature', and his condition today. Seeing the natural world as a place which is innocent and good, he sees man in a state of nature as happy, innocent and good also. Lacking reliable information about the early history of *homo sapiens*, Rousseau is able to paint the rosy picture of man's first state in a confident, absolute and uncomplicated way.

The opening contrast is essential. Rousseau writes that his aim is 'to meditate upon the equality which nature established between men, and the inequality which they have since set up' (Rousseau, *Œuvres complètes*, vol. 2, ed. M. Launay, Paris, 1971, p. 204). Equality — inequality: for Rousseau, the division is profound, and shameful.

Inequality marks the slave, and slavery is what Rousseau sees in modern society. Wild animals which have been domesticated – the horse, the cat, the bull – are all stronger and more admirable in their wild state; all have become effeminate when tamed. Rousseau adds, 'It is the same with man himself: as he becomes a creature of society and a slave, he becomes weak, fearful and servile' (p. 217).

The inequality is not merely one of strength. It is one of *possessions*. Part II of the *Discours sur... l'inégalité* begins with the famous lines 'The first man who, when he had enclosed a plot of land, thought of saying: *This is mine*, and found people simple enough to believe him, was the true founder of civil society.' If property is evil, how much more so are those possessions which *increase* the degree of inequality between those who are masters, and those who are slaves? Rousseau attacks luxuries, which most earlier *philosophes* had agreed were necessary as part of the fabric of industry, even if their equitable distribution might be improved. In 1714 the Englishman Bernard Mandeville had put the position firmly if outrageously in his *Fable of the Bees*, by claiming that all transactions which encouraged the circulation of money were a help to society – even if they were, like prostitution, considered by some to be 'immoral'. In 1721, in the *Lettres persanes* (letter 106), Montesquieu had approved 'le luxe' as giving needed employment to the city's poorer inhabitants, and in 1736, in his poem 'Le Mondain', Voltaire contrasts Adam and Eve, living in crude, ape-like discomfort, with the modern world, in which the busy circle of commerce is completed by the trade in luxuries:

> Le superflu, chose très nécessaire
> A réuni l'un et l'autre hemisphère
>
> [Our luxuries are such a needful thing,
> They've joined as one the new world to the old] (Voltaire, *Mélanges*, ed. J. van den Heuvel, 1961, p. 203.

Rousseau turns his back on the entire argument by saying that not only should it be unnecessary to have to find work for the poor, but that the whole fabric of *le luxe* – all non-essential industries – is pernicious – 'From society and from the luxuries which it brings forth are born the liberal and mechanical arts, trade, letters, and all the frivolities which make industry flourish, and enrich and destroy the State' (p. 253). Rousseau would not reform all this, nor 'redistribute' the wealth or the objects of luxury. No. He would abolish the lot.

One more political matter in the *Discours sur. . . l'inégalité* needs to be mentioned — the 'contract' which he postulates between a monarch and his people. For some while French writers had seen (rightly or wrongly) the peaceful replacement of the British king James II by William of Orange, in the 'Glorious Revolution' of 1688, as the model of a contractual relationship between a monarch and his people (here represented by Parliament). As the Hanoverian succession appeared more and more assured, and the strength of Parliament and general British prosperity both continued to grow, the *philosophes* were drawn inevitably to compare this situation with that in France, where there was no such contract, nor an effective parliamentary system. Rousseau's remarks about the illegality of arbitrary rule (i.e. without any 'contract' between a monarch and his people) and the nature of the contract which should be *supposed* to exist between the one and the other are not therefore new. But their context — the condemnation of property and privilege, the statement that modern man is no better than a slave in the toils of society — gives them a new force. In the *Discours sur. . . l'inégalité* he sees 'the establishment of the body politic as a genuine contract between the people and the leaders whom it chooses for itself; a contract through which both parties bind themselves to obey the laws which it enumerates, and which form the basis of their union' (p. 239). Not only are the *people* the ones who choose their leaders; these leaders have a 'right to abdicate', and, should they behave despotically, they would have brought inequality to its highest degree, and their deposition or assassination would be an act of justice (pp. 245-6).

Here Rousseau recapitulates his view that modern society is utterly corrupt, and based on inequality — the last phrases of the *Discours* indicate 'that it is patently against the law of nature. . . that a handful of people should have a surfeit of luxuries, while the hungry multitude lacks the necessaries of life' (p. 247). When in 1762 Rousseau published *Du Contrat social*, his theory, so hostile to the *ancien régime* of Louis XV, and the concept of the 'volonté générale', the 'general will' which was to be implemented with such ferocity in the French Revolution during the period of the Terror, had been largely lifted out and away from the consideration of man in a state of nature, and had a direct application to the *status quo* in France which no one could ignore. When Rousseau begins the first chapter of *Du Contrat social* with the words 'Man is born free, and everywhere he is in chains,' the 'everywhere' applies particularly to France. When, in the same year, Rousseau's *Emile, ou de l'éducation* was published, it too began with similar phrases: 'Everything is good that comes from the Creator's hands, everything degenerates in the hands of man.' Again, the 'everything' applies to France. Though these two works are manifestly aimed at the France of Rousseau's own day, they aim not at reforming, but at destroying the society with which they are concerned.

Society is bad, nature is good — and the original inhabitants of the unspoiled natural world are good also. Their representative is the 'noble savage', a person already briefly referred to in discussion of Prévost's *Cléveland*. Rousseau more than any other writer concentrates interest on this figure, and again the *Discours sur... l'inégalité* is a crucial text, together with his *Emile, ou de l'éducation*.

I have already mentioned the speculations which the discovery of 'wild children' had aroused. Rousseau lists several of them in note (c) to the *Discours sur... l'inégalité* (p. 248). In the *Discours* he considers the original nature of the first man with profound approval, seeing in him an admirable creature whose happiness depends on the absolute absence from his life of that corruption which even the most basic forms of society entail — even agriculture.

The natural way of life, he says, is 'simple, uncomplicated and solitary' (p. 216), so simple that disease was unknown, so uncomplicated that considered thought, 'reflexion', was unnecessary and so solitary that even the union of male and female for propagation was a matter of sudden, satisfactory yet brief encounter. And man in a state of nature was *good*, with an innate inclination to kindness, pity and compassion which the subsequent artificiality of society tends to inhibit (p. 224), and with an equally natural *gentleness*, which prevents him absolutely from doing any harm to other human beings (p. 230). How great a change from the Hobbesian view that man, in his dealings with other men, is naturally a wolf — *homo homini lupus*! But the new attitude is characteristically Rousseauan, and exactly parallel to his liking for gentle natural scenes.

For Rousseau then, men in a state of nature lived 'free, healthy, good and happy' (*Discours*, p. 231), and he says firmly that 'this state is the true childhood of the world', from which every step forward in the progress of mankind has been a step towards degeneracy and servitude. The frontispiece to the *Discours sur... l'inégalité* carries a large part of Rousseau's message. It shows a superb young savage wearing only a sheepskin, with a sword attached, and with a necklace round his neck. At his feet is a bundle of clothes (a hat with a plume protrudes), while a group of Europeans, fully clothed and hatted, listen to one side as he addresses them. The text which illustrates the scene is in note (p) to the *Discours* (p. 261), where Rousseau quotes an anecdote from Prévost's *Histoire générale des voyages* concerning a Hottentot who had been brought up in European ways by the Dutch governor of the Cape. After some years away he was able to re-visit his Hottentot tribe. When he came back from this visit, he had taken off his clothes, and put on the sheepskin, carrying the European things in a bundle, which he set on the ground in front of his benefactor, the governor, with these words:

> I renounce this apparel for ever; and I also renounce the Christian faith for the whole of my life; it is my resolve to live and to die in the religion, the ways and customs of my ancestors. The sole favour which I ask of you is to leave me the necklace and the sword which I carry; I shall keep them out of love for you (*Discours*, p. 261).

The frontispiece bears the caption 'Il retourne chez ses égaux' — 'He returns to his equals.' It might equally have been addressed directly to the reader, with a 'Go thou and do thou likewise,' so wholly does Rousseau condemn the society we live in. Certainly, many romantics took Rousseau's message in this way, trying to shed their city-dwellers' ways and 'return to nature'. Rousseau himself adopted his distinctive but simple 'Armenian dress' in 1762, partly for personal convenience, and partly as a rejection of European artifice, while the more extreme step of 'living in a state of nature' is obviously a part of the fascination of Bernardin de Saint-Pierre's *Paul et Virginie* (1788), and of Chateaubriand's *Atala* (1801) and *René* (1802). By the end of the nineteenth century all sorts of experiments in 'going native' have been tried — Gauguin's escape to paint native scenes in Tahiti is the most famous. In 1906 the supreme descendant of Rousseau's noble savage appeared in print — *Tarzan of the Apes*, by Edgar Rice Burroughs. If Sherlock Holmes is descended from Voltaire and the rationalist *philosophes*, Tarzan (or Lord Greystoke) comes just as truly from Rousseau. He is, *exactly*, the noble savage, born of aristocratic parents, reared in the jungle by giant apes, good, and uncontaminated by society. When, in the subsequent volumes, he is tempted by the offers of society, we see him again and again as Rousseau's Hottentot, who returns to his equals, spurning European ways, and re-adopting the primitive life in which he was reared.

Rousseau himself does not say how the modern European can 'return to his equals'. But in his *Emile, ou de l'éducation* (1762) he develops a scheme of education for a child who is naturally good and innocent at birth, and to whom no harm can befall, provided he grows up uncontaminated by society. The child, Emile, is therefore enabled to live in sole contact with nature, and the main task of his tutor, whom we may imagine to be Rousseau in person, is to facilitate Emile's learning-from-nature by keeping society-and-corruption away from him. In this we see again Rousseau's liking for gentle nature, and his blind eye for the sublime. Emile does not drown, nor poison himself, no viper bites his leg, nor does a weasel snap at his tender extremities. Instead, he learns 'naturally', urged always by curiosity, and at times by a moderate amount of hunger, thirst and anxiety; and continues in this way, learning 'at his own pace', for many years. Rousseau's confidence in the rightness of his method is so strong that Emile does not read until he is fifteen − and then only La Fontaine's *Fables* and Defoe's *Robinson Crusoe* − and is not thought to be ready for contact with others until he is well into adolescence. To me, this shows Rousseau at his most perverse, a literary and pedagogic ostrich, denying the very existence of society which makes 'education' a necessity, and in which all modern people must live. But I am outnumbered by the pro-Rousseauans, who saw, and continue to see, his rejection of society as a glad alternative to the failures of traditional methods of education. From Rousseau come the Swiss Pestalozzi in the 1800s, and the 'play way' of Dalton, in America a century later, and then the freedom allowed by Bertrand Russell and his colleagues at Bedales in the 1930s; and at last, the long-continued, much-abused and heroic experiments of A. S. Neill, especially at Summerhill school, in the 1950s. And meanwhile, in fiction but not at all in the groves of Academe, is the noble Tarzan, whose jungle education matches Emile's country education more closely than Edgar Rice Burroughs or the Rousseauans might like to admit. True, Tarzan meets tougher foes in the jungle than does Emile in the woods, but he was born with (as it were) 150 years more experience of nature in the mind of his creator. When they are shown in the process of *learning*, Emile coping with elementary geography, or the lodestone, and Tarzan learning, on his own, to read from the books in his slaughtered parents' tree-house, they are brothers at the bosom of a loving and generous mother nature: were they to meet, we should surely hear the words 'Me Tarzan you Emile.'

Returning to the 1980s, we must alas! see Rousseau's idea of the noble savage as unreal. But in the 1760s, Rousseau and most educated Europeans knew precious little about the life of primitive peoples. Rousseau's ideas encouraged the hope that in some part of the world, such 'noble savages' might still exist. In the *Nouvelle Héloïse*, St Preux had visited Juan Fernandez and Tinian, and has seen Tinian as a place from which the 'peaceful Indians' had been expelled by 'avaricious Europeans' (book iv, letter 3). Once again uninhabited, Tinian had become a natural paradise, in which 'the fortunate animals' lived without fear, since they were 'for the greatest part of their year. . . the sole lords of this happy soil'. These last phrases are from Richard Walter's account of Anson's *Voyage round the World*, and the source of Rousseau's knowledge of these Pacific islands. Surely such places might still be discovered, lands in the great Pacific ocean, still largely unexplored? When, in the late 1760s, British and French mariners made their spectacular Pacific discoveries, it was not surprising that they should hope to find some noble savages among the inhabitants. Without Rousseau, and without Burke, these European expeditions would have seen the south Pacific with far less romantic eyes.

7

Ossian

Hot on the heels of Burke, contemporary with Young, came the 'Ossianic' poems produced by James Macpherson (1736-96). These poems were supposedly translated by Macpherson from geniune Gaelic originals, but were largely his own invention. They are the first really important imaginative works to spring from the recent theoretical writings on the primitive and the sublime.

Macpherson showed specimens of these poems to friends in 1759, and hinted that they could be followed by a longer work by 'Ossian', 'related to the wars of Fingal'. In 1760, his *Fragments of Ancient Poetry, Collected in the Highlands of Scotland, and Translated from the Galic or Erse Language*, was published anonymously, with an unsigned preface by his admirer Hugh Blair. *Fingal* was published in 1762, backed up by Blair's *Critical Dissertation on the Poems of Ossian* in 1763, and completed by *Temora* and other poems by Ossian in 1763.

Following the bards of Blackwell, Young and Gray, and probably influenced by P. H. Mallet's *Monumens de la mythologie et de la poésie des Celtes* (1756), Macpherson presented a 'real' bard, the old, blind poet Ossian. Macpherson always maintained that his publications were translated from Gaelic originals — the 'Preface' to *Fragments* asserts that 'The public may depend on the following fragments as genuine remains of ancient Scottish poetry.' The setting for these poems went back earlier than, say, the time of Elizabeth or the Normans, and ignored both the Saxons and King Arthur — *all* of these would have had, perforce, traces of Roman or Latin culture in them. Instead, Ossian's poems relate the adventures of the early Celtic inhabitants of Ireland and Scotland, in which the ways of these people are displayed without any moderating, weakening influence of a Christian, Mediterranean or urban kind. The characters know nothing of Christianity, they have no towns, they cannot read. Their poet, Ossian, appears therefore as a northern Homer, blind, illiterate, and educated not by 'art' but by 'nature'. In Blair's *Critical Dissertation* the comparison between Ossian and Homer is made many times — 'both poets are eminently sublime' — and the 'sublime' aspects of Homer are singled out as his greatest qualities (in 'actions and battles', for example), and his quieter, conversational or more mundane passages are treated with less approval — 'some of them trifling; and some of them plainly unseasonable'.

Above all, the setting of Ossian's poems is primitive. The opening of book II of *Fingal* shows this to perfection:

Connal lay by the sound of the mountain stream, beneath the aged tree. A stone, with its moss, supported his head. Shrill through the heath of Lena, he heard the voice of night. At distance from the heroes he lay; the son of the sword feared no foe!

The hero — given a strange, unfamiliar name — sleeps in the open, on the bare mountain-side. The tree beside him goes back into the past, it is 'aged', like the 'moss' which softens his primitive pillow. The noises of the wild natural world are directly part of his experience — he lies 'by the sound of the mountain stream', and hears the night wind 'shrill through the heath of Lena'. Yet — being a warrior, with a heroic appellation, 'son of the sword', he does not need to sleep close by his lesser, but still heroic, comrades.

Another passage underlines the resigned melancholy of Ossian's verse. This comes from the first of the 1760 *Fragments*. The warrior Shilric, foreseeing his death in battle, speaks sadly to his lover Vinvela:

If fall I must in the field, raise high my grave, Vinvela. Grey stones, and heaped-up earth, shall mark me to future times. When the hunter shall sit by the mound, and produce his food at noon, 'some warrior rests here', he will say; and my name shall live in his praise (J. J. Dunn (ed.), *Fragments of Ancient Poetry*, p. 11).

Battle is natural for the noble man, and death the acceptable result, with a primitive, anonymous grave as a memorial. Whether Ossian's warriors remember the identity of those who lived before them is indifferent — their way of life will be the same. 'Some warrior rests here,' says the hunter in years to come, admiring the fact that he was a *warrior*, and died in battle.

With its wild and un-Mediterranean characteristics, Ossian's poetry moves deliberately away from the nature-poetry written earlier in the century. However 'accurate' Thomson and Brockes tried to be, their writings were intentionally reflecting their modern cultures and attitudes. With Macpherson's 'translations' of Ossian, readers felt they were plunging into an only slightly diluted presentation of a profoundly different world. Ossian's poetry was admired precisely because it appeared to be 'irregular and unpolished'. Blair's comments, in 1763, suggest that he may have read Diderot's *De la poésie dramatique*, for his argument proceeds from the sublime to a consideration of the conditions which encourage or inhibit sublime poetry. In discussing the 'barbarity' of Ossian's poems, he says this is 'a very equivocal term' — on the one hand, barbarity 'excludes polished manners', but it is also 'not inconsistent with generous sentiments and tender affections' (which, as Diderot had pointed out, were less likely to flourish in a cultured society). This 'barbarity' was 'favourable to the sublime':

> Accuracy and correctness; artfully connected narration; exact method and proportion of parts, we may look for in polished times... But amidst the rude scenes of nature, amidst rocks and torrents, and whirlwinds and battles, dwells the sublime. It is the thunder and lightning of genius. It is the offspring of nature, not of art. (H. Blair, 'Critical Dissertation' in *The Poems of Ossian*, 1805, I, 229-30).

As Diderot wrote, 'la nature veut quelque chose d'énorme, de barbare et de sauvage'; and Blair would agree. But Diderot (like Thomas Blackwell before him) went on to point out that we, living and acting in the present, cannot really be part of a wild and barbarous society any more. Blair, in contrast, has no such qualms in discussing Ossian, since Ossian — for Blair — is genuine, and his poems come untainted from a remote, uncomplicated age: 'His imagery is, without exception, copied from the face of nature, which he saw before his eyes.' This direct, unimpeded vision is then detailed in a list which could serve as a model for the sublime subject-matter of the early romantics:

> The sun, the moon, and the stars, clouds and meteors, lightning and thunder, seas and whales, rivers, torrents, winds, ice, rain, snow, dews, mist, fire and smoke, trees and forests, heath and grass and flowers, rocks and mountains, music and songs, light and darkness, spirits and ghosts; these form the circle, within which Ossian's comparisons generally run (ibid.).

Naturally, we may see this 'circle' as related to Diderot's, where he catalogues the subjects for true poetry; it is proper to reflect, as well, how far away these subjects for poetry, especially Ossian's, have moved from 'the imitation of men in action' prescribed by Aristotle, or from Socrates' concern with 'the men who dwell in the city, and not the trees or the country'.

Among the 'irregular and unpolished' qualities Ossian's poetry was admired for was its spontaneity. Macpherson's 'translations' were thought to be all the more genuine since they were in 'measured prose', unlike Pope's translation of Homer, done into rhyming couplets, or Gray's ode 'The Bard', written in rhyming stanzas. Had Macpherson written in blank verse, like Thomson, in rhyme like Brockes, or even in Greek metres like Klopstock, this would have added a layer of artifice − of modernity − to the otherwise simple and primitive material of the poems. His 'measured prose' is in fact a form of free verse, where 'the cadence and the length of the line' are 'varied, so as to suit the sense', and Macpherson is the first to develop this technique extensively, modelling his style on the English of the Authorised Version. (Mallet's *Monumens. . . de la poésie des Celtes* of 1756 had also contained prose translations of old Danish poems, which may have encouraged Macpherson to use prose.) It is yet another departure from the formality of the late seventeenth century, which will be extended further by Blake, whose use of invented names is also reminiscent of the outlandish names (to English ears) of Ossian's heroes.

Ossian's spontaniety appears also in the actual form of the poems. Macpherson's first volume was entitled *Fragments of Ancient Poetry*, and the 'fragmentary' nature of these first fourteen poems is characteristic of all, even the longest, such as *Fingal* or *Temora*. The poems have the dimensions of the feeling which pervades them. No careful 'introductions' or 'expositions', no 'exhortations' or 'moral conclusions' open, direct, or complete these poems, there are no lines from poet to reader, no careful 'distancing' of the poet from his subject. Instead, the poems open instantly with the matter and the *emotion* of the moment; and when this is dealt with, they close. Although the long, epic poems have a 'story', even in these it is the presentation of the emotion − grief, pride, anger, yearning, despair − which controls the poems' form; and in the shorter poems, this often gives a feeling that we are reading the essence, the central and most *moving* part, of the matter. In poem ten of the *Fragments*, the opening lines set the scene of the poem:

It is night; and I am alone, forlorn on the hill of storms. The wind is heard in the mountain. The torrent shrieks down the rock. No hut receives me from the rain; forlorn on the hill of winds.

But in 'setting the scene', Ossian or Macpherson has also established the emotional atmosphere, and this is what matters in the poem. Such directness and freedom from elaborate introductory or concluding comment is unthinkable in the poetry of Thomson or Haller. While Thomson's shepherd, freezing to death in the snow, might have said a few words, short and to the point — and no more; and while Haller claimed that his mountain-lover sang love-songs of artless directness, Thomson and Haller themselves could not write without artifice. Later in the century, the technique of *in medias res*, with no flashbacks and no lengthy conclusion, was brought to a pitch of intensity by Goethe, both in the poems of his 'Sturm and Drang' period, and in the startling brevity of some scenes in the *Urfaust*. By the 1800s the cult of the 'fragment' will be so elaborated, by artists, poets and musicians alike, that a special value will be attached to works which are *interrupted, incomplete* or *preparatory*. The most famous of these 'fragments' is Coleridge's 'Kubla Khan'. But this is a long way on. In 1760, the apt comparison is with the *ruin,* whose present imperfect outlines still contain powerful and moving hints of what once was there.

The emotional content of Ossian's poetry — the *feelings* which control its form — was finely understood by Goethe, in a way which is intimately part of the structure of his novel *Die Leiden des jungen Werthers* (1774). Blair had contrasted Ossian with Homer, saying that Homer fell away from the sublime through his 'cheerfulness' and 'loquacity', in other words because he sometimes dealt with day-to-day matters in an unemotional, practical and even humorous way. Not sublime. In contrast, Ossian's is *'The Poetry of the Heart'* — it is all emotion. Coming to *Werther*, we find that the hero at first thinks much of Homer, and tries to be active and useful. However, Werther is not really a 'high-flyer', and his efforts do not succeed. The second half of his story tells of his growing despair and final suicide, and it is exactly appropriate that his *livre de chevet* should now be not Homer, but Ossian. Earlier on, in the first reference to Ossian in the novel, it is in terms of *emotion* that the book is mentioned. Werther is already deeply in love with Lotte, and reacts violently when conventional attitudes are expected of him. If asked 'how he likes her', he reacts at the inadequacy of 'like' to convey his fullness of feeling, and caps his indignant response with 'Recently someone asked me how I liked

Ossian' (I, 10 July). 'Liked' is part of polite vocabulary, unconnected with the waves of feeling which sweep this feeble, sensitive creature to his destruction.

Ossian's poems are also replete with ghosts. While earlier writers had tinkered with them — in the graveyard poetry of Young and Robert Blair, for example — and while Voltaire, seeing the ghosts in Shakespeare's plays, had awkwardly slipped a *spectre* into *Sémiramis* (1748), with disastrous box-office consequences — no one had dared to go against the generally sceptical attitude of the age until Macpherson produced the poems of Ossian. Here ghosts appear, or whisper, in almost every poem, sad wraiths with 'how weak a voice', 'like the breeze in the reeds of the pool'. The passage describing the warrior Connal lying awake on the windy mountainside (*Fingal*, book II), is followed immediately by the appearance of the ghost of Crugal:

> The hero beheld, in his rest, a dark red stream of fire rushing down from the hill. Crugal sat upon the beam, a chief who fell in fight. He fell by the hand of Swaran, striving in the battle of heroes. His face is like the beam of the setting moon. His robes are of the clouds of the hill. His eyes are two decaying flames. Dark is the wound of his breast! ... Dim, and in tears, he stood and stretched his pale hand over the hero. Faintly he raised his feeble voice, like the gale of the reedy Lego!

Such an apparition is not out of place in the nocturnal setting Ossian has described. We may believe in these ghosts, since they are part of a remote poetic world, completely different from our own. In Ossian's far-away world, described by a poet dead a thousand years before, the readers of the eighteenth century could see a convincing similarity between the ghost of Crugal and the ghost of Patroclus in book 23 of the *Iliad*; though Ossian, and though Homer, may have believed in ghosts, the readers did not need to worry whether such ghosts might trouble them in London, Paris or Strassburg. Within a year or two of the *Fragments* and *Fingal*, other writers were to experiment with supernatural themes, like Horace Walpole in *The Castle of Otranto* (1765), and the attempts have gone on, with no more than occasional success, until our own times. In the eighteenth century, the anti-supernatural propaganda of the *philosophes* was so strong that such inclinations were generally made less direct by disguising them in antique clothes. This, after all, is what Macpherson had done, but his followers were less thorough in the disguise they used. Generally, a 'medieval' or vaguely old-fashioned setting was claimed, as in Walpole's 'gothic' novel; but the connection with modern life was never severed so completely as it was in the poems of Ossian. In *The Castle of Otranto*, as in the novels of Mrs Radcliffe, in Schiller's *Der Geisterseher*, Cazotte's *Diable amoureux*, and even in the novels of Sir Walter Scott, we are, alas! aware from time to time of the author *pretending* that the story is merely an old manuscript re-written, and not a work written in 1765, or 1796, or 1814. Even Fuseli, the most ardent delineator of ghosts and visions (see p. 208), shows them as *illustrations* to the works of earlier writers, Shakespeare, Dante or Homer.

Western Europe in the eighteenth century was drastically restricted in its belief in the supernatural. While all sorts of beliefs had been possible — if often disapproved — in the seventeenth century, the Age of the Enlightenment had set itself so firmly against any manifestations of an 'other' world that when, in the 1720s and 1730s, an epidemic of vampire-fear erupted in eastern Europe, the reaction in the west was one of mockery and indifference (see my article 'The Year of the Vampire: an undying memory' in *Essays for Peter Mayer*, ed. C. Thacker, 1980). The events in Serbia of 1727 and 1731 were centred round the occurrence of numerous deaths in the village of Medweyga, and the discovery that the corpses had not decomposed after burial. To the villagers, influenced by Greek Orthodox attitudes, this showed that the dead had become vampires — that their souls were restless, remaining in the vicinity of their graves, and bringing about further deaths among their surviving relatives. When news of these matters reached western journals in 1732, they were received in virtual silence. In eastern Europe interest in vampire-fears continued on and off until the end of the century — a measure of the sustained strength of religious and superstitious beliefs in those parts of the world — but the subject was ignored in the west until 1747-8, when the young Lessing translated back into German (in the *Naturforscher*, nos. 47-8) a French account which had been printed in 1734. And then again silence. By the 1760s, the public in England, Germany and France was avid for instances of the sublime, and the aged Ossian's many ghosts, pale and fleeting, with whispering voices and vanishing forms, gave exactly the thrill which the supernatural aspects of the sublime should provide. Vampires, in contrast, were still far too frightening, and too difficult to fit into the new apparatus of sublime art, and it was not until much later that Fuseli could paint forms of vampire in his *Nightmare* compositions (*c.* 1785). Full use of vampires by romantic artists does not occur until 1816, when Polidori and Byron both begin their short vampire-romances, on the same occasion which prompted Mary Shelley's *Frankenstein*.

I have inserted this comment on vampires partly as a reminder that, while the romantic impulse grew and grew in the middle decades of the eighteenth century, the forces of the Enlightenment — rational, preoccupied with social, political, economic and material matters — were still at their strongest. The years of Macpherson's Ossianic publications are also those of the completion of Diderot's *Encyclopédie*, finished in 1772. Some years ago, working on Voltaire's *Candide*, I needed to consult a letter which Voltaire had addressed, publicly, to Stanislas, the ex-king of Poland, in the *Journal encyclopédique* of 15 October 1760, pp. 105-9. It was intriguing to find that it was printed immediately before a long piece entitled 'Fragmens d'anciennes poësies, recueillies dans les montagnes de l'Ecosse' — i.e. extracts from Macpherson's *Fragments of Ancient Poetry* — one of the very earliest translations of Ossian into French. The contrast between the two items is astonishing — the one urbane, precise, sarcastic, and the other vague, primitive and dreamlike, so much so that it might exist without any need for Voltaire, the Enlightenment, and the concern of 'men who dwell in the city' at all.

8

'That Long Labyrinth of Darkness'

The melancholy appeal of the Ossianic ghosts was immense, and spread over from their remote and primitive setting into more familiar regions. In the eighteenth century, the possibility of all supernatural phenomena had been challenged and indeed derided by rationalist philosophers, while the concept of the benevolent Creator of a perfect universe intended for man's benefit did not leave much excuse for ghosts either. But, as Burke had indicated, mystery, obscurity, uncertainty were a part of the sublime feelings which *darkness* encouraged; and at night, these feelings included the fear of 'ghosts and goblins'. From the 1760s onwards, 'ghosts and goblins' appear often and alarmingly in the art and literature of western Europe. While they may be 'excused' by the ghosts in Ossian, and also by the ghosts in Shakespeare's plays, they may be explained as well as part of a recurrent human conviction that there may be more to existence than a totally material explanation allows. In the second half of the eighteenth century the hankering after the supernatural grows steadily, and is at last, after the anti-clerical excesses of the French Revolution, channelled into the emotional and mystical enthusiasms of revived and romantic forms of Christianity.

In Horace Walpole's 'gothic story' *The Castle of Otranto* (published at the end of 1764, but dated 1765, and under the pseudonym 'Onufrio Muralto'), the author is some three parts serious, and one part tongue-in-cheek. Since 1747 he had been gradually converting his buildings at Strawberry Hill into a gothic paradise. In his letters, he is sometimes flippant about what he is doing; yet his endeavours continued until his death in 1797, until Strawberry Hill was a complete and composite, occasionally incongruous assemblage of all that eighteenth-century taste considered to be 'gothic' — battlements and pointed windows, towers and cloister, fan-tracery and panelling; armour and heraldic bearings, stained glass, furniture and tapestry, with a collection

111

of 'curiosities', 'objets de vertu' and other works of art so numerous that Walpole himself had a *Description of the Villa of Mr. Horace Walpole* printed in 1784 (see Plate 18). By 1764, Walpole had lived in this evolving gothic creation for seventeen years. It was a part of him — waking and sleeping. On 9 March 1765 he wrote to the Reverend William Cole, describing the manner of the novel's composition, and its inspiration — a dream, set in the gloomy chambers of a fantasy-castle based on Strawberry Hill. He wrote:

> When you read of the picture quitting its panel, did you not recollect the portrait of Lord Falkland, all in white, in my Gallery? Shall I even confess to you, what was the origin of this romance! I waked one morning, in the beginning of last June, from a dream, of which, all I could recover was, that I had thought myself in an ancient castle (a very natural dream for a head like mine filled with Gothic story), and that on the uppermost banister of a great staircase I saw a gigantic hand in armour. In the evening I sat down and began to write, without knowing in the least what I intended to say or relate.

This letter is both true and a simplification, like the more famous explanation Coleridge wrote of how he came to dream the poem which he named 'Kubla Khan'. The gothic intricacies of Strawberry Hill; memories of Shakespeare's ghosts, and the unghostly chatterings of Juliet's nurse; the growing taste for wild and melancholy ruins, both in gardens and in the literature of the time, and a shrewd assimilation of the qualities listed by Burke as essential in the creation of the sublime, these and other impulses come together in this 'gothic story' with thrilling success. Walpole has no hesitation in using supernatural events as the focal points of his novel, and this is precisely because they are mysterious and incomprehensible. In the second and third paragraphs an event is described which might be an illustration to Burke's treatise. The wedding of Prince Manfred's son, Conrad, is due to take place, but Conrad himself does not arrive. A servant sent to fetch him 'came running back breathless, in a frantic manner, his eyes staring, and foaming at the mouth. He said nothing, but pointed to the court. The company were struck with terror and amazement. The princess Hippolyta, without knowing what was the matter, but anxious for her son, swooned away.' At last the servant cries out 'Oh! the helmet! the helmet!' and Manfred himself goes out into the courtyard to learn what has happened:

The first thing, that struck Manfred's eyes, was a group of his servants, endeavouring to raise something, that appeared to him a mountain of sable plumes. He gazed, without believing his sight. 'What are ye doing?' cried Manfred, wrathfully; 'where is my son?' A volley of voices replied, 'Oh! my lord! the prince! the prince! the helmet! the helmet!' Shocked with these lamentable sounds, and dreading he knew not what, he advanced hastily; but, what a sight for a father's eyes! He beheld his child dashed to pieces, and almost buried under an enormous helmet, a hundred times more large than any casque ever made for human being, and shaded with a proportionate quantity of black feathers (Horace Walpole, *The Castle of Otranto*, ed. W.S. Lewis, 1964, pp. 16-17).

'Indeed terror is... the ruling principle of the sublime,' wrote Burke, having said shortly before that 'astonishment' is 'the passion caused by the great and sublime in nature', adding the comment that 'astonishment is that state of the soul, in which all its motions are suspended, with some degree of horror' (*Enquiry*, II, i, ii). The servant who discovers the monstrous − and inexplicable − helmet is speechless with horror, and the company present are instantly affected by his terror *because they do not know* what has caused it. When Manfred goes out to see what has happened, the *size* of the fatal helmet is beyond his comprehension, while those trying to lift the helmet can only utter single, incoherent words, 'the prince! the prince! the helmet! the helmet!'

We might adapt Burke's words, and say that 'all the motions of the prince's soul were suspended, with some degree of horror' − and indeed Walpole's next lines convey the full effect of the sublime:

The horror of the spectacle, the ignorance of all around how this misfortune had happened, and, above all, the tremendous phenomenon before him, took away the prince's speech (*Otranto*, p. 17).

It says much for Walpole's inventiveness that he is able to continue with any success beyond this memorable moment. Yet he does. The fatal helmet, with its sable plumes, comes into the story several times to give mysterious reminders of doom, and is matched with a gigantic sword, which takes 'an hundred gentlemen' to carry it, a giant hand in armour, and at the last 'the form of Alfonso [the owner of the mysterious helmet], dilated to an immense magnitude', rising above the walls of the castle which have been shattered by his appearance. And there is 'the picture quitting its panel', of which Walpole wrote to Cole. It is a portrait which hangs over a bench where Manfred has just been making foul suggestions to the young and innocent Isabella. The portrait 'uttered a deep sigh, and heaved its breast', and was then seen to 'quit its panel, and descend on the floor, with a grave and melancholy air' (*Otranto*, pp. 23-4).

I mention the moving portrait last, because it appears at the point where Walpole brings in another aspect of the sublime, hugely productive of terror, and allied with the fear of the supernatural. This is *darkness*, inseparable from the idea of the gothic novel, since so many thrilling moments in these books take place at night, or within the ill-lit confines of subterranean caverns, passages, stairways or dungeons. As Burke said, 'how greatly night adds to our dread', and again 'all artifices calculated to produce an idea of the sublime ought rather to be dark and gloomy'. Walpole uses 'night' and 'darkness' lavishly. As Manfred declares his near-incestuous intentions to Isabella, the moonlight 'presented to his sight the plumes of the fatal helmet, which rose to the height of the windows, waving backwards and forwards in a tempestuous manner, and accompanied with a hollow and rustling sound'. The portrait leaves its panel, and Manfred follows the 'spectre' of the portrait. This gives Isabella her chance, and, running away, 'she recollected a subterraneous passage' — the first of hundreds in subsequent gothic novels, down which tender, trembling virgins will flee, helped by a flickering candle, and pursued by evil, murderous or — oh horror — lascivious men. Walpole's is a sublime beginning, and, even though his novel is the first of the *genre* (Walpole himself gave it the subtitle, 'A gothic story'), this passage contains most of the elements which later writers will use to distraction:

> The lower part of the castle was hollowed into several intricate cloisters; and it was not easy for one, under so much anxiety, to find the door that opened into the cavern. An awful silence reigned throughout the subterraneous regions, except, now and then, some blasts of wind that shook the doors she had passed, and which, grating on the rusty hinges, were re-echoed through that long labyrinth of darkness. Every murmur struck her with new terror (*Otranto*, p. 25).

There is much more, all related to the fear which the situation inspires in both the victim, and the sensitive reader. The gothic novels which follow will, for the most part, swell only occasionally to such fullness of terror, violence and mystery, their purple passages being spaced by long interludes derived from the sentimental novels of, say, Prévost or Richardson. But writers knew that Walpole's novel was a success, and tried, fumblingly, to turn his triumph to their advantage. In France, the gothic element reinforced the attraction of 'English' themes. For a work of fiction to have as its subtitle 'histoire anglaise' – 'an English tale' – was to imply a degree of acceptable *exotisme* whose elements might include a character of a moody and even suicidal inclination, or with a dark secret, or a cruel elder brother; and whose setting might be rural, remote, mountainous – and, with the advent of the gothic, ancient crumbling and mysterious. Yet this was all promise, unmatched by performance. Typical is the novel *Varbeck* (1774) by Baculard d'Arnaud. The title and an early footnote promise a tale of rebellion, the story of Perkin Warbeck, set in the dark past of English history. But the content is English only in the names of people and places, and not at all antique. The few attempts at the gothic are feeble, and the most extensive, to do with a cave, has to be justified with a footnote:

> Let us go forward – I think I have found one of the underground caves which were made at the time of the civil wars.*

> *Many of these artificial caverns are to be found in England, some made even before the time of William the Conqueror (*Varbeck*, p. 290).

In England however such timidity was uncommon. Walpole's followers might be inept, but their attempts to recapture the *frisson* of *Otranto* are unremitting. Observe the young hero of *The Hermitage; a British Story* (anonymous, 1772):

> As he walked pensive to and fro, on a sudden, behind him, at the further end of the gallery, he heard a clash of armour: Turning hastily, he observed the buckler and shield to shake which once his great ancestor Norban wore... Again, he looked up, and perceived the coat of mail to tremble on the crooks where it hung, and the gauntlet moved as if it beckoned him. [The hero finds a 'small onyx cross, which hung concealed by the armour', and puts it on.] Soon as the amulet had touched his bosom, from every point of the cross, there fell warm drops of blood; and, with a horrid clangour, the armour shook in every joint! Surprise now

changed to fear (*The Hermitage*, pp. 13-16).

By 1774, the ingredients of the gothic tale were seen to be both enjoyable, and distinct from, say, tales of city life or intrigue at court, and a 'codifying' was attempted rather like Burke's analysis of the sublime in 1756. It appears in the *Miscellaneous Pieces in Prose* by John Aikin and his sister Anna Laetitia Aikin (who became better known as the novelist Mrs Barbauld), especially in two essays — 'On the Pleasure derived from Objects of Terror; with Sir Bertrand, a Fragment', and 'An Enquiry into those kinds of distress which excite agreeable sensations'. Their titles are replete with the sublime, and their content shows how far — to the authors' minds at least — the gothic enthusiasm had progressed. In the second essay, the authors remark that so much in the way of horror has been exploited — done to death, we might say — that 'books of entertainment', their authors and their public are eager to discover 'a new torture, or non-descript calamity'. Justifying this taste with the words 'suspense', 'surprise' and 'imagination', they say in the first essay a most perceptive thing — *the more the better*: 'Hence, the more wild, fanciful, and extraordinary are the circumstances of a scene of horror, the more pleasure we receive from it.'

The first essay concludes 'with Sir Bertrand, a Fragment' (pp. 61-5). Already in discussing Ossian I have remarked on spontaneity as an element of 'genius' and 'original' poetry. The 'fragment' is not only spontaneous; it is, in a gothic context, *mysterious*. In the original version of 1774, the piece opens with '— After this adventure, Sir Bertrand turned his steed towards the woulds, hoping to cross those dreary moors before the curfew tolled' — i.e. the hero had only just finished with one set of excitements, which must remain unknown. Five thrilling pages later, the fragment stops with 'After the banquet was finished, all retired but the lady, who, leading back the knight to the sofa, addressed him in these words: —' and 'these words' remain as unknown to the reader as the 'adventure' which Sir Bertrand has just concluded at the beginning of the 'fragment'. Above all, 'Sir Bertrand' is more atmospheric than the *Castle of Otranto*. While the events are similar, they are described with a feeling for suspense which surpasses Walpole's brisker shudders. The fragment is richer in adjectives of *mood* — 'the sullen toll of a distant bell', 'a dim twinkling light', 'by a momentary glimpse of moonlight' — and this is augmented by deliberate delay:

All was still as death. He looked in at the lower windows, but could not distinguish a single object through the impenetrable gloom. After a short parley with himself, he entered the porch; and, seizing a massy iron knocker at the gate lifted it up, and, hesitating, at length struck a loud stroke. The noise resounded through the whole mansion with hollow echoes. All was still again. He repeated the strokes more boldly, and louder. Another interval of silence ensued. A third time, he knocked; and a third time all was still ('Sir Bertrand', p. 62).

Although the gothic novel has still room to develop, the essentials are present in *The Castle of Otranto* and in 'Sir Bertrand'. The passage I have just quoted would serve to paraphrase many an anticipatory scene in Hammer films of the 1960s — two centuries after the gothic novel began.

In 1768 Horace Walpole published a play, *The Mysterious Mother*, which is every bit as violent as the *Castle of Otranto*. So far as I know, this tragedy has not been performed on the stage, and Walpole wrote in his 'postscript' that 'the subject is so horrid, that I thought it would shock, rather than give satisfaction to an audience'. In 1768, it might indeed. Modelled on Racine's *Phèdre* more than any other source, it treats not of the dread possibility of incest, but of its repeated occurrence. The heroine, the Countess, has a young daughter, Adeliza, who is of marriageable age. The Countess, who is guiltily melancholic and obsessively given to religious meditation, also has a son, Edmund, whom she has banished, but who has returned secretly, hoping to gain his mother's pardon. A wicked priest, Benedict, is anxious to harm the Countess when she will not make a full confession to him of what past misdeed leaves her so guilty; he guesses eventually that the Countess may, long ago, have slept with her son, and that Adeliza is the daughter of this incestuous union; and so, for revenge, Benedict plots to join Edmund and Adeliza in marriage. He succeeds, and when the full truth is revealed, the Countess stabs herself, Adeliza resolves to take the veil, and Edmund leaves to seek death in the wars.

The Mysterious Mother is in would-be Shakespearian blank verse. Walpole's talents as a writer are more for narrative prose than for conversation, and not for verse of an extended kind at all. We are left with a feeling that Walpole has deliberately sought out the most 'horrid' story he can imagine; and that then, pen in hand, he has been subtly and cruelly restrained by misconceptions of how such a play should be written — so that the monstrous theme is tamed into failure. He

117

observes the 'three unities' with care — this is Walpole, the punctilious city-dweller, the courteous correspondent of Mme du Deffand; and yet he writes *à la Shakespeare* — this is Walpole, creator of Strawberry Hill, hankering after the language, as well as the architecture of the past. The theatre in Britain had a strange and uneasy renaissance in the eighteenth century, and *The Mysterious Mother* is a minor part of it. While urbane — indeed classical — comedy reached a peak with the work of Sheridan, and reached fair eminence in plays by Garrick and Colman, or by O'Keefe, tragedy was both spurred on and bedevilled by the spectre of Shakespeare. Given new and spectacular life on the stage by the actor-playwright David Garrick (1717-71), Shakespeare's plays served as an inspiration not only in Britain, but also in France and in Germany. But in Britain, while the plays could be triumphantly revived, their language was no longer that of Georgian society, and when Georgian writers like Walpole tried to imitate, rather than write with equal freedom, discipline and genius, they created an unhappy nonsense. Looking back, Byron saw and understood Walpole's dilemma. In 1821, he called *The Mysterious Mother* 'the last tragedy in our language' ('Preface' to *Marino Faliero*).

In France, the situation was far worse. Though Shakespeare had been admired by Voltaire in the 1730s, and translated by P.-A. de Laplace in 1745-8, and again by Le Tourneur in 1776-83, the hold of the seventeenth-century classical theatre was so firm that no tragedies could be presented unless they were of a Cornelian or Racinian kind. Voltaire's vain struggles to emulate his predecessors, and to incorporate the occasional Shakespearian ghost, are well enough known already — though it is still instructive here to say that his play *Sémiramis* (1748), written in dull but easy Alexandrines, and with its echoes of Racine's *Phèdre*, and with its ghost borrowed from *Hamlet*, is a failure for the very reasons which make *The Mysterious Mother* a failure too. In neither play could the author make something *of his own* from the splendid yet dangerously powerful materials of the past.

In Germany, the situation was different. Here was no vigorous national theatre from the previous century towering up to say 'Imitate me.' Instead, the writings of Diderot and the example of Shakespeare were received in Germany in the 1760s with enthusiasm. While Lessing, who had been one of the translators of Diderot into German, adapted the didactic aims of the *genre sérieux* for his own plays, culminating in his masterpiece *Minna von Barnhelm* (1767), other writers, such as Hamann, Lenz and Herder, seized on Diderot's praise of the genius, and urged German writers to respond to the challenge, since Diderot

himself in his plays had failed to do so. And — though Diderot said
little about him — there was Shakespeare as a supreme model. And
then (a breathless style is appropriate, for it was a breathless age)
there was Ossian; and again, there was Dante, whose *Divine Comedy*
had recently come into view, after long neglect, through the 're—
discovery' of his poetry by Bodmer in the 1740s, a 're-discovery'
which was also made in England in the mid-1750s. For the Germans
of this period, Dante as much as Shakespeare was *sublime*. In Shakespeare, they found, as did the British, violence and ghosts, and an
apparent indifference to the conventions of the classical theatre,
and in Dante, they found an itinerary through Hell, made lurid by
the stories of one monstrous criminal after another, and contrasted
by the piteous fate of the innocents who had suffered at the hands
of these evil-doers.

From Dante comes the theme of the first sublime play in German,
H. W. von Gerstenberg's tragedy *Ugolino* (1768). It is clearly governed
by the same wish to inspire fear which dominates Walpole's *Mysterious
Mother*, published in the same year, and the *Castle of Otranto* of 1764.
Even more than the 'gothic' *Otranto*, with its 'long labyrinth of darkness', it is a tragedy of night and imprisonment, and like *Otranto* may
well have been written with the scenes of Piranesi's *Carceri* as a
visual inspiration. Piranesi had produced his first collection of prison
fantasies in the late 1740s, and then in the early 1760s re-issued them,
under the title *Carceri d'Invenzione*. In this new edition, he added two
extra scenes, while reproducing the original fourteen plates in an
altered form. His alterations are to the mood. Already, they were
gloomy, but now, darker, heavier and more oppressive, they have
become scenes of intolerable yet inescapable repression (see Plate 19).
It is as if Piranesi had read Burke — which, indeed, he might have
done, prompted by his English patrons at the time — and had seen,
in Burke's analysis, how his own vision of the power of Roman architecture could be strengthened. His style becomes more formidable
at this time, and there is here a web of connections, leading from
Burke, which helps to explain the dark imaginings of Piranesi, of
Walpole and of Gerstenberg. In his *Anecdotes of Painting* of 1771, Walpole urges modern artists to 'study the sublime dreams of Piranesi'
(iv, p. 398). By then, Walpole could have seen many of Piranesi's
most accomplished plates of Roman architecture; but it is the *Carceri*
which are the true background of the *Castle of Otranto*, and of *Ugolino*.

Ugolino is the first, and easily the greatest, of prison-plays. From the *Inferno*, canto xxxiii, Gerstenberg takes the story of Ugolino Gherardesca in the 'tower of famine'. The story is simple: captured by an enemy, Ugolino and his sons are imprisoned and left to die. When Gerstenberg re-tells this story in 1768, he gives it a setting which is sublime, and equally simple:

> The story of this drama is known from Dante.
> The characters are Ugolino, count of Gherardesca, and his three sons.
> The time – a stormy night.
> The scene – a poorly lighted room in the tower.

With such a setting, we are predisposed to pity the victims, and our feelings are increased, as we learn that Ugolino is imprisoned, not for his crimes, but for his virtue, while the youngest son, Gaddo, is ill.

Francesco, the oldest son, discovers a hole in the roof, and the possibility of escape. Francesco leaps, and then, at the beginning of the third act, two coffins are brought into the prison chamber. One holds Francesco – alive – and the other his mother, Ugolino's wife. She is dead, and Francesco relates the harrowing story of her death, his shameful treatment by Ruggieri, and his return in the coffin.

In a soliloquy – act iv – Ugolino broods over his fortunes. Beside his wife's coffin he sees himself once great, now reduced to misery. Lifting the coffin-lid he exclaims:

> Here, I was king! Here I was a friend, and a father! Here, I was adored! And I hungered for more. I wanted to see slaves tread in the dust of my footsteps. . .

Like so many of Shakespeare's fallen kings he is brought to impotence and solitude: 'O lonely earth! I grieve.'

The characters, dying of hunger, grow weaker and yet more frantic. Little Gaddo is delirious, and his innocence, given a Rousseauan totality, is poignant. We have already been told that he is too young to know what hate is. Now he cries out, 'O, everyone loves me, and I love everyone. But still no one wants to help me.'

The frenzy grows. Francesco dies – from poison given him by Ruggieri during his brief while in freedom – and Anselmo, the second son, torn with hunger, thinks not to devour his brother since there is poison in his flesh, but turns to gnaw his mother's corpse. Just in time, Ugolino prevents him, and raves with despair. Gaddo dies – virtually as did Falstaff, 'a' babbled of green fields' – and Anselmo, consumed with remorse, offers his own body to Ugolino. Ugolino hits him – dreaming, in his frantic state, that Anselmo has turned into the archfiend Ruggieri. Weakened, Anselmo dies, forgiving his father, who is at last left alone to die in a noble elevation of spirit, transfigured by grief and suffering.

While all this is deeply indebted to Shakespeare – the imprisoned Clarence, or Richard II deprived of power, or Lear near to madness in his misfortune – Gerstenberg retains the firmest hold on the construction of the play, which could serve as an example of adherence to the 'three unities' of time, place and action. Gerstenberg had already written with much approval of Shakespeare in his *Briefe über Merkwürdigkeiten der Litteratur* (1766-70), together with praise of Spenser, Ossian and old Norse poetry, and in 1766, two years before *Ugolino*, his *Gedicht eines Skalden* had given German readers a lengthy poem of a 'nordic' kind, modelled both on Ossian and on Mallet's Scandinavian translations of 1756. Gerstenberg's title page has a vignette of a primitive burial monument – a vast flat stone surmounting three rough pillars, erected on a mound.

Other early literature was re-read with fresh, romantic insight, or rediscovered, or, simply, invented. Usually under the influence of Burke and Young, the seekers, editors and inventors believed that they might find qualities of originality, genius and the sublime in the literature of the past. As the century progressed, the search became more discriminating, and the sense of historical – and geographical – division between periods, countries and cultures grew finer. But in the 1760s, the essentially romantic criterion of difference from the everyday overrode other doubts there may have been. Milton and Spenser had already been admired by Addison in the *Spectator*, and in 1732 J. J. Bodmer had translated Milton into German. From the middle of the century Milton's Lucifer, a rebellious angel, still mighty and still beautiful in his ruin, stands beside Shakespeare's Iago, Lady Macbeth and Edmund as a tempestuous, fear-inspiring – and therefore sublime – figure of evil. Mallet's publication of Scandinavian poetry in French in 1756 was translated into English by Bishop Percy in 1770, while in 1748 Bodmer published the 'Minnelieder' found in the Manesse codex, and a version of the *Nibelungenlied* in 1757.

In England, Bishop Thomas Percy produced his *Reliques of Ancient British Poetry* in 1765, containing an immense quantity of verse from the fifteenth, sixteenth and early seventeenth centuries. Above all, this collection stimulated interest in poetry of a direct and simple kind (or at least thought to be so, in contrast to the artificial and periphrastic verse of Augustan England), especially in the *ballad*, which romantics were to adopt as one of their most characteristic forms of expression at the end of the century. A few old ballads had already been published – in 1711, Addison had praised the beauties of 'Chevy Chase' in the *Spectator*, nos. 70, 74 – but Percy's *Reliques* gave the decisive impulse towards the writing of 'folk poetry' and narrative verse in 'ballad' form.

The great 'imitation' – or forgery, if you prefer – of literature of an ancient kind was the body of Ossianic poetry published by Macpherson from 1760 onwards; but there were other examples, large and small, flippant and serious. In 1764, Walpole had published *The Castle of Otranto* under an Italian pseudonym, claiming that the work had been translated from a medieval Italian text – though he soon admitted he was the author. But other inventors – or forgers – were not so ready to admit their originality. Fuseli, who 'invented' the Dantesque legend of Ezzelin and Meduna in the 1770s, did not admit the fact until 1814 (see p. 207 below), when another painting on the theme prompted Byron to ask him where the story came from. Macpherson never admitted that he wrote the poems of Ossian. And the same applied to Chatterton's 'Rowley' poems.

Thomas Chatterton (1752-70) wrote an immense amount of verse in his brief career (see Chatterton, *Complete Works*, ed. Donald S. Taylor, 1971). Some, conventional in style, is acknowledged, but a large proportion of his writings is in deliberate and carefully studied forms of antique English (approximately Chaucerian in construction and vocabulary), and these poems he claimed were written by genuine poets from the middle ages, whose work he had copied from old manuscripts. He attributed most to a poet-priest of his own invention, Sir Thomas Rowley.

Though he did not follow the direction for long, one early inspiration for his forgeries was undoubtedly Ossian. Whether he suspected Macpherson or not is uncertain; it is sure, however, that the instant popularity of a northern 'bard' urged him to emulate the *Fragments* and *Fingal*, and among his poems not in conventional language are seven 'Ossianic' poems, of which the longest, 'Godred Crovan', describes the events surrounding a two-day battle on the Isle of Man soon after 1066.

In their way, the 'Rowley' poems are as remarkable as Macpherson's Ossian. The success of Percy's *Reliques* in 1765 may have led Chat-

1. (right) *Pons Diaboli*, the 'Devil's Bridge', from Scheuchzer's *Beschreibung . . . des Schweizerlands* (1708).

2. (below) Turner's view of the *Pons Diaboli* (1804), sketched from virtually the same spot as Plate 1.

3. (left) God's handiwork in the Creation: the Fifth Day, from Scheuchzer's *Physica sacra* (1731).

4. (below) The Blocksberg, engraved by Bestehorn (1732) — a mountain, a place of fear and a haunt of witches.

5. (right) An ideal and arcadian landscape, the *Falls of Tivoli*, by Gaspard Poussin, painted *c*. 1670.

6. (below right) William Williams' *Thunderstorm with the Death of Amelia* (1784) illustrating the death by lightning of an innocent maiden, in Thomson's *Summer*

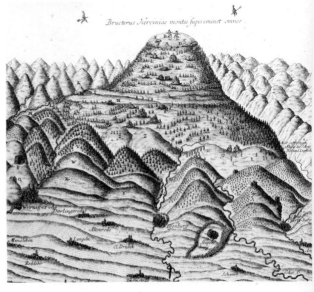

Stonehengs.   TAB. XIV

Surprennante Structure
des Rochers en Angleterre
dite
Stonehengs.
Chorea Gigantum
ou la danse des geants.

Cest près de Sarisbury dans une plaine
un arrangement de pierres d'une
hauteur prodigieuse, qui sont elevées
l'une contre l'autre et portent en haut
d'autres grosses pierres posées à la
traverse pour joindre celles d'en
bas et pour en former une espece
de porte. Cette structure est moins
surprennante par la grandeur des
pieces, que par l'entreprise de les
ranger. L'on voit d'abord, que ce
sont des monumens d'un age, qui
ne nous laisse le plus de memoire de
leur verité. Mais ceux, qui les
prennent pour d'autres monumens
que de sepulture, se raisonnent aisement
peu à peu qu'ils soyent reflexion sur la
plus ancienne facon des tombeaux
de la enterrer de pierres levée. L'on en
voit des essaim dans les estampes de
Sveca illustrata et dans les monumens
Danois de Wormius. Un autre oncle de
Rochers près d'Ochel et de Pellerich leur
confirme cette verité. Voyez, Guelon Antiquita

Wunderfame
Felsen=Höhle.

Unweit Salzburg bey dem Erz-Bischöfl:
Lusthause Hellbrunn, an welchem die
Natur selber den Bau geführet, mit
einem solchen Ansehen, den die Kunst
ihm nicht zuwege zu bringen vermocht
hätte. Indeme zwey unterschiedene
freystehende Felsen bogen dazu die
Öffnung machen. Die Vertiefung
bedarf gleichfals keiner andern als
seiner natürlichen Auszierung zur Vor-
stellung der Schauspiele welche öfters
daselbst mit sonderbarer Wirckung
des Wiederhalls vorgestellet werden.

7. (left) 'The grand ethereal bow' — William Kent's engraving of 'Spring' for the 1730 edition of Thomson's *Seasons*.

8. (below left) Primitive monuments juxtaposed — Stonehenge and the Rock Theatre at Hellbrunn — in Fischer von Erlach's *Entwurf einer historischen Architektur* (1721).

9. (above) Pacific monuments seen through European eyes — from Anson's *Voyage round the World* (1748). Compare this with Hodges' *Monuments of Easter Island* (Plate 34).

10. (below) Roman ruins, submerged in the debris of time. The temple of Jupiter tonans, by Piranesi (1748).

11. (above) Fischer von Erlach's version (1721) of the Chinese 'Cliffs made my Art', derived from Nieuhof's *Gezantschap . . . aan den grooten Tartarischen Cham* of 1665.

12. (below) J.G. Köppel's view of the 'Grotto of Æolus' at Sanspareil, inspired by the 'Cliffs made by Art' (Plate 11).

13. (right) Baroque agitation — Matthias Braun's statues of the vices and the virtues at Kukus.

14. (below right) The hospital at Kukus, from Stillenau's *Leben des . . . Grafen von Sporck*, 1720. Braun's statues line the balustrade in front of the hospital.

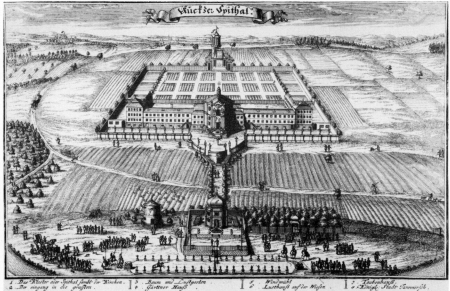

15. (left) Braun's sculpture of St Garino (1731-3), carved in the woods at 'Bethlehem', near Kukus.

16. (below) *Nebuchadnezzar*, by William Blake (1795).

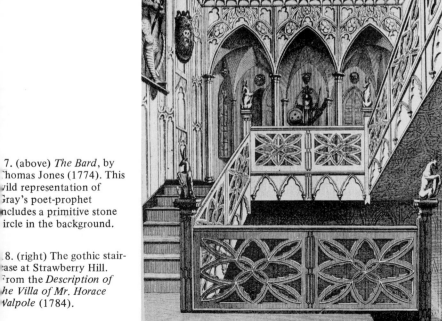

7. (above) *The Bard*, by
Thomas Jones (1774). This
wild representation of
Gray's poet-prophet
includes a primitive stone
circle in the background.

8. (right) The gothic staircase at Strawberry Hill.
From the *Description of
the Villa of Mr. Horace
Walpole* (1784).

19. (left) From Piranesi's *Carceri d'Invenzione* (*c.*1760), a much more forbidding version than in Piranesi's *Carceri* of the 1740s.

20. (below) Proposal for a hermitage (*c.* 1770). 'It might be built with old wood . . . It might be don in a fortennight.'

21. (right) Engraving of a *Tempest* by Vernet. The original was bought by Diderot in 1768.

22. (below right) *The Earth-stopper* (1773), by Joseph Wright of Derby – nocturnal, English and sublime.

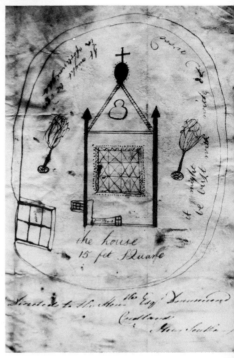

23. (left) Joseph Wright of Derby, *Landscape with Rainbow* (*c*. 1794-5). The storm is imminent, and man of little consequence.

24. (below left) Peter Scheemakers, *Horse Attacked by a Lion* (1743), based on a classical model.

25. (above) *Horse Attacked by a Lion*, by George Stubbs (*c*. 1765). The same subject as Scheemakers' sculpture (Plate 24), now vibrant with fear.

26. (right) Nature, observed indirectly, 'A man sketching, using a Claude glass', by Gainsborough, *c*. 1750-5.

27. (above) A view of Matlock, by William Gilpin – a composition rounded and softened by the use of a Claude-glass.

28. (left) 'This sublime view' – the eruption of Vesuvius on 8 August 1779, painted by Pietro Fabris.

29. (above right) The crater of a dormant volcano, painted by Fabris, in Sir William Hamilton's *Campi Phlegræi* (1776).

30. (right) *Vesuvius*, by Joseph Wright of Derby. He saw the volcano erupting in October 1774.

31. (left) Fierce, exotic, and un-European —
'Man of New Zealand', by Sydney Parkinson.

32. (below) 'And ice, mast-high, came floating
by' — 'The Ice Islands', 'drawn from nature' by
William Hodges (1773).

33. 'Resolution Bay in the Marquesas', by
William Hodges. He was one of the first to
appreciate the un-European qualities of such
scenes.

terton to think that there was room for another 'new' poet from the past, an English Ossian as it were; although the language in which he wrote, much more obscure than that of the poems in Percy's collection, unfortunately put his work beyond the reach of many readers eager to devour the poetic, but modern, language of Macpherson's 'translations'. Chatterton attempted all kinds of verse-form, from epigrams to the epic narrative of *The Battle of Hastings*. He also wrote a short verse play, *AElla*, which describes the conflict between Saxons and Danes in early tenth-century England, and the ill-fated love of AElla and Birtha. *AElla* was probably written in 1769, within months of Walpole's *Mysterious Mother* and Gerstenberg's *Ugolino*. Like Walpole's play, I doubt if it has ever been acted – its language prevents it, unless someone were to translate it first. But like Walpole, and like Gerstenberg, Chatterton is urged on by the example of Shakespeare. Chatterton did not know French – he was largely self-educated – and probably knew nothing of Diderot's *Discours sur la poésie dramatique*. But *AElla* fits in to Diderot's vision of 'epic' times, when poetry responded to the sublimity of human activities and their natural surroundings. Lines 350-77 show this well, where AElla and Birtha are about to enjoy their wedding-feast, but are stopped by the news of a Danish invasion:

AElla:
I lyche eke thys; goe ynn untoe the feaste;
Wee wylle permytte you antecedente bee;
There swotelie synge eche carolle, and yaped jeaste; [yaped =
                                                          comic
And there ys monnie, that you merrie bee;
Comme, gentle love, wee wylle toe spouse-feaste goe,
And there ynn ale and wyne bee dreyncted everych woe.
                                       [dreyncted = drowned
Enter a Messenger.
Messenger:
AElla, the Danes ar thondrynge onn our coaste;
Lyche scolles of locusts, caste oppe bie the sea,
Magnus and Hurra, wythe a doughtie hoaste,
Are ragyng, to be quansed bie none botte thee; [quansed =
                                                     quenched
Haste, swyfte as Levynne to these royners flee: [Levynne =
                                  lightning royners = destroyers
Thie dogges alleyne can tame thys ragynge bulle.

Haste swythyn, fore anieghe the towne theie bee, [swythyn =
                                                 swiftly
And Wedecesterres rolle of dome bee fulle.
Haste, haste O Ælla, to the bycker flie, [bycker = struggle
For yn a momentes space tenne thousand menne maie die.
Ælla:
Beshrew thee for thie newes! I moste be gon.
Was ever lockless dome so hard as myne!
Thos from dysportysmente to warr to ron,
To chaunge the selke veste for the gaberdyne! [gaberdyne =
                                                armour
Birtha:
O! lyche a nedere, lette me rounde thee twyne, [nedere = adder
And hylte thie boddie from the schaftes of warre. [hylte = shield
Thou shalte nott, must not, from thie Birtha ryne,
Botte kenn the dynne of slughornes from afarre. [slughornes =
                                               clarions
Ælla:
O love, was thys thie joie, to shewe the treate,
Than groffyshe to forbydde thie hongred guestes to eate?
                                 [groffyshe = grumpily
O mie upswalynge harte, whatt wordes can saie
The peynes, thatte passethe ynn mie soule ybrente? [ybrente =
                                                burnt

Later in *Ælla* comes the 'roundelaie' sung by 'mynstrelles' to Birtha
(ll. 961-1020). Birtha grieves, since Ælla has gone to fight the Danes,
and she fears he will be killed, and so her companion calls the minstrels
in to sing to her, and cheer her up. Yet their song is a tragic one, with
its refrain

    Mie love ys dedde,
    Gon to hys death-bedde,
    Al under the wyllowe tree.

These are the last three stanzas

    Wythe mie bondes I'll dente the brieres [dente = twine
    Rounde hie hallie corse to gre [hie = his gre= grow
    Ouphante fairie, lyghte youre fyres, [Ouphante = elphin
    Heere mie boddie stylle schalle bee.
      Mie love ys dedde. . .

124

Comme, wythe acorne-coppe and thorne,
Drayne mie hartys blodde awaie;
Lyfe and all yttes goode I scorne,
Daunce bie nete, or feaste by daie.
    Mie love ys dedde. . .

Waterre wytches, crownede wythe reytes, [reytes = reeds
Bere mee to yer leathalle tyde.
I die; I comme; mie true love waytes.
Thos the damselle spake, and dyed.

Keats knew and admired Chatterton's verse, and used to 'recite,
or *chant*, in his peculiar manner' the lines beginning 'Comme, wythe
acorne-coppe and thorne'. I would suggest that Chatterton's lovely
'roundelay' is the first fine poem to be inspired by the ballads in
Percy's *Reliques* — and that, in turn, it is in part the inspiration of
Keats' 'La Belle Dame sans Merci' of 1819.

In 1770 Chatterton poisoned himself, poor, exhausted, ill, and
lacking the recognition he craved. He was not quite eighteen. To the
romantics who followed, he was in his writing and in his brief life
a glowing, meteor-like example of genius, rejected by a philistine
society. While Wordsworth, in 'Resolution and Independence', called
him

The marvellous boy,
The sleepless soul that perished in his pride

Alfred de Vigny put him beside the doomed poets Gilbert and Chénier,
in his *Stello* (1832), and expanded his tale of Chatterton's last hours
in the tragedy *Chatterton* (1835), using him as a symbol of the true
poet at all times, who — according to Vigny — must inevitably suffer
the neglect, scorn and even hatred of society.

Before Wordsworth and Vigny, however, Chatterton had already
been given ample posthumous acclaim. One who praised him was the
irascible Philip Thicknesse, known to his enemies as 'Dr Viper'. He
had included a monument 'Sacred to the Memory of THOMAS CHAT-
TERTON — Unfortunate Boy!' in the grounds of St Catherine's Hermitage, near Bath. In his guide to the 'hermitage' Thicknesse wrote:

I had scooped out a cave on the side of the dingle, under the spreading roots of an ash tree, and turned a rude arch in front of it; and

there placed, cut in relief, the head of that wonderful genius.

When his daughter Anna died, she was buried at this spot, for, as Thicknesse wrote,

> as she was virtuous, dutiful, and not void of some genius, we have deposited her body beneath the only monumental stone raised in *Britain* to the Greatest Genius *Britain*, or perhaps any other nation under the sun, has produced.

Thicknesse was also an enthusiast for garden monuments of a primitive kind — as well as 'the Hermit's Hut', at St Catherine's Hermitage, he had already made the 'Hermit's Cave' in his garden at Felixstowe Cottage on the Suffolk coast in the 1760s, containing a realistic full-size model of a hermit, and in 1768-9 proposed to erect 'a little Stone-Henge' dedicated to Wilkes and Liberty in the hills near Abergavenny. In their different ways, Chatterton's 'Rowley' poems and Thicknesse's garden monuments are alike striving after aspects of the primitive which we discover in the past. While the gothic novel was in its early years, the primitive and the antique in nature was being eagerly sought, discovered, and, when necessary, invented.

By the 1760s and 1770s, the fascination which hermits and hermitages had for lovers of nature is thoroughly a part of early romanticism. In books it coincides with admiration for people who live a solitary, meditative life, remote from society (Robinson Crusoe, though far from being a 'hermit' as regards meditation, is a model for his isolation, leading to the hermit-hero of Edward Dorrington's *The English Hermit* of 1724). Prévost's Cleveland, though not on a desert island, is another such model, through his various experiences of isolation, combined with melancholy introspection. By mid-century, these solitary figures are common — in an English setting, in the 'Man of the Hill' in Fielding's *Tom Jones* (1749), in a slightly exotic setting in Johnson's *Rasselas* (1759) — and from the 1770s onwards they are near-to-indispensable in the popular and now forgotten novels of the period — such as John Potter's *Arthur O'Bradley* (1769), or the anonymous *The Hermitage; a British Story* of 1772 from which I have already quoted, or Richard Graves' *The Spiritual Quixote* (1772).

In painting, the best example is by Joseph Wright of Derby (1734-97). In the late 1760s he painted several pictures showing contemporary people involved in speculation of a scientific or aesthetic kind, in a nocturnal setting where their features and posture are revealed by lamp or candlelight — the most famous are *Three Persons Viewing the Gladiator by Candlelight* (*c*. 1764-5), *A Philosopher Lecturing on the Orrery* (*c*. 1764-6) and *An Experiment on a Bird in the Air Pump* (*c*. 1767-8). All these we may say, without hesitation, are activities which a *philosophe* such as Voltaire or Diderot would appreciate. In the *Experiment on a Bird in the Air Pump*, they would understand and applaud the kinds of attention and interest shown by the spectators as being representative of the widely differing types of which society is composed. But only a few years later — in 1770-1 — Wright painted two pictures in which the theme of study in a nocturnal setting is repeated, but taken far away from 'men who dwell in the city'. In the *Hermit Studying Anatomy*, the scene is a cave in wild countryside, with light — as in the *Experiment* — from a single lamp within, and from the moon outside. Here, the moonlight shows up the savage nature of the surroundings — there is no sash-window to keep the world of nature at a distance — and the hermit studies on his own, a solitary contemplator not of the marvels of post-Newtonian science, but of a skeleton. At the entrance to the cave there are two young men, who by their pose and expression have just arrived. But the hermit does not know they are there. He meditates, while the youths look on, not joined with, but separated from, the old man and his unworldly concerns. Somewhat similar is *The Alchymist, in Search of the Philosopher's Stone, Discovers Phosphorus*, begun in 1770 or 1771. Here the setting is no longer modern, but gothic. The moon shines through small leaded panes, set in pointed windows, and the ancient, white-bearded alchemist himself wears monk-like clothes. His expression, like that of one of the young assistants in the background, is again immensely different from the expressions in the first group of three paintings by Wright of Derby mentioned above. This is no moment in a lecture; here is no rational analysis, but rather the instant of unexpected discovery — of uncomprehending amazement, in which there is an element, albeit a small one, of fear.

In gardens, the real, three-dimensional hermitages became wilder, and were occasionally inhabited by flesh-and-blood hermits, employed for the purpose. Charles Hamilton had advertised for one, for the hermitage on his estate at Painshill in Surrey, and there was even an instance of a landowner being asked, by a complete stranger, if he would allow the stranger to come to live on his estate *as a hermit*. The letter, undated but probably written in the 1770s, is addressed to Mr Drummond, of Cadland House in Hampshire:

127

Honered Sir

I have tacking this fredom to aquaint your honnor it is to ask a faver as never yet was nown for human kind to do that if your honnor pleases to Buld a small hut as a hermetage Near your honers house in a wood with a high wall round It your honer might hear of a man to Live in it for 7 years with out seing any human Creature that is to se what Nature would turn to in that time.

I mean not to cut my hair nor yet my Beard nor my Nayls in that time. I shud wish to have all Neseres of Life Brought to me in a privat plase without seing any Body and if your honner will give proper encoredgement for them years I would

Be at your honners
Servise directley
the soner the Better

I have not disskribed my Name hear to your honnor but I shall hear when it gose on and I hope then to troble your honer with a feawe lines for anser

God Bles your honor.

On the second page the would-be hermit illustrates the hermitage which he would like to build (see Plate 20). While he is brisk enough about the specifications — 'the house 15 fet Square' — and about the provisions he would need — 'I shud wish to have all Neseres of Life Brought to me in a privat plase without seing any Body' — the kind of life he proposes to lead has nothing specifically religious in it. It is, however, Rousseauan. It is a total withdrawal from society, with an aim which Rousseau himself had not the determination to pursue, 'to se what Nature would turn to in that time'. No reply to the letter has been preserved.

Odd though the project may seem, it was not unique. In the same period, one of the wildest of all hermitages was begun at Hawkstone in Shropshire, the seat of Sir Rowland Hill, who died in 1783. The exact date of the work is not known, but it was visited by Dr Johnson in 1774, and is fully detailed in T. Rodenhurst's *Description of Hawkstone* (2nd edn, 1784). The park at Hawkstone is extraordinary in its contrasts, since the generally flat terrain — towards Cheshire to the north and west, and back into Shropshire on the south and east — is interrupted by huge spurs of sandstone, which rise up in a dramatic sequence of near-vertical cliffs and towers. The grotto or hermitage follows the highest edge of the tallest of these cliffs, the tunnels extending over a hundred yards, with numerous chambers, side-turnings, and glimpses of giddy depths and far-away prospects. When Johnson was there, he referred to the grotto as a 'place without any dampness', which 'would afford a habitation not uncomfortable', and in Rodenhurst's *Description* of 1784, there is not only an account of the grotto, but also of

> a well designed little Cottage, which is an Hermit's summer residence. – You pull a bell, and gain admittance.
>
> The HERMIT
>
> Is generally in a sitting posture, with a table before him, on which is a skull, the emblem of mortality, an hour-glass, a book, and a pair of spectacles.

Rodenhurst goes on to describe the behaviour and character of 'the venerable bare-footed Father, whose name is Francis'. In the edition of 1784, 'he seems about 90 years of age, yet has all his senses to admiration', and in the 9th edition, of 1807, the text is unaltered, so that 'this solitary Sire', still 'about 90 years of age', must have been either a perpetual nonagenarian, or well over 110 years old. In its heyday, the high-sited grotto at Hawkstone boasted 'costly shells selected from the remotest regions of the sea', illuminated 'through some exquisitely fine painted glass. . . particularly a Philosopher at his Studies, by Mrs PEIRSON', but now only the sandstone labyrinth remains, with the open framework of a spacious chapel-shaped chamber, surmounted by a single archway overlooking the 'AWFUL PRECIPICE'. Dr Johnson's interest in Hawkstone was indeed to do with the sublimity of the natural scene, and this must soon be considered (see p. 144 below). I suspect that, had the venerable Francis been there in 1774, Johnson would have mentioned him, and with less approval than the landscape. In 1779, five years later, Richard Graves' satirical *Columella* brings together the general craze for hermitages in literature, painting and gardens, when he makes fun of the hired hermits in contemporary landscape gardens. The frontispiece of his novel, by C.W. Bampfylde, sums up the ridiculousness which could result. On a far hill-top a version of the temple of the Sibyl is illuminated by a setting – and thus Claudian – sun; a Roman bridge crosses the stream in the middle distance, while in the foreground, the view from the grotto or hermitage is disfigured by a herd of pigs, stampeding across the scene.

In the 1770s the *painting* of nature extends to much wilder scenes – and not merely of hermitages. The French painter, Claude-Joseph

Vernet (1714-89) had become known since the late 1740s for his marine pictures, of storms and shipwrecks, and of contrasting tranquil scenes, and although it is considered that his development as an artist does not progress much after his completion of the series of paintings of the 'Ports of France' in the mid-1760s, his storm-scenes become wilder as the years pass. In his *Salons*, especially for the year 1767, Diderot discusses Vernet's calm or stormy seascapes at length, with a characteristic mixture of attitudes — thrilled by the violence of the storms, yet seeing their main interest as a human one, for the pitiful 'stories' he imagines round the shipwrecked victims. In his *Salon* of 1769 he admits that the Vernet *Tempête* has been bought by himself (in 1768 — see Diderot, *Salons*, ed. J. Seznec, 1967, IV, 87-9). In his notes for the *Salon*, he adds that the painting hung in his study, his most precious possession. If God reproaches him with self-indulgence, he will give up everything — except the Vernet: 'Ah, leave me the Vernet. It is not the artist himself, but Thou who created it' (p. 389). This recalls Diderot's own description of the genius in 1757, who 'in the silence and obscurity of his study is able to envisage and be moved by the wonder of nature — in the tempest he is seized with fear'. His Vernet, bought in 1768, would help if his imagination needed stimulation (see Plate 21).

Vernet lived and painted in Italy for nineteen years, until 1753; his painting then included many views of a post-Claudian kind of the Italian landscape. Among the contacts which Vernet had with other artists was a fruitful acquaintance with Richard Wilson (1714-82), whose residence in Italy was from 1750 until 1757. Both Vernet's and Wilson's Italian landscapes have a common affinity with views of the campagna by Claude. When Wilson returned to England, he not only continued to paint scenes of Italy but incorporated a Claudian atmosphere into his paintings of English or Welsh scenery. Most memorable examples are his two versions of Snowdon, both painted *c.* 1765, and now in the Walker Art Gallery, Liverpool, and the City Art Gallery, Nottingham. Were we not told that the scene was in Wales, we might think that it was in Italy — from the 'glow' which suffuses the landscape, and from the resemblance which the lake in the foreground has to the water-filled crater of an extinct volcano, such as Lake Albano, which Wilson had sketched several times. And the fishermen by the edge of the lake could be not Welshmen, but Italians, figures from an arcadian past. But though Wilson's British pictures continued to say 'remember Italy' — and no doubt this helped to get him commissions — he did in his last years develop an interest in scenery which was rougher and more barren. His painting of *Llyn-y-Cau, Cader Idris* (*c.* 1774), in the Tate Gallery, is a good example. While the echoes of Lake Albano are still audible, this is no longer a scene where a palace — like Castelgandolfo — might perch on the brink of the crater. It is barren, harsh, with an overall colouring of rusty red and slaty blue-grey. The small human figures and scattered cattle could find water enough in such a landscape, but no vegetation — only rocks. The echoes of this painting have changed — to the newly appreciated sights of the volcanic region near Naples — Vesuvius, Solfatara, Lake Avernus and the rest. Wilson's *Llyn-y-Cau*, painted long after his leaving Italy in 1757, coincides with the brisk surge of interest in volcanoes which began in the late 1760s. It is an interest which was prompted in several ways — we should not forget the concern with seismology which was current just before and after the Lisbon earthquake of 1755 — and among these are certainly the admiration focused on the sublime after Burke's treatise, the fortuitous occurrence of a series of spectacular eruptions of Vesuvius in the 1760s and 1770s, and the equally fortuitous posting of Sir William Hamilton as British Envoy to the court at Naples throughout this period (see p. 145 below). In 1774, the probable date of Wilson's painting, Joseph Wright of Derby was in Italy, and in the very region of Naples and Vesuvius, observing and recording the eruption of the volcano.

But before we advance to the brink of the volcano, other aspects of the sublime in nature must be surveyed. As I have said, Richard Wilson's painting of landscape was permanently affected by his experience of Italy. Himself the first of the great British landscape artists, his British patrons accepted him as a worthy successor to the painters of Italian landscape — a British Claude — and in the 1760s he could make no greater compliment to his patrons than by showing their country, and their estates, as extensions of arcady. Joseph Wright of Derby, much younger than Wilson, was also more versatile, and more accessible to the influences of both rational and romantic attitudes. Just before his departure for Italy in 1773, he painted another night-scene, *The Earthstopper on the Banks of the Derwent*, which is, after so much landscape of a Claudian kind, amazing (see Plate 22). It may indeed have ancestors — art historians have suggested that it is reminiscent of moonlight landscapes by Aert van de Neer — but by 1773 these are unimportant. This painting is natural; I think it is English, and it is sublime. A single lantern lights the digging man, his rootling dog, and the broad backside of his waiting horse; its light spreads over to the swollen stream, which is also lighted from the sky above. Behind the solitary digger rises a stumpy cliff, the rock irregularly veined, and covered from above with over-hanging branches. To the left, on the far side of the Derwent, a tall, dead tree is outlined against the clouds. Near to the lantern and the digging man, another, shattered trunk sprawls across the rushing stream. Compare this painting with Wright's *Experiment*, or with the *Philosopher Lecturing on the Orrery* of a few years before. It is almost as if the painter had *wished* to show a scene which was not concerned with 'men who dwell in the city', but with the vast, dark and frightening world of nature — in which the single man has only a minor role.

Just how small that role could be becomes clear in Wright's paint-ings of Vesuvius; but in Italy his interest in the sublime was roused in several ways — in depicting the sea-shore caves near Naples, rocky arches looking out to the moonlit sea, and especially in the versions of his *Virgil's Tomb* painted between 1779 and 1790, after his return from Italy. Here the tomb of the Roman poet is so shattered that it appears more like a cave than a ruinous building. It is seen at night — the moon shines through a gap in the clouds, and its light passes into the tomb through a hole on the far side. In most versions the painting has no human figures, but in one there is the figure of Silius Italicus within the tomb, honouring, or almost worshipping, the poet's remains. He kneels, and his arms are raised up in ecstasy. It is, like the scene in the *Hermit* or the *Alchymist*, a moment of solitary emotion, not of thought. It seems that *Virgil's Tomb* was not conceived until Wright came back to England, and it may be compared with several rocky scenes in Britain which he painted in the later part of his career — *Matlock High Tor*, for example, in 1777-80, or *Chee Tor* (late 1780s), or the *Cut through the Rock, Cromford* (*c*. 1790) — in which the sublimity of the landscape is shown in a northern and un-Italian setting. In the last years of his life, his *Landscape with Rainbow* (*c*. 1794-5) has lost all trace of foreignness (see Plate 23). The lowering sky above and gloomy trunks of trees to each side are oppressive enough to give a touch of foreboding, while the vivid contrast of the rainbow has moved far away from the gay arc of optimism in William Kent's engraving for 'Spring' (Plate 7). One *might* argue from Wright's rainbow that this was 'God's promise'; that it was all based on 'the SYSTEM'. But it does not seem likely, any more than it does in Turner's even more sombre painting *Buttermere, with part of Crummockwater...*

132

a Shower, which was exhibited in 1798 with lines from Thomson's 'Spring' referring to 'the grand ethereal bow'. These paintings have little connection with the Enlightenment. Unlike the *Philosopher Lecturing on the Orrery,* they have scant space for man. Wright's *Landscape with Rainbow* shows a bridge, a horse and cart, Turner's *Buttermere* has a figure in a rowing boat — and in his original sketch (1797), there was neither rainbow nor boat. The lecture has stopped. Man is no longer necessary as the logical and unique centre of the universe.

There may be a clear progression in this direction in Wright's paintings, although he continues with social themes to the last. But it is clear that while the *Philosopher Lecturing on the Orrery* and the *Experiment* are early on in his career, his numerous paintings of wild nature come later, during and after his visit to Italy. With the painter George Stubbs (1724-1806), there is a more definite division, rather than a progression. In this respect Stubbs is astonishingly similar to Diderot in France, in that throughout his career he divides his attention sincerely and profoundly between matters which we may term 'social' and 'beautiful' and matters which are 'natural' and 'sublime'. With Diderot, there is enough evidence to show that he himself was aware of the division, and indeed of the contradiction between his interests — the simplest example being the fictional dialogue *Le Neveu de Rameau* (see p. 261 below). With Stubbs there is a dearth of written material, and we must therefore go straight to his pictures. On the one hand, his social or scientific works; on the other, those which touch the sublime — either hesitantly, or with total conviction.

Stubbs is the supreme painter of horses. In 1754 he went to Rome — he might have met Wilson — and on his return journey, landing at Ceuta, in north Africa, he is supposed to have witnessed the attack made by a lion on a horse which became one of his most celebrated subjects:

A lion was observed at some distance, directing his way, with a slow pace, towards a White Barbary horse... The lion did not make towards the horse by a regular approach, but performed many curvatures, still drawing nearer... till the lion, by the shelter of a rocky situation, came suddenly upon his prey. The affrighted barb beheld his enemy, and, as if conscious of his fate, threw himself into an attitude highly interesting to the painter. The noble creature then appeared fascinated, and the lion finding him within his power, sprang in a moment, like a cat, on the back of the defenceless horse, threw him down and instantly tore out his bowels (*The Sporting Magazine*, May 1808).

This episode we may imagine in Stubbs' mind, as he returned to England. In the late 1750s, he got to grips with a project which had already been in his thoughts for some time — the meticulous dissection, drawing and etching of the horse, which culminated in *The Anatomy of the Horse*, published in 1766. It has equal scientific and artistic importance, being, at a stroke, the most authoritative and detailed study of equine anatomy, and a volume in which the objective and abstract delineation of the subject, bare of all embellishment, has a monumental dignity, wholly unemotional, firmly realistic and convincing. *The Anatomy of the Horse* was published in the period when the volumes of 2,000-odd plates illustrating the *Encyclopédie* appeared, and, although Stubbs' single work is artistically far superior to the (none the less excellent) French plates, produced by a wide variety of artists, they all have in common the paramount aim of presenting useful information in a clear and effective way. Though different in some technical respects, Stubbs' work has the same approach as that of Diderot's artists, and it could have formed a superior part of the *Encyclopédie*. While engaged on *The Anatomy of the Horse*, Stubbs was also becoming known as a painter of horses, and of scenes in which horses have an important part. Such paintings may be considered as 'social' presentations of the horse, in settings where the horses are clearly trained and controlled, portrayed as admired, beautiful — and expensive — belongings of the patrons who commissioned the paintings. The horses have been thoughtfully bred and successfully tamed by their human owners. The greatest of these paintings is Stubbs' life-sized *Whistlejacket*, now at Kenwood House, and painted not later than 1762. Here the horse is shown rearing up on his hind legs, doing a *levade*. There is no rider, the horse has no saddle or harness of any kind, and the background is plain. While *The Anatomy of the Horse* portrays the horse in superb abstraction, *Whistlejacket* is the portrait of the essence of a horse, alive, in perfect condition, and displaying his perfection. Yet, though majestic — the *size* of the painting is almost enough to ensure that — the horse is not wild or violent. We respect the horse's strength, but we are not frightened. There is sufficient regularity, smoothness and general lightness and openness in the painting for it to be much

134

more 'beautiful' than 'sublime'.

In contrast, and in the same period as *Whistlejacket*, Stubbs painted the first of his sublime studies, in which a horse is shown in conflict with a lion. Stubbs treated the subject many times, varying the moments in the encounter – from the horse first suspecting the lion's stealthy approach, to the later, frantic stages where the horse sinks to the ground with the lion on its back. Stubbs' studies, in several different media, and in widely differing sizes, from life-size paintings to enamels painted on copper barely larger than miniatures, were made over a period of more than thirty years. His interest may have been aroused by the incident at Ceuta; but he also had a recent sculptural model to prompt him, the group of the horse attacked by a lion carved by Peter Scheemakers in 1743, and displayed in the garden at Rousham (see Plate 24). Stubbs and Scheemakers were both employed by Lord Rockingham in the early 1760s, and could have discussed the composition together. Scheemaker's group is itself based on classical models, and one of these – the two groups of a bull attacked by a lion – had been in England, at Castle Howard in Yorkshire, since early on in the eighteenth century.

What distinguishes Stubbs' paintings of the horse attacked by a lion from Scheemakers' group, and from all Stubbs' other paintings of horses until the last years of his life, is the *emotion* which pervades them (see Plate 25). While his other paintings all show or imply human discipline, these are wild pictures, in which human beings have no place. Instead, *fear* governs them, with a completeness which places them wholly on the side of the sublime. Burke himself had contrasted the 'useful beast', which 'has nothing of the sublime', with the horse in wilder scenes, 'whose neck is cloathed with thunder, the glory of whose nostrils is terrible, who swalloweth the ground with fierceness and rage'. Stubbs might well have read these passages, and we may see his paintings as illustrations of what Burke meant. In varying degrees, the lion and the horse are in kinds of solitude – in waste and desolate settings, with no other horses, and no men, who might drive the lion away; in some versions, the background is dark and gloomy; and in all, there are forms of 'astonishment' – 'and astonishment' (in Burke's words) 'is that state of the soul, in which all its motions are suspended, with some degree of horror'. In *The Castle of Otranto*, it was the 'astonishment' of the supernatural which roused 'horror' in the feelings of the characters, and of the readers. In Stubbs' paintings, it is the 'astonishment' of danger, the terror of death which 'effectually robs the mind of all its powers of acting and reasoning'. If Stubbs was fascinated (it is the *mot juste* for the subject), so was his public, and it was his patrons who continued to commission the different versions of the horse frightened, attacked or devoured by a lion, for as long as he was willing to paint them.

Roughly in between Stubbs' principal paintings of horses of a 'beautiful' kind, and his sublime paintings of horses attacked by lions are his many paintings of rare, wild and exotic animals from abroad. Burke had claimed that 'in the gloomy forest, and in the howling wilderness', we meet the sublime 'in the form of the lion, the tiger, the panther, or rhinoceros'. Stubbs' paintings don't quite fit Burke's phrases, for his lion, tiger, leopard, cheetah or rhinoceros tend to appear not in 'the howling wilderness' or 'the gloomy forest', but in settings which are only mid-way to the sublime. Some of his tigers are in sultry lairs, and the *Cheetah with Indian Servants* (Manchester City Art Galleries) has wild mountains behind, and a lavish addition of *exotisme* from the two huntsmen, dusky, turbaned and with tip-tilted shoes. Yet the stag beyond, poised for flight, stands against a river and hillside which could more likely be Scottish than Indian. His *Moose* (Glasgow) has a craggy background just as unconvincing, while the *Zebra*, in the Mellon collection, stands foursquare on a path, with trees behind from any of a hundred English parks; and Stubbs' *Kangaroo*, now at Parham Park, has a background far closer to Richard Wilson than Australia. It is curious that his landscape backgrounds to his paintings of horses, whether the scene is suburban, rural or wild, are generally apt, and often enough are no less than exactly and genially judged – we should remember that there are a few paintings by Stubbs which are masterpieces in the landscape *genre*, like the *Rubbing-Down House on Newmarket Heath* (Mellon Collection), or *The Reapers* and *The Hay-Makers*, in the Tate Gallery. But the settings for his foreign animals remain obstinately English – only that for the *Green Monkey* (the Walker Art Gallery, Liverpool), with the profusion of peaches, looks as exotic as the creature it displays. The successful painting of exotic scenery had to wait until the artists had been there and seen it – and Stubbs' problems with the zebra or the kangaroo are no greater and no less than Chambers' with the pagoda at Kew, erected in 1759-60. The building, like the zebra or the kangeroo, is fine, based on reasonable information. But the surroundings are English, and wrong; and this makes the few genuine observations of wild and 'foreign' scenery at this time, in the South Seas or in the Hebrides, all the more impressive (see p. 163 below).

Stubbs continued to paint his studies of the horse and the lion for some thirty years; and to paint scenes with English horses and their owners until his death. His versions of the sublime and the beautiful are created virtually side by side all through his career. At the turn of the century, he painted two pictures which suddenly unite the English scene with the sublime emotions which had dominated the horse-and-lion paintings. I refer to *Hambletonian Rubbing Down* (1799), and to *Freeman, Keeper to the Earl of Clarendon* (1800) (Mellon collection). *Freeman* portrays the gamekeeper bending over a dying deer, with a lively hound which has obviously just run up, and which the keeper is holding back from the deer. It is a moment as tense, and as precisely seized, as those involving the horse and the lion. The keeper looks up, straight out of the picture, as if interrupted, and the deer seems also to be directing its last glance at the spectator. Behind, the background of thickly leaved trees is dark and oppressive. Not a comfortable picture, but one of gloom and apprehension. In an instant, the deer will be dead. *Hambletonian* has, in contrast, a background which is firmly matter-of-fact and unmysterious — the level heath at Newmarket, with the 'rubbing-down' house at one side — but the horse 'Hambletonian' completely dominates this scenery, as if it, the horse, were a giant and the rubbing-down house and other buildings were made for pygmies. It is a huge painting — nearly 7 feet tall, and 12 feet broad — and 'Hambletonian' fills the canvas. All Stubbs' other paintings of horses in an English setting show them clearly or implicitly controlled by their riders, masters, jockeys and grooms. Here, however, the horse is master. No one else. Two human beings stand by the horse — a groom holding the bridle, a boy with a rubbing cloth in one hand, the other up over the horse's neck. But these humans are like dwarfs, or servants to the horse — both small in size, and fearful in their posture. The groom looks out uncertainly, as if he should not divert his attention from the giant horse, who threatens to push him out of the picture, while the boy with the cloth can barely reach to the horse's neck. The horse himself, bare but for his bridle, is like an animated and *menacing* page from the *Anatomy* (indeed, without the study which produced the *Anatomy of the Horse*, the exactness of delineation of *Hambletonian* would be unthinkable); or a 'Whistlejacket' turned vicious and unpredictable. Where 'Whistlejacket's' pose, caught at the high point of the *levade*, was perfectly controlled — disciplined, and therefore unthreatening — 'Hambletonian' is shown in a moment of continuing movement, which the horse himself is directing, not the humans beside him. Two of his hooves are raised in impatience, and the great muscles of his neck are tense, ready to snatch his head away from the puny groom. This horse is no longer 'domestic', but has become fierce and masterful — he 'swalloweth the ground with fierceness and rage'.

Stubbs' progress from the horse-and-lion pictures to *Hambletonian* consists of a movement from a partial to a complete reality — from 'real' horses and lions, seen in poses which were either *derived* from earlier models, or vividly remembered from a single experience in 1754 or 1755, and set in imaginary landscapes, to a single 'real' horse, drawn from life and set in a landscape of equal and unimpeachable verisimilitude. This progress is, with variations, the theme of this whole history, and it is especially clear in the appreciation of nature and natural phenomena in the decades following Burke's treatise on the sublime. While the newly discovered beauties — and sublimities — of nature are at first savoured via the protective 'excuse' of their resemblance to a remote classical arcadia, and particularly their resemblance to *paintings* of such scenes, they come at last to be appreciated directly, *for themselves*, and for the feelings which they inspire in the beholder.

This is exactly the case, in the growing appreciation of wild nature in the 1760s and 1770s. Just as painters themselves — Wilson, and then Wright of Derby — moved from Claudian scenes to a closer and more accurate vision of the landscape, so tourists and writers came to shed — slowly and in stages — their way of looking at scenery as if it *ought* to be a painting. I say, 'in stages', for one development in this process was to move on from a liking for 'Claudian' scenery to scenery of a sort which Salvator Rosa might have painted.

The travel-notes of the poet Thomas Gray are instructive here, since he left records of visits to 'sublime' areas at three different times. In 1739, he visited France and Italy, travelling for much of the way with Horace Walpole. Together, they wrote back enthusiastically to England describing their feelings at the sight — and sound — of the scenery and torrents of the Grande Chartreuse. Walpole is appropriately breathless:

'Precipices, mountains, torrents, wolves, rumblings, Salvator Rosa' (letter to Richard West, 28 September 1739, in Horace Walpole, *Correspondence*, ed. W. S. Lewis, 1948, XIII, p. 181).

Gray writes more coherently, first to his mother, on 13 October 1739:

> On one hand is the rock, with woods of pine-trees hanging over head; on the other, a monstrous precipice, almost perpendicular, at the bottom of which rolls a torrent, that sometimes tumbling among the fragments of stone that have fallen from on high, and sometimes precipitating itself down vast descents with a noise like thunder, which is still made greater by the echo from the mountains on each side, concurs to form one of the most solemn, the most romantic, and the most astonishing scenes I have ever beheld.

A month later, on 16 November 1739, he writes to West in lines which are now well known, and which, with our later knowledge of Burke's treatise, can be seen as foreshadowing the essence of the sublime in nature:

> In our little journey up to the Grande Chartreuse, I do not remember to have gone ten paces without an exclamation, that there was no restraining: Not a precipice, not a torrent, not a cliff, but is pregnant with religion and poetry. There are certain scenes that would awe an atheist into belief, without the help of other argument. One need not have a very fantastic imagination to see spirits there at noon-day: You have Death perpetually before your eyes, only so far removed, as to compose the mind without frighting it (Thomas Gray, *Correspondence*, ed. P. Toynbee and L. Whibley, 1935, I, pp. 71, 74).

Taken together, these three passages show an excitement at landscape which has been fed by Thomson's *Seasons*; yet Gray's reactions of astonishment, of exclamation, and of mingled poetic and religious rapture are especially memorable since they all involve his feelings. 'Scenes that would awe an atheist into belief, without the help of other argument' — how different from Thomson's, or Scheuchzer's, praise of the scientific wonders of nature, since they reflect the wonders of a rational Creator!

It is not surprising that when Walpole read Gray's 'The Bard', he should remark — praising lines 15-18, where

On a rock, whose haughty brow
Frowns o'er old Conway's foaming flood,
Rob'd in the sable garb of woe,
With haggard eyes, the Poet stood

— that only Salvator Rosa was capable of painting 'up to the horror' of the scene; nor surprising that Gray should admire the 'Salvatorian' qualities of 'Horror... and thrilling Fears' which shone from certain paintings — in a list of several works, the most violent is 'Hannibal passing the Alps; the mountains rolling down rocks upon his army; elephants tumbling down the precipices'.

In 1765, twenty-six years after his visit to the Grande Chartreuse and the French Alps, Gray went to Scotland. Meanwhile, there had been Burke, and Gray writes in summary of his experiences 'in short, since I saw the Alps, I have seen nothing sublime till now' (to Dr Wharton, 14 September 1765, *Corr.*, I, p. 412), and again 'The Mountains are extatic, and ought to be visited in pilgrimage once a year. None but those monstrous creatures of God know how to join so much beauty to so much horror' (to William Mason, 8 November 1765, II, p. 415). Gray's following lines, cheerily written to the clergyman-author of *The English Garden*, show how great the gap had grown between the new fashion — or appreciation — of the sublime, and the gentler, arcadian tradition of the first half of the century:

A fig for your Poets, Painters, Gardiners, and Clergymen, that have not been among them; their imagination can be made up of nothing but bowling-greens, flowering shrubs, horse-ponds, Fleet ditches, shell-grottoes, and Chinée-rails.

Four years later, in 1769, Gray went to the Lake District, and to Yorkshire. In describing Gowdar-crag (near Keswick), Ingleborough (beyond Lancaster towards Settle), and Gordale Scar, near Malham, he shows a fearful pleasure in the wildness of these mountainous scenes which is unequivocally part of the sublime, and more wholly so than his liking for the Grande Chartreuse. 'Fearful pleasure', 'pleasurable fear'? He *enjoys* it, though the danger is — to him, in 1769 — greater than it was in 1739. Then, he wrote, 'you have Death perpetually before your eyes, only so far removed as to compose the mind without frighting it'. Ingleborough, like the Scots mountains, is 'that huge monster of nature', while the *threat* of Gowdar-crag ties his tongue, while urging his pen:

the rocks atop, deep-cloven perpendicularly by the rains, hanging loose and nodding forwards, seem just starting from their base in shivers. The whole way. . . is strew'd with piles of the fragments strangely thrown across each other, and of a dreadful bulk. The place reminds one of those passes in the Alps, where the Guides tell you to move on with speed, and say nothing, lest the agitation of the air should loosen the snows above, and bring down a mass, that would overwhelm a caravan. I took their counsel here and hasten'd on in silence (to Dr Wharton, 18 October 1769, *Corr.*, II, p. 506).

Ten days later, Gray saw Gordale Scar. Fear — and pleasure — were at their most sublime conjunction:

> on the cliffs above hung a few goats; one of them danced and scratched an ear with its hind foot in a place where I would not have stood stock still
> for all beneath the moon.
> As I advanced the crags seem'd to close in. . . the rock on the left rises perpendicular with stubbed yew-trees and shrubs, staring from its side to the height of at least 300 feet; but these are not the thing! it is that to the right. . . that forms the principal horror of the place. From its very base it begins to slope forwards over you. . . and over-shadows half the area below with its dreadful canopy. . . in one part of the top, more exposed to the weather there are loose stones that hang in air, and threaten visibly some idle spectator with instant destruction. . . The gloomy uncomfortable day well suited the savage aspect of the place, and made it still more formidable: I stay'd there (not without shuddering) a quarter of an hour, and thought my trouble richly paid; for the impression will last for life (II, p. 511a).

Well away from painting by now, the reader might think — there's no word of Rosa here. Yet in the next lines, Gray says, 'At the ale-house where I dined in Malham, Vivares, the landscape-painter, had lodged for a week or more; Smith and Bellers had also been there, and two prints of Gordale have been engraved by them.' It is fair to say that by the turn of the century, English artists would paint Gordale Scar in ways which were true to the subject, and no longer masked it with an Italian atmosphere — there is Thomas Girtin's watercolour, *c.* 1801, in the British Museum, and James Ward's gigantic oil painting of 1810, in the Tate. But this is 1769, and Vivares was not a Girtin. And if we look at nearby passages in Gray's description of his travels, we find that

141

he is, as often as not, viewing the scenery in an *indirect* manner which translates what is there into something which has the feeling of a painting. He is using a *Claude-glass* — a round or oval convex mirror, with a dark backing, which reflects the objects or scenery which you view with softened and reduced brightness, and 'rounded' at the outside limits. The reflection of a landscape in this mirror was therefore given a slightly duller and uniform tone — as in, say, a sepia drawing — and a rounded and 'composed' look, as if it were instantly apt as a scene for a painting. The softness of the tones led easily to the instrument being named after Claude, though it is not known if he himself ever used it. By the 1740s they were fairly common — William Shenstone ordered one in 1748, and there is a sketch by Gainsborough, *c*. 1750-5, in the British Museum (ref. Oo.2-27) showing 'a man sketching, using a Claude glass' (see Plate 26).

To return to Gray: while visiting the Lakes, he saw them via his Claude-glass — near Appleby and the river Eden, the views 'gave much employment to the mirror' (III, p. 505); near Derwentwater, he wrote, 'I . . . saw in my glass a picture, that, if I could transmit to you, and fix it in all the softness of its living colours, would fairly sell for a thousand pounds' (III, p. 508); and, during the excursion to view Gowdar-crag, when he had 'hastened on in silence', he had seen Walla-crag — 'pray think', he wrote to Wharton, 'how the glass played its part in such a spot'. Earlier on the same day, near Borrowdale, he had rejoiced at the 'changing prospect every ten paces'. His preoccupation with 'the glass' — for you had to look into it with your back to the scene to be viewed — doubtless led to his accident another day:

> Fell down on my back across a dirty lane with my glass open in one hand, but broke only my knuckles: stay'd nevertheless, and saw the sun set in all its glory (III, p. 506).

'Saw the sun set'? I doubt it. With the Claude-glass intact, he saw its reflection — obliquely, and over his shoulder, like the artist in Gainsborough's sketch. The Claude-glass was the *vade mecum* of a generation of tourists to the wilder parts of Britain, especially after the 'picturesque tours' of the Reverend William Gilpin had begun to appear, beginning with his *Observations on the River Wye. . . Relative Chiefly to Picturesque Beauty; Made in 1770* (1782). Gilpin's aim was to describe and illustrate 'that kind of beauty which *would look well in a picture*' (*Observations on the Western Parts of England*, 1798, p. 238), and with this as a principle, the Claude-glass which he used so regularly led not

142

only to the frequent use of an oval format for his illustrations (see Plate 27), but to such deformation of his scenes that there was often a great gap between the original landscape and Gilpin's picture of it. It is certain that descriptions and illustrations of the wilder parts of Britain, like Gray's account of the Lakes (published in 1775), or Gilpin's series of *Observations*, or, to a lesser extent, the several *Tours* in the British Isles published by Arthur Young from 1768 onwards, encouraged many others to visit these remoter areas of the country; but these publications all depend to some extent on the 'picturesque' approach, which was both a pretext, an excuse for visiting and responding to the wildness of nature, and sometimes an obstacle to seeing nature more clearly. As Horace Walpole had perceived, 'this country exhibits the most beautiful landscapes in the world when they are framed and glazed, that is, when you look at them through the window'.

'Framed and glazed', 'through the window', reflected in a Claude-glass – or appreciated via the contrived alternations of scenery of the landscape garden. Gray's emotional response to the Grande Chartreuse in 1739 is paralleled in the garden – the *ferme ornée* – of The Leasowes, near Halesowen, created by William Shenstone from the mid-1740s onwards. Here the visitor was meant to follow a long, meandering route through and round the arcadian property, looking both at the beauties within and at those of the surrounding countryside, and to experience an extended sequence of emotional sensations, prompted by the scenery itself, and by the sensitively composed inscriptions and modest urns, statues and other monuments placed at telling points along the route. When Rousseau was in England in 1766-7, not long after Shenstone's death in 1764, he visited few gardens – he had already begun to reject the entire idea of the 'garden' as an artificial and stultifying approach to nature – but he might, I think, have appreciated and even enjoyed The Leasowes for its gentle, elegiac and emotional atmosphere, and have found in its walks and groves the poetic stimulus to 'virtue' which St Preux had experienced in the 'Elysée'. Gray had already made a similar claim for 'certain scenes' near the Grande Chartreuse, 'that would awe an atheist into belief', and by the 1770s such expectations, that the natural beauties of the garden were to be appreciated emotionally and morally, had become commonplace. In 1774 the anonymous *Essay on the Different Natural Situations of Gardens* (possibly by Robert Dodsley, Shenstone's friend, and the author of the long 'Description of the Leasowes' in 1764) divides gardens into four 'different dispositions of grounds distinct from each other' – approximately (1) highland, (2) romantic vallies and woods,

(3) gentle, and (4) flat — 'which create distinct and separate sentiments'. So while a mountainous terrain will induce noble sentiments,
a flat garden — being dull — 'appears to create little or none'. At the
beginning of the century, garden manuals had still made their principal
division that of size. The more powerful you were, the greater your
control over the land surrounding your palace — or your house. Now,
in this *Essay* of 1774, your garden will reflect your temperament rather
than your political power, and — *à la* Rousseau — influence *your*
disposition as well. As Julie's 'Elysée' reflected the outpouring of her
virtuous nature, so St Preux imbibed virtue from the 'Elysée'. In the
words of the *Essay* (p. 4), 'Nature not only creates these different
sentiments upon the view of these different situations, but also creates
a love and attachment for one or other of them, according to the different tempers of men.' While a flat, monotonous garden will please
'a person of no taste or feeling', 'a man who is fond of great projects,
or great exploits, or who has an high regard for the splendor of his
ancestors' will love a mountainous garden, and the melancholy atmosphere of vallies and woods will appeal to 'a man in misfortunes', who
will 'naturally retire' to such places. This reads a little as if it implied,
mainly, an attraction of 'like for like'; but three years after the *Essay*,
in 1777, there is a powerful claim that nature's influence is felt by
those not initially in sympathy. It comes in Joseph Heely's *Letters on
the Beauties of Hagley, Envil and the Leasowes*, where, praising the
'beauties' of the park at Hagley, Heely writes, 'Here, methinks, if any
where, among such tranquil bowers, where peace and pleasure seem to
dwell, the villain would be disarmed from executing his dark and
bloody purposes; and every passion that corrodes the human breast,
be lulled into a perfect calm' (I, pp. 152-3).

None of the early romantics ever suggested that there might be
other natural scenes which might inspire vicious thoughts or actions —
and with the growing fashion for seeing *all* that was 'natural' as 'good',
this was unlikely. But while Gray, Rousseau and Heely claimed that
different aspects of nature had a moral power, not all those who
viewed the wildest scenes said as much, even though, with and after
Burke, they were appreciative of their sublime qualities. On 25 July
1774, Dr Johnson visited Sir Rowland Hill's wild and craggy park at
Hawkstone, near Hodnet. Johnson, not a lover of wild nature, was
deeply impressed. Hawkstone was 'a region abounding with striking
scenes and terrific grandeur' — 'terrific' meaning literally 'giving terror'.
He was by 1774 aged 64, heavier than he should be, and not used to
climbing precipitous slopes of any size. Johnson wrote, simply, 'The

whole circuit is somewhat laborious,' and goes on to describe the grotto at the top of the main sandstone cliff. His main comments contrast Hawkstone with Dovedale — a natural valley — and with the garden at Ilam in Derbyshire. He classes it above Dovedale, since, most clearly, it is more fully sublime. He writes that 'it excells Dovedale, by the extent of its prospects, the awfulness of its shades, the horrors of its precipices, the verdure of its hollows and the loftiness of its rocks', and extends this description with the summary that 'the Ideas which it forces upon the mind, are the sublime, the dreadful, and the vast. Above [he is thinking of the cliff-top grotto], is inaccessible altitude, below, is horrible profundity.' No doubt, Johnson was impressed — 'He that mounts the precipices at Hawkstone, wonders how he came thither, and doubts how he shall return. His walk is an adventure, and his departure an escape'. In his next sentence, he is not merely impressed, he admits to enjoyment of the sublime. At Hawkstone the visitor 'has not the tranquillity, but the horrour of solitude, a kind of turbulent pleasure between fright and admiration'. This last phrase — 'a kind of turbulent pleasure between fright and admiration' — is Johnson's own. It was Johnson who felt the 'turbulent pleasure'. But it could have come direct from Burke. And, as in Burke, and in contrast with Gray or Rousseau, there is no touch of moral improvement. Indeed, Hawkstone is so 'turbulent' that its most suitable inhabitants would be giants, 'men of lawless courage and heroic violence' — brigands, we might say, huge *banditti* from a painting by Rosa. Ilam, in contrast, has a 'grandeur tempered by softness', and this, Johnson claims, might involve moral improvement — as the visitor 'looks up to the rocks his thoughts are elevated, as he turns his eyes on the vallies, he is composed and soothed'. Ilam, in short, 'is the fit abode of pastoral virtue'. Yet even here Johnson is not by any means a Rousseauan. The background of these pleasing scenes helps to elevate, to compose and soothe. But it is the visitor himself who does the thinking. He does not — as Rousseau is already doing in France in the mid-1770s — abandon his thought to nature's cradling care.

With a closely similar attitude to Dr Johnson is Sir William Hamilton (1730-1803), in his extended discussion of Vesuvius. Hamilton was posted to Naples as British Envoy in 1764, and remained in Italy for thirty-six years, until the summer of 1800. In the course of the first fifteen or so years Vesuvius erupted frequently and with violence, and Hamilton not only studied the volcano himself with unprecedented care, but encouraged others to show interest — in particular, the artist

Pietro Fabris was supervised by Hamilton to become a wonderful painter of the volcano, and, among the many foreign visitors to Naples, Joseph Wright of Derby was also given hospitality while he painted Neapolitan scenes, and vivid pictures of Vesuvius in eruption.

Many people had written about volcanoes, and Vesuvius especially, centuries before Hamilton went to Naples. In the mid-seventeenth century, Athanasius Kircher published his *Mundus subterraneus* (1665), of which a rather mangled digest appeared in English in 1669, *The Vulcanos: or, Burning and Fire-vomiting Mountains*. Kircher's curiosity, and his efforts, were immense. Looking at this work, and his *oeuvre* as a whole, we may see him as a kind of literate, learned and indefatigable jackdaw, picking up and heaping together all the information he can find. In discussing Vesuvius and other volcanoes, he collects mytho-logical references, travellers' accounts and theological and approxi-mately scientific comments to produce the most comprehensive book on the subject written until his time. If there is any guiding principle, it might be the *a priori* assumption that the Creator's works are wonder-ful, and infinitely diverse — that there is, in the end, no knowing and no rational understanding the complexity of the universe. Though he was a sincere believer, Kircher does not *admire* this aspect of the Crea-tion, and through all his curiosity about volcanoes comes the conviction that volcanoes are dangerous and horrid. There is even the reference, which he does not contradict, to earlier theologians who 'have not incongruously placed the greatest of all the Fire-conservative Abysses in the Centre of the Earth, for an eternal Jakes and Prison' (*Vulcanos*, ch. 1, p. 4). In Scheuchzer's *Physica sacra* of 1731, there is an equal energy in gathering facts, but these are governed, not by general curio-sity, but by a belief in the logical perfection of all aspects of the uni-verse. This post-Newtonian view enables Scheuchzer to see the Creation as beginning in Genesis, and to trace the causes, relationships and phenomena of the natural world back to the first books of the Bible. His presentation of the Creation, the Flood and of the rainbow have been mentioned earlier — see p. 21. In vol. I, Plate CLXVII of the *Physica sacra,* 'Fulmen et septum in Sinai', he illustrates Exodus xix, 16-18. His plate shows the sublimity of the mountain, enveloped in the storm. It is a parallel to Thomson's 'In Winter dreadful thou!' God is present at every point.

By the time Sir William Hamilton was in Naples, the Enlightenment was dominating the intellectual activity of Europe, and Burke had published his treatise on the sublime. Hamilton's main writings on Vesuvius extend from his *Observations on Mount Vesuvius. . . and other Volcanos: in a Series of Letters, Addressed to the Royal Society* of 1772 (of which the earliest letter is dated, from Naples, 10 June 1766) to the three volumes of the *Campi Phlegræi* — two volumes published in 1776, the *Supplement* in 1779. Hamilton spared no effort to investigate Vesuvius, studying, analysing, discussing, measuring and exploring the volcano with amazing thoroughness — and amazing also since he was busied with many other matters, artistic, antiquarian, diplomatic and social, at the same time. On page 2 of the *Supplement to the Campi Phlegræi* of 1779, he writes, 'the last visit to the crater of Vesuvius . . . was my 58th, and to be sure I have been four times as often on parts of the mountain without climbing to it's summit'. To observe the mountain more easily when it erupted — as it did often when he was in Naples — he acquired a country residence, the villa Angelica, near Portici, 'at the foot of Vesuvius, and close by the sea-side'. When Dr Charles Burney, the musicologist, visited Naples in 1770, he had to go out there to meet Hamilton, and was invited to stay there, both for music and to view the volcano, which was then in eruption. On Friday 26 October Burney and a Captain Forbes went out together. The description — in Burney's *Music, Men and Manners in France and Italy 1770*, edited by H. E. Poole, 1969, pp. 176-7 — reveals the complex attitude which Hamilton maintained towards the volcano and his other interests:

His Villa Angelica is but a small house which he [Hamilton] fitted up himself — situated opposite and within 2 miles of the foot of Mount Vesuvius. . . After dinner we had music and chat till supper. Mr. H. has 2 pages who play very well one on the fiddle and the other on the violoncello. . . As soon as it was dark our musical entertainment was mixed with the sight and observations of Mount Vesuvius, then very busy. Mr. H. has glasses of all sorts and every convenience of situation etc. for these observations with which he is much occupied. He favoured me with a sight of his MS. of which he has just sent a copy to our Royal Society [one of the letters in the *Observations* published in 1772] . . . Tho' at 3 miles distant from the mouth of the mountain, were heard the reports of the explosion. . . the stones and red hot matter thrown up. . . we were certain that they mounted near 1000 feet above the summit of the mountain. The sight was very awful and beautiful, resembling in great the most ingenious and fine fireworks I ever saw. M. H. who has studied very closely this mountain and all its symptoms for upwards of 6 years read us very entertaining lectures upon it. . .

After supper we had a long dish of musical talk relative to my history [the *History of Music* upon which Burney was beginning. He wanted to know of anything to do with Greek or Roman music which might have been recovered in the excavations at Herculaneum and Pompeii].

Hamilton mingled his musical, social and antiquarian interests here in an entirely characteristic way; and the eruption of the volcano is both an entertainment – a background of an exotic kind to the 'music and chat', and compared to 'ingenious. . . fireworks' – a subject for prolonged scientific enquiry, and, we should not forget, the cause of the submergence in ash and lava of the Roman cities from which Burney, and Hamilton himself, hoped eagerly to recover antique remains. In his writings on volcanoes, Hamilton is most of the time dispassionate, empirical, an English *philosophe* – a typical phrase in the *Campi Phlegræi* of 1776 refers to 'several curious experiments relative to this phenomenon' (I, p. 89). He stresses repeatedly the 'utility' of his study. He is adding to the stock of human knowledge about the physical universe, by recording and enquiring fully and systematically. In the *Supplement* of 1779, which describes the violent eruption of August 1779, he says firmly, 'As many Poetical descriptions of this eruption will not be wanting, I shall confine mine to simple matter of fact' (p. 5).

None the less, in the *Campi Phlegræi*, and even more in the *Supplement*, Hamilton does wax poetical. He points out that the eruptions are more colourful and more beautiful by night, and at times sees them in terms of entertainment. As Burney had referred to fireworks in 1770, so Hamilton himself writes, 'It is impossible to describe the beautiful appearance of these girandoles of red hot stones, far surpassing the most astonishing artificial fireworks' (*Campi*, I, p. 17). In 1779, in the *Supplement*, after saying on page 5 that he will confine his description 'to simple matter of fact', he does the contrary. His description is of the scene in Fabris' second plate in the *Supplement* (see Plate 28). In the sky was 'a black, and extensive curtain' made up of 'puffs of smoke as black as can possibly be imagined', against which the fire from the volcano was displayed:

The fiery fountain, of so gigantick a size upon the dark ground abovemention'd made the most glorious contrast imaginable, and the blaze of it reflecting strongly on the surface of the sea, which was at that time perfectly smooth, added greatly to this sublime view (p. 10).

148

Completing his description, he again uses words which are not 'matter of fact' — 'Thus, Sir, have I endeavour'd to convey to you at least a faint idea of a scene so glorious, and sublime, as perhaps may have never before been view'd by human eye, at least in such perfection' (p. 13). Johnson and Hamilton are not far apart, when they write on Hawkstone and Vesuvius. Both know what the 'sublime' is meant to be — Johnson was a friend of Burke's, Hamilton had met him at the Literary Club — and both acknowledged the attraction of such perilous yet majestic scenes. But they were both men of the city, loving converse more than solitude. Neither of them would say, echoing Gray in Scotland or the Lakes, 'those montrous creatures of God the cliffs at Hawkstone', or 'that huge monster of nature Vesuvius'.

In the *Campi Phlegraei*, p. 5, Hamilton says that he 'employed Mr. Peter Fabris, a most ingenious and able artist' in early 1773 to depict the scenes of and round Vesuvius for his book. The pictures are a marvel, not only for their brightness and exactness, but for the range of topics which they cover — under Hamilton's direction. Many views are of the landscape, coast and islands in the region of Vesuvius, all related to the volcanic phenomenon. Commissioned by Hamilton, and praised by him for their accuracy, they were often made on the spot and at the time of each phase of the eruptions. They are not merely colourful — they could do that without exaggeration — but record the more violent aspects of the volcano with romantic admiration and excitement. While science is served, with numbered views of the changing profile of the volcano, and meticulously detailed studies of the different kinds of stone and ash produced from the eruptions, so is topography, even of a classically related kind, for was not Lake Avernus the crater of an extinct volcano; and was not the grotto of Pausilipo, of volcanic creation, known to the ancients? Plate XVI in the *Campi Phlegraei*, showing this grotto, indicates the site of Virgil's tomb, and Plate XXIX, of Lake Avernus, indicates with numbers not geological features, but places with classical associations. Entertainment is there as well: Plate XXXVIII in the *Campi*, showing a 'Night view of the current of lava. . . 1771' might illustrate Burney's experience the year before, with a large crowd which has travelled out to the nearest safe vantage-point to enjoy 'a beautiful Cascade of fire. . . the finest effect, that can possibly be imagined'. In the foreground is the king of Naples, and with him Sir William Hamilton, explaining, demonstrating, rather like an infernal lecturer-cum-conductor. *This* is a 'spectacle'.

But in other plates, Fabris shows the sublimity unsoftened by human presence, or on a scale which leaves us merely as indications of how little we are, compared to the power of the volcano. Plate IX in the *Campi* shows an interior view of a crater, with small humans walking round the edge, obviously 'observing' in a *philosophe*-like manner. The next plate, in contrast, shows the volcano in eruption, glowing and smoking, with lava pouring down its sides. No people are there – or if they are, they are far too small to be seen. Nature is in full, and terrible, control. Plate XIV (see Plate 29) shows the interior of a crater of a dormant or extinct volcano. Here, more observers pick their way, dwarfed by the harsh, wildly contorted and jagged rocks. This scene, in its presentation of nature and humans, is akin to Wilson's view of *Llyn-y-Cau, Cader Idris*, painted around 1774 (see p. 131). Both scenes are sublime – the barrenness and the size of the crater, related to the puny human figures, leave the spectator uneasy, since man and his activities are so wholly unimportant. Diderot might say, 'it is the presence of man which gives interest to the physical world', but here nature doesn't care a hoot. Fabris' most spectacular painting is Plate II in the *Supplement* (see Plate 28). A night scene, 'taken from an original drawing' made on 8 August 1779, it shows Vesuvius in lurid pyrotechnic eruption, across the bay of Naples. Flame, smoke, rocks shoot high into the air, while lava courses down the slopes of the mountain. The light illuminates a boat, sailing across the dark water, and shows in silhouette the human figures in the foreground, who stand on the shore, looking in amazement at the terrific scene. A woman, on her knees, might be praying, or holding up a relic to propitiate the angry volcano, while to her side a man gestures, his arm stretched out in a frenzy of excitement. Like Stubbs' paintings of the lion and the horse, it is a moment of emotion seized and captured – terror, yes, and astonishment, where our thoughts 'are suspended, with some degree of horror'; and admiration, that such vastness and strength and glory in nature should be so lavishly displayed.

Soon after Hamilton had engaged Fabris to illustrate his writings on Vesuvius, Joseph Wright came to Italy to study painting, and was given hospitality in Naples by Hamilton. Wright was fortunate in witnessing an eruption of the volcano in October 1774, made several studies of the subject during his visit, and continued to paint pictures of Vesuvius and of other Italian scenes long after his return to England at the end of 1775. When in Rome, where he spent most of his time, Wright had been attracted by the firework display at the Castel Sant'-Angelo. His studies and paintings of this scene, the 'Girandola', go together with his interest in Vesuvius, and when he returned to England, he twice exhibited pairs of paintings, *Vesuvius* and the *Girandola*, in 1776 and 1778. To put the two subjects together stresses the element of 'spectacle', of 'entertainment' which the eruption of Vesuvius was thought to provide — Hamilton had used the terms 'fireworks' and 'girandoles' in his descriptions, Burney had agreed, and there is an element of this in several of Fabris' pictures. But at least two of Wright's volcanic studies, both painted while he was in Italy, and both now in Derby Museum and Art Gallery, have a violence and directness which disassociates them from 'entertainment', and brings them entirely into the region of the sublime. One, a gouache, shows the volcano erupting in the daytime, with a blue but smoke-darkened sky beyond. Glowing, orange lava surges down the mountain, and pours in a broad band across much of the foreground, leaving only the strip of brownish earth and rock nearest to the spectator untouched. Though the sky is overcast, with the billowing smoke, and given vivid contrast by the flames shooting high up out of the crater, the colouring of the lower part of the study is not harsh, but 'warm', and I think *pleasing* in its effect on the eye. The *shock* which follows is one wholly appropriate to the sublime, as the spectator sees, and feels, that this foreground is not 'warm' — as it might be, say, in a later Impressionist painting of a cornfield ablaze with poppies — but *glowing* with molten lava, destructive, irresistible and utterly unconnected with humankind.

The other picture, an oil painting simply called *Vesuvius* (see Plate 30), shows the interior of the crater. On either side walls of raw, irregular rocks tower up. Some spurs lean forward as if they might thunder down into the fire and molten lava in the centre, others, sloping backwards, have pitch-black fissures from which thick, sooty smoke belches out and upwards to the smoke-cloud covering the top of the scene. In the very middle, fire, rocks, gases shoot upwards from a crater which is itself surrounded by the surging waves of lava. It might be urged that this painting is composed in a theatrical style, rather in the manner of a backdrop to illustrate 'pandemonium'. So it might. But it would have to be a play without people, for no man could survive an instant in this lethal scene. It is an imagined scene — no more violent 'landscape' in the whole of nature could be found. Wholly illuminated by fire (no light from the sky could ever pierce such clouds), it is a storm-scene, of a fiery sea in which no ship ever sailed, and on whose burning shore no Lucretian observer (a Diderot, or a Vernet) could ever stand.

Returning to England, Wright painted more Vesuvian scenes, and several of these are indeed 'theatrical'. But his perception of the sublimity of nocturnal fire was fully and successfully transferred to one

English scene, the painting of *Arkwright's Cotton Mills, by Night* (*c*. 1782-3). Like the *Earthstopper*, or *Virgil's Tomb*, it is a night-scene in which the illumination comes partly from the sky — the moon is visible, half-covered by a band of cloud — and partly from artificial light, here glowing through the rows of windows in the mill. I do not know whether Wright intended to be critical of the Industrial Revolution and of its impact on the English landscape, but it is true that the new, violent and lurid effects of factories within a previously rural scene had been noticed for some time — Arthur Young, passing through Coalbrookdale by night in 1776, had said that it was 'horribly sublime', and by 1801, Philip de Loutherbourg will make his *Coalbrookdale by Night* (in the Science Museum, London) look more like a volcano than furnaces. In *Arkwright's Cotton Mills, by Night*, the scene is not infernal, like *Vesuvius*, but English; yet sinister. People there must be, within the mill, but we do not see them. They are too far away, and the mill-walls enclose them. On either side the landscape is dark, and to the right it rises up in a wooded crest, towering high above the mill. In the foreground a horse and cart, with a man walking behind, are vaguely silhouetted against the red light from the mill. Their path, slow and uphill, leads out of the picture, as if they have nothing to do with that fiery scene in the valley beyond.

9

The Noble Savage

As the taste for wilder surroundings grew stronger, so curiosity about their inhabitants increased. The admiration for several of the types of person considered suitable has already been outlined — peasants, peasant-poets, the bard, the genius; hermits, and individuals of a solitary disposition; solitary lovers, and lonely figures from the distant past. These different types have been seen to be more 'interesting', the more their responses were emotional, impulsive, and uncontrolled. 'Feeling' was genuine — reasoning was false. This attitude was given authority by Rousseau, in his *Discours. . . sur l'inégalité* of 1755, when he stated that the most primitive state of man was the most virtuous, that modern man is degenerate, and that 'a state of reflection is a state contrary to nature — the man who meditates is corrupt' (*Discours*, p. 216).

Rousseau's claim could be accepted by his admirers without difficulty, since there was no practical way of proving him right or wrong. Then, by chance, in the 1760s, the opportunity to satisfy this curiosity about the 'noble savage' arose, when a series of navigators sailed round the world, exploring regions in the Pacific previously untouched by Europeans.

The Pacific voyage of Commodore Anson in the 1740s has already been mentioned in connection with the primitive monuments on the island of Tinian, and with the influence of his account on Rousseau in the *Nouvelle Héloïse* (see pp. 48, 93, above). Anson's 'perception' of the monuments on Tinian was essentially governed by his early eighteenth-century outlook, and the garden landscape which he was to create on his return to England at Shugborough remained, in essence, Claudian.

In the 1760s, the voyages of exploration made by Byron, Carteret, Wallis and Cook were, in a different respect, still governed by an early eighteenth-century principle, which, though it went far back to the earliest classical geographers, was given additional strength by post-Newtonian views of the universe. For these explorers were all instructed to search for the 'southern continent'. If, as was known, the northern hemisphere was composed mainly of vast land-masses – Asia, Europe, north America, and a large part of Africa and south America all lying north of the Equator – it was reasonable to suppose that a globe made by a Creator whose Creation obeyed mathematical principles would be 'balanced' top and bottom. In other words, there *ought* to be a *terra australis* of a sufficient size to match the land masses north of the Equator, thus assuring a proper symmetry to the proportions of the globe. If we think back to the 'aesthetic of Versailles'; or to the views of Thomas Burnet on the symmetry of the globe before the fall of man; or to the post-Newtonian writings of Scheuchzer or Thomson, such an idea of the necessary balance of the world's surface is not as naïve as it might otherwise seem today. Maps often indicate with dotted lines the area where this land might be, labelling it *terra australis incognita*, 'unknown southern land'. The more hopeful phrase *terra australis nondum cognita*, 'southern land *not yet* known', is occasionally used, although the possible area of this southern land shrank, ever southwards as successive discoveries showed the Pacific to extend more completely to east and west, and further and further to the south. As late as 1754, Philippe Buache's *Carte des terres australes* shows a highly conjectural mapping of the 'terres antarctiques', in which New Zealand is an enormous promontory sticking up from the southern continent. Later still, in 1767, Alexander Dalrymple's *Account of the Discoveries Made in the South Pacifick Previous to 1764* has a section discussing 'what may be further expected in the South Sea', where he argues from the proportion of land to water in the northern half of the globe that a similar proportion 'will probably be made up in the Southern Lands and Islands not yet discovered'. This shows 'a seeming necessity for a Southern Continent'. In 1764-6, John Byron's circumnavigation had, as part of its aim, the discovery of this southern continent (although he did not find it), and his ship, the *Dolphin*, had not long returned to England before she left on another circumnavigation, commanded this time by Samuel Wallis. Wallis received a task similar to Byron's. His orders stated that there was

> reason to believe that Lands or Islands of great extent, hitherto unvisited by any European Power, may be found in the Southern Hemisphere. . . in Latitudes convenient for Navigation, and in Climates adapted to the produce of Commodities useful in Com-

merce (quoted in George Robertson, *An Account of the Discovery of Tahiti*, ed. Oliver Warner, 1955, p. 7).

On 19 June 1767, the crew of the *Dolphin* had sighted Tahiti, and Robertson wrote in his journal 'we now supposed we saw the long-wished-for Southern Continent, which has often been talked of, but never before seen by any Europeans'. A year later, Cook's orders for *his* first circumnavigation beginning in 1768 likewise included the search for the 'Great Southern Continent'.

I have quoted long phrases from Wallis' secret orders, since they show the practical reasons for the exploration — 'convenient for Navigation... Commodities useful in Commerce'. Though the initial argument might be both naïve and *a priori*, that the 'southern continent' *ought* to exist, the reasons for its prompt and efficient discovery were pressingly real: politics and trade. The approach, the despatch of expeditions to find out in a practical, empirical way if there was a southern continent, where it was, how big it was, and what it contained, was one which the French *philosophes* who created the *Encyclopédie* would have approved. Often, the *a priori* theories which these explorers were expected to verify were theoretical to the point of whimsy — such as the idea, fostered by Maupertuis, that the natives of Patagonia might be a race of creatures midway between the ape and man, and might even sport a rudimentary tail — but they were dealt with practically. Commodore Byron had reported that the natives on the shores of the straits of Magellan were indeed exceptionally tall, but Wallis scotched the 'giant' theory by going ashore and measuring the Patagonians on the spot.

Up to and including Wallis, the fortunate discoverer of Tahiti in 1767, Pacific explorers do not appear to have read or have been influenced by Rousseau. Although George Robertson, who recorded this voyage of the *Dolphin*, shows that Tahiti was a place of delight for the crew — they stayed there for six weeks, enjoying an abundance of food, good weather and sexual recreation which have come together but rarely in the experience of man — he makes no suggestion that the natives might be happier or better than their British visitors, nor is there any extended speculation about the differences between the Tahitians and the sailors.

Wallis and his crew left Tahiti in July 1767. In November 1766, Louis-Antoine de Bougainville began his voyage round the world, setting out from Nantes in the *Boudeuse*, joined a while later by the *Etoile*. In April 1768, after long delays in South America and a grim passage of the straits of Magellan, he reached Tahiti. As for Wallis, this landfall was a delight, and a necessary one. But there was a difference. Wallis, Robertson and the other sailors on board the *Dolphin* do not seem to have known about Rousseau. Bougainville had. His *Voyage autour du monde* of 1771 is a splendid example of French *philosophe* prose — clear, succinct, dedicated to recording and analysing the events of the voyage. It is therefore to be compared with Anson's *Voyage* published in 1748. But once or twice, Bougainville leaves his plain, mariner's style to write in an emotional way. In South America, he waxes eloquent, and anti-clerical, condemning the regime of the Jesuits in Paraguay. This we may pass by — many a *philosophe*, like Voltaire in *Candide*, neglected tolerance when dealing with 'l'infâme'. Yet when he reaches Tahiti, only three or four days after writing that 'la géographie est une science de faits' — 'geography is a science of facts' — that is to say, theories must not be allowed to deflect our vision from the facts which are before our eyes; on reaching Tahiti, he succumbs to a pre-conceived idea of an unspoiled island paradise which can only be attributed to Rousseau. Here was an island uncorrupted by Europeans (though Bougainville was later to claim that one at least of the more signal evils, the pox, had come to Tahiti through Wallis and his crew the year before), and where a still-existing arcady might be found. Bougainville's descriptions reveal this belief in the most poignant way, since, however rose-tinted his view may have been, the harm which followed the arrival of the Europeans corresponded with terrible exactitude to the decadence described in Rousseau's *Discours . . . sur l'inégalité.*

Before they had even set foot on the Tahitian shore, Bougainville and his crew had ample reason to be impressed. They were greeted by more than a hundred canoes, of which the first 'had a crew of twelve naked men who offered us branches from the banana tree, and from their gestures it was clear that this was their olive branch' (Bougainville, *Voyage autour du monde*, intr. M. Hérubel, 1966, p. 182). The sign of peace was accompanied by a piglet and a great cluster of bananas, for which the Frenchmen gave objects in exchange. Meanwhile, the majestic landscape which they were approaching offered them 'the most pleasing prospect', with a stupendous cascade dashing down the wooded mountainside, while the lower slopes opened out into meadows and groves of bananas and coconuts. While the *Boudeuse* and the *Etoile* were still seeking a safe anchorage more canoes approached, one native calmly spent the night on board the *Etoile*, and the Frenchmen began to cast appreciative eyes on the beautiful Tahitian women who now came out in the canoes – women 'whose pleasing features are equal to those of most European women, and whose beautiful bodies are clearly superior to them all' (p. 185).

'Most of these nymphs were naked', adds Bougainville, and speaks of 'countries where the freedom of the golden age still prevails'. While the Tahitian males made signs to the French sailors, to show just what they could do with the women when they came on shore, one of the girls climbed on board the *Boudeuse*:

> Carelessly the young girl allowed the loin-cloth she was wearing to slip off, and she appeared before our eyes just as Venus had displayed herself to the Phrygian shepherd: and she had just such a celestial form (ibid.).

'The golden age', 'Venus' and the Judgement of Paris – these are not terms which Wallis had used, even though his sailors enjoyed the amorous welcome of the islanders every bit as much. Bougainville had only one serious quarrel with them, when three or four natives were killed, and their otherwise wholly peaceful and most friendly behaviour may have been due to the show of force Wallis had been obliged to make at the beginning of his time at Tahiti a few months before. Bougainville was clearly convinced that he had found an island paradise of a Rousseauan, deist kind, such as might theoretically have existed before property, and towns, and inequality began. His sailors wandered unarmed wherever they wished. Everywhere they were welcomed, fed freely, and urged to join in bouts of public love-making with young and beautiful women. 'Venus is here the goddess of hospitality. There are no mysteries in her worship, and the enjoyment of her rites becomes the occasion for a national festival' (p. 195). Bougainville suggests that he himself did not join in, though his sailors did. In the meanwhile he walked into the interior of the island, 'transported into the garden of Eden' – and found a country and inhabitants which seemed made for each other. A perfect climate, and a fertile, beautiful countryside yield 'the treasures of nature' in abundance, so that 'everywhere we saw that hospitality reigned, with tranquillity, a gentle joy, and all the signs of happiness' (ibid.). Elsewhere he says, 'you would think you were in the Elysian Fields' (p. 207) – as in this scene:

> We were halted by a handsome islander, who was reclining in the shade of a tree. He offered to share with us the grassy bank which served as his couch. We accepted. This man then leant towards us,

157

and in a gentle tone, accompanied by a flute through which another Indian was blowing with his nose, he slowly sang us a song, no doubt anecreontic. It was a charming scene, worthy of Boucher's brush (p. 191).

Bougainville does not stop at the description of idyllic scenes. The *Discours. . .sur l'inégalité* had linked the 'golden age' of the noble savage with his political and economic independence, and Bougainville sees the political system on Tahiti in a similar light. The islanders' good faith was maintained, apart from incessant petty theft of the Europeans' personal belongings. Hospitality and justice were apparent in general trading, as well as in the social and sexual meetings of the Frenchmen and the Tahitians. Among themselves, the Tahitians did not appear to steal, and their houses were all open, without locks, bolts or guards (p. 194). One long passage might almost have been modelled on Rousseau's *Discours*, so absolute does the Tahitians' political happiness appear:

> To us the character of the people seemed gentle and kindly. There does not appear to be any civil war in the island, nor any private enmity, although the country is divided into small territories, each with its independent ruler. It is likely that among themselves the Tahitians act with a good faith which is not called into question. Whether they are at home or not, by night or by day, their houses remain open. Each gathers fruit from the first tree in his path, or takes it in whichever house he may enter. It would seem that, as regards things which are absolutely necessary to life, there is no private ownership, and that these things are held in common (pp. 212-3).

As if to complete this poetic picture of an innocent race, living in uncorrupted happiness, Bougainville includes among those who observe the first landing of the Frenchmen an old man, venerable, dignified, and, we are to imagine, wise. He alone among the Tahitians perceives the danger which the Frenchmen represent to the established and happy order of things. Unlike the other natives, who are in a 'kind of ecstasy' at the sight of these newcomers, he is almost indifferent:

> his air of thoughtfulness and concern seemed to show that he feared lest these happy days, which he had passed in the bosom of peace, should now be troubled by the arrival of a new race (p. 190).

158

Bougainville sighted Tahiti on 2 April 1768; landed on the 6th, and sailed away on the 15th. Not a long stay, not long enough for the idyllic vision to be seriously disturbed — though he does add one passage (p. 227 of the *Voyage*) in which he admits that the islanders lived not in near-total equality, but with marked and extreme differences of rank and privilege. The general picture is of an island paradise — and Bougainville's naturalist, Philibert de Commerson, left an even more absolute judgement: 'I can state that it is the only place in the world where there live men with no vices, no prejudices, no needs, no strife... They know no other god but Love' (Appendix to Bougainville, *Voyage*, pp. 391-2). It is not surprising that Bougainville and his classically educated officers named the island after the home of Venus, calling it *Nouvelle-Cythère*, 'New Cythera'.

Bougainville's old man, concerned at the arrival of strangers, was right. A year later, almost to the day, Captain Cook came to Tahiti. He stayed there for six weeks, set up a camp on shore, and surveyed the island. That was during his first voyage round the world, from 1768 to 1771. During his second (1772-5), he came to Tahiti twice, and again for a long stay in 1777 during his last voyage to the Pacific (1776-9). Then came other Europeans; and diseases and missionaries. The life of the Tahitians, utterly untouched by European ways until 1767, was irremediably changed.

While Bougainville's happy visit marks the first meeting between Europeans with Rousseauan attitudes and an untouched primitive race, it was too short for the rosy impression to be dispelled, and this impression was transmitted to Europe in Bougainville's *Voyage* and the other accounts of the French stay on Tahiti. With Cook's voyages, not only was the study of Pacific and Tahitian life more thorough, but his changing teams of naturalists and artists recorded their perceptions in a far more complex way. Their vision was also Rousseauan — to a certain extent, and varying from person to person — and not averse to the idea of the 'noble savage'. They appreciated both the *exotisme* and the wildness. And their combined experience was long and varied enough to allow them to confirm, reject or modify their views far more profoundly than Bougainville and his companions had done. Above all, their views, of whatever kind and on whatever topic, were subjected to the test of experience. Many of the topics, comprising their main reasons for making these voyages, were firmly to do with trade, or science, and had nothing to do with Shaftesbury, Rousseau, Burke or the sublime. For example, on his first voyage, Cook was to search for the 'southern continent', and in so doing charted the whole coastline of New Zealand and the eastern coast of Australia; and he was to observe the transit of Venus at Tahiti; on his second, the existence of the 'southern continent' was to be ascertained more exactly, by a careful circumnavigation of the southern oceans in latitudes as far to the south as could be managed; and his third voyage was meant to confirm, if possible, the truth of another theory, the existence of a *north-west* passage — by sailing north through the Bering Strait and attempting to find a sea route eastwards round the top of the American continent. But while making these empirical investigations Cook and his companions were also the first to try out, in an extended test of experience, Shaftesbury's long-simmering claim that 'The wildness pleases,' and Rousseau's more recent belief in the 'noble savage'.

To take the 'noble savage' first. The belief, in its entirety, would not hold water. Cannibalism was all too frequent. On his first visit to New Zealand Cook had suspected that the Maoris sometimes devoured their enemies; yet many Europeans had not wanted to believe this. During the second voyage these fears were horribly confirmed when a shore party from the *Adventure*, the companion ship to Cook's *Resolution*, was ambushed and several sailors were eaten. On board the *Resolution* only a week or so earlier (23 November 1773) Cook and his companions observed natives eating pieces of human flesh, cut from the head of a native who had just been slain.

Yet this did not prove that all natives in the South Seas were like the Maoris. On board the *Resolution* was a Tahitian native, Oedidee or Hitihiti, who watched as the Maoris ate the flesh. One officer, William Wales, said in his journal that at the sight the Tahitian 'became perfectly motionless, and seemed as if Metamorphosed into the Statue of Horror... He continued in this situation untill some of us roused him. . . and then burst into Tears nor could refrain himself the whole Evening afterwards' (quoted in *The Journals of Captain James Cook: II, The Voyage of the Resolution and Adventure*, ed. J. C. Beaglehole, 1961, p. 819). Could the Tahitians therefore be blameless? Even this proved a vain hope — together with Oedidee on the *Adventure* was another Tahitian, Omai, much more important in this history, who was to travel back to England, stay there while Cook's third expedition was in preparation, and return to his homeland with Cook in 1777. When questioned by Cook, Omai admitted that in the frequent wars between the Tahitian islanders, cannibalism did occur.

Cook's account of the cannibalism which he had witnessed is remarkable for its detachment and understanding, in contrast with the remarks of the French navigator J.-M. Crozet, who had witnessed the death of his captain, Marion du Fresne, and sixteen sailors at the hands of the Maoris in 1772. Crozet concluded angrily that the 'noble savage' was 'the most treacherous. . . the fiercest and most dangerous' of the enemies of 'educated' men (*Nouveau voyage à la mer du sud*, 1783, pp. 127-9). Cook's entry (23 November 1773) begins: 'That the New Zealanders are Canibals can now no longer be doubted'. A few lines later he adds, 'few considers what a savage man is in his original state', and then explains the reasoning which the Maoris might employ to justify eating the flesh of their enemies. The Rousseauan attitude might, at first glance, seem the very target of Cook's words. But even if Cook might be disproving claims that primitive man was an entirely innocent creature, he adds that these same natives have excellent qualities — 'their behavour to us has been Manly and Mild, shewing allways a readiness to oblige us'. Cannibals, yes, not 'noble savages'. But not wholly reprehensible; rather, human beings like ourselves, but in hugely different circumstances.

A few months before, in his journal for 2 June 1773 (*Journals*, II, pp. 174-5), Cook had written sadly of the harm which his expedition had brought to New Zealand. While the Maori women had seemed 'more chaste than the generality of Indian Women' on his first visit, now this was not the case. The fault was that of the Europeans:

Such are the consequences of a commerce with Europeans. . . we debauch their Morals already too prone to vice and we interduce among them wants and perhaps diseases which they never before knew and which serves only to disturb that happy tranquillity they and their fore Fathers had injoy'd.

'Happy tranquillity'? Cook concludes in a tragic tone: 'If any one denies the truth of this assertion let him tell me what the Natives of the whole extent of America have gained by the commerce they have had with Europeans.' In considering 'what a savage man is in his original state', Cook saw — through experience — more truly than Rousseau, and more truly than Bougainville. But, unlike a Voltaire or a Walpole, he did not therefore think savages inferior. They lived in circumstances so different from those of Europeans that they were indeed virtually in another world. It was a world which might in some ways be admired, in others abhorred, but which was weaker than the European world, and incompatible with it.

In 1777 Cook returned to Tahiti, bringing back from England the young Tahitian, Omai. Cook himself had only a middling opinion of him, although in England Omai was seen by many as a living proof that Tahiti was the home of the 'noble savage'. Returning Omai at last to the island of Huahine, near Tahiti, Cook did his utmost to set him up in comfort, with the plethora of European tools and toys which the British authorities had thought fit to give him. Cook was depressed at Omai's less than 'noble' performance on his return from Europe, and felt that Omai, and the Tahitians as a whole, had suffered harm which could not be put right:

> I own I cannot avoid expressing it as my real opinion that it would have been far better for these poor people never to have known our superiority in the accomodations and arts that make life comfortable, then after once knowing it, to be again left and abandoned in their original incapacity of improvement (*Journals*, II, ed. Beaglehole, 1961, p. 459).

The clock cannot be put back. They were not 'noble savages', but their life was more than tolerable. In a wise and tragic phrase which puts him above both the single-minded lovers of the natural life, and the blinkered *philosophes* who could admire only the city, Cook writes, 'Indeed they cannot be restored to that happy mediocrity in which they lived before we discovered them' (ibid).

Cook then left Tahiti for the last time, in December 1777. Early next year he sighted the Hawaiian islands, and returned again in the winter of 1778. On 14 February 1779, Cook was killed by natives, in the course of a muddled, scuffling riot on the shore of Kealakekua bay. Not long before, Cook had written of the Hawaiians that they were 'an open, candid, active people' (*Journals*, III, ed. Beaglehole, 1967, p. 281).

The naturalists and artists who made these voyages to the South Seas went on widely different routes, though they all had experience of Tahiti. On the first voyage the main naturalists were Joseph Banks and Daniel Solander, and the artists were Sydney Parkinson and Alexander Buchan. Buchan died only a few days after the *Endeavour* had reached Tahiti in April 1769, and Parkinson died much later on the voyage, in January 1771. Banks had intended to go with Cook on the second voyage, but withdrew after disagreements, and so, while Banks went on a different expedition into the north Atlantic (see p. 172 below), Cook took on his second voyage different naturalists — the German J. R. Forster and his son J. G. A. Forster — and a new artist, William

Hodges. A different group again went on the third voyage, including the artist John Webber.

Few of these travellers failed to appreciate the extent and interest of the discoveries which were made, and their separate journals often support or modify what Bougainville and then Cook had written about Tahiti, the 'noble savage' and cannibalism. But it is more valuable in this history to see how Cook's artists in particular reacted, not only to the natives whom they saw, but to the physical world which they explored.

On the first voyage, they saw the Patagonians on Tierra del Fuego. Buchan made several sketches of them, singly, or in a group within a hut, showing indeed that these natives were not giants, nor 'noble savages', but were people living a life which no European could envy. Reaching New Zealand, the Maoris provided far more exotic material. They might be cannibals, but their appearance, like that of the chief depicted by Parkinson (see Plate 31), their encampments on cliffs overlooking the sea, and the fantastic carvings on their canoes were neither squalid nor uninteresting. Here was the wild, the primitive and the sublime in nature and in man, and in forms which Europeans had not seen before. Though Bougainville and even Banks had used terms from Greece and Rome to interpret what they saw, these scenes, as seen by Buchan and Parkinson, were neither Greek nor Roman. During Wallis' visit to Tahiti in 1767, one of the sailors wrote of the native canoes which had 'very pretty carved work on them, much resembling the Doric Order of Architecture'. European commentators, translators and interpreters of what Cook, Buchan and Parkinson had written or drawn might pervert their evidence back into this Grecian style (see p. 170 below), but the originals, text or drawing, leave no doubt that *their* vision saw beyond 'the Doric Order' and beyond 'New Cythera' to a culture and a natural world which was entirely new. An interesting in-between example is that of the kangaroo. With difficulty, Cook's sailors had shot one on the Australian coast. Parkinson had sketched it, and from his sketch and from the skin and skull of the animal, Stubbs had painted the picture which is now at Parham Park. While Stubbs' animal seems faithful enough, the background is, as I have already said, neither here nor there. Stubbs never saw nature in the Pacific. Cook's artists did. They were the first to depict these new, wild, terrible and beautiful scenes.

On the second voyage two main groups of scenery were observed. First, the polar landscapes, of sea, icy coasts and towering icebergs. These had been explored with heroic thoroughness by Cook and his men in the search for the 'southern continent', so that Cook could write on Tuesday 21 February 1775 that through his voyage there had been 'a final end put to the searching after a Southern Continent, which has at times engrossed the attention of some of the Maritime Powers for near two Centuries past and the Geographers of all ages' (*Journals*, II, p. 643). He admits that 'there may be a Continent or large tract of land near the Pole', but goes on to explain that the region, being covered in eternal ice, can be of no use to anyone. He discusses the ice-fields, and ends with lines which convey his experience and attitude with eloquence and conviction:

> If this imperfect account of the formation of these extraordinary floating islands of ice, which is written wholly from my own observation, does not convey some usefull hints to some abler pen, it will however convey some Idea of the Lands where they are formed, Lands doomed by nature to everlasting frigidness and never once to feel the warmth of the Suns rays, whose horrible and savage aspect I have no words to describe; such are the lands we have descovered, what may we expect those to be which lie more to the South, for we may reasonably suppose that we have seen the best as lying most to the North, whoever has resolution and perseverance to clear up this point by proceding farther than I have done, I shall not envy him the honour of the discovery but I will be bold to say that the world will not be benefited by it (p. 646).

Thomson, writing of 'wish'd, wint'ry Horrors' in 1726 had not thought of anything so barren as this; I doubt if he could have imagined these 'Lands doomed by nature to everlasting frigidness'. Cook himself, devoted to his task of exploration and a brilliant navigator, was — and it was a part of his genius to be this so consistently — eminently practical. Earlier in his polar circumnavigation, he had exposed himself and his crew to hardship and danger, and he would do so again. But at this point, his attitude is exactly that of Locke in 1690, insisting that our search for knowledge should be confined to 'what may be of use to us'. Land further south there might be, but Cook turns away, believing 'that the world will not be benefited by it'.

We, armchair explorers, may think lightly of Cook's decision; and I suppose the imaginative leap to such unrewarding danger is beyond us. One episode from Georg Forster's *Voyage round the World* of 1777 (republished 1968, ed. Robert L. Kahn) may bring the peril nearer to our understanding. Earlier on the same voyage, in December

1772, when Cook was beginning his circumnavigation in the southern oceans, the *Resolution* and the *Adventure* had reached a region of giant ice-floes, and by the 14 December 'a vast number of islands of ice' stretched before the ships 'as far as the eye could reach'. The following morning 'it was almost calm, but very foggy', and so, 'to try the direction of the current', a boat was launched, and, writes Forster, 'Mr Wales the astronomer, and my father [J. R. Forster], took this opportunity to repeat the experiments on the temperature of the sea at a certain depth [which they had been making some days before]'. Then the horror, which Burke would have had no difficulty in classifying:

> The fog encreased so much while they were thus engaged, that they entirely lost sight of both the ships. Their situation in a small four-oared boat, on an immense ocean, far from any inhabitable shore, surrounded with ice, and utterly destitute of provisions, was truly terrifying and horrible in its consequences. They rowed about for some time, making vain efforts to be heard, but all was silent about them, and they could not see the length of their boat. They were the more unfortunate, as they had neither mast nor sail, and only two oars. In this dreadful suspence they determined to lie still, hoping that, provided they preserved their place, the sloops would not drive out of sight, as it was calm. At last they heard the jingling of a bell at a distance; this sound was heavenly music to their ears; they immediately rowed towards it, and by continual hailing, were at last answered from the *Adventure* (*Voyage*, p. 73).

Over two years later, Cook turned away from this quest. In the meanwhile, Hodges had made some amazing drawings and paintings of Antarctic scenes (see Plate 32) which are nothing if not sublime in the barrenness which surrounds the British ships. 'The world will not be benefited' by further exploration to the south, Cook had written, but we, looking back from a comfortable reading of John L. Lowes' *The Road to Xanadu* of 1927, know that the ice-floes and frozen seas found in Cook's voyages, whether drawn by Hodges or William Wales, or described by Hawkesworth or Cook or by Forster, crossed Coleridge's path:

> And now there came both mist and snow,
> And it grew wondrous cold:
> And ice, mast-high, came floating by,
> As green as emerald ('The Rime of the Ancient Mariner', II.51-4).

Cook, Wales, the Forsters and Hodges all saw many exotic scenes during the second circumnavigation. Whether Buchan and Parkinson on the first, and Webber on the third voyage may have been more 'objective' in their recording — or, in other words, less excited by what they saw — is not important here. What does matter is that William Hodges (1744-97) is the first painter of note to visit, see and record with an eye of excitement the wild and exotic scenes of the south Pacific. Hodges had already studied for seven years under Richard Wilson, and had been occupied in painting 'Wilsonian' scenes — i.e. landscapes of British subjects suffused in Claudian light — when he was appointed to sail with Cook's second expedition. He had also shown some interest in primitive scenes, for in 1767 he exhibited a 'View of a Druid's Altar in Pembrokeshire'. While with Cook Hodges made portraits of natives, and paintings of many native scenes, peaceful or less so. Above all, he recorded the landscape of the Pacific islands, capturing for the first time the combined and complex *exotismes* of island-mountains rising steeply from the sea, the un-European vegetation which clothed the land, the barbaric shapes and decoration of the Maori or Tahitian war-canoes — no 'Doric' in these (see Plate 33) — and the unusual and again un-European colourations of the clouds and sky which, as in some of his Antarctic pictures, gave a distinctive feeling to the whole. While Cook was charting the shores of New Zealand, on 17 May 1773, the crew of the *Resolution* saw no less than six water-spouts near to the ship. Cook describes them (*Journals*, II, pp. 140-2) in matter-of-fact terms, even though one of the water-spouts, first seen 'at the distance of two or three miles at least from us', at last 'pass'd within fifty yards of our stern'. Hodges painted the scene at least twice. One version was engraved as Plate III for W. Wales and W. Bayly's *Original Astronomical Observations* (1777). The authors explain that Hodges' drawing, 'taken at the time', 'exhibited the appearance of one of them in three several states, and also the appearance of that which approached so near to the ship' (p. 346). This version by Hodges was therefore intended in part as a full and faithful record of the event. His other version, now in the National Maritime Museum at Greenwich, is less scientific, and more dramatic — a masterpiece in the genre of storm scenes, transposing the sublime excitement from Vernet's well known formula into a new and arresting form.

In March 1774 the *Resolution* came to Easter Island and to scenes which were not wholly new to Europeans. This remote island had been discovered by the Dutchman Jacob Roggeveen in 1722, and brief descriptions of the tall stone statues found there had been published.

166

A Spanish ship had also passed by Easter Island in November 1770. But Cook and his companions were the first to view the strange monuments on Easter Island as objects which might be admired *because* they were strange, and *because* they were primitive. In their descriptions Cook, Wales and Forster consider the monuments with admiration, but without eloquence. Fifty years before, Roggeveen had written of 'some particularly high erected stone images', which had at first caused astonishment, since he could not understand how 30-foot high images could have been erected by the natives. He then adds, 'but this astonishment ceased with the discovery. . . that these images were formed from clay' (*The Journal of Jacob Roggeveen*, tr. & ed. A. Sharp, 1970, pp. 97, 98). Roggeveen was wrong: the monuments were made of stone, not clay. But his total indifference to their *appearance* is characteristic of his time — in 1722 it would have needed a Stukeley, or a Fischer von Erlach, to wax eloquent in their praise. Cook admires the skill of the builders of these 'Stupendous stone statues', which stood on platforms 'faced with hewn stones of a vast size, executed in so masterly a manner as sufficiently shews the ingenuity of the age in which they were built' (*Journals*, II, p. 353). He wonders what they represented — gods, or departed rulers — he remarks, 'I my self saw a human Skeleton lying in the foundation of one'; and he wonders, only half seriously, whether one of the accounts derived from Roggeveen was right, that they were built by giants '12 feet high', which might explain how the statues, with their heavy, separate stone cylinders on the top, were set up. Both Wales and Forster travelled across this small island, saw more of the monuments, measured and discussed them. Wales calls them 'Colossean Statues', 'stupendous Figures', 'prodigeous Masses of Stone' (in *Journals*, II, pp. 826-7), while Forster suggests that the cylinder on top of the monuments 'resembled the head-dress of some Egyptian divinity'. Forster admits that the Europeans could not fathom how the natives then present on the island, few in number and clearly not up to any advanced form of architecture, could have made the figures. He suggests that the figures are 'the remains of better times — times before a possible earthquake or volcanic eruption had made the island as barren as it now was' (Forster, *Voyage*, 1968, pp. 325-39).

In their accounts, Wales and Forster both mention that Hodges was active in drawing the monuments, and Wales tells in happy detail how a native 'walked past Mr Hodge snatched his hat off from his head and ran away with it' (in *Journals*, II, p. 822). Hodges did not seem to mind — Wales said that

He sat like Patience on a Monument
Smiling at Grief.

He was too busy to respond, for he must have been working on his landscape of *The Monuments of Easter Island* now in the National Maritime Museum (see Plate 34). We have only to compare it with the engraving from Anson's *Voyage* of the monuments on Tinian (see Plate 9) to see how far Hodges has moved from the shelter of the Greco-Roman tradition, and how fully the different aspects of the sublime have been brought together. Like his painting of the water-spouts, it is one where the spectator is faced with astonishment. In the former, it is with fear, wondering what will happen to the ship; in the latter, it is with fear at the total strangeness of the scene. Sinister, more than melancholy, with the human bones; barren, with the arid landscape round the monuments; and, with the harsh colours of the stone and sandy ground, with the size and strangeness of the monuments, a deeply menacing scene. Hodges, as I have said, had already painted at least one scene of a 'Druid's Altar' when in England. It might have resembled, say, Thomas Jones' stormy, nocturnal version of *The Bard*, painted in 1774 (Plate 17), but we do not know. Here in *The Monuments of Easter Island* he has seized the sublime, and shown it even more terrible in daylight. We do not have to 'invent a story', as Diderot so often does in his *Salons*, to feel uneasy. In front of those towering images — made by whom? meaning what? — the tiny skull is unforgettable.

Two other paintings by Hodges must be mentioned, both involving volcanic activity. One, in the Art Gallery and Museums at Brighton, is provisionally entitled *The Inner Crater of Mauna Loa, Sandwich Isles* — a landscape of a roughly circular area, ringed by jagged rocks, and with patches of smoke rising irregularly from vents in the ground. There is no vegetation at all — it is a rock-scape, and the only relief is in the puffs of smoke, and a few Europeans who scramble awkwardly up the side of the 'crater', or who walk, tiny and unimportant, across the shallow centre. We might think that Hodges painted it on Easter Island, which was a place with rocky scenes reminiscent of an extinct volcano (and Forster at least had thought an eruption had devastated the island). Alternatively, the scene might be on the island of Tanna, where the *Resolution* called in August 1774. There an active volcano was shooting fire, smoke and stones up into the air, scattering the Europeans with sooty ash. Cook and his companions tried hard to explore the inner part of the island, in order to approach the crater of the volcano, but the natives would not let them, and guided them, again and again, back to the coast. Though they failed to reach the crater, they several times reached an area of lesser volcanic activity, where steam or smoke puffed up from the ground, and which they called the 'solfatara', after the similar region near Naples, not far from Mount Vesuvius. In their journals, both Cook and Forster show great interest in the 'solfatara' at Tanna, and it seems likely to me that the painting by Hodges which has been described is a depiction of this spot.

Hodges' other volcanic painting is also of Tanna, and shows the landing of a party from the *Resolution*, faced by hostile natives, with the volcano erupting in the background. It is, if not a nocturnal, at least a twilight scene, and the figures of the natives and the Europeans are lit from one side by the lurid flames from the volcano while, behind them on the other side, the jungle stands dark and mysterious. Neither this painting, nor the one I have just described of the smoking volcanic rockscape, has the full power of Hodges' *Monuments of Easter Island*; but they are equally attempts to portray the sublime, and the sublime in nature's most violent manifestation, the volcano. If the 'Landing at Tanna' is too crowded — the ingredients jostle each other, as if Hodges were trying to squeeze two subjects, the landing, and the land-scape, into one canvas — the rockscape is (and I think intentionally) too bare. If Wright of Derby's *Vesuvius* (see Plate 30) is 'theatrical' in its enclosing shape and frenzied, fiery activity, Hodges' broad, bare crater belongs to a theatre of the dead, in which humans are equally out of place.

Exploration didn't end with Captain Cook; nor did the recording of new and exotic scenes end with Hodges. On Cook's third expedition (1776-79/80) the main artist was John Webber (1750-93), and he added to the work of Hodges on Tahiti numbers of drawings and paintings, both of landscape and of native activities, including a sketch of an elaborate ceremony of human sacrifice, with Cook himself present as a solemn witness, and the Tahitian, Omai, beside him explaining the ceremony. That was in 1777. As recently as 1768, Commerson had claimed of the Tahitians 'they know no other god but Love'. Later on this voyage, Webber recorded scenes in the Hawaiian islands of compar-able strangeness, such as the open-air temple or *heiau* at Waimea; and then at Nootka Sound, on the coast of Vancouver Island, there were natives from a different, more northerly culture to be drawn, and still further to the north he drew the snow and ice and towering mountains on the coast of Alaska.

The exploration of the *Resolution* and the *Discovery* continued after

Cook's death in 1779, with another brief attempt to find a 'North-West Passage'; and then there were other explorations and other regions, islands, races and tribes still to be discovered. But none of them could sail to spots yet unknown to Europe, and innocent of European knowledge, with quite the same expectations. How could they? The test of experience had proved that the 'noble savage' was not simple, but complex; not a creature of instinct, of kindness and peace, but occasionally scheming, treacherous, ferocious and cruel; and even, at times, a cannibal.

Just as Bougainville, Cook and their companions had come to Tahiti with certain theories and expectations, so their accounts and depictions of their experiences in the Pacific were received and transmitted in ways which sometimes prolonged the wished-for Rousseauan theory of the 'noble savage' and the unspoilt natural paradise. This happened especially in the presentation to the public of Cook's first voyage. Cook's own account was extensively 'edited' by John Hawkesworth, who published *An Account of the Voyage Undertaken for Making Discoveries in the Southern Hemisphere* in 1773. No doubt Bougainville's *Voyage*, published in 1771 and translated into English by J. R. Forster in 1772, helped to urge the Rousseauan viewpoint, which appears strongly in Hawkesworth's sections on Tahiti, and is also coloured by views of the 'bard' which had become common in England in the 1760s. So Hawkesworth writes of 'the bards and minstrels of Otaheite', and sums up the idyllic picture by writing 'the whole scene realizes the poetic fables of Arcadia' (*Account*, II, p. 83). This attitude is also maintained in Hawkesworth's illustrations, all the more easily since Cook's first artists, Buchan and Parkinson, were both dead, and unable to ensure the faithful engraving of their drawings. Many were given an idyllic cast, often absent in the original, and the strangeness of the Maori or Tahitian costumes and artefacts – huts, wood carvings and canoes – were also softened. The most notable example is in the engraving of Buchan's drawing of Tierra del Fuegan natives in a hut – cramped, cold, dirty and squalid – where the hut is transformed into a leafy cabin, and the inhabitants appear graceful, lively and clean-limbed.

Although Cook's later voyages were related to the public with much greater fidelity, the myth of an arcadian Tahiti continued to survive. It was strengthened in England by the visit of the Tahitian, Omai, which lasted from July 1774 until June 1776 – practically two years. Unlike Aoutourou, who had been taken by Bougainville to Paris, and had proved a dull fellow, Omai was well received. With Banks to provide introductions, he went the rounds of British society, was introduced to the king, George III, and was fêted, written about, and drawn or painted – both by William Parry, by Nathaniel Dance and by Reynolds. Parry's painting, now at Parham Park, shows Omai barefoot in Tahitian dress beside Banks and Solander. Reynolds' portrait, however (now at Castle Howard), shows Omai on his own, as does Dance's drawing. Again barefoot, and in Tahitian clothes, handsome, dignified, he *looks* everything a 'noble savage' should be. Even Dr Johnson, who met Omai, could not deny the courteous manners of the Tahitian – but avoided attributing them to his savage origin. Instead, he claimed that Omai 'had passed his time, while in England, only in the best company; so that all he had acquired of our manners was genteel'. While in England, Omai stuck firmly to one aim – to return to his native islands, and there to avenge his father, who had been killed in an inter-island raid.

The British took him back to the Tahitian islands faithfully enough, which he reached safe and sound in August 1777. With him he brought all sorts of useful items – tools, furniture, domestic animals and horses – and other items less useful, and, we may reflect, hardly congruous with the status of a 'noble savage'. For example, there were fireworks, and a jack-in-the-box, a portable organ, and even a 'Lectrifying Machine', presumably a device to produce a small current which would create a sudden tingling sensation in the fingers of those who were touching it when it was operated. And while in England Omai had been inoculated against the smallpox, a disease then unknown in Tahiti. The Tahitian Aoutourou, whom Bougainville took to France, died at Madagascar on his way back to Tahiti, from smallpox. He had already acquired that other European disease, the pox, in Tahiti, where it had been introduced either by Wallis' sailors in 1767, or by Bougainville's a few months later in 1768. It is ironic that Omai seems to have been free of venereal disease until his return to Tahiti, when, according to William Bayly (in Cook, *Journals*, III, p. 193), he caught the pox from a Tahitian girl who also stole many of his belongings.

Omai's return was not particularly successful, nor was it tragic. He quickly used up his stock of gifts and valuables, but seems to have lived on in some style for nearly three years after Cook sailed away in 1777. He died a natural death.

Britain did not learn of Omai's last days for many years. Meanwhile Cook had been murdered in 1779, and his death – or rather the depiction on canvas of his apotheosis – was to form the climax of a lavish pantomime to do with Omai. This was *Omai, or a Trip round the World*

(1785). It was written by John O'Keefe, and its décor — stage-setting and many native costumes — was designed by Philippe de Loutherbourg (1740-1812), with help from John Webber, several of whose Tahitian drawings were followed for the stage-settings. Work by Hodges was also consulted by Loutherbourg.

Using the real Omai, his ambitions for revenge, and his visit to England in a most fanciful way, O'Keefe's story takes Omai from Tahiti to London, where he falls in love with Londina, the daughter of Britannia. Then, via Kamtchatka and the Sandwich Islands, Omai and Londina return to Tahiti, and natives from all the countries explored by Captain Cook file on to the stage. When Omai has been declared king of Tahiti, the painting of the 'apotheosis of Captain Cook' is let down, and the cast sing an anthem in praise of Cook.

Preposterous though this may seem, it is no more foolish or untrue than the 'pageants of Empire' which I saw as a child, or similar pageants to celebrate 'the solidarity of the workers' or 'ethnic harmony' which are staged today. *Omai, or a Trip round the World* is important in this history, since it shows more vigorously than any other example how exotic scenery, barely known before Cook's voyages, had become attractive to the public; and how sympathetic the idea of the 'noble savage', the inhabitant of such scenery, had also become. Near the end of *Omai*, an earthquake helps to resolve the hero's difficulties, and a similar pageant, by Arnould, called *La Mort du capitaine Cook*, produced in Paris in 1788, and in London a year later, was said to have had a volcano as part of its scenic attraction.

Truly the wildness pleases. Joseph Banks had differed with Cook after the first voyage, and, instead of going round the world again, he went to Iceland with Solander in 1772, and, *en passant* as one might say, visited the island of Staffa in the Hebrides. Banks left no surviving journal, and we must see his visits obliquely, through the accounts and the drawings of his companions. These were published in Thomas Pennant's *A Tour in Scotland, and Voyages to the Hebrides 1772* of 1774, with an 'Account of Staffa, communicated by Joseph Banks, Esq.', and in Uno von Troil's *Letters on Iceland . . . Made during a Voyage Undertaken in the Year 1772, by Joseph Banks* (1780).

During his voyage Banks observed superb examples of natural wildness. In the Hebrides, the small island of Staffa was strangely comparable to Easter Island which Cook was to visit soon afterwards, since it was, even in 1772 and a part of the British Isles, virtually *terra incognita.* Only one topographer, the Scot Buchanan, had mentioned it before, and Banks felt that he was here a discoverer. Here were unknown wonders of nature — and how much more marvellous they were, than anything humans could create:

> Compared to this what are the cathedrals or the palaces built by men! mere models or playthings, imitations as diminutive as his works will always be when compared to those of nature (Banks, in Pennant, *Tour*, II, p. 262).

The columns of rock, rising straight up or curving out of the sea, were even more *regular* than anything which man might boast of — and regularity was 'the only part in which [man] fancied himself to exceed his mistress, Nature'. Above all, the cave drew Banks' praise. It was, he wrote, 'the most magnificent, I suppose, that has ever been described by travellers' (II, p. 262). A palace, a cathedral, but greater than man had made, and made by nature. How should it be named? Banks' question, the answer, and his misunderstanding are not just a matter of linguistic ignorance. It is to do with the strength of romantic feeling at the time, which had led Bougainville, Banks and Hawkesworth to see Tahiti through arcadian spectacles, and now led Banks in the Hebrides to see Staffa via the poems of Ossian. Banks asked what the cave on Staffa was called. 'Said our guide, the cave of *Fiuhn*', and Banks adds to this 'whom the translator of *Ossian's* works has called *Fingal*; how fortunate that in this cave we should meet with the remembrance of that chief, whose existence, as well as that of the whole *Epic* poem is almost doubted in *England*' (II, p. 263). Banks had been misinformed by his interpreter, since the Gaelic name for the cave meant 'the cave of music', 'an-ua-vine', and not 'an-ua-Fine', 'the cave of Fingal' (see B. Faujas-Saint-Fond, *Voyage en Angleterre... et aux îles Hébrides*, 1797, II, p. 69n). While belief in Ossian has shrunk, Fingal's Cave has kept its sudden renown, and this is due at first to the sublimity of the views of Staffa, by Banks' artist J. F. Miller, engraved for Pennant's *Tour* (see Plate 35). As with the pictures and descriptions by Gray, Fabris, Wright of Derby or Wilson of wild, mountainous or volcanic scenes, we could run through Burke's requirements for the sublime: astonishment, vastness, irregularity and the rest. Banks had certainly stressed that nature was here more regular than in any of the works of man. Yet the 'regularity' of the basalt columns, which Banks measures with empirical keenness, is thrown into disorder by a volcanic upheaval. In the most famous view of Staffa, visitors in a tiny dinghy advance within the cave. Like a cathedral nave, it is indeed 'regular', with pillars rising smoothly and perfectly upwards on either side. But overhead rocks of a different formation squeeze down with a terrible weight, and outside, half submerged by the sea, jumbled heaps of basalt testify to the earth's irresistible convulsions in the distant past. Although Miller's view is not a patch on Hodges' 'Monuments of Easter Island' either for subtlety or strength of composition, both pictures agree in their juxtaposition of man and nature. Man is tiny, and ineffectual. In Hodges' painting, no more than a skull and scattered bones; in Miller's view, man is at least alive, but present only as a midget, observing and measuring for just so long as the weather − another part of nature − is favourable. (I would suggest that Mendelssohn's overture 'Fingal's Cave' (1829), through which the island is now best known − and through which the name of Fingal also continues to be remembered − has a surging movement which conveys the strength and ceaseless activity of the ocean, rather than the static and barren immensity of the rocks. But that is fifty years later than Banks and his artist Miller, and part of another story.)

Soon afterwards Banks reached Iceland, and studied an active volcano. Uno von Troil, whose descriptions probably reflect Banks' attitude, is firm in admiring the sublime more than the beautiful: 'It is true, beauty is pleasing both to our eyes and our thoughts; but gigantic nature often makes the most lasting impressions' (*Letters*, p. 4).

Banks' party advanced towards 'gigantic nature', 'to mount Heckla itself', where Uno von Troil and Banks were 'the first who ever reached the summit of this celebrated volcano'. Though Hecla did not erupt, the travellers were well satisfied with several geysers, spouting hot water out of the ground. Of the first, von Troil wrote, 'it was one of the most beautiful sights I ever beheld', and explained that the explorers were able to boil mutton, salmon trout and ptarmigan in one of its vents. A while later, in a countryside which was alternately rocky, covered in ice or snow, or else intolerably hot, von Troil wrote: 'So much is certain, at least, nature never drew from anyone a more cheerful homage to her great Creator than I here paid him' (pp. 10-11). The writer was a clergyman, being the Bishop of Linköping. His tone is like Thomson's, with 'In Winter dreadful thou!', but his admiration is for a scene which Thomson might have found hard to swallow: 'Here a poet would have an opportunity of painting a picture of whatever Nature has of beautiful and terrible united.' Snowy, cloud-covered mountains were on one side, with Hecla on another, covered both with clouds and with smoke, and on another, a 'ridge of high rocks, at the foot of which boiling water from time to time gushes forth;

and further on extends a marsh of about half a mile in circumference, where are forty or fifty boiling springs, from which a vapour ascends to a prodigious height' (pp. 257-8). In the middle was the geyser. I doubt whether Rousseau would have seen anything 'beautiful' here at all. But the scene was appreciated by these travellers in 1772. It is apt, and fascinating, and persuasive, that nature's supreme wildness in the volcano should have attracted the attention and admiration of so many Europeans in these years — Hamilton, Fabris, Burney, Wright in Italy; Wilson in Wales; Hodges and others in the South Seas, and Banks and his companions in Iceland. While the 'noble savage' might have his defects, even the wildest of nature's manifestations could still be appreciated, and with enthusiasm.

In surveying attitudes in the 1770s to the noble savage and his surroundings, it is proper to conclude with the visit of Dr Johnson and Boswell to Scotland and the Hebrides in 1773. Each wrote a travel journal, each journal was published. Johnson wrote *A Journey to the Western Islands of Scotland* (1775), Boswell *The Journal of a Tour to the Hebrides* (1785). References are to the edition by R. W. Chapman, combining the two works, of 1978.

Their journey is, in a way, a parallel to Banks' voyage to the Hebrides and Iceland the year before. Banks went, full of his Pacific experiences, and Johnson and Boswell went with a wish to see the remote parts of the British Isles for themselves, and to see the inhabitants of these rarely visited regions. Both of them were well read, both keenly interested in the vogue for wildness and the noble savage, holding opinions which were often at odds. Johnson was Britain's staunchest supporter of the Aristotelian city-centred outlook, while Boswell, much younger, was infected with romantic enthusiasms. By August 1773, a lot had already appeared to do with recent Pacific voyages — Bougainville's *Voyage* and Hawkesworth's *Account*, for example — and from the texts of Boswell and Johnson it is clear that they had also heard of Banks' discovery of Fingal's Cave. Several of the most noted travellers of the age, as well as the theoreticians of the sublime, were well known to Johnson and Boswell, being members of the Literary Club — for example Banks, Hamilton, Burke and the Wartons.

For Samuel Johnson (1709-84), the city-lover and vitriolic disapprover of Scotsmen, this journey was a test of experience of no little difficulty. He was aged sixty-three when he reached the Hebrides and, as Boswell wrote, 'large, robust, I may say, approaching to the gigantick, and grown unwieldy from corpulency' (Chapman, p. 171). Much of the journey was made in country without roads, and no wheeled vehicles, and so Johnson rode, awkwardly, on a horse, or grotesquely on a donkey, or proceeded on foot, using a stick. James Boswell (1740-95), had already pursued *his* romantic inclinations by travelling to Corsica, to meet the patriot, General Paoli, after first meeting Rousseau in France, and discussing with him the need of the Corsicans for independence, and the constitution for a Corsican republic which Rousseau had been asked to draw up. Much of this is related in Boswell's *Tour to Corsica* of 1768. And Boswell was a Scot, proud of the fact, and proud to show Johnson his country.

Johnson was cantankerous, vehemently prejudiced and often prompt to mock or exaggerate what he thought to be faults in the opinions or characters of others. Yet his vision was broad, and he was capable of adapting, almost of changing, his own opinions in the light of experience — experience acquired during these onerous travels. In this, he may be contrasted with that other lover of the city, Voltaire. Boswell met Voltaire in 1764, and told him of his and Johnson's plan to visit the Hebrides. At this, Boswell writes, 'he looked at me, as if I had talked of going to the North Pole, and said "You do not insist on my accompanying you?" — "No, sir" — "Then I am very willing you should go"', (p. 167). The attitude of Horace Walpole, the English Voltaire, was similar. When an artist was being sought to sail on Cook's second voyage, the opportunity was given to Johan Zoffany; but he decided not to, preferring to go to Italy, and Walpole said of this that it was 'better than his going to draw naked savages and be scalped with that wild man, Banks' (to Sir Horace Mann, 20 September 1772, in *Horace Walpole's Correspondence with Sir Horace Mann*, ed. W. S. Lewis *et al.*, vol. VII, 1967). (Zoffany's preference for the art of Italy, descended from that of Greece and Rome, shows only too sadly in his painting in the heroic style of 'The Death of Captain Cook' (*c.* 1795), where the figures in his composition are neither English nor Hawaiian: merely echoes of poses from classical sculpture.)

Johnson set off with the view that the city should be the centre of his interest, since that is where most men were, and where they could best use their minds. Logically, those places where men were less numerous, or where they could not use their minds, were of less interest. Wild nature therefore, of the kind discussed in this history, had little to recommend it. Seeing a barren area of sand, which had drifted over and smothered good meadow-land, 'near two miles square', Johnson said 'he never had the image before. It was horrible, if barrenness and danger could be so' (Chapman, p. 355). The Scottish mountains are, according to Johnson, a wide extent of hopeless sterility. The appearance is that of matter incapable of form or usefulness, dismissed by nature from her care and disinherited of her favours, left in its original elemental state, or quickened only with one sullen power of useless vegetation (pp. 34-5).

Of the Hebrides, he writes similarly 'Of these Islands it must be confessed, that they have not many allurements, but to the mere lover of naked nature' (p. 142). His view is wholly opposed to that of Gray, referring to the Scottish mountains as 'ecstatic', 'those monstrous creatures of God'.

But Johnson gives his reasons. If the Hebrides 'have not many allurements', it is because 'the inhabitants are thin, provisions are scarce, and desolation and penury give little pleasure'. When Boswell (who would surely have approved of Gray's attitude) said that he fancied living a solitary, meditative life in the Hebrides, Johnson replied, 'Ay, sir; but if you were shut up here, your own thoughts would torment you: you would think of Edinburgh or London, and that you could not be there' (pp. 354-5).

During their stay in the Hebrides, Johnson often thought 'of Edinburgh or London'. On Friday 8 October, Boswell wrote, 'Dr Johnson appeared today very weary of our present confined situation. He said, "I want to be on the main land, and go on with existence. This is a waste of life"' (p. 358). Happily, nine days later, they came to a small island which was obviously more cultured:

As we walked up from the shore, Dr Johnson's heart was cheered by the sight of a road marked with cart-wheels, as on the main land; a thing which we had not seen for a long time. It gave us a pleasure similar to that which a traveller feels, when, wandering on what he fears is a desert island, he perceives the print of human feet (p. 378).

'The print of human feet' — this is the essential. Yet if the humans live in 'desolation and penury', they are unable to live intelligently. 'Without intelligence man is not social, he is only gregarious; and little intelligence will there be, where all are constrained to daily labour' (pp. 123-4). Johnson would, I think, have admitted that even in the city a person 'constrained to daily labour' would be 'only gregarious' — and Johnson's own definition has an animal sense, 'going in flocks or herds'.

Johnson was, however, open to instruction. In the Highlands he writes: 'It will very readily occur that this uniformity of barrenness can afford very little amusement to the traveller.' But this is a blin-kered, stay-at-home state of mind. If we are to judge rightly, we must travel, and see for ourselves. If not to the shores of the Mediterranean, at least to the less welcoming parts of our own land:

> Regions mountainous and wild, thinly inhabited, and little culti-vated, make a great part of the earth, and he that has never seen them, must live unacquainted with much of the face of nature, and with one of the great scenes of human existence (p. 35).

Johnson's reaction did him credit. In the next valley, a shade more fertile, he paused, and admitted that here at least nature pleased him:

> I sat down on a bank, such as a writer of Romance might have delighted to feign. . . The day was calm, the air soft, and all was rudeness, silence, and solitude. Before me, and on either side, were high hills, which by hindering the eye from ranging, forced the mind to find entertainment for itself. . . here I first conceived the thought of this narration (p. 35).

Johnson's change of mood is a famous one. Throughout the rest of his 'narration' he shows the sharpest attention to the human qualities of his hosts and their dependants, and with few lapses – at sixty-three, and 'unwieldy from corpulency', he did better than we would have done – he kept his eyes and his mind triumphantly open. There were defences, of course – 'no man should travel unprovided with instru-ments for taking heights and distances' (p. 133), i.e. the benighted Highlanders had no rulers – but he sometimes admitted his liking for scenes of sublimity. Early on, at Slanes Castle, he had written of 'all the terrifick grandeur of the tempestuous ocean'. We may imagine him aware of Boswell listening, when he adds:

> I would not for my amusement wish for a storm; but as storms, whether wished or not, will sometimes happen, I may say, with-out violation of humanity, that I should willingly look out upon them from Slanes Castle (pp. 16-17).

Nearby was the 'Buller' or 'Bouilloir' of Buchan, a deep fault in the rock-face where the 'boiling' sea could be watched in safety. Johnson appreciated that this was 'terrour without danger', merely 'a volun-tary agitation of the mind that is permitted no longer than it pleases'

(p. 18). This was merely play — like the 'imaginations excited. . . in the artificial solitudes of parks and gardens', contrasted with the real dangers in 'an unknown and untravelled wilderness' (p. 36). As he went on towards the Hebrides, the 'terrour' and the 'danger' came closer together. On Saturday 26 September, at night in a small boat, 'Dr Johnson sat silent and patient. Once he said, as he looked on the black coast of Sky. . . "This is very solemn"' (p. 332). On Sunday 3 October they sailed from Skye, and a storm rose. Johnson 'grew sick', and in a while 'was quite in a state of annihilation', while Boswell, sick too, stayed on deck to experience the tempest. Johnson, down below, missed this, but Boswell the romantic wrote, 'There was something grandly horrible in the sight. I am glad I have seen it once' (pp. 347, 349). Now Boswell became 'very ill', while Johnson was void, and 'lying in philosophick tranquillity'.

At last, in another boat, Johnson was brought to the full avowal of his pleasure:

> As we sailed along by moon-light, in a sea somewhat rough, and often between black and gloomy rocks, Dr Johnson said, 'If this be not *roving among the Hebrides*, nothing is' (p. 384).

Johnson had admitted to the joy of adventure. Elsewhere, back on the mainland, he once praised 'the rough musick of nature', when 'the wind was loud, the rain was heavy, and the whistling of the blast, the fall of the shower, the rush of the cataracts, and the roar of the torrent' combined into a noble chorus (pp. 143-4). But his greatest concession to romanticism was on the island of Skye. The alternation between danger and security, between a frail boat and the medieval solidity of castle walls, brought out one splendid statement. They had left one host rather late, 'in the gloom of the evening'. They had a guide, who led them to their next host. 'But what' — asks Johnson — 'must be the solicitude of him who should be wandering, among the craggs and hollows, benighted, ignorant, and alone?' Next day, Johnson wrote down his impressions:

> The fictions of the *Gothick* romances were not so remote from credibility as they are now thought. In the full prevalence of the feudal institution, when violence desolated the world. . . the adventurer might very suddenly pass from the gloom of woods. . . to seats of plenty, gaiety, and magnificence. Whatever is imaged in the wildest tale. . . would be felt by him, who, wandering in the

mountains without a guide, or upon the sea without a pilot, should be carried amidst his terror and uncertainty, to the hospitality and elegance of *Raasay* or *Dunvegan* (p. 69).

This is as far as Johnson goes towards Boswell's liking for romantic things. The primitive past is boring — 'to go and see one druidical temple is only to see that it is nothing, for there is neither art nor power in it; and seeing one is quite enough' (p. 243). He is willing to look back at recent Highland or Hebridean manners, thinking back to their simple way with 'a generous and manly pleasure' (p. 82). But that is past, and when it comes to the suggestion that the Scots once had poets of a 'Homeric' kind among them, he is scathing. In Scotland, 'the state of the Bards was. . . hopeless. . . the Bard was a barbarian among barbarians, who, knowing nothing himself, lived with others that knew no more' (p. 105).

This brings us to Ossian, and to Macpherson. Johnson was implacable in opposing the authenticity of the poems — 'I look upon McPherson's *Fingal* to be as gross an imposition as ever the world was troubled with', he said (p. 320). If, in his prejudice, he claimed that the Scots had only been cleanly after 'the Union made them acquainted with English manners' — before, their houses were 'filthy as the cottages of the Hottentots' (p. 24) — he was no less pitiless about Ossian. A similar link with a primitive race ensures the same contempt:

If we know little of the ancient Highlanders, let us not fill the vacuity with *Ossian*. If we have not searched the *Magellanick* regions, let us however forbear to people them with *Patagons* (p. 108).

Patagons are the Patagonians, thought by some to be a race of giants (see p. 155 above), and in 1773 just beyond the verge of credibility — as Johnson felt Ossian should be.

Johnson's intransigence with Ossian is easy to grasp. His general approach to Highland life is more complex, governed by his profound concern with people. When he first came across a cottage in the Highlands, he was fascinated: 'This was the first Highland Hut that I had seen; and as our business was with life and manners, we were willing to visit it' (p. 27). Johnson's approach is utterly at odds with that of the Rousseauan romantics such as Bougainville. *They* hoped to see, in Tahiti, people living a life of idyllic happiness. Johnson, whose 'business was with life and manners', wanted to see how he and the Highland cottagers compared. 'Men and women are my subjects of enquiry; let us see how these differ from those we have left behind.'

10

The Wildness Pleases

'The road of excess leads to the palace of wisdom'
(William Blake, *The Marriage of Heaven and Hell*, *c*. 1789)

After Shaftesbury wrote 'The wildness pleases,' it took most of a century for Europeans to learn what wildness was, and to learn to like it. In the last twenty-five years of the eighteenth century, the liking is shown with an assurance which is greater than ever before, which reaches its most extreme expression in several different forms, and which has a practical outlet in the political and social violence of the French Revolution. Such extremes are the business of this chapter.

When William Hodges returned to England at the end of Cook's second voyage, he was occupied for a time in finishing his paintings of Pacific scenes; and then in 1778 he went to India, where he stayed for six years. There, he painted, he drew and he wrote. In his *Select Views in India* of 1786, and his *Travels in India* of 1793, he reinforces his vision of the individuality of atmosphere of different parts of the globe, and adds a note of *sic transit* which is generally lacking in his paintings from the Pacific. There, the barbaric canoes, their tattooed and strangely adorned warriors, and the towering cliffs and vivid jungle behind them were utterly unfamiliar, but emphatically in the present – like the handsome, amiable Omai; even *The Monuments of Easter Island*, depicting objects from an unknown past, are menacing, not melancholy. But nearly all Hodges' Indian scenes are of monuments, palaces, fortresses which are falling into ruins, abandoned, partly overgrown; with few or no inhabitants, and occasionally depicted at night, by moonlight. The titles in the *Select Views* are evocative: 'A view of the tombs of Gazipoor', 'View of a mausoleum at Etmadpoor', 'A view of part of the tomb of the emperor Akbar at Secundra', and Hodges' text adds to the feeling. Beneath 'a view of part of the ruins of the city of Agra', he writes that it is 'taken from. . .a Building that was once the Palace of the Emperor Arungzebe', and adds that along the banks of the river Jumna there are 'for many Miles similar Monuments of once human Greatness now dissolving in the Dust'. Hodges' *Tomb and distant view of Rajmahal hills* of 1782, in the Tate Gallery, is characteristic in conveying both the individuality of the exotic scene, and its melancholy (see Plate 36).

Joseph Wright of Derby made one outstanding excursion into the exotic at this time, in *the Indian Widow* of 1783-5, in Derby Art Gallery (see Plate 37). Were it not for the widow's head-dress and the tomahawk on the tree behind her, we might imagine the scene to be rather Pacific than American; and Wright was surely influenced by Hodges. To the left, lightning streaks down from a stormy sky to the raging sea — as in Hodges' painting of water-spouts — and to the right a glowing volcano (which no 'Red Indian' ever saw) reminds us both of Vesuvius, known to Wright, and of the volcano on the island of Tanna, seen and depicted by Hodges. In the centre, the widow — were it not for her head-dress — might mourn one of Ossian's vanquished warriors, and the windswept bush by her side could be heather. Yet her head is outlined against a brighter patch of sky, and in this Wright declares himself, between Rembrandt and Turner, one of the great explorers of light. When I first saw this painting, I was perplexed, as it seemed a scene exactly out of Chateaubriand's *Atala*, published in 1801. Yet Wright died in 1797. What I had thought to be Wright illustrating Chateaubriand was in fact painted fifteen or more years before; Chateaubriand in 1801 was still as imbued with Ossian when he described Red Indians to a European audience as was Wright in the 1780s.

Wright's *Indian Widow* is sublime; but others were attracted by gentler *exotismes*. The writer J.-H. Bernardin de Saint-Pierre (1737-1818) is remembered for his praise of Rousseau, and for his Rousseauan *Etudes de la nature* (1784), which demonstrate at length, and optimistically, how wonderfully the Creation is made, and how man is the principal beneficiary; and for his novel *Paul et Virginie*, which was first published in 1788 as the fourth volume of *Etudes de la nature*. Here in a natural paradise derived from the ideal situations postulated in the *Discours sur. . .l'inégalité*, the *Nouvelle Héloïse and Emile* — and from Bougainville's Tahiti — two young and innocent European children grow up together. They are on the tropical, fertile island of Mauritius, which Bernardin de Saint-Pierre had visited in 1768. They are idyllically happy, for nature smiles, and the corruption of society is unknown. It is the gentle nature beloved of Rousseau, and it is as if his Julie and St Preux were free to develop as they felt in such surroundings — and as if the constraints of property, custom, class and society were as unknown as the hardship and violence of nature. This dream lasts for most of the book, and is shattered when Virginie travels to France to be educated.

There she learns not truth, but artifice — not virtue, but a false, prudish modesty — and returns to Mauritius a 'young lady'. As her ship comes within sight of the island, a terrible storm arises — the first and only 'sublime' natural manifestation in the story — the ship is wrecked, and, given the chance to reach the shore if she will only strip off her cumbersome clothing, Virginie chooses rather to preserve her new-found and artificial modesty, and drowns. The symbolism is plain: Virginie's contact with European 'refinement' has made her unsuitable for this innocent and natural environment, and so she must die. It is an odd, violent and unconvincing end to a story which is unconvincing, albeit enjoyable for most of its length, since the scenes, characters and events are so consistently colourful, gentle and innocent. While St Preux and Julie's *situation* is at least truthfully described — society would say 'no' to their marriage — Bernardin de Saint-Pierre dodges the need to be truthful (in other words, to remember that man is a 'social animal') by keeping Paul and Virginie away from society, and from the responsibilities which come with adolescence. It is no wonder that such happy escapism appealed to Flaubert's frustrated heroine Emma Bovary when, in the 1830s, her yearning, misguided imagination longed for anything which might be *different* from the banality of her modest life in Normandy.

The storm which destroys the island-idyll of *Paul et Virginie*, though out of place in a story otherwise so optimistic, was chosen by Vernet for one of his last paintings, *The Shipwreck of Virginie* of 1789, in the Hermitage, Leningrad. Long before, in his *Salon* for 1769, Diderot had reproached him for painting to a formula, for failing to imitate himself well enough; but here the violence of the scene goes beyond his earlier paintings. The tremendous waves are snatched up by a fiercer wind, the clouds are blacker and fill the entire sky, and the ship — Virginie's *St. Géran* — heels sideways at a more fatal angle. Vernet has included few of the comforting ingredients which indicate man's at least partial control over nature. Here, the shore is as wild as the sea and sky; and in the foreground two despairing figures, Paul and his faithful servant, are useless to help. Virginie, clothed in virginal white, lies drowned on the beach between them. The painting seems less 'believable' than the best of Vernet's earlier *naufrages*, and one might ask whether Vernet's experience of natural violence had been extended in his old age, or whether he was simply responding to the public's craving for ever stormier storms.

At this time, creators of gardens are equally eager to bring the wild and the exotic into their landscapes. Easily the most remarkable are

Wörlitz, in Saxony, and Fonthill in England, and something must be said of each. The park at Wörlitz, near to the town of Dessau (now in East Germany), was created during the long rule of Fürst Leopold Friedrich Franz von Anhalt-Dessau (1740-1817), who became enthusiastic about landscape gardening after two extended visits to England in the 1760s. The area of the park was vast, and was gradually adorned in the 1770s and after with temples, monuments and other features whose number and variety must recall the gardens at Stowe, created, for the most part, in the first half of the century.

Wörlitz, some decades later than Stowe, contains both the beautiful and the sublime. The gentler aspects of nature are commemorated in the small island dedicated to Rousseau, where an urn, surrounded by poplar trees, recalls his tomb on the île des peupliers' in 1778. Elsewhere, in the Temple of Venus, a grotto in the foundations was dedicated to Æolus, and contained an Æolian harp. The gothic was also welcome — the prince had experienced difficulties with his wife, and preferred to live not in his castle, but in the 'Gothisches Haus', which is powerfully reminiscent of Walpole's Strawberry Hill. Wörlitz has, though, a somewhat different 'message' from that of Stowe. There, for several generations, it was, above all, a political statement which the Cobhams wished to build into their landscape — as, for example, in the Temple of British Worthies, designed by Kent, where the choice of 'worthies' to illustrate Britain's greatness is directed by the political sympathies of Lord Cobham. Here at Wörlitz the aim is rather more of the Enlightenment, a didactic one, showing the visitor the riches and marvels of the world — natural, scientific and historical — which the wisdom of the ruler had chosen to exemplify in the monuments erected in his park. So at Wörlitz we find an 'iron bridge', modelled directly on Telford's creation in cast iron at Ironbridge in Shropshire (1779), one of the world's wonders among the burgeoning productions of the Industrial Revolution. To set this object in the park at Wörlitz must have been comparable to a modern gardener who would include in his landscape a space module like the one in which Armstrong travelled to the moon. And, to return to the eighteenth century, it was comparable to the monument to Captain Cook which was erected at Stowe in 1778. Looking back at Cook, or Bougainville, or Anson, it is deceptively easy for us to see them all as explorers *in the past*; but at Stowe in 1778, Cook, and his discoveries in the Pacific, were as recent as Armstrong to ourselves, or the far side of the moon. So, at Wörlitz, there was also a 'Pavillon' in which a group of objects brought back from Tahiti by the Forsters, father and son, were displayed — just as there was at Hawkstone in Shropshire, the park which Dr Johnson had visited in the mid-1770s and admired for its sublimity. At the turn of the century, Rodenhurst's *Description of Hawkstone* was amended to include a passage on the 'SCENE AT OTAHEITE', which had at its centre 'a low building, constructed of sticks and reeds...taken from...Captain Cook's Voyages', with a small collection of items from the Pacific inside, and 'with several *Otaheite* plants growing at the door.' While the fragile Tahitian huts at Hawkstone and Wörlitz have long since disappeared, both parks retain their most sublime features — at Hawkstone, 'the GROTTO', looking out over 'an AWFUL PRECIPICE', and 'rugged rocks bulging with terror!'; and at Wörlitz, the volcano.

Unlike the cliffs at Hawkstone, which are a natural, if unusual, formation, the volcano at Wörlitz is wholly artificial. Called 'der Stein', 'the rock' — or 'Vulkankrater', 'Vulcan's crater' — it was made after 1788, and probably more or less completed by 1790. It occupies an island some 300 yards in circumference, on a branch of the main lake, and its cone rises up prominently in the flat terrain to a height of about eighty feet. But it is not a natural hill carved or excavated to look like a volcano; it is enturely man-made, and it is hollow, so that it may 'erupt' when the proper materials are ignited inside. Seen down the lake, from the direction of the castle, it is like a small Stromboli, and the reddish-black stones round the summit do indeed suggest that its crater has been overflowing with fiery material not so long ago (see Plate 38). It seems that its 'eruptions' were planned as nocturnal spectacles — the gardeners who stoked the fires inside the crater with coal, sulphur and other materials were also employed to pump up water to the 'lip' of the crater, where it was made to flow down as a cascade, passing over glass-covered ports set in the side of the crater, through which coloured lights were shone, thus producing the effect of glowing lava. There is an engraving of 1797 which shows this happening, while spectators in a boat watch the lurid scene. Flames and sparks shoot up into the night sky, 'lava' flows down the side of the 'volcano', and the still waters of the lake reflect the light up again on to the overhanging branches of the trees which line the sides of the lake. It is a small recreation of one of Fabris' paintings of Vesuvius by night. But not so small. The *Stein* at Wörlitz is the size of a young hill, and voyagers to Italy would have known that lesser volcanic vents in the vicinity of Vesuvius were no larger. The sublime scenes which travellers had recently seen in Italy, or in the Pacific — Hamilton, Wright of Derby, Hodges — were now reproduced in a garden landscape. Not just described, nor painted, but made in a three-dimensional and amazingly solid form. Such emulation of the wildness of nature is, I am sure, unthinkable in earlier decades of the eighteenth century; though we can see how, little by little, this audacious act could at last become a reality. So far as I know, the first, and for years the only, reference to a volcano within a garden comes in the far-from-serious *Dissertation on Oriental Gardening* of William Chambers, in 1772. Chambers' aim was to show how the Chinese achieved admirable effects in their gardens by means of repeated and violent contrasts. In describing the sublime 'scenes of terror' which alternate in their gardens with 'pleasing' or 'surprising' scenes, he mentions 'founderies, lime-kilns, and glass-works' which simulate the noise and smoke of volcanoes. That is all, and *en passant*, and tongue in cheek, like the use of 'gibbets, with wretches hanging in terrorem upon them'. Fürst Leopold von Anhalt-Dessau was well read, and knew of Chambers — he had built a high-slung, swaying and frightening Chinese 'Kettenbrück' or chain-bridge imitated from Chambers' instructions (which Chambers had drawn from the picture and description in Fischer von Erlach, known also to the Fürst von Anhalt-Dessau) but he was well travelled also, had been to Italy, and had known Hamilton in Naples. The *Stein* at Wörlitz is, like Hamilton's *Campi Phlegræi*, a complicated presentation of a volcano, not merely sublime, but intellectual as well. If we approach the volcano from the other side, we see that a house in Italian style is built on its slopes — and learn that this is called the 'villa Hamilton', in memory of Hamilton's villa from where so many travellers such as Burney and the Prince of Anhalt-Dessau, had viewed Vesuvius (see Plate 39). And if we were to approach the volcano by boat, we should probably land at its foot in a cave-like recess, ornamented with fragments of basalt columns reminiscent of those in Fingal's Cave, discovered in 1772 and swiftly known to the wide circle of Anglophiles and readers of travel literature throughout Europe. Entering a door in this cave, we should then find ourselves in a maze of corridors and chambers in the heart of the 'volcano'. The Prince de Ligne was there soon after the *Stein* was built, and wrote:

> Jumping from your boat, you plunge into caves, catacombs and scenes of horror, through fearsome darkness and stairways. You emerge for a breath of air, right into a fine roman amphitheatre. . .
>
> And now new fears seize you, you wish to escape, and must, perforce, climb up a narrow stairway. The darkness becomes more complete. . . a sudden brightness dazzles your sight. . . a door opens; light gleams from a beautiful statue in the middle of a room, and you realise. . .that it has come through yellow, star-shaped panes in

the roof of this chamber, and that an etruscan entablature is set in the velvet blackness of the stones forming the walls...

You are still less than a third of the way through the tour... A dwelling on another peak of this very rock... It is a house which looks most simple and straightforward from the outside. Inside it is utterly magnificent, the whole of *Herculaneum* (Prince Charles de Ligne, *Coup d'œil sur Belœil*, in *Mélanges*, IX, 1795, pp. 162-6).

Certainly the *Stein* was meant to be sublime. The descriptions of the Prince de Ligne in 1795, of J.G. Grohmann in 1795, of C.A. Boettiger in 1797, of A. Rode in 1798, all agree on this. But they all reveal that the *Stein* had a more complex, general purpose, which I would name didactic, and in which the sublime is only a part. De Ligne had seen this complexity when he wrote 'These are the only gardens where genius and reason go hand in hand' (p. 166). Long before, Pope had exhorted visitors to his rock- and shell-encrusted grotto at Twickenham to 'Approach! Great Nature studiously behold!', and such an appeal might, more or less, have still applied at Hawkstone. But at Wörlitz the many features in the park, and the many sections of the *Stein* in particular, are too diverse to be summed up as 'Great Nature'. They are, rather, a summing up of the world and its marvels, both natural and cultural and scientific. Two of the descriptions, Boetigger's *Reise nach Wörlitz* of 1797, and Rode's *Wegweiser* of 1798, imply this when they both compare the park, the *Stein* and its marvels to the villa and gardens of the Emperor Hadrian at Tivoli, where, according to Spartian, he had wished to recreate memorable scenes from all over the world – for example, the town of Canopus in Egypt, the vale of Tempe in Greece, the portico of the philosophers in Athens – and, for completeness, 'he even made a Hades' – 'etiam inferos finxit' (*Vita Hadriani*, 24).

Vaster, more extravagant, and directed with passionate intensity towards the sublime is the park at Fonthill, created by William Beckford (1760-1844). Beckford inherited the Fonthill estate and an enormous fortune from his father, Alderman William Beckford, who died in 1770, soon after he had completed a new Palladian mansion – Fonthill Splendens – to replace his previous residence, which had been burnt down in 1754. Alderman Beckford had also enlarged a group of fishponds into a 'landscape lake' of the kind made fashionable by Capability Brown, and had built various features on the estate, such as an imposing entrance-gateway, and a cavernous, heavily rusticated boathouse.

In his youth, William Beckford lived extravagantly at Fonthill

Splendens, and travelled extensively, and again extravagantly, on the Continent. In Switzerland he united the fashionable admiration of mountain scenery to the equally fashionable admiration of the solitary genius — on 30 October 1777 he wrote to his half-sister Elizabeth Hervey 'Were I not. . .to see a Genius or two sometimes, to go. . .to the Mountains very often, I should die' (quoted in J.W. Oliver, *The Life of William Beckford*, 1937, p. 22).

A year later, in June 1778, he visited the monastery of the Grande Chartreuse. His impressions, recorded in 'An Excursion to the Grande Chartreuse in the year 1778', are even more ecstatic than those of Gray or Walpole in the 1740s (see p. 138 above. I quote here from Beckford, *The History of. . .Vathek; and European Travels*, 1891, pp. 270-93). The wild, lonely natural setting — 'the vast extent of the forests, frowning on the brows of the mountains' — and its religious connections stimulated his fantasy. His guide pointed out a tall peak, 'which he called the Throne of Moses', and Beckford adds, 'If that prophet had received his revelations in this desert, no voice need have declared it holy ground, for every part of it is stamped with such sublimity of character as would alone be sufficient to impress the idea.' Precipices, waterfalls, mists, lightning, 'the luxuriant foliage of the wood', mountains 'tinged with a pale visionary light', views over 'immense tracts of distant countries', seen from a situation 'too dizzy to allow a long survey', all these were coupled with the solemn life of the monastery. Though only seventeen years old, Beckford had been welcomed warmly and respectfully by the monks, for on his estates was the site of the earliest Carthusian settlement in England, Witham Priory, and they greeted him as the custodian of this relic of their order. On his second night at the Grande Chartreuse, he made a 'wild excursion' into the woods, thinking of the founder, St Bruno, and his life here centuries before. He returned at midnight, and wrote an 'ode' describing an imaginary appearance of the saint:

> Anon, before me full it stood:
> A saintly figure, pale, in pensive mood ('An Excursion', p. 288).

The poem is not a good one — Beckford was only seventeen. But his excitement was extreme. Going to bed, he was slow to fall asleep, and then, he writes:

> I was suddenly awakened by a furious blast, that drove open my casement, and let in the roar of the tempest, for the night was

troubled. In the intervals of the storm. . .the faint sounds of the choir stole upon my ear; but were swallowed up the next instant by the redoubled fury of the gust, which was still increased by the fall of the waters (ibid., p. 289).

It is a scene from a gothic novel — as from 'Sir Bertrand', published in 1774, or from any of the romances which Mrs Radcliffe was to write in the 1790s. Yet Beckford was himself the hero, and a large part of his contribution to the romantic movement comes from his extraordinary, lavish and continued efforts to make the sublime, in its varied manifestations, the major dimension of his own life. As he left the Grande Chartreuse, the monks declared to him 'that if ever [he] was disgusted with the world, here was an asylum' (p. 293).

Beckford came of age in 1781. To celebrate, he held a Christmas party lasting several days at Fonthill Splendens, to which only a small number of his closest friends were admitted. This party was not austere, but wildly exotic. The Palladian formality of his father's mansion was transformed into an Eastern richness. Daylight, and the outside world, were excluded, while the interior was given over to the care of Philippe Jacques de Loutherbourg, an artist already famous for his stage decorations, and whose collaboration with John Webber in designing the décor for *Omai* (in 1785) has already been mentioned. Another artist present at this party was Alexander Cozens (*c*. 1717-86), who encouraged Beckford to read Persian and Arabic stories, and to whom Beckford had already confided, in a letter written in 1777-8, his ambition of building a great gothic tower at Fonthill, enriched with stained glass to provide gorgeous and unusual colour effects. What happened at Beckford's party we do not know; but it is reasonably conjectured that the exotic, occasionally erotic, and frequently sultry pages of *Vathek*, Beckford's oriental-cum-gothic novel, owe part of their inspiration to this event and its rich but oppressive setting. Begun and mostly written in 1782, *The History of the Caliph Vathek* was published in 1786 (see p. 210 below).

Travelling abroad again in 1782, Beckford took with him as his artist Alexander Cozens' son, John Robert Cozens (1752-97), and Cozens' drawings and water-colours of scenes in Italy and France give an idea — though obviously not an exactly parallel one — of the scenery which Beckford himself admired. At Naples, they stayed in the villa Angelica, on the slopes of Vesuvius — Beckford and Sir William Hamilton were related — and Cozens took many views of the volcano and the surrounding countryside. Nearby, Cozens sketched the wooded slopes of the park at Astroni, which extended over the bed and sides of an old crater. Between Naples and Rome, he also sketched the two lakes, Lake Albano and Lake Nemi, which filled the craters of extinct volcanoes, and where, perched on the lip or brink, palaces had been built, Castelgandolfo at Lake Albano, and the Palazzo dei Cesarini at Lake Nemi. After only four months on the Continent, Beckford returned to England, leaving Cozens to stay on in Italy for another year.

In 1783 Beckford married, and his wife bore him two daughters. When she died in 1786 Beckford seems to have decided to withdraw from the world, and to create within his estate at Fonthill a private yet sumptuous paradise, making real the dream which he had cherished since his letter to Alexander Cozens in 1777-8, and which was given an austere yet colourful direction following his visit to the Grande Chartreuse in June 1778. If 'disgusted with the world', he would make his own 'asylum' within his estates at Fonthill. His plans were not established all at once, but by the late 1780s he had begun to plant quantities of trees, and to consider the idea of a ruined 'hermitage' on a hill within his grounds. His activities aroused interest, and neighbouring landlords, not all of them friendly, irritated him by hunting across his land. In 1793, the decisive step was taken — to avoid being observed, and to prevent these incursions, he would have a wall built round his property. At first the wall, twelve feet high, was to be a modest seven or eight miles in circumference, enclosing 509 acres, but when complete it extended for over twelve miles, enclosing 1900 acres. At the centre, Beckford built not a ruined hermitage, but an enormous and eventually complete 'gothic' creation, Fonthill Abbey, the most extensive and expensive of all eighteenth-century follies. This gothic extravagance must be discussed again shortly, in terms of its architectural romanticism; here, it is important to note its solitary situation, and the wildness of the huge park which surrounded and concealed it from outsiders. In its extravagance Beckford's *œuvre* is comparable to that of Fürst Leopold von Anhalt-Dessau. In its extreme insistence on solitude, it is immensely different. The social concern of the German ruler is replaced by a self-isolating and inward-looking concentration. Beckford traced a labyrinth of paths through his private paradise so that he could ride for no less than twenty-seven miles without ever travelling along the same route twice. Or so it was said. Though some areas were cultivated — a medieval herb garden, a rosarium, and an area under glass — and some were exotic, such as the 'American plantation', the general emphasis was on immensity and on wildness. Beckford was not content with the long landscape lake his father had made — Fonthill lake — but made another called Bitham or Bittern lake. This was in a much remoter part of the estate, set in hilly ground, and surrounded with forest trees to make it seem like the crater of one of the extinct volcanoes he and Cozens had seen in Italy. A comparison of Bitham lake itself with one of Claude's paintings of Lake Albano — showing Castelgandolfo on the lip of the crater — and with one of Cozens' water-colours is instructive. While Claude's view (in the Fitzwilliam Museum, Cambridge) is suffused in a characteristically golden sunlight, Cozens' numerous views are tinged with the approach of night. Though the palace in Claude's painting is in the distance, it is a point to which our eyes continually return. Though the landscape as a whole is arcadian, this palace says 'here live many people, the rulers of this peaceful region'. In Cozens' water-colours, in contrast, the trees are thicker, darker, and the landscapes less inhabited. There may be the same, or similar palaces in roughly the same hillside position, but they are now dark, in silhouette, and unconnected with the few peasants or shep-herds whose business takes them elsewhere, under the gloomy trees. I suggest that, while the lake in Claude's painting is, *tout court*, a tranquil lake deep-set in embracing hills, providing the interest and contrast which is its quality, Cozens' lakes are ever so slightly menacing in their dark stillness; and I suggest that when Cozens, and Beckford his patron, and we the spectators all *know* that these were once volcanoes, this knowledge contributes some small part of the solemn feeling which the scenes inspire. (I would venture a similar contrast between the mood of Cozens' water colours, and the oil painting by Corot of Castelgandolfo, painted in 1855-60, and now in the Davies Collection, Cardiff. While Cozens' views are serious, sombre, Corot's painting is once again light in its mood. There is no hint of the 'extinct volcano', and the dancing couple in the foreground is wonderfully carefree and idyllic.)

Beckford's vision of sublime nature was best recorded by J.M.W. Turner, who was one of the few artists to paint the scenes at Fonthill in their brief perfection. In 1799 Beckford commissioned him to make sketches and water-colours of the Abbey and the Fonthill landscape, and several of these are now in the British Museum. One view, 'Land-scape with distant hazy view of Fonthill Abbey, looking up from Bitham lake', shows the lake surely as Beckford wished, deep-set in the forest-thickness of the park. 'The lake looks as if God had made it, it is so natural,' Beckford himself once wrote, and Turner's painting has captured this truth to nature. Unlike the *Stein* at Wörlitz, which is artificial in its complexity, Turner's view of Bitham lake is wholly sublime — wild, solitary, dark, mysterious — and in brooding contrast

191

to the insubstantial shapes of the Abbey which hover in the sunset sky. Wildness is the key to Turner's interpretation of Fonthill, seen again in his sombre view of Beckford's landscape, with the Abbey tower silhouetted, stern and gothic, on the horizon, which was engraved to accompany the anonymous poem 'Fonthill' in *The Anniversary* (1829, see Plate 40). Beckford had sold Fonthill in 1822, and in 1825 the tower of the Abbey had collapsed. Round the ruins of the Abbey, the landscape was already changing. The poem concentrates on the ephemeral nature of what Beckford had tried to create, but adds that

> Turner, with a wizard's power,
> Has fixed in splendour tree and tower;
> And bravely from oblivion won,
> A Landscape steeped in dew and sun.

Splendour and sun, if not the dew, are essential in Turner's landscape with Bitham lake. In the engraving of the second view, equally sublime, the splendour is gaunt and unwelcoming; I know no picture of a 'landscape garden' as forbidding as this. 'The wildness pleases'? The scene is natural, it is sublime; it pleased William Beckford, but it was wilder than any 'garden' had been before, and no one would ever go so far again.

Near the beginning of this history it was proper to remark that the first stirrings of romanticism took place in the midst of a strong current of rational and unromantic attitudes – the Enlightenment. It is equally necessary to remember that, while enthusiasts were fascinated by the sublime, others still delighted in nature's gentler side, or, if they admired the sublime, admired it with circumspection. I have already mentioned that the pastoral tradition continues throughout the century, beside the growing and diverging approval of wild, un-pastoral nature. Marie-Antoinette's Hameau or dairy farm at Trianon was only completed in the 1780s. Parallel with this is the continuing liking for gentle, or moderately gentle, nature, like the exotic but kindly scenes described in *Paul et Virginie*. Wholly characteristic is the attitude of the two 'Ladies of Llangollen', Lady Eleanor Butler and Miss Sarah Ponsonby, who lived together in exile in north Wales from 1778 until nearly half a century later. Their farm cottage was converted into a small gothic treasure house, and their cottage garden was made romantic with – modest – ruins and arches, an ancient font, and a gothic seat where they read the poetry of Ossian. And, in the 1790s, they had, like Wörlitz and like Fonthill, *their* volcanic effects. In 1792 they enlarged their cottage to include a library, and the upper part of the library door was filled with 'a kind of prismatic lantern. . .of cut glass variously coloured'. The light from this lantern 'resembles that of a volcano – sanguine and solemn' and 'gloomily glaring' (Anna Seward, *Collected Letters*, 1811, IV, 99, and *Llangollen Vale*, 1798, p. 8). Yet this light was not frightening – how could it be, in such a 'dear, minute Lyceum'? It was accompanied by the 'aërial music', especially cherished at twilight, of an Æolian harp,

What strains Æolian thrill the dusk expanse,
As rising gales with gentle murmurs play.

Mrs Seward's praise of the 'gentle murmurs' might have been expected. Anna Seward, 'the Swan of Lichfield' (1747-1809), was renowned for her emotional response to nature, and was supposed to 'collect' interesting storms, rather as a modern boy might collect cricketers' signatures. Another visitor was the novelist Mme de Genlis. When she spent the night there in 1792, the Æolian harp had been hung beneath her window. There was a storm, and the harp emitted 'the most melodious sounds . . . a vague and celestial melody . . . an enchanting harmony'; and the sensitive guest reflected: 'It is natural enough that such an instrument should have originated in an island of storms, amid tempests, of which it softens the terrors' (Mme de Genlis, *Memoirs*, 1825, III, pp. 295-6). The two ladies of Llangollen had been glad to welcome her as the authoress of *Adèle et Théodore, ou lettres sur l'éducation* (1782), in which the touching tale was told of a noblewoman imprisoned by a jealous husband for nine years in a dungeon, deprived of all light, and having as only sounds the noise of her odious husband, bringing her bread and water, and the rumble of occasional thunderstorms:

I cannot express, how eager was my desire to hear some kind of noise: when the thunder was especially loud, I could hear it; it is beyond my powers to tell what I felt at these moments; it seemed to me, that I was less alone. I would listen to that majestic sound with rapt attention, and when it had entirely finished, I would relapse into deep, profound sadness (II, p. 298).

Turner too painted a scene with an Æolian harp, 'Thomson's Aeolian harp' in 1809, showing the Thames at Richmond in a Claudian light; but Turner's taste was usually for more violent scenes; and, unlike Mme de Genlis, who gave her heroine so preposterous a situation that it bore no conceivable relationship to reality, he had himself experienced and studied and drawn these phenomena on the spot. Much later, in 1842, he had himself lashed to the mast of a ship in a storm (just as Vernet had done) — and was in this position for four hours. He said afterwards, 'I did not expect to escape, but I felt bound to record it, if I did.'

Turner's studies of sublime Fonthill, in 1799, have been mentioned. The year before, in 1798, he exhibited his 'Buttermere lake with part of Cromackwater. . . a shower' (in the Tate Gallery), which combines mountains and storm clouds with a rainbow in a way which wholly exceeds the Newtonian thought of Thomson or Kent. A similar comparison may be allowed between Turner's views of the 'Pons diaboli' (Plate 2) and the 'Passage of the St Gothard' in Switzerland, taken in 1804, and the crude view of the same scene made by Melchior Füssli and described by Scheuchzer almost a century before (see p. 20 and Plate 1 above). Turner's views are wholly sublime, while Scheuchzer's description and surrounding texts come back repeatedly to the divine origin of these natural marvels, of which we are remined by the rainbow near the waterfall, and the marine shells (relics of the Flood) found on the mountain tops.

Others before Turner had begun to explore the little-known subject of mountain-painting, departing gradually from the formulae of Claude, Gaspard and Rosa. Painters of volcanoes I have already mentioned, but there are also the Swiss painter, Caspar Wolff (1735-83), whose Alpine views in the 1770s are exceptionally gaunt and bleak; and A.L.R. Ducros (1728-1810), who painted scenes of storm-wracked mountains in Italy, such as the melodramatic 'Civita Castellana' (c. 1786), now at Stourhead; and the versatile de Loutherbourg, first noticed by Diderot, in his *Salon* for 1767, as painting a 'Shipwreck' (now in the National-museum, Stockholm) which could reasonably be compared with one of Vernet's. De Loutherbourg worked with Caspar Wolf in 1770-1, and his mountain, rock and storm scenes include 'travellers attacked by banditti' (1793, Southampton Art Gallery), and the 'Avalanche' of 1803, in the Tate Gallery, which was well known to Turner and influenced his 'Fall of an avalanche in the Grisons' of 1810.

Such lists, of painters and their paintings, can be matched by lists of writers — travellers , novelists, poets — who respond as eagerly to mountains and to storms in the last decades of the eighteenth century; long catalogues and analyses have already been written by Daniel Mornet and Paul van Tieghem (see the Bibliography). But having written, at length, of the century's interest in volcanoes, it is not really instructive to go over this ground again. I choose to complete these references with the *Recherches sur les volcans éteints du Vivarais et du Velay* by B. Faujas de Saint-Fond (1778), since they have at one point a connection with another aspect of the sublime, and since, in the late eighteenth century, this connection was not considered inappropriate. Most of Saint-Fond's large volume is, like Hamilton's writings on Vesuvius, detached and scientific. Saint-Fond had read the *Campi Phlegræi* of 1776, and approved Hamilton's text and the *vérité* of Fabris' coloured illustrations. Coming to the château of Rochemaure, however, near Montelimar, he describes and illustrates a part of an extinct volcano on which a ruined, medieval castle is perched; the ruins of the natural phenomenon are matched with the ruins of man's making:

> The château. . .must once have been immense; it is fortified with massive scarps of basalt. . .nothing now but ruin and confusion. Here there are vast chambers, either cast down or open to the sky; at several spots you may see ancient frescoes, which have kept all their original colour; they have figures and coats of arms, the last monuments of feudal rule. . . It is all on a vast scale, but all of it is marked by disorder and destruction (p. 260).

Faujas de Saint-Fond does not write in an emotional way; he thought of himself as a serious investigator (we might say a 'scientist'), and was to continue his volcanic enquiries for many years — in 1798, he was to visit Fingal's cave to examine the basalt columns there. But this one instance, the château of Rochemaure, moves him to perceive the appeal of gigantic dilapidation, and this interest, entirely part of the sublime, is one which is not fully developed until this late stage in the century. The château, he writes, had been built using the natural basalt for its walls. It should, he implies, have been indestructible. 'But time has changed all this, and you see with surprise and admiration the ruins of nature mingled with the ruins of art' (p. 271). Passing through these ruins, he reaches the last courtyard of the château, and is 'truly impressed' by the sight before him:

> It is a spur of basalt of a prodigious height; one is seized with amazement. . . I had a sketch made of this scene. . .the last stronghold, an inaccessible donjon dominating the defences (p. 271. See Plate 41).

Even now, the description is not complete. Climbing to the summit of this highest tower, he is 'seized with astonishment and a kind of horror' at its vertiginous elevation, and *then* discovers a gorge on the other side, a further reminder of the extinct volcano:

> A stream of water clatters down where once flowed a river of fire. . . a vast, profound gash, a kind of abyss all the more fearful, since the colour of the ground here is black and burnt, and there is no doubt that this was once a mouth of the volcano (p. 271).

Nature's most sublime manifestation: a volcano; a gigantic example of man's past violence: a gothic castle; and both ruined, dead, irrecoverable. This is the characteristic of most of the extreme examples of gothic or primitive architecture which are admired, painted or even constructed in the last decades of the century, and it is a characteristic which goes far beyond the amateur, antiquarian enthusiasm which prompts Horace Walpole's Strawberry Hill, or the Gothic Temple at Stowe; and beyond the gentle melancholy of Vernet's or Wilson's Italianate and Claudian scenes, of Young's *Night Thoughts*, and of Sanderson Miller's factitious ruins at Hagley. Now, for the real enthusiasts, only the most extreme will do. Horace Walpole lives on, until 1797, and the gentle ladies of Llangollen will continue to adorn their gothic cottage under the shadow of Strawberry. But the wilder themes of Walpole's *Castle of Otranto* begin to call for more than literary repetition. Though *Otranto* may have been born in the surroundings of Strawberry, admirers of the novel would soon need far rougher settings to satisfy their tastes, and most of them will incorporate ruins in their roughness.

At Hohenheim, close to Stuttgart, Herzog Karl Eugen von Württemberg (1737-93) had not a ruin, but an entire region of ruins built, scattered over several acres of ground to give the impression that here, long ago, there had been an ancient city; in among the ruins, beside them, or built on top were modern rustic dwellings — habitations of later, inferior people, scratching a living in the debris of an earlier age. This scheme was begun in 1774, and had some sixty different features; but the effect was only partially maintained, as the styles were absurdly mixed — gothic, Roman, Chinese, rococo and Moorish. Describing the park in 1786, the Prince de Ligne praises details, such as 'three splendid, partly-buried columns', but blames the indiscriminate mixture of buildings.

Other attempts at this evocation of the distant past were more convincing. At Schloss Fantaisie, a few miles to the west of Bayreuth, the landscape park was adorned with a sinister, and I think unique, complex of catacombs in the 1790s, tunnelled into the limestone slope. Darkly shaded by pine trees, and ornamented with shelves for coffins like an early Christian refuge, they are far gloomier than the fragments of chapel, abbey or cloister which spring up in other eighteenth-century gardens and parks. Going further back into the past, prehistoric monuments were constructed – in England, at Park Place, Remenham, on the Thames, an entire stone circle was set up in 1787, the genuinely prehistoric stones having been transported there from their original site on the island of Jersey. Horace Walpole, so often sarcastic about other people's excursions into the sublime, called it 'little master Stonehenge'. Yet older still, seeking to emulate the original dwellings of the earliest men, are the extraordinarily wild grottoes, mainly in Wiltshire, built by Josiah Lane (1753-1833) in the last years of the century. His most 'primitive' grotto is the jagged masterpiece of 1792 at Wardour Castle, which is like the vertebral crest of a mountain-range – yet hollow. Peering out, we might be inspired with the feelings of a cave-man – I do not exaggerate, for in the same decade, in Egypt at the time of Napoleon's expedition, Geoffroy de Saint-Hilaire claimed that, reclining on the banks of the Nile, he felt stirring within him the 'instincts of the crocodile'.

But Lane's most extensive grotto-work in Wilshire brings us back to William Beckford. At different points on the Fonthill estates Lane made several 'primitive' grottoes. Above ground, there is the 'rude erection in imitation of a Cromlech'; the 'Hermit's Cell' is an artificial cave dug below in the chalky slope; and on the far, eastern side of Fonthill lake is a long, convoluted sequence of caves and chambers, corridors and stairways, with their higher points emerging in the beech woods, and with openings lower down at the level of the lake. In the quarry nearby is a cartouche, carved 'J. L. 1794', and Beckford himself described the grottoes – as 'Lord Mahogany's cave' – in mocking yet delighted terms in his *Modern Novel Writing* of 1796. In 1709, Shaftesbury had claimed that 'the rude *Rocks*, the mossy *Caverns*, the irregular unwrought *Grotto's*' were superior to the 'formal Mockery of Princely Gardens', and, after nearly a century of experiment with shells and crystals and coral, garden-makers had learnt how such 'irregular unwrought *Grotto's*' were to be wrought.

If we are hostile, we must always see the artificiality in these attempts to re-create, to re-enter and re-live ages, cultures and experiences which are not our own. These writers, artists, *dilettanti* or amateurs in the eighteenth century were all trying, clearly or confusedly, with or without intelligence, and with degrees of sincerity or hypocrisy – for fashion forces us, if we are weak, ambitious, idle or sycophantic, into postures which are as fatuous as the trousers we wore five years ago — these men and women in the eighteenth century were trying to respond to Shaftesbury's 'wildness pleases', in its multiple, exciting and difficult forms. In this effort, which was for most of them an effort to escape from what they were — viz. 'men who dwell in the city' — the less successful must often be sneered at as 'artificial'; but we should admire them more than we condemn. Some of them — like Herzog Karl Eugen at Hohenheim — struck before the iron was properly hot; they made a hames of the job. Some — like Vernet or de Loutherbourg — were entangled in the restraints of an earlier tradition, and could barely avoid academic formality even when they laboured to be 'wild'. Some were too timid — like the sweet 'ladies of Llangollen' — and others, like Fürst Leopold of Anhalt-Dessau, were committed to the contrary cause of Enlightenment.

Beckford's achievement, in this end-of-century crescendo of agitation, is to have devoted his genius, wealth and opportunity to a single and sublime *œuvre*. The parts — the park at Fonthill, the grottoes, the Abbey, the treasures it contained, and the writings which expressed his thoughts — may each be discussed separately. But they are all best and properly seen as components of a many-sided work at whose centre William Beckford lived his solitary life, directing and elaborating his creation. The Abbey — unlike the earlier park at Hohenheim — was conceived and built when understanding of what was 'gothic' had advanced far beyond the essentials of battlements and pointed arches; and Beckford had energy and money enough to proceed wholeheartedly. The gigantic enclosure round his park — he himself called it 'the great wall of China' — was adequate to prevent interruption. Fonthill Abbey, conceived, commissioned and directed by Beckford, was designed by the architect James Wyatt, and its complicated, interrupted and evolving building took from 1793 until 1813. When complete — not a 'ruined hermitage', as first imagined — it was the greatest, most daring and most absolute of all gothic follies, taller and more extensive than the great English cathedral churches it emulated (see Plates 40, 42). Though it was not ruined, its isolation in the huge, wild park gave it added strangeness. For all its size, and the incomparable richness of its contents, it was the home of a recluse, with few friends and few visitors. Twenty of the paintings he collected are now in the National Gallery — yet few saw them once they had gone to Fonthill, until they were sold at the great sale of 1823, or at some lesser sale. And in 1822, Beckford left Fonthill for Bath, and never returned.

Soon after Beckford made his early journeys to the Continent, a

French financier, de Monville, had the most extraordinary of all artificial ruins built in his landscape park near Marly. The park, called the
Désert de Retz, was acquired by de Monville in 1774, and over the next
eleven years he built there a variety of garden features, seventeen in all,
including a large 'Chinese house', in which he lived after 1776. The different styles of the buildings did not clash with one another, as they
were carefully dispersed in the landscape. In 1780-1, the 'colonne
détruite', the 'broken column' was built, and this we may compare with
any of the primitive or gothic monuments built elsewhere in the eighteenth century. A few years before, in the mid-1770s, the Marquis de
Girardin had built a small version of the temple of the Sibyl at Tivoli, in
his park at Ermenonville. Others, beginning with William Kent at Stowe
(see p. 34 above) had built versions of this temple, but Girardin was
the first to have it built in a ruined state; and he did so deliberately, to
invest the structure with an elaborate atmosphere of melancholy
rêverie. But Girardin's Temple of Philosophy, as it was called, though
picturesque, though gently romantic, was not sublime. It was too small.
The same comment applies to the 'naumachie', the incomplete and
broken oval line of columns round the lake in the Parc Monceau, and
the Egyptian tomb or pyramid nearby, begun in the late 1770s. Both
are picturesque, beautiful, but too small to be sublime. In contrast, de
Monville's column was gigantic, even in its ruin. It was built to resemble
the lower sections of a Grecian column, with a simple base and plinth
and a section of the main, fluted shaft above, terminating jaggedly at
the top. The column is nearly fifty feet in diameter, and the portion
above ground rises for over sixty feet; but the proportions are such as
to show that the column, *were it to be complete*, would rise to a stupendous 350 or 400 feet. It looks, therefore, like a fragment of a
titanic architecture, whose top must have been destroyed in a storm of
incomparable violence; and which can only have been built by a mighty
race of men, or giants, who have since vanished from the earth. Coming
closer to the ruined cloumn, we see that there are windows set in the
flutings of the shaft. Human beings, ordinary ones, of a stature like our
own, live within the column, like pygmies, or ants, inhabiting the
abandoned fabric of a building designed for creatures far greater than
themselves (see Plate 43). While contemplating the lovely pyramid in
the Parc Monceau, we may enjoy a delicious melancholy; before the
broken column in the Désert de Retz, and in the catacombs at Schloss
Fantaisie, we are invited to be afraid.

Such fear, at the immensity and gloom and vanished power of earlier
monuments and cultures, is powerfully apparent in the later works of

Piranesi. His first *vedute* of Roman monuments, modern and ancient, and his imaginary prison-scenes, the *carceri*, dating from *c.* 1745, have already been discussed (see p. 51 above). We might say, superficially, that Piranesi's later works are simply a more powerful extension of what he had already begun; and it is true that while Piranesi is both important and unique in the eighteenth century, his works illustrate a fairly narrow range of subjects. Overwhelmingly concerned with architecture, he has hardly a traceof the gothic, so dear to his contemporaries, in his work; although his studies of architectural objects, especially of those from Roman antiquity, often show them in decay, and succumbing to the invasive and destructive forces of nature, nature *per se* without an architectural target is as rare as battlements or a pointed arch; even Vesuvius, so fascinating a subject for visitors to Naples in the 1770s, and whose eruption was the means of preserving the ruins of Pompeii which he studied in the same period, appears only once, as a large, gently smoking hill in a decorative border, in one of his engravings. And, quite as great a gap, since so many of his works aim to produce an emotional, rather than an intellectual, response, the people who appear in his *vedute* have only the simplest and barest of features. Emotion is conveyed by their minuteness in relation to the buildings; and by their gestures, of ever-repeated astonishment among the ruins, or whispering conspiracy in the prison scenes. The emotion comes, not through the features of the people in his vast, crumbling or oppressive scenes, but through the immediate exploration which the beholder's eye makes of the buildings before him, invited by the eager or frantic signs of the spectators in the picture, and encouraged by the intricacies of stairways and galleries in the prisons, and by the commanding perspectives leading deep into the ruins of ancient Rome.

In Piranesi's early works, the views of ruins were, by and large, tinged with melancholy, and the views of prison interiors were more directly disquieting, conveying fear. In the 1760s, he re-issued the series of the *carceri*, renaming them *Carceri d'invenzione*, and adding two plates to the original 14. But one look at an earlier plate and its later version shows that Piranesi had not simply brushed the dust off the old plates. The entire composition has been made darker and more solid, with heavier stonework and shadows near-to-impenetrable; and the composition has been made more complicated, with the addition of further steps and stairways, glimpses of more passages or galleries or ladders, which, like the original ways in the first plates, lead the spectator's eye on a perplexing and always unsuccessful journey — a flight — into and round the prison, from which no path leads out (see Plate 19).

From the 1750s he recorded the buildings of ancient Rome, with an overriding wish to demonstrate their greatness as persuasively as possible — especially in contrast to the architectural remains of the Greeks. In an amazing series of works issued from the late 1750s until just before his death in 1778, Piranesi presented the heroic grandeur of all kinds of Roman architecture — palaces, funeral monuments, aqueducts, fortifications, temples — with the passion of a propagandist. Showing views, or plans, or details of the buildings in their original state, he stresses the size, complexity, exactness, difficulty and magnificence of the Roman achievement — above all the gigantic size; and recording these buildings in their present state, he stresses the wonder of these qualities by showing how puny and crude their modern inhabitants appear, small and ignorant, incapable of building such marvels for themselves, while the surging and enveloping growths of moss, creepers and bushes remind us of the centuries which separate these peasants from the glory of Rome.

In the early 1750s he began work on a series of plates — 250 in all — which appeared in 1756 as the four volumes of the *Antichita Romane*. In volume IV, Plate IX is of the 'Foundations of Hadrian's Mausoleum'. In this his scene cuts out not only all nearby modern accretions to the masonry, but blocks out the superstructure, which we feel to be towering up beyond the top of the frame. Our first glance shows a complicated series of buttresses rising precipitously from the bottom to the top of the engraving, with platforms or ledges at several points. The stones are evidently hewn exactly to size, and laid with scrupulous accuracy, yet their size is gigantic, as we see when we look more closely. The 'closer glance' reveals the human beings who have clambered on to the ledges — among the tiniest figures in relation to buildings which Piranesi ever drew. On the lowest platform, the figures stand only a fraction taller than a single course of stones. One peers downwards over the edge, while another gestures, possibly upwards to another waving man far higher up and minutely silhouetted against the sky. Were this a painting by Caspar Wolff, the 'foundations' would be a mountain in the Alps, and the men mountaineers. Yet it is a building — just *part* of a building — made by men. The discovery of the human beings in the engraving produces a vertiginous effect — on the central ledge of this 'cliff' of masonry, another man clings precariously. He could easily fall, like the jumble of blocks of stone at the bottom of the scene. Many times larger than the nearby man on the lowest ledge, they bulge out, over the edge of the engraving, and the shadow of the lowest, most jutting stone spreads downwards, darkening the text which runs beneath and, I think, threatening the modern beholder. We, not merely the persons within the picture, are amazed and frightened by this monstrous memorial.

In the next years, and into the mid-1760s, Piranesi prepared and published many more plates to demonstrate the architectural and engineering achievements of the Romans, and all share some of the emotional technique apparent in the 'Foundations of Hadrian's Mausoleum'. In 1762 he published the *Descrizione e disegno dell' emissario del lago Albano*, a study of the 1500-yard long tunnel built by the Romans as an outlet for the waters of Lake Albano, together with an appendix, *Di due spelonche...*, on two caves on the shore of Lake Albano which had been enlarged and ornamented in Roman times. Some of the plates in these two collections continue the awesome presentation of antique masonry in savage settings reminiscent of Salvator Rosa (unlike the 'Foundations of Hadrian's Mausoleum', which has no vegetation), and the combination of gigantic size, intense gloom and natural wildness runs parallel to the increase in terror apparent in the re-issued *carceri*. In the 'View of the entrance to the Emissarium', one side of the foreground is cluttered with jagged baulks of timber; the other side shows the handful of spectators. So much for the present age. The rest of the engraving shows the colossal masonry, dominated by an archway of stupendous size and majestic simplicity. The little light reaching this cavernous scene comes obliquely from above, and shows, beside the archway, trees of comparable stature growing from the upper ledges in the masonry. Hardly any foliage is shown, merely the dark, contorted trunks — apparently as dark, as old and as strong as the building from which they grow, and with which they are united. In this view of antique architecture Piranesi has moved far beyond the melancholy of his first *vedute* of Roman ruins. Here we experience an awe, a fear which is aroused in a way which matches Burke's prescription of size, power and darkness as ingredients contributing to the terror which is 'the ruling principle of the sublime'. I would add Burke's 'solitude' to these ingredients in Piranesi's views, since, although there are usually several spectators in each of the *vedute* — they 'give scale' — these spectators, like the beholders outside the picture, are isolated from the scene which is the subject of the picture. In his first *vedute* Piranesi may have suggested melancholy, since the (beautiful and admirable) ruins were gradually being destroyed by the forces of neglect, nature and time. As there was a 'struggle', the spectators, ourselves, might 'take sides', and participate emotionally. In this *veduta*, nature and the antique architecture are united, not enemies — we do not think of the

'Emissarium' as a building which is 'crumbling away' — and they are united against the inadequacy of the present age. Against ourselves: hence the fear.

In the last years of his life, in 1777-8, Piranesi travelled to the south of Italy, to the gulf of Salerno, to draw the ruined temples at Paestum. Most of his drawings are in the Soane Museum, in London, and the twenty engravings from these were completed and published by his son Francesco Piranesi in 1778, just after his father's death, as the *Différentes vues...de Pesto*. These temples — three of them, built by Greek colonists in the 'primitive Doric' style—had been gradually 're-discovered' by western Europeans in the middle years of the eighteenth century. At first they were a curiosity, not an inspiration, rather like the primitive monuments on the island of Tinian recorded during Anson's voyage in the 1740s, or like the first garden temples built in the primitive Doric style at Hagley and Shugborough in 1758. When the architect James Adam had seen the temples at Paestum in 1761, he said they were 'of an early, an inelegant and unenriched Doric that affords no detail and scarcely produces two good views', and the clear but pedestrian engravings in Thomas Major's *Ruins of Paestum* of 1768 show that the ruins were extensive and in the primitive Doric style, but do not reveal any emotional response in the artist. This Piranesi's views undoubtedly do (see Plate 44). In a curious *volte-face*, having scorned Greek architecture in favour of Roman for so many years, Piranesi uses the simpler and heavier forms of primitive Doric to stress the immense age of the ruins; and though the forms are essentially more clear-cut than those of the later Roman styles, he shows in the heavy weathering of each section of every column and in the luxuriant hairiness of the plants growing from the cracks in the stonework how remote and mysterious the creation of these temples must have been. By 1778 we are into the years when the sublime is triumphant all over Europe; it is in 1780-1 that Monville had the 'ruined column' built at the Désert de Retz, and although this monument has a simple base at the foot of the column and cannot therefore count as 'primitive Doric', its emotional aim of an Ozymandian dismay in the beholder is like Piranesi's in depicting the temples at Paestum. A year later, while travelling with Beckford in 1782, J.R. Cozens went to Paestum and sketched the temples. In each of the two finished water-colours (now in the Oldham Art Gallery) which he made from these sketches, it is fascinating to note that he filled in the sky with storm clouds, not apparent in the original sketches, to make the desolate ruins even more a part of nature, and further from 'men who dwell in the city'.

This 'Ozymandian dismay' at the disproportion between the achievement of the past and the present beholder, coupled with the relentless, destructive advance of time, is a part of the early romantics' vision of previous ages, decades before Shelley's poem of 1817. In the work of Piranesi it is, as I have said, transmitted from the picture to ourselves, rather than to some principal figure within the composition. But another work, roughly contemporary with Piranesi's last drawings of the temples at Paestum and with Monville's 'ruined column' at the Désert de Retz, states this moment of dismay, isolation and fear in an intensely personal way. It is the chalk and sepia wash study of 'The Artist in despair over the magnitude of antique fragments' (*c.* 1778-80) by Henry Fuseli (see Plate 45). At the bottom of the picture, a human figure, the 'artist', sits beside a great pedestal, on which he rests one elbow, his face hidden by his hand. On the pedestal is a gigantic foot, of stone, as long as his entire body, and of far greater volume. The artist's other hand and arm, fully extended, stretch across the instep of the foot but only reach part-way. On another pedestal, above the foot, is an equally gigantic hand, with its index finger not rigidly, but gently, extended. The gesture of the hand is calm and confident. The two antique fragments indicate simply yet fully how great the entire statue must have been, and how masterful its pose – in contrast to the limp and despairing figure of the artist, who may only sit and grieve at the destruction wrought by time, and at his inadequacy to recreate such awe-inspiring works of art.

Burke would again have seen the sublime in this study – the huge yet fractured nature of the sculpture, the despair and isolation of the artist. Many of the early romantics were fascinated by the wildness of the feelings which they experienced in 'sublime' situations; Fuseli's study illustrates but one of the innumerable forms of extreme emotion which were explored, exploited, suffered and enjoyed at this time – and most often with the 'artist', the writer or painter himself as the distinctive central figure, the 'hero'.

The fascination with the particular vision, and the confidence that this vision was of value precisely because it was particular rather than one common to many, is wholly characteristic of Fuseli and his art. Johann Heinrich Füssli, known later by his English name Henry Fuseli (1741-1825), spent most of his long career glorifying the person and the experiences of the exceptional individual: himself, the artist, other artists, and great and extraordinary men and women of history and mythology – great, that is, in terms of the sublime. Though scenes of sublime nature did not much interest him, the sublime in human life provides the inspiration for practically all his art. He excels in capturing moments of grandeur, tension, violence; of obscurity, doubt and mystery; of pain, madness and fear. His career and achievements are remarkable in several ways – first, for his glorification of the sublime in the life of the individual, and second (at least in this history) for his exceptional role as a transmitter of the ideas and enthusiasms of art and literature. Living in Zürich until he was twenty-two, in an intelligent and artistic family, he left for London in 1764, moved from London to Italy in 1770, back to Switzerland in 1778, and from 1779 until his death he lived in England. In a lesser excursion to France in 1766 he met Rousseau. The following year he published, anonymously, a passionate, breathless *apologia* for Jean-Jacques, the *Remarks on the Writing and Conduct of J.J. Rousseau*. With his long life and such wide and lengthy travels, he had as broad an acquaintance with European culture as any man of his age. Before leaving Switzerland he had become a devotee of Shakespeare, and translated *Macbeth* into German. At this time he came to know Johann Jakob Bodmer (1698-1783), the critic and translator, and from him learnt to admire, or worship, Dante, and medieval German literature. When he returned to Zürich for a while in 1778, he saw the aged Bodmer again, who was nearing the completion of his translation of Homer's *Iliad* and *Odyssey* into German – it was published in 1781. After the 1778 meeting Fuseli began a moving picture of himself 'in conversation with J.J. Bodmer', now in the Kunsthaus, Zürich (see Plate 46). Bodmer sits on one side, looking sternly across at Fuseli, his right hand extended in admonition. His index finger has the same full assurance as the index of the 'antique fragment' which Fuseli sketched in Rome. On the other side is Fuseli. Like the 'artist' beside the giant foot, he is passive, though here he is receptive and meditative, not despairing. One hand rests on his knee, the other with two fingers touching his temples, supports his head. He does not look at Bodmer, but concentrates on the old man's message, his gaze directed in front of him. In the background, filling much of the space between the old man and his young disciple, is a large yet shadowy bust of Homer, which hovers over them, mysterious and almost ghostlike. The central points of the composition form a diamond shape – presiding at the top is Homer, the genius of ancient times; to one side, Bodmer, the great teacher of the last age, looking keenly at his pupil, the hope of the future, on the other; at the bottom, Bodmer's hand also points directly at Fuseli's face; while Fuseli's finger-tips, touching his head, reinforce the concentration on the young man in this moment of inspiration. It is, we might say, a conceited picture, for Fuseli has shown himself as

205

the spiritual inheritor of both Bodmer and Homer. We might see even greater conceit in Fuseli's attitude if we compare his presentation of himself in this painting with Michelangelo's painting of Adam in the 'Creation of Man' in the Sistine Chapel. Fuseli was profoundly and permanently influenced by Michelangelo's vision of the human body, and in taking over Adam's gentle and passive pose to depict himself he was as a draughtsman doing no more than any other figure-painter of his time might have done. Yet the thematic connection is audacious. In the 'Creation of Man', God reaches through space, and with his finger-tip gives life, energy and purpose to Adam's languid clay. In Fuseli's painting, the artist himself is likewise languid, to be inspired by the brooding Homer and the stern-eyed mentor, Bodmer. But while Adam, in Michelangelo's painting, looks mildly and almost blankly towards his Creator — waiting for the divine touch — Fuseli's head has turned away from Bodmer, and he thinks, or dreams into the future, absorbed with what *he* now has to do.

Fuseli's vision of himself as an exceptional person — as a *genius* — is at the centre of the early romantic fascination with the individual. If wild nature was more interesting than nature in a gentle mood, so too was the individual, the exceptional person, in preference to the ordinary and unexceptional man. The ways in which the individual saw himself were varied, but they all accepted separation from the 'men who dwell in the city'. At the most exalted level, there was the man with more talent, far more talent, than the rest: the *genius*. Comparable with the *bard*, his creative power was rarely the result of formal education such as society could provide, but came either from solitary (and there-fore exceptional) study, or as a gift of nature, unsolicited, an accident of birth, or through communion with the sublime forces of nature — again a solitary business. Fuseli's studies of himself made in the late 1770s and 1780s show this kind of man, derived from the ideas of Blackwell, Young, Diderot and Rousseau. Beside the genius was the *hero*, saving his people through some exalted and incomparable act of sacrifice, beyond the power and even beyond the comprehension of ordinary men. The hero, like the genius, is a solitary figure, misunder-stood, exiled, hunted; and his sublime achievements will often cost him his life. Fuseli, and his contemporaries, found just such figures in the tragedies and history plays of Shakespeare, or in the cantos of Dante. Given the proviso that the character was exceptional, Fuseli found as much to admire, artistically and emotionally, in the victims, sufferers and even the villains whom Shakespeare or Dante described. His first paintings submitted to the Royal Academy in the 1770s were both of scenes from Shakespeare, one of 'Lady Macbeth sleepwalking', and in the same period he made many illustrations from the *Inferno*, including studies related to the story of Ugolino (contemporary therefore with Gerstenberg's play of 1768). His most striking drawing, of 1774, shows Virgil and Dante on the ice of Cocytus, where the heads of various sinners protrude. Dante has just reached the heads of Ugolino and his enemy and murderer, Ruggiero. As Ruggiero starved Ugolino and his sons to death, he has been condemned to have his own head gnawn by Ugolino for the rest of time; and Ugolino pauses in this task to tell Dante his tragic history. The horror which could be gleaned from these scenes in the *Inferno* appealed to him so strongly that he even 'invented' an episode of a Dantesque kind, to do with the crusader Ezzelin Bracciaferro, who, after he returned from his travels, suspected his wife had been unfaithful, and executed her. At least two of Fuseli's sketches for this 'sublime' story exist, one of 1779, showing Ezzelin 'musing over the dead Meduna' (in the British Museum: Fuseli produced a painted version of this composition in the same year), and the other of 1817 of 'Ezzelin and the Repentant Meduna' (in the Kunsthaus, Zürich). In each composition, the hero is alone — isolated, before the execution, by his implacable virtue, and isolated afterwards by the ferocity of his revenge, and the restless fear that his wife may, after all, have been faithful. Pain, isolation, fear, despair, these emotions are all felt in the contemplation of Ugolino and the vast gallery of Dante's villains and victims. In his essay on dramatic theory of 1774, the *Anmerkungen übers Theater*, J.M.R. Lenz even suggested that the whole (not just a part) of the *Divine Comedy* would be suitable as a subject for the 'new' theatre he proposed, that Hell would be a fine stage setting, and that the proper author must be none other than 'ein Genie' — a *genius*.

Finding themselves at odds with traditional attitudes — like those of Dr Johnson, or Voltaire — the early romantics made a virtue of their solitude, and admired — or professed to admire — the solitary man, the outcast, the exile, whatever the reason for his solitude, since, in itself, it implied a distinction from those who went along with the crowd. In this vein Fuseli paints 'The Blinded Polyphemus' (1803), to illustrate the pathetic moment when the giant, tormented by the pain of his single, blinded eye, feels the backs of his sheep as they pass by him out of his cave, carrying Odysseus and his men beneath them. We may compare with this Francisco Goya's monotype 'Giant' of *c.* 1800, who broods, silhouetted against the night sky, isolated by his size from the rest of mankind; while later, in 1809 or 1810, Turner — the painter of light — made a first sketch entitled 'Ulysses Poly', which at last in 1829 evolved into 'Ulysses deriding Polyphemus' (in the National Gallery, London). I am sure a part of the poignancy of this master-work lies in the spectator's knowledge that Polyphemus, shadowy and immense beside the mountain, is blind to all the sunset glory of the scene.

Extreme though these situations and characters may be, Fuseli goes further still in his pursuit of sublime experience – to depict people so overwhelmed by the strength of their feelings that they have gone mad; or suffer hallucinations and nightmares; and beyond these – with Fuseli, there is no distinct dividing-line – he draws episodes involving the supernatural, witches with apparitions, and ghosts and demons. In 1785, he exhibited 'The Mandrake', of which Horace Walpole said 'Shockingly mad, mad, mad, madder than ever', and his etching of 'The Witch and the Mandrake' of c. 1812-13 confirms the uncanny mood of the painting – night, clouds across the moon, an owl in flight; with an ugly, barefoot witch crouching down on the mountain-side to lift the Mandrake, half root, half man, and ready to effect her evil purposes. In 1772, he first attempts a composition called 'The Mad House', which was used again in 1792 as an illustration for the English edition of Lavater's *Essays on Physiognomy*, and of this picture Lavater commented:

Fury and force, an energy uniformly supported, and ever active. . . Spectres, Demons, and madmen; fantoms, exterminating angels; murders and acts of violence – such are his favourite objects (quoted in N. Powell, *The Drawings of Henry Fuseli*, 1951, p. 41).

In 1772 it would have been less likely for such a résumé to have been made of Fuseli's repertoire, but by 1792 Lavater had plenty of examples to choose from. From the late 1770s onwards, Fuseli's illustrations and paintings from Shakespeare, practically all of sublime scenes, included a sizeable number of ghostly apparitions – from *Macbeth, Richard III, Henry VI, Hamlet* – while the witches from *Macbeth* provided a variety of spectral scenes, culminating in *The Three Witches*, painted soon after 1783. *Lady Macbeth Sleepwalking*, one of his first submissions to the Royal Academy, he painted a second time in 1781-4. Other literary and mythological sources provided other suggestive and supernatural moments, one of the most grisly being a sketch of c. 1774-8 to illustrate Odysseus' visit to the underworld (*Odyssey*, xi, 96ff.), where Odysseus holds back with his sword the clustering souls of the dead, while the ghost of the prophet Teiresias laps up the sacrificial blood which Odysseus has poured into a trench. Blood – the life denied to departed souls, and, though Fuseli probably did not reflect on this, the same blood which vampires so desperately crave (see p. 109 above). Among Fuseli's most famous paintings is *The Nightmare* (1781), now in the Institute of Arts, Detroit (see Plate 47). On a dimly visible couch, a young woman in a nightdress lies on her back, her head and extended arms hanging limply downwards. On her belly squats a dwarf, swarthy, misshapen, hardly human in form, while nearer to her knees and feet, the head of a horse looks through the curtains into the gloomy room, its eyes blazing. I need hardly repeat what followers of Sigmund Freud have read into this painting — they might even be right, seeing here an expression of Fuseli's own sexual fantasies. But for Fuseli and his contemporaries, *The Nightmare* and its predecessors (*The Changeling* of 1780, for example) and successors up to *The Erinyes beside Eriphyle's Corpse* of 1810, and the similar painting of 1821, were pictures expressing the essence of that familiar dream in which we lie powerless and terrified, while a demon — incubus, devil, ghost or vampire — squats, crushing our resistance, and draining our life away. Again, Burke would acknowledge this as part of sublime, when it is dark, and we are alone, and a prey to ugly fantasies and 'the notions of ghosts and goblins'.

Others at this time, following Walpole in *The Castle of Otranto*, were tempted by the thrill of the supernatural. For decades, the *philosophes* and their fellow-travellers had rejected all belief in ghosts, apparitions and the like as even more feeble-minded than a belief in revealed religion. We may be glad that with this, witches were no longer burned to death, but by the 1770s there was at least a *hankering* after the supernatural thrills which were so lacking in the reasoned world of the *encyclopédistes*. Fuseli, like Walpole, was a leader in responding to this need, and both saw that they must give to their versions of the supernatural a certain remoteness from the clear light of the present day. *Otranto* was in its very subtitle 'A Gothic Story', while Fuseli's spectres are mostly linked to glorious literature — in the past. Even *The Nightmare*, which you or I may experience or fear, occurs in darkness, far from the midday sun.

The followers of Walpole, therefore, and of Fuseli, mostly chose to shroud their ventures into the other world in darkness, in settings of a ruinated, fear-inducing gloom, or in ages and countries far removed from western Europe at the end of the eighteenth century. One of the few French 'gothic novels', *Le Diable amoureux*, by Jacques Cazotte (1772), takes the readers by night to the — Piranesian — obscurity of Roman ruins at Portici to witness the hero make a pact with the devil.

The pact is Faustian — give me pleasure now, and you have my soul later. And in such antique surroundings, we are less incredulous when a camel's head responds to the daring summons, exactly like the horse's head in Fuseli's *Nightmare*, to ask in abrupt Italian 'Che vuoi?' — 'What d'you want?' A similar pact, but more serious and with greater rewards and a direr punishment, is struck between the devil and the Spanish monk Ambrosio at the end of the century, in M.G. Lewis' *The Monk* (1796), and in between there is a lumber-room full of gothic novels — the best by Mrs Ann Radcliffe — which offer mysterious noises, lights in the distance, hurrying shrouded forms, and ghosts — or at least the tingling dread for fifty or a hundred pages that ghosts are somewhere to be feared.

The experience of the supernatural is a solitary business. Rare are the ghosts in a happy crowd on a hot summer's day. Cheery, sunlit crowds have nothing to do with ghosts, or the sublime, or the solitary genius. The genius of the early romantics is of necessity a lonely figure — even if the solitude is only partly desired. William Beckford in his own life and conduct at Fonthill Abbey was patently an 'eccentric', a man living remote from the 'centre', viz. the city; and long before he himself began to reside in Fonthill Abbey, his oriental-cum-gothic novel *Vathek*, begun in 1782 and published in 1786, has in its finest and sombre closing pages the picture of an outcast, condemned, noble and unique — Eblis, the ruler of the infernal empire. His subjects are the damned, and are inspected and joined by the Caliph Vathek and his beautiful companion Nourounihar. This evil couple have long persevered in wickedness, and make a pact — like Faust, or the hero of *Le Diable amoureux*, or Lewis' monk Ambrosio — to be allowed to visit Eblis' underground realm.

Within, they descend 'with an ardent impetuosity', as if 'falling from a precipice', and are led to a place which 'though roofed with a vaulted ceiling, was so spacious and lofty that at first they took it for an immeasurable plain' (*The History of the Caliph Vathek*, 1891, p. 84). Gorgeous in the extreme, with the pavement strewed over with gold dust and saffron, 'censers in which ambergris and the wood of aloes were continually burning', and tables bearing 'a profusion of viands' and 'wines of every species', the infernal halls are enlivened by 'a throng of Genii and other fantastic spirits of each sex' dancing lasciviously in troops. Yet the scene is not one of delight, but gloom and terror, for Eblis' subjects are in perpetual agony:

a vast multitude was incessantly passing, who severally kept their right hands on their hearts, without once regarding anything around them; they had all the livid paleness of death; their eyes, deep sunk in their sockets, resembled those phosphoric meteors that glimmer by night in places of interment. Some stalked slowly on, absorbed in profound reverie; some, shrieking with agony, ran furiously about, like tigers wounded with poisoned arrows; whilst others, grinding their teeth in rage, foamed along, more frantic than the wildest maniac. They all avoided each other, and, though surrounded by a multitude that no one could number, each wandered at random, unheedful of the rest, as if alone on a desert which no foot had trodden (*Vathek*, pp. 84-5).

'Frozen with terror', Vathek and Nourounihar ask, 'why these ambulating spectres never withdraw their hands from their hearts'. An immediate answer is denied them, and they are instead ushered into the throneroom. There, 'upon a globe of fire, sat the formidable Eblis' (p. 85). This ruler has no doubt a resemblance to Milton's Satan in *Paradise Lost*; but the Halls of Eblis are in part a memory of the 'Egyptian Hall' and neighbouring rooms of Fonthill Splendens, transformed by de Loutherbourg into the scene of an oriental fantasy for Beckford's private, three-day coming-of-age party at the end of 1781. Eblis, the prince of darkness, was also to resemble Beckford himself in later years — even if Beckford did not know this in 1782:

His person was that of a young man, whose noble and regular features seemed to have been tarnished by malignant vapours; in his large eyes appeared both pride and despair; his flowing hair retained some resemblance to that of an angel of light.

And when he spoke, his voice was 'more mild than might be imagined, but such as transfused through the soul the deepest melancholy'. Beautiful, but damned; corrupt but admirable, and so in the last decades of the eighteenth century immensely more appealing than an ordinary person.

Eblis welcomes the daring couple into his empire, 'to enjoy whatever this palace affords' (p. 86). Encouraged, Vathek and Nourounihar begin to make the tour, led by a Giaour. They see more melancholy inhabitants, noble and once incomparably powerful — the Preadamite Kings, among them the loftiest, Soliman Ben Daoud — and each holds his right hand 'motionless on his heart'. Soliman tells his story, and explains at last that he is 'in torments, ineffable torments!' With his last words, 'an unrelenting fire preys upon my heart', he 'raised his hands towards heaven. . . and the Caliph discerned through his bosom, which was transparent as crystal, his heart enveloped in flames' (p. 88).

Vathek and Nourounihar are seized with fresh horror, and their guide the Giaour then confirms that the same fate will soon befall them. In the concluding paragraphs we read that 'their hearts immediately took fire', and they 'plunged into the accursed multitude, there to wander in an eternity of unabating anguish' (p. 92).

Beckford's ambitions to build a 'ruined hermitage', fired by his visit to the Grande Chartreuse in 1779, have already been discussed; and his passionate wish for privacy, and the miles of wall which he had built round the Fonthill estate. The fantasies of *Vathek* are also a part of his dream, private, unique, extravagant and tragic at the same time – and both Beckford's 'great wall of China' and the intensely private garden-paradise it enclosed, with the costly gothic tower-palace-abbey he was building for himself alone at the centre are among the influences which fired the imagination of Coleridge, when in 1798 he wrote of the 'stately pleasure-dome' built by Kubilai or 'Kubla Khan' in Xanadu, set in the centre of an immense and fabulously exotic garden park.

> So twice five miles of fertile ground
> With walls and towers were girdled round

wrote Coleridge; and though he thought first and foremost of Kubilai and China, Beckford's Fonthill, with its wall, paradise and solitary, eccentric writer-builder-owner within were also a part of the inspiration of 'Kubla Khan'.

While Fuseli was celebrating the sublimity of the genius in his drawings and paintings, his contemporaries in Germany were celebrating the genius, the rebel, the outcast and the outlaw in literature. These writers, forming what is known as the 'Sturm und Drang', cannot be considered a 'movement' – they did not all know each other, for a start – but they have a common interest in their advocacy of a freer, more turbulent and less conventional way of conduct (as exemplified by the behaviour of the genius), and their opposition to traditional restraints, both in the arts and in society. The name 'Sturm und Drang' – 'Storm and Stress' – is the title of a play written in 1776 by F.M. Klinger (1752-1831), and was applied, after the event, rather to the general *mood* of these writers than to any conscious literary association between them. Klinger himself first wished to call his play *Wirrwarr* – 'Turmoil' – which exemplified the general neglect of order which is apparent both in their work and in the unruly characters they depict. While their dramatic theory was mainly derived from Diderot, they turned to Shakespeare for practical examples of a free and 'natural' drama, and some − Herder and Hamann − even reproached Diderot for writing such timid plays when his theory was so bold. Their ideas of the genius and the 'natural' man came, like Fuseli's, from Young, Diderot and Rousseau. The drama of the 'Sturm und Drang' begins properly with Gerstenberg's *Ugolino* in 1768, and for the next two decades a torrent of 'wild' plays appears. Gerstenberg himself began to write a play, *Der Waldjüngling* (c. 1771) about that most solitary 'natural' character, the 'wild boy of the woods', but did not complete it. While Shakespeare's 'wildness' may be seen as a source for much of the passionate dialogue of *Ugolino* − scenes from *Timon of Athens* come easily to mind − the prescriptions of Rousseau in the *Discours sur. . . l'inégalité* lie behind the *Waldjüngling* − indeed, Gerstenberg's short manuscript includes two sides of preparatory notes in which direct quotations from the *Discours* appear.

Although there are many writers who may be considered as part of the general movement of the Sturm und Drang, one writer, Goethe, is outstanding for his full and varied treatment of the solitary genius in the early 1770s. Johann Wolfgang Goethe (1749-1832) had a life and travels as long and as varied as Fuseli's, and a career of far greater distinction. Unlike Fuseli, whose fascination with the *extremes* of human experience provides the continuing inspiration for practically all his art, and who is, therefore, the principal artist to depict the human manifestations of the sublime, Goethe is a writer whose concerns and whose works have an almost universal scope. Before 1770-1, his early writings had been mostly restrained and traditional in style and content, and in the later 1770s − approximately from 1776, after his arrival at Weimar the year before − his work acquired a seriousness and breadth which, while not rejecting the sublime, no longer allows it the central importance which it has for Fuseli throughout his career.

In 1770-1, however, Goethe came into lengthy contact with Johann Gottfried Herder (1744-1803), and through him received instruction and inspiration to study Young, Ossian (some of whose poetry Goethe translated) and Shakespeare, and the 'national' poetry and art − such as gothic architecture − of northern countries, while learning to suspect and even reject the formal and rational attitudes of the French *philosophes*. In 1771, Goethe wrote his first draft of the play *Götz van Berlichingen* (called at first *Geschichte Gottfriedens von Berlichingen mit der eisernen Hand*), which has for dramatic precedent Shakespeare's history plays, with their lengthy action, multitudinous *dramatis personae*, and frequent changes of scene from one country to another, from town to battlefield, and from noble palace to peasant's cottage, including settings of an exhilirating wildness, caves, forests, desert and wilderness, and conditions as wild again — storms and tempests by sea and land. Above all, the dramatists of the Sturm und Drang saw Shakespeare as a genius who was unhampered by the Aristotelian 'unities' and unconcerned by the French regard for the 'bienséances'. Free, therefore, to write as he wished (or so they thought), he could present all manner of violence on the stage — battles, fights and murders — and all manner of wild, exalted and extraordinary human beings: exiled kings, usurpers, villains, murderers; madmen, fools, fairies and monsters, witches and even ghosts. Goethe had already spoken on Shakespeare to an audience in his parents' house in Frankfurt in October 1771 (the essay *Zum Schäkespears Tag*, not printed until 1854), and in *Götz von Berlichingen* he manages to compress many of the titanic qualities which 'Shakespearian' drama was thought to possess. Above all, Götz himself is an exceptional character, strong, violent and passionate; hard, cruel even in his determination, and inspired to heroic deeds by his love of freedom. The 'freedom' of the dramatist is as important as the personal and political freedom for which the hero lives and dies — the scene-changes are so numerous as to seem capricious, introduced precisely because variety, contrast and violence on the stage had been forbidden for so long. Characteristic, and echoing moments from battles in *Henry VI, Richard III* and *Macbeth*, is the brief scene in Act III, 'Forest beside a bog', where two fugitives from the fighting meet. Hardly have they spoken to each other when they hear horsemen galloping up; they hide, one up a tree, the other in the rushes at the edge of the bog. Götz and his horsemen pass through (i.e. across the stage), and when they have gone, one fugitive climbs down from his tree:

First Soldier (*climbs out of the tree*). This is no good. Michel! He doesn't answer! Michel, they've gone! (*He goes towards the marsh.*) Michel! O God! He's sunk. Michel! — He can't hear me, he's drowned. You're dead now, you coward. — We're beaten. Enemies, enemies everywhere!
    Götz. . . on horseback
    Götz. You! Stay there, or you die!
    First Soldier. Mercy! Don't kill me!
    Götz. Your sword!

To turn from Gerstenberg's *Ugolino* of 1768 to the 1771 version of *Götz* is rather like watching, first, a firm, solid, regular cauldron in which a brew of immense potency is bubbling, but remains within the cauldron; and next a similar brew which has surged up and out of the cauldron, and runs boiling and uncontrolled in all directions; while the container, the cauldron, is forgotten. Goethe sent his friend Herder a copy of his play, which he read early in 1772, and Herder wrote back to him ruefully, 'Shakespeare has ruined you.' To this, in July 1772, Goethe wrote back that the essential in drama of this 'Shakespearian' kind was the unity of the poet's feeling – in other words, the *instinctive* control which is the gift of the genius. Herder had already written an essay on Shakespeare, which appeared in 1773 in *Von deutscher Art und Kunst*, which he amended before publication to conclude with praise of Goethe and his play, which was a 'monument' in the German tongue to the spirit of Shakespeare.

Herder may have worried that Shakespeare's influence had led Goethe astray. Yet it was Herder himself who had transmitted to Goethe the ardent belief in the unique and godlike power of the creative genius – derived from Shaftesbury.

Tempestuous – far more than Shaftesbury's – and changing from poem to poem, and even in the course of a single poem, Goethe's attitudes are at this time constant in one respect: the emphasis he gives to the importance of the genius. True to the spirit of the time, he sees this genius as *himself*, or at the least a facet of himself. In 'Wandrers Sturmlied' – 'Wanderer's Storm-song' – written in 1771, the same year as his first draft of *Götz*, Goethe writes in ecstatic praise of the tempest, which is the visible form of the creative principle, Jupiter Pluvius, the 'sturmatmende Gottheit'. Inspiration is given by the tempest, by this god, to the poet Goethe, and raises him to the level of the gods, so that the poet claims

> und ich schwebe
> Über Wasser, über Erde
> Göttergleich
>
> [and I hover
> Over water, over earth
> Like the gods.]

All other inspiration is puny beside that of the storm – Jupiter Pluvius alone is the beginning, end and source of poetry – and Goethe gives himself with implicit trust to his Genius, which will not abandon him. It is

> innre Wärme
> Seelenwärme,
> Mittelpunkt!
>
> [inner warmth;
> Warmth of the soul,
> The central point! In *Goethes Werke*, ed. S.M. Prem, n.d. II, 39-42.]

Unlike Shaftesbury, but much more in tune with the 'Stürmer und Dränger' who were his contemporaries, Goethe does not see the genius simply as God's inspired collaborator, but as the great rebel parallel to the rebellious hero Götz von Berlichingen. In 'Prometheus' (1774), Goethe puts into the mouth of the mythological fire-stealer verse after verse of defiance of the gods. While Shaftesbury's harmonious vision saw the poet as 'a just Prometheus under Jove', and something of this is contained in 'Wandrers Sturmlied', here Goethe concentrates on the proud independence of Prometheus, who has done what he has done *without* the help of Jove or any of the gods:

> Wer half mir
> Wider der Titanen Übermut?
> Wer rettete vom Tode mich,
> Von Sklaverei?
> Hast du's nicht alles selbst vollendet,
> Heilig glühend Herz?
>
> [Who helped me
> Against the Titans' arrogance?
> Who saved me from death,
> From slavery?
> Did you not achieve it all, yourself,
> My holy, glowing heart?] (Quoted in *Poems of Goethe*, ed.
> R. Gray, 1966, p. 46).

'Prometheus' is a hymn in praise of the divine strength *within* the poet, who is, here in this poem, the sole worth-while creator:

> Hier sitz' ich, forme Menschen
> Nach meinem Bilde,

Ein Geschlecht, das mir gleich sei,
Zu leiden, weinen, Geniessen und zu freuen sich,
Und dein nicht zu achten,
Wie ich.

[Here I sit, and make men
Men in my own image,
A race able like me
to suffer, weep,
Enjoy, rejoice,
And care nothing for you,
As I do.] (*Poems of Goethe*, p. 47).

A similar self-confidence comes from 'An Schwager Kronos' ('To coachman Time'), written in the same year, though instead of a stern defiance, the poet is now arrogant in a cheerful and cocky way. He writes as the — single — passenger in the post-chaise driven by Time. The poet gives orders, not requests, beginning 'Spude dich, Kronos!' — 'Get a move on, Chronos' — telling him to hurry on into life, 'Rasch in's Leben hinein!' and climb to its very peak. All must be viewed, enjoyed, and then still more briskly down, drunk with the glory of the sunset, to the dark doorway of Hell. Even there, the poet-hero gives the orders:

Töne, Schwager, dein Horn,
Rassle den schallenden Trab,
Dass der Orkus vernehme, ein Fürst kommt,
Drunten von ihren Sitzen
Sich die Gewaltigen lüften.

[Coachman, sound your horn,
Clatter and rattle fast in,
So all Hades knows, a Prince is on his way,
So down there those mighty ones
Get up off their backsides.] (ibid., p. 53).

Goethe wrote this poem 'in der Postchaise' on his way back from a meeting with Gottlieb Friedrich Klopstock (1724-1813), then one of the most eminent living poets. In 1759, Klopstock had published *his* storm poem, the ode 'Die Frühlingsfeier' — 'The celebration of spring' — and Goethe not only emulated Klopstock's use of Greek rhythms in his hymns at this time, but echoes Klopstock's admiration for all aspects of the storm, in his own 'Wandrers Sturmlied'. Yet how great a difference between the two poems! Klopstock sees the storm as the dark garment of God,

> Wolken strömen herauf!
> Sichtbar ist, der kommt, der Ewige!
>
> [Clouds stream overhead!
> Visibly now, the Eternal approaches!]

but has no fear, because God is good — the storm-clouds bring needed rain, not destruction to the peasants and their crops:

> Zürnest du, Herr,
> Weil Nacht dein Gewand ist?
> Diese Nacht ist Segen der Erde.
> Vater, du zürnest nicht.
>
> [Lord, art thou angry,
> Since night is thy garment?
> This night is earth's blessing
> From thee, Father, not anger. In *Werke*, ed. R. Hamel, *Deutsche National-Litteratur*, n.d., XLVII, 104-7.]

Thomson in 1726 might have agreed with this feeling; but Goethe in 1771 is fearless, because he himself is equal to the gods, however violent they may be. He is 'göttergleich' in the strength of his genius.

Just such confidence in his own destiny inspires 'Harzreise im Winter', written at the end of 1777 when Goethe was making a tour of the Harz mountains, and climbed the Brocken. The poem is less 'comfortable', for his destiny may easily be a solitary one, condemned to the barren and pathless wilderness. He begins with a proud wish — may his song hover like the hawk, as it floats gently, watching for its prey. He wants the wild and difficult life, though it has pain, and he prays for protection through the cold of winter; and towards the end, his request changes into a statement, that this is what the 'Vater der Liebe ' — 'the father of love' — is doing:

> Mit der dämmernden Fackel
> Leuchtest du ihm
> Durch die Furten bei Nacht
> . . .
> Mit dem beizenden Sturm
> Trägst du ihn hoch empor. . .

34. (above) *The Monuments of Easter Island*, by William Hodges (1774). Sinister, and utterly different from Greek or Roman remains, unlike the picture of the monuments on Tinian in Plate 9.
35. (below) Fingal's Cave, drawn by J.F. Miller in 1772. As in Fabris' volcano study (Plate 29), man is dwarfed by nature's creation.

36. (left) 'Once human Greatness now dissolving in the Dust' — William Hodges, *Tomb and Distant View of Rajmahal hills* (1782).

37. (below) In Wright's *Indian Widow*, nature's wildness and primitive humanity are united, as in *The Bard*, by Thomas Jones (Plate 17).
38. (right) The 'Stein' at Wörlitz (*c*. 1790) — volcano, grotto, labyrinth, marvel of nature, and entertaining spectacle.
39. (below right) The 'villa Hamilton' on the slopes of the 'Stein' — recalling Sir William Hamilton's 'villa Angelica' on the slopes of Vesuvius.

40. (above) A menacing pa[ss]
— one of Turner's views of [F]
hill, drawn in 1799. By 182[
when the engraving was pu[b]
lished, the Abbey tower ha[d]
collapsed.

41. (left) 'An inaccessible d[un]
jon', on 'a spur of basalt of
prodigious height' — the cas[tle]
of Rochemaure, engraved in

42. (right) Ticket to admit three visitors to the view, for the great sale at Fonthill in 1823. Only one small extremity of Fonthill Abbey remains.

43. (below) Solitary, strange, immense and incomprehensible – the ruined column in the Désert de Retz (1780-1).

Vue Perspective de la Colonne.

44. (above) One of Piranesi's
views of Paestum (1778). He
stresses the immense age of the
ruins, and their primitive simplicity (cf. Plate 50).

45. (left) Ozymandian dismay –
Fuseli's drawing of 'The Artist in
despair over the magnitude of
antique fragments'.

47. *The Nightmare*, by Henry
Fuseli (1781). Night, and solitude,
'the notions of ghosts and goblins'
— terrifying aspects of the sublime.

46. *The Artist in conversation
with J.J. Bodmer*, by Henry Fuseli
(*c*. 1778). Fuseli gives himself the
role of *genius*.

48. The 'Festival of the Supreme
Being', 8 June 1794. This 'mountain', set up in the Champ de Mars,
has a tree of liberty at the top.

49. (above) *The Altar of Good Fortune* (1777), in Goethe's garden, which marks the re-direction of his life at Weimar.

50. (left) Archway in the Roman House in the park at Weimar. The simplicity of the primitive Doric pillars stresses the sense of serenity and con-trol.

[With a brightening torch
Thou makst light this way,
Through fords at night
. . .
In the ice-biting storm
Bearest him high upwards. . .] (*Poems of Goethe*, p. 57).

In the last stanza, the poet is therefore *with* the divinity on the mountain peak. While the 'Vater der Liebe' looks down from the clouds on the 'Reiche und Herrlichkeit', the 'principalities and powers' below, Goethe has in a way granted himself the wish that his song may hover, like the bird of prey at the beginning 'über der erstaunten Welt', 'over the astonished world'.

A part of Goethe's greatness lies in his seeing a question from more sides than one. At this moment, in the 1770s, the question is the importance of the genius, and the importance of the sublime, in nature and in personal experience. Already the poems discussed show differing visions of the genius in his attitudes to God, existence and the world, though there is a firm view of the nature of the genius at the centre of each poem. Without too much distortion, we may see Goethe himself as the genius. In his two most important works in this period, however, the first draft of *Faust*, known as the *Urfaust*, and *Die Leiden des jungen Werthers* – 'The Sorrows of Young Werther' – the question of the genius is touched on in different and deeply moving ways.

Most of the *Urfaust* was written in the years 1773-5 (quotations are from Goethe, *Urfaust*, ed. R.H. Samuel, 1968). The text was not completed for may years – not until 1790 did Goethe publish *Faust. Ein Fragment*, and the completed text of *Faust I*, immensely fuller and more complicated than the *Urfaust* and the *Fragment*, was not published until 1808. Part of the story, to do with the disgruntled, middle-aged teacher who sells his soul to the devil in return for earthly delights, comes from sources Goethe could have known in Frankfurt and in Strasburg. The other part, to do with the seduction of Gretchen by Faust, and his abandoning her later, comes both from Goethe's own love-affair with Friederike Brion in 1771, and *his* abandoning her, and from his knowledge of the trial and execution in 1771-2 of a tavern girl, Susanna Margaretha Brandt, who had murdered her illegitimate child. While the Gretchen story is therefore partly autobiographical, the main and surrounding story of Faust and Mephistopheles has much stronger non-autobiographical sources.

This main story has a setting which is imbued with the sublime, and a character at its centre, Faust, whose aspirations are towards the sublime. The stage directions for the first scene might have been dictated by Burke:

NIGHT
In a high-vaulted, narrow gothic room
Faust restless on the seat at his desk

Into this dark and gothic room, the inquiring hero invites the supernatural. This is not *The Castle of Otranto*, where the supernatural comes unexpectedly and improbably; but a learned yet dissatisfied man's study, where from ancient text and diagram the mystic summons may be made. A sublime setting, therefore. But not, in himself, a sublime hero. Faust is not a Prometheus, scaling mythological heights to steal fire from heaven; nor a high-souled yet savage robber baron like Götz; nor is he the young, ardent poet-genius-hero of 'Wandrers Sturmlied', 'Schwager Kronos' or 'Harzreise im Winter'. He is a middle-aged failure, embittered that his studies, broad and deep, have brought no satisfaction, either to him or his students. Philosophy, medicine, law, even and alas! theology – no good:

Da steh ich nun, ich armer Thor
Und bin so klug als wie zuvor.

[So here I am, a stupid man
No brighter now than when I began.] (*Urfaust* ll. 5-6).

He is, therefore, not an exceptional, man, but a fairly ordinary man – yet, like Goethe and so many of Goethe's contemporaries, unwilling to accept the earth-bound matter-of-fact and unimaginative attitudes of the Enlightenment as an adequate response to life. He yearns for the godlike qualities of the genius, and for the unique experiences which are the prerogative of the genius. Suddenly as Faust gazes forlornly at the moonlight shining in from the world of nature, into his narrow, cell-like room, he thinks to himself 'Escape!' 'Flieh! Auf hinaus in's weite Land!' – 'Out, and away to the open countryside!' (l. 65) (it is like the poet's imperious, confident orders to 'coachman Time', 'Rasch in's Leben hinein!' – 'Quick, onwards into life!'); and his eye falls on a book of Nostradamus' magic secrets. '*Er schlägt das Buch auf und erblickt das Zeichen des Makrokosmus*' – '*He opens the book, and perceives the sign of the Macrocosm*'. This is Faust's 'chance', an opportunity of a magic and supernatural kind to escape from what he is, and from his surroundings. The sight fills him with excitement, 'junges heil'ges Lebensglück — 'young, holy joy of life', and greater courage to face the divine vision. 'War es ein Gott, der diese Zeichen schrieb?' — 'Was it a God, who wrote these signs?' he asks, and yearns to be godlike himself. 'Bin ich ein Gott?' — 'Am I a god?' (ll. 79-86).

Yet the Macrocosm, the 'great harmony of the universe', is too diffuse for his ambition and he falls into fresh dejection. He wants — like the poet in 'Wandrers Sturmlied' — to be united with the fertile, lifegiving forces of 'nature'. Again he looks at the book, and sees the 'sign of the earth-spirit', the 'Erdgeist'. This time he is braver:

Ich fühle Mut mich in die Welt zu wagen,
All Erdenweh und all ihr Glück zu tragen.

[I feel new courage now to brave the world
And bear all sorrows and all joys of earth.] (*Urfaust*, ll. 111-12).

Summoning the Erdgeist, it proves unendurably hideous. The spirit mocks him, tells him 'Fasst Uebermenschen dich!' — 'Control yourself, you "super-man"', and calls him 'a fearful, cowering worm'. Faust — with desperate courage — stands firm, and dares to assert that he is the 'equal' of the Erdgeist. But the Erdgeist will have nothing of it. 'You are equal to the spirit you can understand. Not me!' (ll. 159-60). The Erdgeist disappears, and Faust, disconsolate, asks himself

Wem denn?
Ich Ebenbild der Gottheit!

[Who is my equal, then?
I, image of the Godhead!] (*Urfaust*, ll. 162-3).

But his supernatural summons has not been in vain. Mephistopheles comes, and though we never learn exactly what his status is (and even Goethe's much fuller version, the *Fragment* and *Faust I* do not make it much clearer), he is undoubtedly a supernatural agent, not a human being. He makes a pact of an unspecified kind with Faust, and brings him, among other things, rejuvenation and the hope of excitement and sublime experience. Not much of this is presented in the fragments of the *Urfaust*, and by the time Goethe has completed *Faust I* the experiences of the 'Walpurgisnacht' and the 'Walpurgisnachtstraum' have aspects which extend Faust's quest into many matters beyond and beside the sublime.

One passage, however, should be considered, in scene 14, 'Marthens Garten', where Faust tries to persuade Gretchen that she can trust him. She asks about his religious belief, ending with the direct 'Glaubst du an Gott?' —'D'you believe in God?' Faust's answer is both evasive — Gretchen sees that he has 'no Christianity' — and assertive in a mystical and approximately pantheistic way. The divine nature of God is everywhere, both in the outside world, and within our souls, active and present in all that we do, and our most powerful and joyous feelings correspond to the divine force that is within us. Faust tells Gretchen:

> Erfüll davon dein Herz, so gross es ist,
> Und wenn du ganz in dem Gefühle selig bist,
> Nenn das dann wie du willst,
> Nenns Glück! Herz! Liebe! Gott!
> Ich habe keinen Namen
> Dafür. Gefühl ist alles,
> Name Schall und Rauch,
> Umnebelnd Himmels Glut.

> [Fill all your heart with this, full as you can,
> And when this whole and blest awareness comes,
> Then call it what you will,
> Call it joy — heart — love — or God!
> Myself, I have no name
> For this. Awareness is all,
> The name just sound and show,
> Mere clouds obscuring Heaven's glow] (*Urfaust*, ll. 1143-50).

'Gefühl ist alles' — 'awareness', I think, 'receptivity', and openness to the infinite range of experience and emotion contained in life, rather than the simple translation of 'feeling'. It is the 'receptivity', the especial sensitivity of the genius, who is, like the poet of 'Wandrers Sturmlied' and 'Harzreise im Winter', raised to the level of the gods by his awareness. Faust, seizing his chance of supernatural help, reaches out to such sublime experience.

Goethe's first novel, *Die Leiden des jungen Werthers*, was written rapidly in 1773-4, and published in 1774. Its composition was therefore within the period of composition of the *Urfaust*, and it is right to see it as running parallel, in some respects, to the drama Goethe was sketching at the same time. It is in letter-form — from Werther to his friend Wilhelm — and has much in common with Rousseau's *Nouvelle Héloïse*. The hero is a sensitive young man, living mainly in the country, and passionately in love with a young woman whom he is not allowed to marry, since she is already bethrothed. Like Rousseau's hero and heroine, Werther is convinced of the virtue and vital necessity of his passion, and like them, with a profound love of nature and simple, spontaneous and 'natural' behaviour, he sees himself in conflict with the frivolous, artificial and restrictive attitudes of society.

At this point, the resemblance to the *Nouvelle Héloïse* ends. Werther is consistently to do with Werther, while the *Nouvelle Héloïse* gives St Preux only a middling amount of attention, and much more to the heroine, Julie, with long and difficult interludes to do with topics such as gardens or rural economy or the Parisian theatre.

More than all this, Werther himself is not St Preux — he never has the decisiveness, nor sufficient 'passion' to get more than sympathy from Lotte, whom he loves. Nor is he the titanic 'ich' of Goethe's 'Wandrers Sturmlied' or 'Prometheus'. Instead, he yearns — he is, I think, far more sensitive to others than St Preux — and longs desperately to love, to live, to create. Like Goethe, and like Faust, he is deeply convinced of his own immense superiority — Goethe, in 'Wandrers Sturmlied', is 'like the gods', while Faust asks, 'Am I a god?', and later answers himself with 'I, image of the Godhead'. Several times, in despair at the impossibility of his position *vis-à-vis* Lotte, or *vis-à-vis* the unfeeling, bourgeois world, Werther speaks of himself suffering as did Christ. Approaching the point of suicide, he sees this act as one of Christ-like self-sacrifice, atonement for the insensitivity of humanity.

Werther's 'act' — his suicide — is negative. Unlike Götz, fighting for liberty, or Goethe in the post-chaise after his visit to Klopstock, or Faust, once he has the magical 'chance', Werther is unable to cope with any but the gentler sides of life. Characteristic is his reaction to the storm (book I, 16 June). In the course of an innocent gathering, a violent thunderstorm frightens the timid members of the party, and Lotte, considerate and resourceful, distracts them with a jolly, noisy game. The storm passes over, and Lotte and Werther look out of the window at the 'glorious rain' which is falling. Tears come to Lotte's eyes, and with her hand resting on Werther's she murmurs 'Klopstock!' This one word (referring to Klopstock's ode on the storm, the 'Frühlingsfeier') overwhelms Werther in a flood of emotions, and he kisses Lotte's hand 'with tears of rapture'. Klopstock's ode ended with the poet's gratitude to God that the danger of the storm had passed away, and had been replaced by the blessing of rain. The Goethe of 'Wandrers Sturmlied' would not have done this — he would have dashed out into the storm, exulted in the danger, written about it triumphantly; and Faust, given his chance, would have been equal to the event.

Not Werther, though. He yearns for the sublime, whether in nature or in love, but is not strong enough to face this wildness when he encounters it, or to seize it for himself, as an artist or a lover. A month after the storm episode, and more deeply in love with Lotte than before, he writes (I, 24 July) that he has never been happier, nor has his 'feeling for nature' ever been so profound, yet his artistic ability to seize, to record any of this — the world of nature, or Lotte's portrait — has gone to pieces. Some weeks later his 'feeling for nature', linked to the see-sawing hope and despair of his love for Lotte, becomes so intense that, having perceived unexpected cruelties in nature, he is reduced to a state of panic. The letter describing this experience (I, 18 August) falls into two sections, the first telling of his delight in the beauty, fertility, variety and strength of nature. It could be a paraphrase from Shaftes-bury, so great is his confidence in the *goodness* of the scene:

> When I used once to look out from the cliff, across the river to the hills, over the fertile valley, and saw everything germinating and springing into life round me;. . . how warmly I took all this to my heart, and felt like a god amid the overflowing fullness, while the glorious forms of the everlasting world moved and inspired new life in my heart.

Throughout nature, from steepest mountains to wilderness, and to the furthest ends of the ocean, all is filled with the kind and caring spirit of the Creator.

And then Werther's mood, and his conviction, changes. After seeing life everywhere, he sees death: 'The spectacle of endless life changes before my eyes into the abyss of an ever-open grave.' While destruction gnaws ceaselessly at all living creatures, no act of one's own, however harmless, can avoid bringing destruction to others, '*one* footstep will shatter the ants' carefully-built abode, and stamp a tiny world into a shameful grave'. For Werther, who is not a great adventurer, the grief is not so much in the gigantic natural disasters, such as earthquakes, but in 'the all-devouring strength' which he sees 'lying hidden in the whole of nature'. And so he is overwhelmed, and concludes, 'I can see nothing but an eternally consuming, eternally re-devouring monster.'

'Gefühl ist alles,' 'awareness is all,' said Faust. Given the unique chance of supernatural help, he reaches out, and dares to seize what he so passionately desires. His very act gives him more strength (this is a most characteristic belief with Goethe), and makes him better able to respond to the opportunities of fuller 'awareness' which follow. Werther likewise believes in the supreme value of 'Gefühl'; but he is weak, and he feels and yearns and suffers without being able to act. He gives way to depression, gives up reading Homer, the poet of heroic activity, and reads the resigned and melancholy Ossian instead. Unlike Faust, with his book of magic, Werther lives in the modern world where magic and supernatural intervention just don't happen. Werther is, in any case, so much less a man of action than Faust that, *were* he given the chance of selling his soul in exchange for the vast ocean of 'awareness', he might not dare to seize it. But there is no question of this in Goethe's novel. Werther is not a genius, but a feeble creature. *His* yearnings do not carry him to sublime heights. They destroy him.

While Faust strove towards wider and greater awareness, and while Werther succumbed under the crushing force of his emotions, another glorification of emotion was about to be written by Rousseau. Already in the *Discours sur. . . l'inégalité* of 1755 Rousseau had claimed that the original life of the 'noble savage' was so simple and uncomplicated that 'réflexion' or 'considered thought' was unnecessary; and in the *Nouvelle Héloïse* of 1760 he had shown the hero St Preux enjoying two hours of supreme happiness in Julie's garden, engaged not in action, or discussion, or 'réflexion', but in a 'rêverie' – a day-dream in which the theme was the innocent beauty of unspoilt nature, and the moral beauty of the virtuous Julie (see p. 92 above).

Rousseau wrote the *Rêveries du promeneur solitaire* in the last two years of his life, in 1776-8, and they were published posthumously in 1782. (Quotations from Rousseau, *Rêveries* in *Œuvres complètes*, ed. M. Launay, Vol. 1, 1967) The 'rêveries' which Rousseau describes – his day dreams, waking fantasies, musings – are moments, minutes, hours of unique and solitary happiness, usually in communion with nature. The first 'Promenade' opens with a statement of his total solitude: 'So now I am alone on the face of the earth, having no brother, neighbour, friend or company apart from myself.' Again and again, he sees society conspiring against him, forcing him willy-nilly into this solitude, and again and again, he sees his reveries not only as the fruit of solitude, but as unique in their quality. They are 'conversations with his soul. . . since it is the only one which men cannot take from me' ('Première promenade'). His 'meditations' on his inner nature have been made with greater care than any other man would bother to take, and his attitudes towards society and towards himself have been established 'after the most ardent and most sincere research which any mortal has perchance ever made' ('Troisième promenade').

His reveries are mostly related to his solitary enjoyment of nature. In the 'Septième promenade', he describes a way of 'herborising', of studying nature, which is in reality not a *study* but a forgetting of himself, an ecstasy in the *contemplation* of nature. He sees himself as old, tired, persecuted, 'avoiding men, and seeking solitude, no longer imagining, and thinking even less' — and by no means trying to *learn* in an academic sense from nature. This is in any case an unprofitable activity:

> I make no attempt to acquire information: it is too late. Besides, I have never seen why knowledge in itself should be important for happiness in life (*Rêveries*, p. 531).

Instead he wanders, not studying, not even thinking. There is no system in his wandering. I take no trouble, he writes, 'as I wander carelessly from one herb to another, from plant to plant'. The first examination may have some 'scientific' origin, but quickly this curiosity develops into a more general, unfactual and emotional delight. He wanders 'carelessly' from plant to plant (p. 531)

> to examine them, to compare their various characteristics, to note their similarities and their differences, in short to observe the formation of the plant in order to follow the growth and progress of these living machines, to seek — sometimes successfully — their general principles, the reason and the purpose of their various structures, and to lose myself in wonder, in grateful admiration of the hand which has allowed me to take delight in it all (ibid.).

Study is quickly over, followed by far longer rapture. Other parts of the natural world may be interesting — mineralogy, or zoology, or even astronomy — but involve work, or disagreeable or complicated preparation and equipment. In contrast, 'la botanique', the study of nature, offers prompt and deep delight:

> Plants seem to have been sown on the earth in abundance. . . to invite us to study nature through the appeal of pleasure and curiosity. . . Plants are there naturally (ibid.).

And in this study, preferring by instinct what is most pleasant in nature, Rousseau drifts in happy, uncluttered and thoughtless solitude:

Botany is the study for an idle, lazy, lonely man: all he needs to observe these plants is a spike and a magnifying glass. He walks, wandering freely from one object to the next, he considers every flower... and in observing them he savours an effortless pleasure which is every bit as real, as if it had cost him a great deal of trouble (ibid.).

Pleasure, yes, 'an attraction... which is on its own enough at these moments to make life happy and sweet'. Rousseau puts this idle, thoughtless happiness in the highest terms. Elsewhere in the 'Septième promenade', he opposes *thought*, which he has rarely undertaken with pleasure, and usually against his will, becoming tired and saddened in the process, to *revery*, which is in its rapturous flights his supreme delight:

During these flights my soul drifts, hovering in the universe on the wings of imagination, in ecstasies which surpass all other enjoyment (ibid., p. 528).

The 'Septième promenade' gives general praise of 'la botanique' as an inducement to solitary reverie. In the 'Cinquième promenade', Rousseau writes in superlative terms of his uniquely happy experience on and round the lac de Bienne, near Neuchâtel. He was there for six weeks, in the autumn of 1765, putting up in a farmhouse on an island in the lake, the 'île Saint-Pierre'. There for a short while he was able to 'forget the world', and be idle. Idly, he amused himself in 'herborising'; this is described, and then he tells how, after a satisfactory day's nature-study, he would eat with the landlord and his household, and then, if the meal was likely to last a long while, and if the weather was fine, he would leave:

I used to slip away, and would go quickly on my own to a boat which I would row out to the middle of the lake when the water was calm; and there, stretched right out in the boat and looking up at the sky, I would float and drift slowly with the current, sometimes for several hours, plunged in a thousand vague but delightful reveries — reveries which, though they had no fixed or definite object, appealed to my fancy a hundred times more than the sweetest things I had found among what we call the pleasures of life (ibid., p. 522).

Even the impulse to reverie which begins from a particular flower or plant has now been abandoned; his reverie, his musing is now adrift like the boat, and without direction. Rousseau then gives it even greater credit. If the weather was rough, he would not row on the lake, but 'herborise' here and there on the island, dreaming idly in the solitary nooks, and gazing at the lake and the fertile countryside which surrounded it; and then in the evening he would come down from the upper parts of the island, and sit on the shore watching the water, listening to the waves, forgetting his worries – and letting himself drift so deeply in 'delicious reverie' that night had often fallen without his noticing. The terms he uses to describe the quality of this reverie are extraordinary:

> The sight and sound of the rising and falling of the waves, swelling and diminishing without pause, ceaselessly in my ears and before my eyes, replaced the inner commotion which reverie had silenced within me, and were enough to make me feel with pleasure that I existed, without taking the trouble to think (ibid.).

A while later, he calls this state of happiness 'la suprême félicité' – 'supreme felicity' – in which he is filled solely and wholly with the awareness of his existence; and asks himself, 'what is it that one enjoys in such a situation?' Rousseau's answer completes the definition, and the valuation which he gives to reverie:

> It isn't anything outside yourself (which you enjoy), it is nothing except yourself and your own existence; for as long as this state lasts, you are sufficient to yourself as God (ibid., p. 523).

Although Rousseau has virtually no liking for the wilder aspects of nature, his love for gentle and unspoilt nature – as opposed to the corrupt and unfeeling forms of society – is as profound and genuine as anyone's in the 1770s. So too is his belief in the absolute value of feeling, of impulse, of emotion – as opposed to the sterile and calculating processes of reason. In the *Rêveries*, emotion liberated by contact with nature is claimed as the 'suprême félicité' and the reverie both serves him as a superb way to forget society, as the proof of his existence, and as the means to make him, momentarily, like God. Though there is little of the 'sublime' in Rousseau's supreme felicity, it is level with Goethe's claim to be 'göttergleich' – 'like the gods' – in 'Wandrers Sturmlied', and far more absolute in its rejection of reason. Faust indeed claimed that in the appreciation of the nature of God, 'awareness is all', but, as I have said, this does not mean mere 'emotion' or 'feeling'. Faust remains a human being, who both feels and reflects, and wishes to experience *all* aspects of life, and to be active; while Rousseau in the *Rêveries* first withdraws wholly from society — his near-to-vegetable solitude is a pre-condition of the state of reverie — and then passionately elevates feeling, emotion, to be the sole ruler of his existence. More than this, the strength and 'beauty' of his feeling is the *proof* to himself of this existence. Long before, Descartes had coined the formula 'I think, therefore I am,' and the next century and a half of city-centred philosophers and writers had taken this to imply not only that man's ability to think was a proof to himself of his existence, but also that man's ability to think was the quality which made him different from, and superior to, other creatures. Man was a thinking animal. By extension, he was a social, and a socially responsible, animal as well. He must act, and work. Now Rousseau was saying, in as many words, 'I feel, therefore I am,' and saying that, while one enjoys a state of reverie, 'you are sufficient to yourself as God'.

In Wordsworth's words, 'I was taught to feel. . . the self-sufficing power of solitude.' At the end of the eighteenth century William Wordsworth wrote the earliest version of *The Prelude*, a text only recently published. I quote from *The Prelude, 1798-99*, ed. S. Parrish, 1977. While later versions of *The Prelude* (1805, 1850) expand, and decline into compromise, this first draft is a marvel of directed vision, the completion of a century's study of nature. Shaftesbury, Thomson and Rousseau are united — in the vision of nature as the garment of the Creator, sublime in its qualities, and accessible through feeling, the direct intuition of the sensitive individual.

This '*ur*-Prelude' is in two parts, of 464 and 514 lines respectively. They contain recollections of the poet's experiences in natural surroundings, presented in the spirit of *rêverie*. The poet describes the scenes far more in terms of what he feels than what he sees, and as scenes which have become a part of his own being:

> Oft in those moments such a holy calm
> Did overspread my soul that I forgot
> The agency of sight, and what I saw
> Appeared like something in myself — a dream,
> A prospect in my mind (II, 397-401).

The term 'dream' is used many times to describe his experience, and he stresses that his perception of the divinity of nature is not rational, but felt — and *only* perceptible through feeling:

        and now at length
From Nature and her overflowing soul
I had received so much that all my thoughts
Were steeped in feeling (II, 445-8).

His perception of the unity of the natural world is accompanied 'with bliss ineffable', like Rousseau's 'supreme felicity'; and it is a perception of a religious kind — 'that spirit of religious love in which / I walked with nature' — 'for in all things / I saw one life and felt that it was joy' (II, 406-7, 459-60). And, like Rousseau and like Shaftesbury, Wordsworth claims that his closeness to nature taught him 'to feel. . . the self-sufficing power of solitude' (II, 76-7).

Wordsworth's love of solitude is more 'creative' than Rousseau's, which was prompted quite as much by his distrust of human company as by his love of nature. For Wordsworth, this was directly allied to his 'first creative sensibility' (II, 409). He is therefore like Goethe, in 'Wandrers Sturmlied', who is 'like the gods', rejoicing in the violence of the storm. Wordsworth's feeling for nature is also broader than Rousseau's, embracing scenes of tranquillity like those at the île Saint-Pierre, and scenes of raw sublimity which Thomson would have appreciated in 1726, the year of 'Winter', but which Rousseau would never have enjoyed:

        Oh, when I have hung
Above the raven's nest, by knots of grass,
Or half-inch fissures in the slipp'ry rock,
But ill sustained, and almost, as it seemed,
Suspended by the blast which blew amain,
Shouldering the naked crag, oh at that time,
When on the perilous ridge I hung alone,
With what strange utterance did the loud dry wind
Blow through my ears! (I, 57-65)

This is the sublime and the enjoyment of the sublime — like Thomson's 'wish'd, wint'ry horrors, hail!' But, unlike Thomson in 1726, it is passionately direct, Wordsworth himself talking about his experiences, his feelings — and talking with such intensity, it is as if he talks more to himself, than to an audience. 'Oh, when *I* have hung / Above the raven's rest', followed by the reinforcing 'when on the perilous ridge *I* hung alone' — this Thomson did not do, but Rousseau, in the *Rêveries*, writing in his imagined solitude, 'alone on the face of the earth' certainly does. Walpole had praised English landscapes — 'when they are framed and glazed' — and Thomson's vision in *The Seasons* had always remained of that kind, seen 'through the window' of indirect and impersonal narration. Eighteenth-century literature and art had at last come to admire the direct and personal statement, but always with at least a little reserve. In Ossian, the directness was excused by the poem's antiquity, in *Werther* it was seen as the expression of a hero to be pitied for his obsession, in Fuseli's vision of fear the subjects were taken from established and respected sources. In this first version of *The Prelude*, Wordsworth speaks uniquely of his recollection of his own youthful experiences; these are entirely set in the Lake District, in the heart of 'sublime' nature; and the whole poem is conceived as the description of how he, the poet, was inspired by the natural — and divine — world around him. All tends

> To the same point, the growth of mental power
> And love of Nature's works (I, 257-8).

In 1709, in *The Moralists*, Shaftesbury's language is rarified, rhapsodic, and the natural scenes he describes are far from 'reality'. Yet his thought leads direct to Wordsworth's first *Prelude* of 1798-9, with the poet acknowledging what Shaftesbury had called 'mighty Nature! wise substitute of Providence! impowerd creatress!' It is as if Wordsworth had applied the test of his own experience to Shaftesbury's claim that 'the wildness pleases', and had found it wholly true, acceptable without reservation.

Wordsworth's poem contains many of the episodes, often sublime, which will be the focal points of the expanding *Prelude* of 1805 and 1850 — for example, the theft of the 'Shepherd's boat', the 'elfin pinnace' (I, 108ff.); the scene of

> A naked pool that lay beneath the hills,
> The beacon on the summit, and more near
> A girl who bore a pitcher on her head
> And seemed with difficult steps to force her way
> Against the blowing wind (I, 315ff.)

and the chill remembrance of how he waited for the horses to be brought, to take himself and his brothers home for Christmas (I, 330ff.). But when these numerous recollections are taken into the later *Prelude*, they are diluted with other subjects. The poem's nature changes.

It becomes diffuse, expanding from the theme 'the young Wordsworth and nature' to become a part of Wordsworth's autobiography. By 1798-9, when he wrote the first thousand lines of the *Prelude*, the French Revolution was ten years old. His initial, passionate approval had been tempered with apprehension, then dismay – and while these doubts at the results of political wildness were kept out of the first *Prelude*, they surface in the *Prelude* of 1805. There the test of experience produces a less satisfying result.

In the *Rêveries*, Rousseau had taken the rejection of reason and the pursuit of non-thinking happiness much further than any of his contemporaries. While Wordsworth might be 'steeped in feeling', and glorify the 'self-sufficing power of solitude', he maintained that the aim of *his* reverie was 'the growth of mental power / And love of Nature's works' – a 'mental power' leading to action, taking place in the world of men. Fuseli for his part was continually fascinated by the irrational, in moments of passion, madness and the supernatural – yet the moments which he depicts are those of crisis, of paroxysm, in which, as in his studies of the 'Nightmare', there has been movement, and in which most violent movement must surely follow. Goethe, during the years of his sympathy with the 'Sturm und Drang', showed Götz von Berlichingen as the most active of rebels, himself as a poet of eager and perilous action, 'like the hawk'. In 'Wandrers Sturmlied', he is 'like the gods', but not in the tranquil, self-sufficient Rousseauan way. Goethe's gods here are Dionysus and Jupiter Pluvius, the 'storm-breathing godhead'. While Rousseau, in the 'Cinquième promenade' of the *Rêveries* speaks of 'most precious idleness' as the first and main goal of his stay on the île Saint-Pierre, and through which his supreme states of reverie were reached, Faust wishes above all to be equal to the utmost extremes of experience which life can offer. Only Werther among Goethe's many *personae*, fictional or autobiographical, is deeply Rousseauan, and he is too weak either to endure the intensity of feeling to which he is subject, or to reject it for a more active life. (Werther himself is paralleled by the young man whom Werther meets, and pities, whose mind has been irretrievably shattered after a frustrated love affair.) While we may argue about Goethe's own view of Werther – did he condemn him, or feel sympathy? – we may be sure that, unlike Rousseau's reveries, Werther's intensity of feeling did not bring him any godlike 'suprême félicité'. In the last quarter of the eighteenth century, the readers of *Werther* (except for the few who condemned the book) ardently pitied the young hero for his sufferings in an unfeeling world. In droves, those readers felt that they were of the same unhappy race, and reached, moist-eyed, for their pistols — though only a handful pulled the trigger. Readers of the *Rêveries* likewise withdrew to self-indulgent islands of reflection, communing with nature and their sensitive souls. At Ermenonville, where Rousseau died in 1778, the Marquis de Girardin erected an altar 'à la rêverie', and in England at least two epitaphs bear witness to the fashion for Rousseauan and Wertherian depth of feeling. In 1789 a Mrs Skinn, *née* Masterman, was recorded in the *Gentleman's Magazine* as dying of poverty and exquisite sensibility, and in 1799 a Mrs Sarah Fletcher died a similar death. Her tombstone is inside Dorchester Abbey, south of Oxford, and begins with this exhortation:

> Reader!
> If thou hast a Heart form'd for
> Tenderness and Pity, Contemplate this Spot.
> The young lady buried beneath was loved by all.
> But when
> Nerves were too delicately spun to
> bear the rude Shakes and Jostlings
> which we meet with in this transitory
> World, Nature gave way; She sunk
> and died a Martyr to Excessive
> Sensibility.

These unfortunates suffered, sometimes succumbed. Had not Rousseau himself said that the *Rêveries* were the work of a man whom society had treated so vilely, that he had no recourse but total solitude — an exile through his 'exquisite' and 'excessive' sensibility?

So much for differences between the early romantics' ways of approaching and valuing the emotional life of the individual. They are immense, verging from one extreme to another: passion, madness, fury, despair, rapture, explosion, silence. Whatever the extreme, they are all admired in different ways (with some, the admiration took the form of an awe-struck shudder), and all admired for the way in which they removed the individual from the everyday life of the ordinary — and therefore uninteresting — man. The 'genius', the exceptional character exposed to unique experiences and emotions, is the ideal man of the early romantics, and it is illuminating to consider how different this ideal man is, from the all-round, 'complete' man of the Renaissance. Such a 'complete' man may be seen, for example, in the life, person and achievements of Alberti; or in Leonardo da Vinci; or, in brief, in Leonardo's single drawing of the 'vitruvian man', the 'human figure in a circle, illustrating proportions', where the proportions and fitness of the human body are linked to mathematical — and therefore universal — perfection. This picture is not of an 'exceptional' man, of the sort whose unique experiences are illustrated by Fuseli, but of an 'ideal' man, at the centre and not at the verge of existence. We may see the 'complete' man of the Renaissance as a being in whom many excellencies are combined, to achieve a balanced, harmonious and fully successful whole. A 'sound mind in a sound body' is not an empty phrase, when we look at the sculpture of Michelangelo, or when we read the programmes of education which Rabelais drew up in *Gargantua*, either for his giant prince, or for his joyous mixed company in the abbey of Thélème. Sound mind and body, sound pupils in a new, sound world.

This ideal may still be seen lingering in Shaftesbury's *Characteristics* — he would at least have thought of his creative artist, the 'just Prometheus under Jove', as living in inspired harmony with God and nature, and as living to enrich the existence of his fellow human beings. But Shaftesbury is also an originator of the division between nature and society, and at the head of the quest for singularity and wildness which has, by the 1770s, reached such extremes of expression. Already in 1757, in the article 'Génie' in the *Encyclopédie*, Diderot had separated the genius from the run of ordinary, balanced men, and notes that, while the genius may save his country through some exceptional feat, he may, being erratic, lose it again if left in charge for too long. Patently not a 'complete' man.

Returning for a moment to the Renaissance ideal: this 'complete' man was admired for his physical perfection — his beauty — which was a necessary complement to his intellectual excellence. By the middle of the eighteenth century such harmony of proportion, such harmonious coordination of the parts is rarely of interest, while the contrary — disproportion, even ugliness, whether physical, moral, intellectual or emotional — excites boundless attention.

The example of Fuseli is a useful one here. As an artist he is still devoted to the figure-studies of the Renaissance, and he echoes, copies and uses the poses and gestures of past artists throughout his career. In discussing his painting of 'The Artist in conversation with J.J. Bodmer' I pointed out the audacity, arrogance even, of his adapting Michelangelo's 'Adam' from the Sistine Chapel to represent himself. But there are nevertheless differences in Fuseli's use of this figure which set it in the 1770s, not in the Renaissance. While Michelangelo's Adam is a 'perfect' man, reclining naked, waiting only for God's vital touch,

Fuseli shows himself fully clothed, his body rather slumped than re-clining, and our attention is barely called to his body. Instead, we are drawn to his face, and to his gaze, as he ponders the inspiration which Bodmer and Homer have passed on to him. Our interest is seized by the feeling, rather than by the figures, and this is practically always the case with Fuseli's works. Again and again his figures are derived from Renais-sance models, and they have a superior strength and development which give them vigorous physical and sexual appeal; yet the interest of Fuseli's pictures is usually emotional, and of a kind which seems to neglect or discount the physical excellence of the people involved. Par-ticularly striking, yet characteristic of nearly all Fuseli's work, is the depiction of the woman or women in the 'Nightmare' series. These women are creatures of superb and majestic beauty — yet they are powerless, gripped by total terror. Though their physique is splendid, Fuseli's men and women are by no means 'complete'. They are excep-tional, and, in their day, were admired in proportion to the uniqueness and violence of their experiences.

These characters and their surroundings all go back, directly or in-directly, to Shaftesbury, to his arguments that 'the wildness pleases' and that the poet is possessed by 'divine enthusiasm'. Seeking 'nature' rather than 'the formal mockery of princely gardens', the early roman-tics turn from the city-centre to the extremes of experience, and this is often, though not always, found in the wilder parts of nature. Rejecting the 'reasonable' ways of society, they discover a new value in what is instinctive, passionate and unique. These things, from their very free-dom and naturalness, cannot have been corrupted by society.

In this history, the words 'society' and 'city' have often appeared. They are, for the followers of Shaftesbury, Burke and Rousseau, the villains. But few of the early romantics were willing to fight 'society' or the 'city'. At best, like Rousseau, they condemned the evil and then turned their backs, gazing desperately at the flowers of the field.

Yet Rousseau had also urged his contemporaries to face society — first, in the *Discours sur. . . l'inégalité*, and then in *Du Contrat social*. While he himself, diseased and declining, lost strength for the struggle, others were inspired to apply the belief in 'nature', 'wildness' and 'impulse' to the arch-villain itself, to society. In the political and social turmoil of the French Revolution the philosophical and aesthetic theories of Shaftesbury, Burke and Rousseau are given their first prac-tical trial. For a short time, the theory that 'the wildness pleases' — even in society — is given credence, support and applause.

Rousseau's praise of the 'noble savage', who is free, virtuous, happy and lives instinctively, trusting to his 'natural' inner conscience, is taken up eagerly in the second half of the eighteenth century as a justification of the 'natural' rights of man − and as ammunition to fire against the defenders of the *ancien régime*. The claim that the 'noble savage' once lived in simple happiness, in a state of freedom and equality, was used to oppose not merely the artificiality and corruption of modern society, but also, to a limited extent, the extreme disproportion between the wealth of the privileged classes and the poverty of the majority. To a much greater extent, it was used to oppose the system of accumulated rights and privileges which elevated the nobility and the clergy above the *Tiers Etat* (the 'Third Estate' or 'commoners'), and the hereditary system by which personal nobility − indicated in France by the *particule nobilaire* 'de' before the surname − was transmitted from generation to generation, irrespective of personal merit.

When in 1783, the commoner-hero of Beaumarchais' play *Le Mariage de Figaro* exclaims angrily to himself, thinking of the count, Almaviva (who is trying to use his aristocratic privilege to secure himself the *droit de seigneur* with Figaro's fiancée),

What have you done to deserve so much? You've taken the trouble to be born − and that's all (Act V, sc. iii)

he is expressing the only deeply revolutionary remark of the entire play. In 1783, French society was already in so unsettled a state that almost any new play which was witty and lively ran the risk of being called subversive; and Figaro, the intelligent, resourceful, ebullient yet thoughtful valet is in vivid and memorable contrast to his self-centred, overbearing and socially irresponsible master. Those who wished to see criticism of the *ancien régime* in this could do so, and easily. But the criticism was not new − Aristophanes, Menander, Plautus and Terence provide a few earlier examples for a start. Only Figaro's 'You've taken the trouble to be born' is categorically attacking the structure of the existing system, since it implies the injustice of a system which denies the freedom and moral equality of all men.

Rousseau had in various writings added a further dimension of strict and puritanical *virtue* to the characteristics of the 'noble savage' − in particular through his approval of the stern and self-denying example of the Spartans, contrasted with the corrupt and luxurious ways of other ancient societies, and with the corruption of modern France. The moral 'purity' of the Spartans and similar societies or groups in classical antiquity was also welcomed in this period as an aspect of the newly discovered attractions of strict, simple and primitive architecture, such as the 'primitive Doric'.

In Britain it was not difficult for these ideas to be accepted, for a while and partially, especially as they were expressed not so much against the British government, as against our traditional enemy, the French. For a fair while the inhabitants of the British Isles had been willing to see themselves as free men, contrasted with the slave-like subjects of the tyrant-kings of Spain or France. It is, in this context, immaterial whether the belief is wholly or only partially true; and, ignoring earlier and later centuries, we need think only of the eighteenth. Long before Rousseau, Addison had, in *The Tatler*, no. 161 (20 April 1710), spoken of liberty as enjoyed and cherished by some nations — the Swiss, the British — and denied to the French; and in 1740 there was 'Rule Britannia', from the *Masque of Alfred*, by Thomson and Mallet, and music by Thomas Arne, with its rousing chorus.

Britons never, never never shall be slaves.

In 1766, Tobias Smollett's *Travels in Italy* appeared, with an entry for 20 January 1764 describing the Mediterranean port of Villefranche, and with a few lines on the Sardinian galleys which he saw there:

I went on board one of these vessels and saw about two hundred miserable wretches chained to the banks, on which they sit and row while the galley is at sea. This is a sight which the British subject, sensible of the blessing he enjoys, cannot behold without horror and compassion.

Smollett then reflects that, even so, this is a practical way to employ malefactors; but he has made his point: in Britain, this sort of thing would not be approved.

In the next year, 1765, James Boswell visited the island of Corsica, recording his experiences in *The Journal of a Tour to Corsica* (1768; quotations are from the edition by M. Bishop, 1951). This book's subtitle is *Memoirs of Pascal Paoli*, and it was to meet Paoli, then struggling to achieve independence for Corsica, that Boswell went to the island. Earlier in 1765, he had called on Rousseau in Switzerland, and discussed the Corsicans' struggle with him — Rousseau had already been approached by them for advice to do with their proposed new laws and constitution.

Boswell's view of Corsica and its inhabitants is Rousseauan — his book opens with his discussions and correspondence with Rousseau, and near the end he returns to the *Contrat social* and to Rousseau's possible role as a legislator for the Corsicans. In between, he describes the islanders, and principally his hero Paoli, as people exercising the virtue of the ancient Romans. Paoli himself finds his nation superior in this — Boswell quotes him as saying, 'I defy Rome, Sparta or Thebes to shew me thirty years of such patriotism as Corsica can boast' (p. 81) — and Boswell admires his household for its simplicity. After one incident, he writes, 'I thought myself sitting in the house of a Cincinnatus' (p. 65).

As a Rousseauan — and as a young man, still in his twenties — Boswell enjoys travelling simply with his Corsican guides, eating raw chestnuts with them when hungry, and when thirsty drinking direct from the first brook they find. He adds, 'It was just being for a little while, one of the "prisca gens mortalium, the primitive race of men", who ran about the woods eating acorns and drinking water.' Soon after, he addressed a group of them, urging that they should remember always to live so simply — their poverty was a condition of their virtue: 'They were much happier in their present state than in a state of refinement and vice. . . therefore they should beware of luxury' (pp. 66, 67). Partly in emulation of these noble people, he 'got a Corsican dress made', in which he 'walked about with an air of true satisfaction' (p. 85). I say 'partly', since he may likely have been emulating his other hero Jean-Jacques as well, who had taken to wearing a distinctive loose-flowing 'Armenian dress' since 1762; and 'partly' again, since the 'air of true satisfaction' suggests a joy in dressing-up, in playing at being exotic, which he was to repeat in England — he wore his Corsican dress to visit Pitt, the Prime Minister, in London in 1766, and again at Stratford, at the Shakespeare Jubilee in 1769.

Boswell's enthusiasm for Corsican liberty is doubtless Rousseauan; but it is British as well — when in 1773 he travelled to the Hebrides with Dr Johnson, it was with pride that he showed Johnson the continuing independence of attitude of his fellow countrymen; and when he was with Paoli in Corsica, he 'promised to send him some English books', adding in a note that he had sent him the works of seven or eight British writers 'in favour of liberty' (p. 73).

Boswell's unguarded admiration for Rousseau may have provoked a part of Johnson's disapproval — when he was asked his view of Rousseau he replied, 'I think him one of the worst of men,' and when Boswell demurred, he went on:

Rousseau, Sir, is a very bad man. I would sooner sign a sentence for his transportation than that of any felon who has gone from the Old Bailey these many years. Yes, I should like to have him work in the plantations (Boswell, *Life of Johnson*, year 1766).

Yet Johnson would have yielded to no one in his approval and esteem of a man — any man — for what he was and what he had achieved, irrespective of his birth; and such a view, not rare but widespread in late eighteenth-century Britain, led to deep sympathy with the forces of reform and even revolution in France in the last years of Louis XVI. A man of moderate political views, the peripatetic farmer Arthur Young (1741-1820) could express vigorous disapproval of the French aristocracy in 1787, during the first of his three travels in France (*Travels in France*, 1791). Himself appreciative of sublime scenery, and its emotional appeal, his attitude to agriculture is generally practical, empirical, matter-of-fact. In his first crossings of France, from the Channel down to the Pyrenees, up to Paris and back again to England, his calm descriptions are disturbed most of all by his disapproval, even anger, at the harm done to agriculture, and to the common people, by the neglectful behaviour of the aristocratic landlords, whose abuse of inherited privilege enables them to exist while impoverishing the peasants who depend on them. After several attacks on the intolerance and fecklessness of the *grands seigneurs*, he produces the damning verdict 'whenever you stumble on a Grand Seigneur, even one that was worth millions, you are sure to find his property desert', and exclaims 'Oh! if I was the legislator of France for a day I would make such lords skip again' (29 August 1787). A few weeks later, in Paris, a different sight makes him write sarcastically 'Pass the Bastille; another pleasant object to make agreeable emotions vibrate in a man's bosom' — it is a symbol of the repression which he perceives in France, and which has produced a near-to-revolutionary disquiet. While the government is inept, the alternative — he thinks — is fraught with alarming uncertainty. The impotence of the king's ministers makes the recall of the *Etats* imperative, but such a step, which the French monarchy had refused or avoided since 1614, he thinks 'impossible. . . without a revolution in the government ensuing' (13 October 1787). Behind the discussions, he perceives 'a great ferment. . . and a strong leaven of liberty, increasing every hour' (17 October 1787).

This 'strong leaven' worried Young, and his anxiety is mentioned later. Others, in England, less practical or more taken with the ideal of liberty, applauded the Revolution and hoped to see in its progress the destruction of tyranny – not only in France, but all over the world, and even in England. While some stayed in England, some were in France already or went there on purpose to observe what was going on. A year after the fall of the Bastille (on 14 July 1789, only a short while after the sitting of the *Etats* or States-General on 5 May 1789), the novelist Helen Maria Williams hurried to Paris, panting to witness the millennium. She arrived the day before the federation ceremony in the Champ de Mars on the first anniversary of the fall of the Bastille, and congratulated herself. A day later, and 'I should have missed the most sublime spectacle which, perhaps, was ever represented on the theatre of this earth' (*Letters Written in France*, 1790, p. 1). Throughout this volume, her language is breathless, and with hardly an instant of regret. Fear, yes, of the sort Burke had made fashionable, but the vast scene she contemplates is admirable though sometimes frightening. How privileged she is, to 'witness an event so sublime as the French revolution' (p. 65). Both humanity as a whole, and its leaders, are here to be trusted and applauded. What she saw at the Champ de Mars was 'the triumph of human kind; it was man asserting the noblest privileges of his nature', and she, a witness, feels herself 'a citizen of the world' (p. 14). The Revolution, she feels, is sure to prosper, since its leaders 'are men well acquainted with the human heart. They have not trusted merely to the force of reason' (pp. 61-2). A while later she sees the 'lanterne' at the corner of the Rue de la Vannerie, where summary executions have occurred, and writes 'for the first time I lamented the revolution' (p. 81), but only at the end of her 1790 volume does she write with a little more caution, hoping that the National Assembly will make a constitution which will 'render the French nation virtuous, flourishing, and happy' (p. 223). Until then, Paris in 1790 is an inspiring marvel of man's liberation from a slave-like past. Arthur Young had shuddered at the Bastille while it stood; now she shudders as she visits its harmless remains, seeing what was left through the blinkers of a gothic romance:

> We drove under that porch which so many wretches have entered never to repass. . . descended with difficulty into the dungeons, which were too low to admit of our standing upright, and so dark that we were obliged at noon-day to visit them with the light of a candle (*Letters*, pp. 22-3).

Down below, the cells are 'in a constant state of humidity', and 'a noxious vapour issued from them, which more than once extinguished the candle' (p. 23).

While Helen Maria Williams made this visit — going to the Bastille in a carriage, and enjoying fashionable dinners, one of which must be mentioned later — other foreigners watched the Revolution approvingly, but from a distance. The fall of the Bastille was instantly seen as a symbolic destruction of tyranny, and William Blake's description of this monument is even more 'gothic' than the lines I have just quoted. William Blake (1757-1827) had already absorbed an immense amount from earlier British writers who favoured the sublime and the gothic. Chatterton's Rowley and Macpherson's Ossian were to his mind genuine poets who had flourished, and composed, centuries before their eighteenth-century discoverers had presented them to the public. In 1785, he was exhibiting a water-colour drawing illustrating Gray's 'Bard', in 1796-7 he produced the huge series of illustrations for Young's *Night Thoughts*, and in 1804-5 the drawings for Blair's 'Grave'. With these romantic enthusiasms went a belief in the God-like supremacy of the poetic genius, which bursts out in the impassioned exclamations of *The Marriage of Heaven and Hell* (*c*. 1790), 'When thou seest an eagle, thou seest a portion of genius: lift up thy head!' (one of many lines similar in feeling to Goethe's poems on genius written in the 1770s, though Goethe and Blake knew little or nothing of each other). And with belief in the genius goes the related admiration for the rebel, and for freedom.

Blake eagerly welcomed the events of 1789 in France. He is supposed to have taken to wearing the red bonnet of liberty in these early days of the Revolution, and discussed the progress of events with other enthusiasts under the aegis of the publisher Joseph Johnson. In 1791 Johnson began printing Blake's poem *The French Revolution*, which has a subtitle *A Poem in Seven Books*. Blake probably wrote only the First Book (in mid-1790), and the page-proof of this which survives, printed by Johnson, may never have been converted into a published work. The poem deals with the events in Paris and Versailles between the meetings of the newly constituted *Assemblée Nationale* in June 1789 and the fall of the Bastille on 14 July. In this First Book, of 306 lines, Blake does not describe the actual attack on the Bastille — we may imagine that this, and the fall of the Bastille, were to be the matter of subsequent books, and that indeed Blake's enthusiastic hope of brisk and millennial reform in 1789-90 led him to believe that the Revolution came to a head on the *quatorze juillet* and that its work would then be completed in a matter of months. That this did not happen and that the course of events became much more protracted and more sinister explains, or helps to explain, why the First Book was itself probably never published, and why Blake did not complete the poem.

Yet the First Book survives, and lines 18-53 describe the Bastille. Blake was rarely interested in accuracy of factual description — what matters is the reality of the emotion which he feels. With the Bastille, which he never saw, he wished to convey the sense of the tyranny which it represented in his mind. When it was attacked, in July 1789, it had a military governor, M. de Launay, with a garrison of some 130 men, and contained seven prisoners. Blake converts the governor from a tolerably unremarkable man into a monster of repression, raises the garrison to a thousand, and gives the Bastille seven separately named towers, each containing a separate prisoner condemned to particular and terrible punishment. His description is one of the high points of gothic writing — were it in prose, it could be set beside that other fragment of 1774, 'Sir Bertrand', by John Aikin (see p. 116 above), as containing the essence of the gothic sublime. First, the governor:

> In its terrible towers the Governor stood, in dark fogs
>   listening the horror.
> He is uneasy, for his age, the age of repression, is passing:
>   Sudden seized with howlings, despair, and black night,
>   he stalked like a lion from tower
> To tower, his howlings were heard in the Louvre; from
>   court to court restless he dragged
> His strong limbs. . .
>   . . . in his soul
>   stood the purple plague,
> Tugging his iron manacles, and piercing through the
>   seven towers dark and sickly,
> Panting over the prisoners like a wolf gorged. (Quoted from
>   *Poetry and Prose of William Blake*, ed. G. Keynes, 1961,
>   p. 167).

Then Blake describes the towers and their prisoners. Sometimes the tower is called a 'den', so that we are not sure whether the place is high up in the château, or deep below the ground — and this, for gothic mystery, is proper. The first three towers, or dens, are named *Horror*, *Darkness* and *Bloody*, while the others have ironic names, *Religion*, *Order*, *Destiny* and *Tower of God*, similar in their inversion to the use of opposites in *The Marriage of Heaven and Hell* — 'heaven', 'hell', 'God' and 'the Devil', for example — in the sense contrary to the usual one. Each prisoner, peculiarly punished, has been imprisoned for a different crime — in each case, a crime which, to Blake's eyes, was an act of virtue, thus hated by tyrants:

> ... the den named *Horror* held a man
> ... confined for a writing prophetic...
> In the tower named *Bloody*, a skeleton yellow remained
>   in its chains on its couch
> Of stone, once a man who refused to sign papers of
>   abhorrence; the eternal worm
> Crept in the skeleton (ibid.).

Another, 'in the tower named *Darkness*' has 'a mask of iron on his face' — an echo of the seventeenth-century mystery of the 'man in the iron mask', imprisoned and anonymous, punished for the threat he was supposed to constitute to Louis XIV. The seventh and last prisoner is

> Mad, with chains loose, which he dragged up and
>   down; fed with hopes year by year, he pined
> For liberty; vain hopes: his reason decayed (p. 168).

This passage from *The French Revolution* is, I think, the only instance where the paraphernalia of the gothic is brought to bear on a contemporary and political event. No gothic novelists in the eighteenth century *wanted* to have it thought that their stories were set in the present — they would seem too improbable. Blake, on the contrary, deeply versed in the writing and imagery of his romantic predecessors, wished to transfer the emotional power of these murky scenes to support the cause of present liberty. For Blake, as passionately as Rousseau, believed in the innocence and blamelessness of emotion, in contrast to the sterility of reason — Jesus, he maintained in *The Marriage of Heaven and Hell*, 'was all virtue, and acted from impulse, not from rules'. Some years later, in 1795, two of his most famous coloured monotypes, 'Newton' and 'Nebuchadnezzar', express, as a part of their meaning, the extremes of two evils which come from a rational and unfeeling approach to life. Newton, once the darling of Thomson and Pope, 'discovering' nature at the beginning of the century

> — God said, 'Let Newton be!' and all was light —

is for Blake related to the God of the Old Testament, cruel, rational and revengeful — and lacking love, compassion, feeling; Nebuchadnezzar is the material man, so gross that he has become bestial. For Blake, both Locke the empiricist and Newton the mathematician were symbols of a mechanical and therefore feelingless attitude to life:

> I turn my eyes to the Schools and Universities of Europe
> And there behold the Loom of Locke, whose Woof rages dire,
> Wash'd by the Water-wheels of Newton. . .
> . . . cruel Works
> Of many Wheels I view, wheel without wheel, with cogs tyrannic,
> Moving by compulsion each other, not as those in Eden, which,
> Wheel within Wheel, in freedom revolve in harmony and peace
> (*Jerusalem*, I, 15, in Blake, ibid., p. 449).

(Just such an objection to the concept of the universe as a purely mathematical marvel made by a celestial watchmaker comes in the writing of Novalis in his essay *Die Christenheit oder Europa* (1799, published 1826). He saw the rational attitudes of the Enlightenment as no less than a 'hatred of religion',

> which transformed the infinite creative music of the universe into the monotonous rattling of a monstrous mill – a mill driven by the stream of chance. . . a mill *per se*, with neither architect nor miller, a mill which was indeed a veritable *perpetuum mobile*, a mill which ground by itself (Die Christenheit oder Europa, ed. O. Keuschele, 1980, p. 34).

The Bastille fell, Blake wrote the beginning of *The French Revolution*, and some of the companions whom he met at Joseph Johnson's shop were also eager to celebrate the coming of a new age. Fuseli was there, who wrote excitedly in the *Analytical Review* in December 1789 (V, p. 463) that this was 'an age pregnant with the most gigantic efforts of character, shaken with the convulsions of old, and the emergence of new empires'. There Fuseli met the writer and feminist Mary Wollstonecraft, whose Rousseauan *Vindication of the Rights of Women* Johnson had published in 1791. She fell in love with Fuseli, and in 1792 made plans to go to Paris with him to observe the Revolution at first hand. Mrs Fuseli was not cooperative, and Mary Wollstonecraft went to Paris on her own. Another in this circle was Tom Paine, the first part of whose *Rights of Man* was published in 1791. Tom Paine also went to France, and with Blake's assistance, in 1792. In this year, fear of the Revolution grew in Britain from uneasiness to open hostility. War had been declared by Louis XVI against the Empire in April, in August the French royal family had been evacuated from the Tuileries and were held in strict confinement in the Temple, and in the same month the 'guillotine' had been used for the first time to execute a political prisoner. In September there had been an outbreak of hysteria in which some 1,300 royalist prisoners were massacred – and shortly after, on 20 September 1792, the armies of revolutionary France had defeated the forces of the Empire and their allies led by the Duke of Brunswick at the battle of Valmy. Blake's reactions to this mixed bag sum up the perplexities which confronted free-thinking Englishmen at the time. Out of prudence – and maybe discouragement at the savagery of the September massacres – he did away with the *bonnet rouge*; and out of prudence and friendship, he urged Tom Paine (whose *Rights of Man*, part two, had recently appeared) to hurry straight on to France and not to go home. This was in September, when Paine had already been voted a French citizen by the *Assemblée Nationale*, and more recently a member of the Convention. Tom Paine escaped from the agents of the British government, and reached France and the land of the Revolution in safety. Meanwhile, out of jubilation and yet out of prudence, Blake had celebrated the victory of Valmy in 'A Song of Liberty' which he added as a conclusion to *The Marriage of Heaven and Hell*. Jubilation, yes – 'Empire is no more!' – 'For everything that lives is holy' – but also prudence. He had already torn off his 'white cockade' and 'never wore the red cap again', according to Alexander Gilchrist, his biographer; and in 'A Song of Liberty' the triumphal words nowhere say to the reader 'This is Valmy.' We could be celebrating *any* victory of good over evil. From this point in 1792 Blake's works become politically harmless. Names are no longer named, unless they are so obscure that they only mean something to Blake himself.

Valmy, and the September massacres just before, mark the point of crisis for foreign observers, if not for Frenchmen themselves. On the other side of France, within sound and shot of Valmy, Goethe had witnessed the battle. Unlike Blake, he was not on the revolutionaries' side, yet he too understood what this victory meant. After the battle, he sat among a quiet, disconsolate and hungry circle of German soldiers. At last, they asked him his opinion, which he gave: 'This very day marks a new age in the history of the world; and you can say, you were there as it began' (*Kampagne in Frankreich*, den 19 September Nachts). Wordsworth, Coleridge and a clutch of nearly forgotten novelists in England would have agreed – Thomas Holcroft, in his *Anna St Ives* of 1792, or William Godwin in *Caleb Williams* (1794). Well after the Terror, the ideal of the rebel against society bobs up again in Mary Hays' *Memoirs of Emma Courtney* (1796), in the trenchant, dogmatic line *'obedience is a word which ought never to have had existence'*.

It is not my business to relate the events of the French Revolution in this history; nor even to try to explain them. I wish merely to show

how the ideals of wildness, naturalness and spontaneity, cherished by writers and artists for some decades, now found *practical* expression in the activity of the Revolution. Yet − to reassure the social and economic historians of these violent years − I would not claim for a moment that the romantic beliefs in wildness and spontaneity were more than a part, and often a tiny part, beside the forces of hunger, poverty, ignorance, ambition, frustration, anger and fear which were then active in shaping the course of French history. But these romantic beliefs did, for a while, have some effect, as shown in the events and people, not unimportant and not unrepresentative, mentioned in the following pages.

In France itself, long before Mary Hays wished to delete *obedience* from the dictionary, there were passionate attempts to begin the world again. The fall of the Bastille was by no means the only event to have symbolic meaning. With Rousseau in their minds, reformers and revolutionaries had long been hoping to replace the old and divided order of society with one which was new and undivided, in which privilege and precedent were swept away by a spontaneity of human brotherhood. In Rome, in 1784, the painter Jacques-Louis David (1748-1825) had begun work on *The Oath of the Horatii* in which the manly simplicity and unanimity of the oath-taking by the brothers − a political 'act' − is supplemented by the austerity of the architectural background, an arcade with pillars in a 'primitive' Tuscan Doric. (Another painter with Rousseauan sympathies at this time, Fuseli, had already sketched in 1779, and painted in 1780, his equally sublime *Oath on the Rütli*.) The political 'oath', in which the individual submerges his identity in a greater common and patriotic cause, is a great unifying act in revolutionary France, and is in symbolic terms the most forceful expression of the desire to establish universal 'natural rights' in place of the divisive orders of the *ancien régime*. In January 1789 the Abbé Sieyès published a pamphlet, *Qu'est-ce que le Tiers Etat?* which opens with three simple questions, and their direct answers:

> The plan of this paper is simple enough. We have to ask ourselves three questions:
> 1º   What is the Third Estate? Everything.
> 2º   What has it been in the political order until now? Nothing.
> 3º   What does it demand? To become something.

This wish of the Third Estate to 'become something' in the body politic was dramatically gratified in June 1789. The three *Etats* of the clergy, nobility and commoners had at last met on 5 May. But the king, court and leaders of the clergy and nobility made it clear that they did not consider the three *Etats* as a single, homogeneous body, but as one in which the *Tiers Etat* was inferior. Quickly, the *Tiers Etat* reacted to this, and adopted for itself the title of *Assemblée Nationale*, the 'National Assembly', fulfilling in this the claim by Sieyès that the *Tiers Etat* was 'everything'. The king's response was to call a royal session to be held in the hall used for the meetings of the *Etats*. This, incidentally and intentionally, prevented the *Tiers Etats* from meeting in the meanwhile. Fearing that they might be muzzled indefinitely, the *Tiers Etat* held an emergency meeting in another place – in the *Jeu de paume* or 'tennis court'. There, on 20 June 1789, the *Tiers Etat*, now *Assemblée Nationale*, urgently swore the *Serment du Jeu de Paume*, the 'Oath of the Tennis Court', to continue in existence and in activity until a constitution for the kingdom had been drawn up and established. The painter David was present, swore the oath, and, in 1790, was commissioned to paint the historic scene. Though the original has gone, his detailed sketches remain, and other peoples' engravings of the painting, enough to convey the tumult of the scene. In the centre, standing on a table, Bailly, the president of the Assembly, administers the oath, with his hand raised; and all round him, hands are raised, like those of the Horatii, in passionate assent. Prominent near the centre, stands Robespierre, with *his* hands on his bosom, not in disagreement, but to restrain the exultant beating of his heart at this triumph of humanity over oppression.

On 14 July, the Bastille was taken; on 11 August the National Assembly declared that it was 'entirely destroying the feudal regime' and set about dismantling the inherited and transmitted privileges of the nobility and clergy. These privileges of the old, currupt society formed an immense *practical* obstacle to a new, united and unfragmented nation. The *theoretical* foundation of this unity soon followed, in the *Déclaration des droits de l'homme et du citoyen*, the 'Declaration of the Rights of Man and the Citizen', whose text was agreed on 26 August 1789.

In contrast to the American Declaration of Independence of 1776, which is much more related to the Colonies' immediate and practical problem of achieving independence from the British Crown, this *Déclaration* is conceived in general, idealistic terms, derived in part (though certainly not entirely) from Rousseau's *Discours sur...* *l'inégalité* and *Du Contrat social*. The preamble begins with implicit belief in man's original virtue and happiness – like that of the 'noble savage' — which has since been lost in the corruption of society:

> considering that ignorance, neglect or contempt of the rights of man are the sole causes of public misfortune and the corruption of government.

The seventeen articles of the *Déclaration* repeatedly speak of the unity and equality of men, and of man's 'natural rights' (in implicit condemnation of the divisive and unevenly distributed feudal privileges which the National Assembly had abolished two weeks before). In article 6, a most Rousseauan phrase appears, 'the law is the expression of the general will', which unequivocally sets it above the *particular* will of the king.

On 6 October, the royal family was taken by force from Versailles into Paris, and obliged to reside in the palace of the Tuileries. Early next year, on 4 February 1790, a 'national oath' to the king and constitution (still in the making) was sworn in Paris by the members of the National Assembly, the process extending swiftly to the electors in each part of Paris, to the populace at large, and out into France as a whole, to provide the semblance at least of what Rousseau had termed the *volonté générale*, 'the general will', in joyous operation. On 19 June 1790, a year after the Oath of the Tennis Court, one of the non-Frenchmen active in the French revolutionary scene — the serious, voluble and alas! comical Prussian, Anacharsis Cloots (1755-94) — presented himself before the National Assembly at the head of a gathering of 36 assorted foreigners, an 'embassy of the human race'. Cloots proceeded to federate humanity to the French nation. After this, the Assembly, fired with egalitarian zeal, voted to abolish all titles of nobility. Cloots himself was a baron, and this he abjured, taking up with pride the appellation of 'orator of the human race'.

For the moment, in 1790, the climax of these demonstrations of fraternity was on the first anniversary of the fall of the Bastille, at the Champ de Mars, where, on a huge mound in the centre of a hastily prepared amphitheatre, an 'altar of the Fatherland' was erected. This was the 'most sublime spectacle', 'the triumph of human kind' which Helen Maria Williams was just in time to witness, and which gave her the feeling that she was indeed 'a citizen of the world'. Similar federative commemorations were held all over France, and 'trees of liberty' planted with enthusiasm. One was planted in front of the Bastille — or rather, the ruins of the Bastille, for the fortress is now in part demolished. In his *French Revolution*, Thomas Carlyle adds (I, xii), that the site of the prison is marked with a cheery sign, *Ici l'on danse* — 'Dancing Here'.

For nearly two years after the fall of the Bastille the Revolution proceeded in a verbose, high-flown and — relatively — moderate manner. While many aristocrats had fled the country, the king and queen, detained in the Tuileries, schemed incompetently and ineffectually to return to power, and other aristocrats joined different republican factions. Among these the most colourful was Philippe, Duc d'Orléans, who had long been in opposition to the king's party, and hoped that, should Louis XVI lose the throne, he might become the next king of France. Promptly after the Oath of the Tennis Court, Orléans had ostentatiously led a party of nobles to join forces with the *Tiers Etat*, and subsequently intrigued and entertained lavishly and flamboyantly at the Palais Royal. It was at one of his dinners that Helen Maria Williams observed the jewellery worn by Mme de Genlis, the novelist who had written *Adèle et Théodore* (see p. 193). She had become the governess of Orléans' children, and probably his mistress; and, as a person of egalitarian sympathies, she had abandoned her titles of nobility, and called herself simply Mme Brulart. Now, at this dinner, she wore

a medallion made of a stone of the Bastille polished. In the middle of the medallion, *Liberté* was written in diamonds; above was marked, in diamonds, the planet that shone on the 14th of July; and below was seen the moon, of the size she appeared that memorable night. The medallion was set in a branch of laurel, composed of emeralds, and tied at the top with the national cockade, formed of brilliant stones of the three national colours (*Letters written in France*, 1790, p. 38).

'*Liberté*. . . in diamonds' — as idealistic, as paradoxical and as ineffectual as Cloots' federating humanity to the French nation.

On 20 June 1791 the king, with the queen, the royal children and a few attendants, escaped from the Tuileries, attempting to reach foreign territory. The coach was halted near the frontier, at Varennes, and the royal party was brought back in disgrace. Documents left behind in the Tuileries showed that the king and the queen had merely been paying lip-service to the ideas of national reform, and had meanwhile been plotting to achieve foreign intervention and the overthrow of the revolutionary government. Hostility to the king and to the aristocrats grew rapidly, linked with the certainty that they were in league with the anti-revolutionary forces, including the thousands of aristocratic *émigrés* who had fled from France. As war became more likely, the conviction hardened that it would not be so much a war between the French and their foreign enemies, as war between the French nation, and all those who opposed the ideals of the Revolution. Within the state, therefore, came a growing suspicion of the aristocrats, and the belief that the nation must be purged of all those who threatened the purity of the Revolution. The process fed itself, up to the 'September massacres' in 1792, and beyond, into the 'Terror' in 1793-4. After the French victory at Valmy, on 20 September 1792, a wave of fresh determination to complete the Revolution surged forward. On the following day, the newly elected Convention met, and instantly stated that a new era had begun. The monarchy was abolished, a republic established, and 21 September 1792 was the first day of the new republic. At this Convention the legislators saw themselves as representing a regenerated nation, and from this point more than any other — more than the fall of the Bastille in 1789, or the execution of Louis XVI on 21 January 1793 — they saw that France was 'beginning again'. When, on 5 October 1793, the new revolutionary calendar was ratified, it took 22 September 1792 for '1 vendémiaire' of year 1. The calendar not only implied that a new era had begun, but in its re-division and re-naming of the parts of the year it severed as fully as could be all connection with the old and Christian order. There were still twelve months, but they were all re-named, after the natural and agricultural characteristics of each part of the year — *vendémiaire* meaning 'grape-harvest' or 'vintage' month; the next, *brumaire*, meaning 'foggy' month; the next, *frimaire*, meaning 'frosty' month, and so on. Each month had thirty days, and five festival days were added during the year to make the 365. The festivals were wholly divorced from the old Christian celebrations of Easter, Christmas and the rest by calling them *sanculottides* — the people's festivals. The months were split, not into the old weeks, revolving round the Christian Sunday, but into three *décades* or ten-day periods, in which the tenth day was the 'day of rest'. It was even proposed to replace the old system of a 24-hour day, with 60-minute hours, by a purely decimal system, but this was rejected. This new era with its 'natural' calendar is the most obvious of the many attempts of the revolutionary regime to replace an old system, heavily loaded with references to the old, corrupt order, by an entirely new one, whose references were universal, abstract, popular or 'natural'. As early as 1789 the National Assembly had proposed an international approach to France's complex systems of weights and measures, suggesting that the Académie des Sciences in Paris might work with the Royal Society in London to create a new system with universal validity. The cooperation did not occur, but after some while the metric system was elaborated, less flamboyant than the revolutionary calendar, but longer-lasting.

In the newly elected Convention, in September 1792, the inventor of the new calendar, Romme, was a member, with many others from the time of the *Assemblée Nationale*. Shortly after the Oath of the Tennis Court in 1789, the Duke of Orléans had shown his revolutionary sympathies by passing openly from the side of the nobility to join the *Tiers Etat*. Now, to show *his* regeneration, Philippe d'Orléans, elected a member, henceforth repudiates his aristocratic surname, Orléans, and asks for a new, revolutionary name: which is given him, *Egalité* – 'equality'. Until his execution on 3 November 1793 – barely a year later – he is known by this name, Philippe Egalité. Above all, two members of the Convention must be mentioned, David and Robespierre, who exemplify the early romantic belief in the virtue of the simple, uncorrupted 'natural man', and the rightness of instinctive behaviour as opposed to the rational, calculating ways of the Old Regime. David has already been mentioned; in the Convention, he supported Robespierre wholeheartedly, declaring in July 1794, at the climax of the Terror, when the opposition to Robespierre suddenly threatened to overwhelm him, 'I shall drink the hemlock with you.' The phrase not only expresses heroic determination to give his life for a noble cause, but puts it in an antique and elevated situation – that of the death of Socrates, a subject which he had himself painted in 1787. Until Robespierre's fall, David put himself and his art at the service of the Revolution. Already at the time of painting the *Oath of the Horatii* he had recommended to his pupil Gros the study of ancient virtue, not the recording of modern frivolity – 'Quick, quick, my friend, search through your Plutarch', he had cried. In 1789, he had been among those who had sworn the Oath of the Tennis Court, and he worked on the huge painting of the scene in 1790-1. The *virtue* of the patriot who submerges his personal wishes in the public cause, as in these two commemorative paintings, is praised in his occasional speeches in the Convention; implicit in his voting for the death of the king in January 1793, and forms the inspiration of his *Marat assassiné* – 'The dead Marat' – completed in October 1793, only three months after Charlotte Corday had stabbed Marat in his bath on 13 July. And until the fall of Robespierre he had been busied with the planning and décor of the several Rousseauan pageants which were held by the Convention to mark the founding and progress of the new age. (It should be noted here that David's painting is generally, and properly, classed as 'classical', both in the academic sense of its balanced composition and careful finish, and in the more general sense that his subjects are — as indicated at the very outset of this history — to do with 'the men who dwell in the city'. What is 'romantic' in some of his work is the admiration of the simple, spontaneous and unanimous reaction which occurs in a moment of peril or exaltation, and, in his arrangement of the pageants, the 'orchestration' of just such praise of natural virtue.)

Robespierre — Maximilien François Marie Isidore de Robespierre (1758-94) — was a passionate admirer of Rousseau. When Rousseau lived out the remaining weeks of his life at Ermenonville in 1778, Robespierre was one of the last people to visit him, and his career reflects his Rousseauan beliefs right up to his own death in 1794. Known as the 'incorruptible' for his modest, fastidious and consciously Spartan self-discipline, he believed above all that the French nation must be led back to a noble simplicity, to *vertu* of a kind enjoyed by Rousseau's 'noble savage' before the corruption of society had made men either into slaves or tyrants. All opposition or threat to the achievement of so complete an aim must be removed, since it is opposition to the supreme good — and tantamount to opposition to the 'Supreme Being', evidence of whose goodness is both felt spontaneously within the individual, and apparent in the world of nature around us. His argument, pronounced on 3 December 1792, for the death of Louis XVI is characteristic — the man must die, because his continued existence threatens the state, and because the very creation of the republic is already a judgement against the king:

> We are not holding a trial here. Louis is not a prisoner before the bar. You are not judges. You are statesmen, no less, representatives of the nation. You do not have to pronounce sentence for or against an individual, but to undertake a measure of public safety, and to execute an act of national providence...
>
> Louis was king; and the Republic was founded: the great question which faces you is decided by these words alone... Louis then cannot be judged; he is already condemned — or else the Republic can never be guiltless...
>
> Have we the right to a will which is contrary to the general will, or to a wisdom which differs from the rightness of the universe?...
>
> With regret I utter this fatal truth... but Louis must die, since the nation must live.

In an argument of this kind, 'reason' has been silenced in the face of an overpowering emotional conviction. In the last months of Robespierre's own life, such indifference to the distracting forces of circumstance became exaggerated to the point of blindness. On 10 June 1794, two days after the *Fête de l'Etre Suprême*, the 'Festival of the Supreme Being', the 'law of 22 prairial' was passed by the Jacobin-dominated Convention, and with Robespierre's blessing. This law, aimed less at punishing than at destroying the opponents of the Revolution, has an absolute, almost religious, belief in the rightness — the *virtue* — of the Revolution — and a corresponding certainty that its enemies must be annihilated. These enemies were allowed no defence:

13. If material or moral proof exists, independently of the evidence of witnesses, no witnesses will be heard, unless this formality should appear necessary, either to discover accomplices or for other important reasons of public interest.

The black-or-white absolutism of the attitude is conveyed in the ruling to do with the verdicts of the court. Only two verdicts were to be allowed — acquittal or death. Between 10 June 1794, the date this law was passed, and 27 July, the day Robespierre fell, 1,376 victims were executed at the guillotine. In his last speech before the Convention on 26 July, his words are vibrant with the persuasion of his own, and his supporters', innate, impulsive and indestructible innocence — and the equally blatant corruption of his enemies. They, vile creatures, had suspected him of coveting supreme power in France. But such an infamous idea 'will appear probable only to those perverse beings who have not even the right to believe in virtue'. He goes on, at length (his speech lasted for four hours):

Yet virtue exists as you can testify, feeling and pure souls. . . ; it exists, that generous ambition to found on earth the first Republic of the world; that egoism of undegenerate men who find a celestial voluptuousness in the calm of a pure conscience and the ravishing spectacle of public happiness. You feel it at this moment burning in your souls. I feel it in mine.

Though Blake would never have been party to the wholesale executions of the Terror, he would have understood this achievement of belief, and certitude of virtue, through depth of feeling. Jesus, as he had written, 'was all virtue, and acted from impulse, not from rules'.

Thinking charitably of the recent events in France, the 'ravishing spectacle of public happiness' Robespierre refers to can only have been

253

one of the deist or pantheist pageants which his admirer David had helped to stage in the last months, in which Robespierre had taken part, and for which legislation had recently been passed. On 7 May 1794, the decree of 18 floréal was passed, acknowledging — no less — the existence of the Supreme Being. The first article reads: 'the French people acknowledge the existence of the Supreme Being and the immortality of the soul'; the seventh article lists five principal and 36 related festivals which are to be celebrated in the course of the year; article fifteen decrees that the main festival, the Festival of the Supreme Being, will be celebrated on the following 20 prairial (8 June 1794), and the decree ends with the statement that David will be responsible for the planning of the event. In his last speech before the Convention (26 July 1794), Robespierre looks back to this particular festival with words of ecstasy:

This day had left all France with a profound feeling of calm, of happiness, of wisdom and goodness. Seeing this sublime assembly of the foremost nation in the world, who would have thought that crime could still exist anywhere on the earth?

There had been many earlier festivals of a similar kind. When, on 10 August 1793, the long-awaited Constitution was agreed, this was celebrated with a 'Festival of Unity and Indivisibility' in various public places to hail, once again, the birth of a new society. At the main celebration a part of the décor, by David, included a 'fountain of regeneration'. Where the Bastille had stood a statue of Nature was set up, spouting water from her breasts, which the attendant delegates from the Convention and lesser bodies duly and formally drank. In the Place de la Révolution (once Place Louis XV), a statue of Liberty was unveiled, and 3,000 birds were released, bearing the idealistic message 'We are free. Imitate us.' Later in the year, on 10 November 1793, the notorious 'Festival of Reason' was held, a ceremony performed in many different churches, with the aim of confounding both the atheists and the Roman Catholic church, by showing that the new republic had a genuine and respectable religion which had replaced the mummery and prejudice of Christianity. Not all the ceremonies were the same, nor did David design them all. There was a strong party in the Convention favouring atheism, while Robespierre was a fervent Rousseauan deist, and David seems to have cooperated mostly in projects which had Robespierre's approval. For Robespierre the 'Reason' which this festival celebrated was infinitely remote from the reason of Descartes; rather was it the emotional conviction of the existence of God which we read in Rousseau's *Rêveries*, experienced in unthinking, but deeply felt, communion with nature. Several of the main Parisian churches were taken over for this festival, and the best-remembered celebration, of a markedly rational and even atheist stamp, was held in the erstwhile cathedral of Nôtre-Dame. A statue of Liberty was 'erected on the site and in the place of the ci-devant Holy Virgin'. During this 'Festival of Liberty and Reason', an actress from the Opera was employed to represent the spirit of Liberty, and during the celebrations members of the Convention sang a 'Hymn to Liberty' composed by Marie-Joseph de Chénier, younger brother of the poet André Chénier. In another Parisian church, Saint Eustache, the romantic décor included 'a landscape decorated with cottages and bosquets of trees', a countryside such as Rousseau would have approved.

Most Rousseauan of these pageants was the *Fête de l'Etre Suprême*, the 'Festival of the Supreme Being', held on 8 June 1794. It began in the gardens of the Tuileries, now re-named the Jardin National. The ceremony, arranged by David, was lavish, popular, and replete with symbolic actions. Robespierre, at the head of the Convention, was to set fire to a briskly inflammable statue of Atheism, and this conflagration would reveal another statue rising up, that of Wisdom shining 'in all its splendour'. Robespierre made two speeches at the Tuileries, the first showing once again the conviction that the French nation was reborn, and beginning a new existence. He exclaimed rapturously:

It has come at last, this ever-blessed day which the French nation consecrates to the Supreme Being. Never did the world which he has created present a spectacle so worthy of his sight.

The Convention then proceeded to the Champ de Mars for the main ceremony. The members, led by Robespierre, were ranged round a 'mountain' which served as an 'altar' for the celebrations, with a tree of Liberty at the top (see Plate 48). The members of the Convention were in turn ringed by a tricolour ribbon, held 'by Childhood adorned with violets, Adolescence adorned with myrtles, Virility adorned with oak-leaves and Old Age adorned with vine-leaves and olives' (reported in the *Moniteur*, XX, p. 700). They all sang a 'Hymn to the Supreme Being', written by M.-J. Chénier, and enjoyed the climax to the occasion, which was typically Davidian. The youths – the ones crowned with myrtles – all draw their swords, and place them in the hands of their aged fathers; they swear to make them everywhere victorious; they swear to bring about the triumph of equality and liberty over tyrannical oppression.

It is a repetition of the *Oath of the Horatii* and the *Oath of the Tennis Court*, but presented as a three-dimensional, theatrical and public event – in which the spectators were to join, applauding the oath sworn by the young men, and spontaneously adding *their* self-dedication to that of the actors in the pageant. In the words of the *Moniteur*,

all the citizens, male and female, merging their feelings in a fraternal embrace, concluded the festival by raising to the heavens this cry of humanity and citizenship: *Long live the Republic*!

In the following weeks, which saw the crisis of the Jacobin Terror (hardly 'the ravishing spectacle of public happiness'), the poet André Chénier was executed; also Philippe Egalité. Tom Paine, author of *The Rights of Man*, and a member of the Convention, was saved by an accident. Anacharsis Cloots, orator of the human race, had already been executed on 24 March.

Robespierre was executed on 28 July 1794, and the apparatus of the Terror was quickly dismantled. David, ally of Robespierre, was imprisoned, and later released – to paint again, and in another vein. Gradually a kind of stability seemed to emerge from the ruins of the Terror. Little over a year later, on 5 October 1795, the last uprising to threaten the Convention was scotched when Barras and his second-in-command, the young Bonaparte, scattered the rebellious demonstrators with 'a whiff of grapeshot'.

In the last chapter of his *French Revolution* (VII, viii), Carlyle begins, apropos of his subject, 'Homer's Epos, it is remarked, is like a Bas-Relief sculpture: it does not conclude, but merely ceases'. Like such a sculpture, the Revolution had 'ceased' with the 'whiff of grapeshot', though its effects could be felt, and imagined, long afterwards. The French Revolution was indeed also like 'Homer's Epos'; it resembled an 'epic poem' in the magnitude and violence of its events, in the heroic and tragic conflicts of its protagonists. Long before the violent outbreaks of 1789, Thomas Blackwell had written of Homer's epics from the secure vantage-point of a Scottish university in 1736. We may regret the lack of 'the Marvellous and Wonderful' in our lives – the qualities which are essential as the 'Nerve' of epic poetry; but, says Blackwell, we have instead the blessings of 'Peace, Harmony and good

Order', and he wishes 'that we may never be a proper Subject of an Heroic Poem'.

Europe had now witnessed the 'proper subject of an heroic poem'. Between 1789 and 1795, the tottering semblance of peace, harmony and good order had been gradually lost in France, exchanged at the worst moments for violence, discord and confusion. For decades such tempestuous possibilities had been increasingly admired in the domain of art and literature, in the realm of nature, and in the vagaries of personal conduct. Now, put to the harshest test of practical experience, in the affairs of 'men who dwell in the city', such wildness was found to produce, not the thrilling shudder of the sublime, but downright destruction.

11

Whiffs of Grapeshot

The roaring of lions, the howling of wolves, the raging of the
stormy sea, and the destructive sword are portions of eternity too
great fot the eye of man! (William Blake, *The Marriage of Heaven
and Hell*)

As clearly as anyone outside France, Blake had seen that the events of
1789 were 'the proper subject of an heroic poem'. He had begun
The French Revolution. His sympathies were, and remained, with the
revolutionaries. But only book I of this projected 'epic' survives. The
ever-increasing violence of the revolution produced such a horror of
'the destructive sword' of the republicans that many who had thrilled
to news of the Oath of the Tennis Court and the fall of the Bastille
now turned away, both from revolutionary and political violence,
and from the other forms of violence which had been admired in the
second half of the eighteenth century. Blake himself was no turncoat.
But he was dismayed by the excesses of the revolutionaries, and only
too aware that it was now imprudent for him, or anyone in England,
to show ardent support for them. (Indeed, in 1804 he himself was
accused of sedition, tried for high treason, and acquitted.) From
1790-1, his poetry and his paintings are removed more and more
from political and present reality, invested with a scheme of private
mythological reference which effectively prevents his art from having
any immediate and 'seditious' impact.

While Blake stayed true to his beliefs — but henceforward declared
them through a veil of obscurity — many more, both inside and outside France were moved by the excesses of the French Revolution to
turn against the 'wildncss' which they had once admired. While some,
who must be discussed in a moment, anticipated this general rejection
of wildness even before the outbreak of the Revolution, others
responded more slowly, and in a partial manner, in the late 1790s. By
the end of the century, so wide a rejection of the different aspects of
Shaftesbury's 'wildness' has occurred that we may see it as a *terminus*
for the first half of romanticism. After the Revolution, romanticism
goes on — and on. But the experience of the Revolution was indelible;
rare indeed are the later romantics who could say, without reserve,

'The wildness pleases,' in the manner of Goethe, or Walpole, or Fuseli, or Diderot, or Burke and Rousseau, in the years before 1789.

Some of these people had died before the Revolution – Rousseau in 1778, Diderot in 1784 – and we can only imagine what *their* reactions to the actual events might have been. Some of them had never implied that 'the wildness pleases' in all possible ways. Walpole, for example, is a passionate admirer of sublime horror in *Otranto* and *The Mysterious Mother*, while remaining a life-long addict of social, literary and political intrigue. Again, Rousseau is eager for freedom of emotion for himself, for his fictional lovers and for his 'noble savage', and freedom from the city-centred and social intrigue which Walpole found so satisfying, while avoiding or ignoring the wilder aspects of nature and the horror of the gothic.

Others, long before the Revolution gave the decisive impetus to these evolving attitudes, had rejected some sublime or Rousseauan enthusiasm which they had earlier shared. Usually, this change in attitude followed the 'test of experience'. While Salomon Gessner in Switzerland could persevere in the painting and description of arcadian landscapes, and Gainsborough could subtly and convincingly evolve his unique pastoral idyll from his vision of the English countryside; and while Marie Antoinette and her circle could play at being shepherds and shepherdesses until the outbreak of the French Revolution, others who had admired this gentle approach to nature, evolved in the first half of the century, decided that it was inadequate when set against the reality of rural life. So John Aikin protested that in England, 'pastoral poetry' was 'a native of happier climes . . . What is reality on the soft Arcadian and Sicilian plains, is all fiction here' (*Miscellaneous Pieces in Prose*, 1774, p. 246). Yet Aikin included in the same volume his thrilling fragment 'Sir Bertrand', where his concern with 'reality' is lost in the terror of 'fiction'. Reality in nature is again the business of the poet George Crabbe, whose *The Village* (1783) is a sternly anti-idyllic portrayal of rural life, and a rejection of the Rousseauan dream of simple rural felicity.

The value for Europeans, if not the existence, of Rousseau's 'noble savage' was also questioned. In 1772, Diderot drafted his essay-dialogue, *Supplément au Voyage de Bougainville*, which comments on the idyllic picture of Tahiti – or 'Nouvelle-Cythère' – drawn in Bougainville's *Voyage autour du monde* of the previous year. He does not deny the truth of Bougainville's picture of Tahitian happiness, nor does he show the European who talks with the Tahitian as lacking in corruption. But he points out, with a stress on the paradoxical aspect of the situation, that the two societies, one simple and healthy, the other complex, devious and even diseased, cannot be combined. As much is said by Cowper in book I of *The Task* (1784), when he reflects on the fate of the Tahitian Omai, brought to England by Captain Cook and returned to his native island after a year's 'experience' of European ways:

> The dream is past; and thou hast found again
> Thy cocoas and bananas, palms and yams,
> And homes tall thatched with leaves. But hast thou found
> Their former charms? (*The Task*, I, 655-8).

Omai's visit to England was, willy-nilly, a practical test of these ideas of the 'noble savage'. Omai returned, and his homecoming, though not as sad as Cowper feared, was certainly muddled, inglorious and tainted with the Europeans' disease. On the voyage from Tahiti back to Europe in 1774-5, the German naturalist Georg Forster had regretfully concluded that the European incursion into the south Pacific was deeply destructive to the 'happy' natives of Tahiti:

> If the knowledge of a few individuals can only be acquired at such a price as the happiness of nations, it were better for the discoverers and the discovered, that the South Sea had still remained unknown to Europe and its restless inhabitants (*Voyage* [1777], 1968, p. 346).

Another practical test of the Rousseauan ideal was made by the *émigré* Frenchman, Hector St John de Crèvecœur, who lived in and travelled in the American Colonies in the late 1770s, experiencing a part of the War of Independence. He visited several of the Colonies, farmed for himself for some time in Orange County, in New York, and wrote down his impressions in the *Letters from an American Farmer* of 1782, and in further essays which were published in 1925 as *Sketches of Eighteenth-Century America* (quotations from Crèvecœur, *The Divided Loyalist*, ed. M. Cunliffe, 1978). In many of these descriptions he is seeing through obviously Rousseauan spectacles, finding 'nature' more beautiful and nearer to the Creator than 'art', finding solace and fruitfulness in the freely growing and abundant produce of the — uncorrupted — American soil. He tells with delight how the fireflies were so bright and so numerous that he would take one 'carefully by the wings' and then, 'carrying it along the lines of my book, I have, when thus assisted by these living flambeaux, perused whole pages and then thankfully dismissed these little insect-stars' (*Divided Loyalist*, p. 187); and again he describes the supremely efficient 'natural society' of an ant-hill, exceeding by far in its economy and discipline the achievements of human beings (pp. 157-60). Elsewhere he writes with horror of the barbaric punishment meted out by Europeans to a negro slave who has killed his overseer (pp. 112-14). But in the twelfth of the *Letters*, 'Distresses of a Frontier Man', written under the stress of war, with his own farm and family liable to be attacked by either side, the idyll is strained. Should he, to save his children from death, go away with them to live with a tribe of Indians? The simple life? To live naturally? Yet the Indians may be treacherous; and if the children survive, their characters may have been so alienated that they will no longer know their own parents. He resolves to 'revert into a state approaching nearer to nature', taking his family to live among the Indians who are 'without temples, without priests, without kings, and without laws' (pp. 134-5). His praise and description of the Indians' way of life reads like a paraphrase from the *Discours sur. . .l'inégalité*. Unlike most of his analyses of American life, this passage is absurdly remote from reality.

The real danger he was in forced him to a practical response. He left the backwoods with his children, left America and returned to Europe. His Letters were sold, profitably, in England, and some years later he returned briefly to New York as French consul. The backwoods had been exchanged for the city.

Most important of those to reject the ideals of wildness, independence from society and the genius before the Revolution are Diderot and Goethe. In the *Supplément* Diderot had cast doubt on the value of the 'noble savage' as an ideal which Europeans would be able to follow. In *Le Neveu de Rameau* (written c. 1761-75, published in German 1805, in French 1821 . . . 1891. Quoted from Diderot, *Œuvres romanesques*, ed. H. Bénac, 1962) the discussion between 'Moi' — the author — and 'Lui' — Rameau's nephew — and the interspersed comments of 'Moi' on the proceedings are given the setting of a Parisian coffee-house, and the subject of Rameau's nephew's doubts and certainties to do with his musical career — singer, composer and creator, and paid teacher. The nephew is a disreputable, down-at-heel parasite, and 'Moi' both pities and despises him, for 'Moi' is responsible, respectable, solvent and self-righteous. But the nephew is also a genius — or nearly so; there lies his problem — he has a spark of creativity which others like 'Moi' do not have (it is a gift, not something one may acquire), which others may envy, which makes him *different* from the rest of society; and which, being only a spark, allows him moments of sublime power, but only to abandon him and leave him, ridiculous, a while later.

Diderot had once admired 'genius' with fervour. But he had quarrelled with Rousseau — who had been, together with Shaftesbury's Theocles, the model for 'Dorval' — and at the same time had become engrossed in the bourgeois, society-centred task of producing the *Encyclopédie*, published between 1751 and 1772. In the *Neveu de Rameau*, the scene is no longer the countryside, but the Café de la Régence. What impressed 'Moi' when watching Dorval, enough to make 'Moi' exclaim that Dorval was 'under a spell' as he indulged in the rapturous viewing of nature, is inadequate when a similar 'Moi' watches Rameau's ageing and unsuccessful nephew in Paris. The nephew tends to burst into 'pantomimes', periods of imitative musical excitement where he sings or mimes actors or instruments — or combinations of these. In the longest pantomime, he 'forgets himself' totally in the triumphant voicing and personation, not only of separate operatic songs, arias, characters and episodes, but in the presentation — all on his own, remember — of the absolute range of the human voice, and of human emotions: 'now in a *basso-profundo* he reached the infernal depths, now. . .he burst upwards to the very heights' (*Neveu*, p. 468). The patrons of the café, and the passers-by, stop to listen, and laugh uproariously at him — but he notices none of this, so seized with his wild enthusiasm that 'Moi' wonders if the newphew ought not to be taken to a lunatic asylum. But he goes on, imitating different instruments, then all the orchestra, and the choir, and at last the entire opera, presenting a universe through his sole mimetic genius. He *is* the vast range of scenes which nature contains:

> a storm, a tempest, the cries of those about to perish, mingled with the whistling of the wind and the crash of the thunder; he was night with its darkness, shadows and silence, for even silence is depicted by sounds (*Neveu*, p. 469).

His sublime repertoire in this 'pantomime' is close to the subject-matter of the epic poet, listed by Diderot in his *Discours sur la poésie dramatique* of 1758. Then, Diderot had expressed his preference for ways which were 'poetic' over ways which were 'civilised'; but here he shows that the poetic and sublime, as portrayed by Rameau's nephew in the confines of a coffee-house, are intriguing, admirable even, but also ridiculous. While the nephew is wholly absorbed (like Dorval in the earlier *Entretiens*) in the moment of inspiration, and sweat runs down his face, streaking the lapels of his coat with grimy powder fallen from his wig, 'Moi' asks himself,

Did I admire him? Yes, I did! Was I moved by all this?
Yes, I was moved; but a touch of the ridiculous was mixed
into these feelings and soured them (*Neveu*, p. 469.).

At the end of the dialogue, the nephew retires with a certain dignity. At least, 'Moi' has not persuaded him to change his ways, though no one, 'Moi' or any of Diderot's readers, would envy the nephew his shiftless character, or consider him of much 'use' in the corrupt, relentless yet unavoidable life of the city.

Most notable of all those who turned against romanticism before the outbreak of the French Revolution was Goethe. In his early twenties, he had shown enthusiastic belief in the wildest forms of the sublime — in works written between 1771 and 1775; and then, in November 1775, he moved to Weimar.

In his first years at Weimar Goethe retained much of his wildness, going on breakneck excursions with the young ruler, Karl August, who had just come of age. Yet while he enjoyed these escapades, Goethe was becoming involved in the court and administrative life of the small dukedom. The Duke had acquired a cottage (now known as the Gartenhaus) in the valley of the Ilm, just outside Weimar, for Goethe to live in, and he moved there in May 1776, delighted to be at a distance from the activity of the court, yet occupied with the problems it offered him of political power. Goethe fell in love with Charlotte von Stein, an older, married and more serious woman than any of the several women he had previously loved — and who steered him towards attitudes of 'seriousness' and 'responsibility'; among his many activities he considered the use and planning of his cottage garden, and of the countryside which surrounded it. In early December 1776, he accompanied the Duke on a visit to Wörlitz, where, as guest of Fürst Leopold von Anhalt-Dessau, they visited the castle and the gardens (which Fürst Leopold was busily enlarging into a landscape paradise), joined in hunting parties, and played boisterous games on the frozen lake. Goethe fell through the ice and was saved with difficulty.

Back in Weimar on 21 December, his creative and literary, courtly and amatory activities began again at once. By the night of the 24 December he had reached a crisis, summed up in his laconic journal as 'pressure, melancholy and belief' (*Goethes Tagebücher ... 1776-1782*, ed. H. Düntzer, 1889). Next morning, on Christmas Day, 1776, his journal includes the Greek words 'αγαΘη τυχη, 'good fortune'. There is no explanation or comment until on 5 April he writes a triumphant 'good fortune erected!' and adds that he has 'invented a myth'.

What Goethe had done was to invent a symbol, an image, to represent the idea of his own 'good fortune' — and this image, presumably conceived in his mind on the night of 24 December 1776, and noted in his journal the next morning, was then created in a three-dimensional form and erected at the far end of his garden, on 5 April 1777. It is the 'Altar of Good Fortune' (see Plate 49), a monument composed of a perfectly plain cube of stone (about 3 feet square) surmounted by an equally plain stone sphere. There is no inscription or adornment at all. Goethe's friend Oeser, with whom he had discussed the project, said that most people thought it was just a stone ball from a gate-post (see Düntzer, p. 74, n. 5). But for Goethe it was deeply important, with a personal meaning which directs all the rest of his career. It marks the real turning-point in his life from the undirected, wilful and self-centered attitudes of the Sturm und Drang to an attitude of directed and responsible effort. For the *sphere* had the sense of movement, change, flux (which had been predominant in the attitudes of the Sturm und Drang), while the *cube* represented solidity, permanence and order. The monument as a whole therefore shows Goethe's desire to reconcile and unite his earlier wildness and instability with a greater order and control.

Amid the proliferating monuments to wildness at this time, Goethe's small and private 'Altar of Good Fortune' passed unnoticed. Its purity of form is in no way 'primitive'. Its simplicity and modest size make it unobtrusive — and the abstraction of its design would have made it incomprehensible to most people before the beginning of the present century. But we may see its private yet profound importance in Goethe's own writings, long before the excesses of the French Revolution brought other people to reconsider their views.

Within a year, he had begun to write satirically of contemporary garden-mania (which he had observed at Wörlitz, though the ultimate wildness of the volcano (see p. 185) had not yet been devised) in the *Triumph der Empfindsamkeit*, making fun of the extremes of sensibility then fashionable. The Prince in the play has such a love of wildness that he has decorated the interior of his castle with arbours, forests and grottoes, and has had screens painted which he takes round with him on his travels, so that a 'portable' wild nature can be erected round him wherever he goes. There is even a court functionary responsible for this, the 'Naturmeister' or 'Directeur de la nature'. Shaftesbury would have seen such silliness as 'rattles', diversions from the serious and moral contemplation of *real* nature (which is concealed by the Prince's painted screens). In his journal, in February 1778, Goethe notes the value of discipline: 'A more definite feeling of limitation and so of true expansion.' It is the discipline imposed on the sphere of movement, when it is anchored on the cube of order.

The 'order' Goethe was turning towards was again related to Shaftesbury's conception of nature, for the universe — even the 'wild' parts — is ultimately a work of harmony. In the *Moralists*, Theocles speaks of the 'harmony of thought' with which he is inspired, as he sings 'of Nature's order in created beings' (p. 98). In 1782 or 1783, Goethe contributed a prose piece, entitled 'Fragment', to the 32nd issue of the *Journal von Tiefurt* (ed. B. Suphan, 1892, pp. 258-61), in which he writes rapturously of the universality and divinity of nature. The passage is derived from the *Moralists* — parts are a paraphrase of Theocles' outburst. But Goethe leaves out of his paraphrase much to do with wildness, saying merely, 'even the most unnatural is nature'. Instead, he stresses man's (and Goethe's) dependence on nature, and the universal (and apparently paradoxical) qualities which make up the completeness of nature. It is almost as if he were describing the opposed but complementary qualities of the sphere (mutability) and the cube (order):

> In her, there is an eternal life, birth and movement, yet she never moves backwards. She is eternally changing; there is no instant when she stands still. She has no understanding of what it is to stay, and she has laid her curse on standing still. She is constant. Her pace is measured, rare are her exceptions, her laws unchangeable (*Journal*, p. 260).

Nature, Goethe writes, is 'kindly. . . wise and calm, whole yet never completed'. And, as if standing before the Altar of Good Fortune, he says 'I entrust myself to her' (p. 261).

A year later, in 1783, he published the poem 'Das Göttliche' in no. 40 of the *Journal von Tiefurt*, where the admiration for nature is much reduced (nature is unfeeling, indifferent, and existence is bound by 'eternal, iron, mighty laws'), but where man (or Goethe himself) has the duty, and the sublime potential, to do good, and to make something permanent from the fleeting, immaterial elements of existence: 'Man alone can make the moment endure.' Here Goethe sees man as the cube in the monument, giving order and value to the shifting elements. Again, it is Shaftesbury whom Goethe echoes, with his artist-creator, a 'just Prometheus under Jove'.

In this first decade at Weimar, Goethe wrote many works, in which there are often themes which may seen contradictory. Yet the general development is apparent, from Sturm und Drang wildness to a calmer and more responsible attitude. It is most readily seen in his play *Torquato Tasso*, which he began in 1780-1 (Acts I and II) and then abandoned for several years, not completing it until 1788. The play repeats the Werther-theme – the 'genius', the 'sensitive soul' who responds so deeply to the beauty and sorrow of the world that he is driven to madness. Goethe himself later admitted that he saw the poet Tasso as 'a fuller and more talented Werther', and in March 1787 he noted that he often thought of 'Rousseau and his hypochondriac wretchedness'. Werther committed suicide, Rousseau retired into the solitude of *rêverie*. But Goethe's Tasso, after offending his friends at court, and imagining that everyone is in league against him, turns for help at the end to the strong, calm and possibly unscrupulous courtier Antonio, embracing him in a symbolic reconciliation. It is not a clear, or a particularly heartening, conclusion – we do not know what will become of Tasso, we cannot admire Antonio without reserve. It is like Diderot's uncertain conclusion to the *Neveu de Rameau*, the reader is left with contradictory impressions of the imperfect and disreputable 'genius' and of his respectable interlocutor 'Moi' – who is both responsible, and dull. But Goethe's conclusion to *Tasso* at least avoids Werther's tragic death, and Rousseau's tragic isolation. The world of men, with its imperfections, has been accepted.

Tasso, begun in 1780 but not completed, was taken up again by Goethe, and given its difficult but 'worldly' conclusion while he was in Italy. Goethe left Weimar for Italy in September 1786 and returned in June 1788, and we might say that in this time he shed all remaining inclinations towards the Sturm und Drang. The conclusion to *Tasso* is characteristic, and may be compared with the evolution in the attitudes of his autobiographical hero Wilhelm Meister, and of his slowly developing portrait of Faust – matters which take Goethe far away from early forms of romanticism. His appreciation of the antique world moved profoundly away from the romantic interpretation of the past, and towards the seriousness of neo-classicism, admiring not the primitive but the pure, not the wild and the dilapidated but the simple and the solid qualities of early architecture. Most illuminating of all his Italian experiences in this respect were his excursions from Naples to see the temples at Paestum. He went twice, in March and in May 1787, and after the second visit he wrote (to Herder, 17 May 1787) that Paestum was 'the last, and virtually the noblest conception' which he would be taking back with him 'in its entirety' on his return journey to Weimar.

Like Piranesi in 1777, like Cozens in 1782, Goethe was aware that the 'primitive Doric' architecture of the temples at Paestum was conceived in a spirit far removed from that of Rome, and the Renaissance continuations of Roman architecture. Like them, he saw the strangeness of Paestum; but unlike them, he did not record an impression of 'terror', or even 'mystery'. Goethe saw the temples at Paestum instead as a foundation, a gigantic and solid beginning for the European architecture which was to follow.

On his return to Weimar in 1788, Goethe, much changed and matured, was to find his ruler, Herzog Karl August, a maturer man as well. In Goethe's absence Karl August had had *his* personal monument set up, the 'Schlangenstein' or 'Snake-stone'. This cylindrical monument, encircled by a twining serpent whose head is poised, alert and open-jawed, on the top, is inscribed **GENIO HUIUS LOCI**, 'To the Genius of the Place'. To Alexander Pope in the earlier part of the century, the 'genius of the place' which the landscape gardener was to respect meant, approximately, 'nature', and 'the natural configuration of the land'. Now, in Karl August's 'Schlangenstein', the sense is deepened. It includes not merely the natural qualities of the park at Tiefurt, but the spiritual qualities of the land as a whole, of which Karl August was the ruler, and to which, in this altar-like monument, he dedicates himself.

A similar seriousness is apparent in an aspect of the 'Roman House', built in the park in 1792-6. Meant as a small country residence for Karl August, its architect was J. A. Arens, but Goethe supervised the project, with the Duke's full approval. While the upper storey with its Ionic portico could have been built at any point in the eighteenth century, the small basement area looking out over the valley is both a demonstration of how Goethe had responded to the temples at Paestum, and a continuation of the sense of his Altar of Good Fortune, erected in 1777. The two pairs of 'primitive Doric' pillars which support the main arch and the upper part of the building are short, widening downwards to suggest immense strength and control. and they back on to unadorned piers of equal solidity. This is the fundamental simplicity and strength which Goethe saw at Paestum — not the wild, primitive and terrifying oldness perceived by Piranesi and Cozens. And it is the order and calm of the cube in the Altar of Good Fortune. The arch above has a pure curve, a shallow segment of a circle, which is 'based' on the pillars, like the sphere on the cube; and through the serenity of this open archway, 'nature — the valley and wooded slopes of the park — is formed into a picture (see Plate 50).

The French Revolution began within a year of Goethe's return to Weimar. He himself had admired, experienced and analysed all kinds of wildness from the 1770s onwards; and, as I have shown, he had come to reject it. When the dramatic hero he had himself created, Götz von Berlichingen, could die with the word 'Freedom!' on his lips, Goethe could himself understand, if he did not accept, the passionate desire for liberty which swept through France in 1789. In 1790 he made a watercolour sketch (now in the Kippenburg Collection) of a sign at the French frontier, showing a pole surmounted by the *bonnet rouge* and tricolour ribbons, and bearing the notice 'Passers-by: this land is free.' Even after the Revolution had plunged into unacceptable excess, he could appreciate the unprecedented nature of the Revolution, the 'newness' of the age which had been brought into being. Valmy, as he said, marked 'a new age in the history of the world'. In the same way Wordsworth, in the 1805 version of *The Prelude*, had seen the Revolution as 'that dawn', in which human nature had seemed to be 'born again' (X, 613, VI, 354), and Johann Georg Forster (who had accompanied Cook on his second circumnavigation) could describe it as 'the explosion and new-creation of a world' (letter of 5 July 1793, in his *Briefwechsel*, 1829, II, p. 460).

'New age', 'dawn', 'new-creation' the Revolution may have been. But the practical ways in which its sublime strivings found expression dismayed its foreign supporters, as did the later attacks by republican France on Switzerland. Napoleon's eventual change into an emperor confirmed their suspicions that liberty led first to anarchy, and then to odious tyranny. At different points, practically all those enthusiasts for the sublime who had welcomed the Revolution came at last to turn against it: Herder and Schiller in Germany, Burns, Coleridge, Southey and Wordsworth in Britain. The travelling farmer, Arthur Young, who had at first welcomed the opportunities for reform which the Revolution presented to the world at large — 'the construction of a new and better order and fabric of liberty than Europe has yet offered' (20 July 1789) — sees soon that 'the present devotion to liberty is a sort of rage' (10 January 1790), and by 1793 has written *The Example of France, a Warning to Britain*, denouncing Jacobin extremism. Helen Maria Williams, who had described with rapture Mme Brulart's medallion made from 'a stone of the Bastille', and with *Liberté* written on it in diamonds (see p. 249) is persuaded that the Jacobins are the source of 'every outrage committed by popular fury' (*Letters From France*, 1794, I, xlii). Soon after, she admits that 'the pure and sublime worship of liberty' has been perverted to 'the grim idol of anarchy' (II, i). She stayed in Paris during the Terror, and was frightened that any journal she kept might be used by the police to justify her execution. Consequently, 'amidst the horrors of Robespierre's tyranny', she turned to translating Bernardin de Saint-Pierre's *Paul et Virginie* into English, as being the most perfectly innocuous occupation she could devise. Her version of this idyllic and non-political story was published in 1795, and is a pointed example of the general retreat from violence which becomes common at this time.

Even Mary Wollstonecraft, who had wanted Fuseli to come with her to France, was several times daunted by the violence she observed, and her *Letter on the Present Character of the French Nation* (1792) is impregnated with her fears that evil and vice had triumphed over virtue in the tumult of the time. By 1794 she had recovered enough confidence in the necessity of the Revolution to write the first volume of her *Historical . . . View . . . of the French Revolution*, but she did not carry her survey beyond the removal of the royal family from Versailles to the Tuileries in October 1789. The Terror she never described.

Fuseli himself did not go to watch the Revolution, though he was at first in sympathy. He had for some years felt that the arts should not be attributed with moral or political importance, and in 1793 he wrote that 'their moral usefulness' was 'at best accidental and negative' (in the *Analytical Review*, XVI, July 1793, p. 242) — a withdrawal from involvement in political innovation, as well as from moral didacticism, which is paralleled by his condemnation of popular rule soon after. He saw the power of the Jacobins 'sinking into despotism', and 'the anarchies that ensue' as 'little more than the temporary contests for rule of factions equally criminal' (XVII, November 1793, p. 242). At that moment 'the tyrant of the ruling party' to whom he referred was Robespierre, supported at the level of artistic propaganda by his ardent admirer David (see p. 251). A few months later, in July 1794, Robespierre fell, and for a short while David was imprisoned.

The Terror ended, David was released, and on 5 October 1795, with the 'whiff of grapeshot', order was assured — by Napoleon Bonaparte. Napoleon's authority grew steadily greater, and in 1799 David openly abandoned his Rousseauan principles, and adhered to the new 'tyrant of the ruling party'. In 1800 he was made official painter to the First Consul, producing *The First Consul Crossing the Alps*. There is wildness in the wind-swept mane and tail of the horse, and the mountains are jagged and bare. So much is still 'sublime'. But Napoleon *controls* this steed — with a single hand — while he points onwards and upwards with assured authority. In the *Oath of the Horatii* and the *Oath of the Tennis Court*, David had given expression to moments of spontaneous and general unanimity, in which the 'hero' is not a person, but the ideal — 'the nation', 'duty', 'freedom'. Here, in contrast, he gives glory to the single man who leads his soldiers — tiny, toiling figures in the background — and who takes credit for the victory. Behind his horse, to the extreme right, a small tricolour completes the column of soldiers struggling up the pass. This is a French army, with the colours of the republic. But the rocks in the left foreground are far more prominent, engraved with the names of individuals who have led armies over the Alps. Partly obscured, two names from the past, 'Karolus Magnus' and 'Hannibal', and — in clear, larger letters — 'Bonaparte'. Public virtue? The common cause? Not a bit. When Napoleon declared himself Emperor, it was perfectly appropriate that David should depict the coronation in 1804, and then be declared *Premier peintre de l'Empereur*.

Fuseli did not observe the Revolution with Mary Wollstonecraft. He did not go over to France until August 1802, when he accompanied Joseph Farington and other friends on a six-week visit to Paris. Farington's long account in his *Diary* (ed. K. Garlick and A. Macintyre, 1979) contains more on painting than on any other topic, and David is often mentioned, Farington's comment being usually introduced by 'we', to include the opinions of Fuseli and the other English painters. Generally their judgement of his work is unfavourable, and this is understandable, considering the differences between English and French approaches to painting at the time. But in discussing David's character there is deep dislike — not only was he a close follower of Robespierre, but he is now a turncoat, the lackey of a new tyrant:

> Inveterate as was his republican Spirit . . . and violent as He was in the days of terror, He now feels it expedient and submits to be an instrument to record the glory of a Despot (*Diary*, V, 3 October 1802, p. 1899).

'He feels it expedient' — the man who had once said to Robespierre, 'I shall drink the hemlock with you.' The Revolution was the harshest test, the test of violent practical experience, applied to the notions of wildness and the sublime. Just as the violence of the Revolution appalled the earlier enthusiasts of freedom, so this violence had to be brought to an end to re-establish civil order. The new ruler of France, Napoleon, not only quelled the last revolutionary uprising, but, as his determination to be sole ruler of France increased, he judged it expedient to reject his boyhood apostle, Rousseau, in favour of Voltaire, the champion of 'men who dwell in the city' — and whom he had despised when younger. Returning from the Egyptian campaign in 1799, Napoleon noted his own change of direction: 'The more I read Voltaire, the more I like him. . . Since I have seen the East, I have lost my taste for Rousseau. The noble savage is a dog' (P.-L. Roederer, *Journal*, 1853, p. 165). Rousseau (like the 'dog' into which the innocent 'noble savage' had turned during the Revolution) had become a menace to the well-being of Napoleon's state. It is amusing, but a little sad, to remember that *one* of Napoleon's romantic heroes was never rejected — the poet Ossian. At Malmaison, Napoleon's admiration is commemorated by Girodet's *Ossian Receiving the Generals of the Republic* (1800-2), and as late as 1813 Ingres painted for Napoleon *The Dream of Ossian* (now in the Ingres Museum, Montauban). Rousseau and the noble savage were dangerous: they had to go. But Ossian, vague, gentle, melancholy, and entirely in another age, might safely be preserved. Like *Paul et Virginie*, Ossian was harmless.

'The wildness pleases,' wrote Shaftesbury, and suggested that the outpourings of the solitary genius were the only means of expressing the sublimity of 'wildness'. Shaftesbury died in 1713, without seeing how others would interpret his words. In 1756 Burke defined the aesthetic nature of the sublime, contrasting it with beauty, and showing its terrible superiority over what was small, gentle, ordered and restrained. Burke lived to see the French Revolution, and was appalled (his opinions are expressed in 1790, in his *Reflections on the Revolution in France*, and the short *Debate on the Army Estimates*). Man's passions could not be kept under control by the individual, since 'his own private stock of reason' was inadequate (*Reflections*, p. 123). Mankind needed the ordered control of institutions and laws — the framework of society, no less — to prevent anarchy. In France, such external control had been lost, and the anarchy which threatened the French would bring 'the excesses of an irrational, unprincipled, proscribing, confiscating, plundering, ferocious, bloody and tyrannical democracy' (*Debate*, p. 33). For Burke in 1790 the term 'democracy' was little different from 'the rule of the mob'. It did not mean what it generally

271

does in western Europe today, with its hopeful sense of 'informed and sensible universal adult suffrage'. Having said this, the qualities of the anarchic popular rule which he fears are barely distinguishable from those of the sublime he had defined in 1756 — the unruly, the terrible, the obscure, the irrational, the ugly — which all stem from fear and pain and terror: 'Indeed terror . . . is the ruling principle of the sublime.' Robespierre's Terror, culminating in 1794, fulfilled the worst of Burke's apprehensions; and, to go by his definition, the Terror was sublime. Expressed in its most direct, tangible way — by means of the guillotine in the centre of Paris — wildness had proved intolerable.

Additional Bibliography

Primary texts have been quoted from editions, original or modern, identified at the point of quotation, and there is therefore no need to list them here a second time.

Alexander, Michael *Omai 'Noble Savage'* (1977)

Allen, B. Sprague *Tides in English Taste* (1937)

Aulard, F.-A. *Le Culte de la raison* (1892)

Babbitt, Irving *Rousseau and Romanticism* (1957)

Bachmann, Erich *Felsengarten Sanspareil* (1979)

Bell, C. F., and Girtin, Thomas *The Drawings and Sketches of John Robert Cozens* (Walpole Society, vol. xxiii, 1935)

Benedikt, Heinrich *F. A. Graf von Sporck 1662-1738* (1923)

Berry, Julian (ed.) *William Beckford Exhibition 1976* (1976)

Biener von Bienenberg, K. J. *Versuch über einige merkwürdige Alterthümer im Königreich Böhmen* (1778-85)

Brett, R. L. *The Third Earl of Shaftesbury* (1951)

Bruford, W. H. *Culture and Society in Classical Weimar, 1775-1806* (1962)

Clark, Kenneth *Civilisation* (1969)

— *The Romantic Rebellion* (1976)

Cobbe, Hugh (ed.) *Cook's Voyages* (1979)

Conisbee, Philip *Claude-Joseph Vernet 1714-1789* (catalogue of Greater London Council Exhibition, 1976)

Constable, W. G. *Richard Wilson* (1953)

Fothergill, Brian *Sir William Hamilton* (1969)

French, Anne *Gaspard Dughet called Gaspard Poussin 1615-1675* (catalogue of Greater London Council Exhibition, 1980)

Füssli, Heinrich *Briefe*, ed. Walter Muschg (1942)

Ganz, Paul *The Drawings of Henry Fuseli* (1949)

Gilchrist, Alexander *The Life of William Blake*, ed. Ruthven Todd (1945)

Gosse, Philip *Dr. Viper . . . Philip Thicknesse* (1952)

Grigson, Geoffrey *The Harp of Æolus and Other Essays* (1947)

Haller, Albrecht von *Récit du premier voyage dans les Alpes*, ed. E. Hintsche and P. F. Flückiger (1948)

Hardman, John (ed.) *French Revolution Documents 1792-95* (1973)

Hazard, Paul *La Pensée européenne au dix-huitième siècle* (1946)

Healey, F. G. *Rousseau et Napoléon* (1957)

Honour, Hugh *Neo-Classicism* (1968)

— *Romanticism* (1979)

Jacobs, M. *Gerstenberg's Ugolino . . . Mit einem Anhang: Gerstenbergs Fragment 'Der Waldjüngling'* (1898)

Joppien, Rüdiger *Philippe Jacques de Loutherbourg R. A. 1740-1812* (catalogue of Greater London Council Exhibition, 1973)

— 'Philippe Jacques de Loutherbourg's Pantomime "Omai" ', see Mitchel (1979), pp. 81-136

Köppel, J. G. *Die Eremitage zu Sanspareil* (1793)

Lloyd, Albert B. *The Singer of Tales* (1960)

Lysaght, A. M. 'Banks's Artists and His *Endeavour* Collections', see Mitchell (1979), pp. 9-80

Manwaring, E. W. *Italian Landscape in Eighteenth Century England* (1925)

Mavor, Elizabeth *The Ladies of Llangollen* (1971)

Mitchell, T. C. (ed.) *Captain Cook and the South Pacific* (1979)

Monk, Samuel Holt *The Sublime* (1935)

Moorehead, Alan *The Fatal Impact* (1966)

Mornet, Daniel *Le Sentiment de la nature en France de Jean-Jacques Rousseau à Bernardin de Saint-Pierre* (1907)

Mortier, Roland *Diderot en Allemagne* (1954)

Nicholson, Benedict *Joseph Wright of Derby* (1968)

Oppé, A. P. *Alexander and John Robert Cozens* (1952)

Parker, C.-A. *Mr. Stubbs the Horse Painter* (1971)

Powell, Nicolas *Fuseli: The Nightmare* (1973)

Price, Lawrence Marsden *The Reception of English Literature in Germany* (1932)

Robertson, George *An Account of the Discovery of Tahiti*, ed. Oliver Warner (1955)

Rosenblum, Robert *Transformations in Late Eighteenth Century Art* (1970)

Røstvig, Maren-Sophie *The Happy Man* (1962-71)

Salerno, Luigi *Salvator Rosa* (1963)

Schiff, Gert *Henry Fuseli 1741-1825* (catalogue of Tate Gallery Exhibition, 1975)

Smith, Bernard *European Vision and the South Pacific* (1960)

Stubbs, George *The Anatomy of the Horse*, ed. J. C. McCunn, C. W. Ottaway and Eleanor M. Garvey (1976)

Thacker, Christopher *Masters of the Grotto: Joseph and Josiah Lane* (1976)

— ' "O Tinian! O Juan Fernandez!" Rousseau's "Elysée" and Anson's desert islands', *Garden History*, vol. V, no. 2 (1977)

— *The History of Gardens* (1979)

Thompson, J. M. (ed.) *French Revolution Documents 1789-94* (1933)

Tieghem, Paul van *Le Sentiment de la nature dans le préromantisme européen* (1960)

Tieghem, Philippe van *Les Influences étrangères sur la littérature française (1550-1880)* (1967)

Tompkins, M. S. *The Popular Novel in England 1770-1800* (1969)

Willey, Basil *The Eighteenth-Century Background* (1962)

Wilton-Ely, John *The Mind and Art of Giovanni Battista Piranesi* (1978)

Wyndham, Violet *Madame de Genlis* (1958)

Index

INDEX